PRINCIPLES OF ENZYMATIC ANALYSIS

Edited by
Hans Ulrich Bergmeyer

in collaboration
with Karlfried Gawehn

Verlag Chemie · Weinheim · New York · 1978

Editor's note

The methods published in this book have not been checked experimentally by the editor. Sole responsibility for the accuracy of the contents of the contributions and the literature quoted therein rests with the authors. Readers are therefore requested to direct all enquiries to the appropriate authors (authors' addresses are listed on pp. XI–XII).

Translated by Express Translation Service, Oxford, and Horst Michael Langer, Hockenheim/Baden

1st Edition 1978

This book contains 99 figures and 30 tables

CIP-Kurztitelaufnahme der Deutschen Bibliothek

Principles of Enzymatic Analysis / ed. by
Hans Ulrich Bergmeyer. In collab. with Karlfried Gawehn.
– 1. ed. – Weinheim, New York : Verlag Chemie, 1978.
ISBN 3-527-25678-4 Verlag Chemie
      0-89573-006-5 Verlag Chemie International

NE: Bergmeyer, Hans Ulrich [Editor]

Composition, Printing and Binding: Passavia, D-8390 Passau
Printed in West Germany

Preface

The trend towards the standardization of methods, particularly in clinical chemistry, and towards the unification of nomenclature, quantities, and units, has brought about considerable changes. A chapter on enzymatic analysis written in modern, unambiguous terms reads completely differently today from what was previously the case. We shall get used to this. Experimental work for the standardization of methods has, however, also brought a flood of new information on how methods can be rationally optimized. The theoretical background of the methods used routinely has become more transparent.

Both the new knowledge and the introduction of new nomenclature, quantities, and units have led to the decision to publish the "Principles of Enzymatic Analysis" as a separate book. The highly-valued Section A of the greater work "Methods of Enzymatic Analysis"* has been a guideline, but it was soon found that it was possible to adopt only two chapters of this with nothing other than inevitable formal changes; all the other chapters have been rewritten, rearranged, and supplemented. Some new contributions have been necessary in order to bring the entire work up to the present state of the art. The extensive experience gained in the editing of "Methods of Enzymatic Analysis" over a period of almost 20 years and the many items of practical information from colleagues in the laboratory have been utilized. The present book is not intended to present theoretical knowledge but rather those principles that are necessary as a basis for practical work, the development of new methods, and their use. Consequently, theory has been copiously illustrated with examples.

The kinetic backgrounds of the individual subjects are presented in such simple and – it is hoped – understandable fashion that the reader needs no knowledge of higher mathematics.

The biochemical nomenclature, the standard guidelines for methods of clinical chemistry, quantities and units, and the citation of the literature correspond to the recommendations of the *International Union of Pure and Applied Chemistry, International Union of Biochemistry*, and *International Federation of Clinical Chemistry*, or legislation based on the *Système International d'Unités* (SI-system). Where necessary, old and new quantities and units are given in parallel, e.g. the catalytic activity of enzymes in units (U) and in katal (kat).

This book is intended to serve all those who wish to deal with the principles and methods of enzymatic analyses and must become acquainted with the new nomenclature and the new quantities and units, whether for teaching or for publication: teachers and students of the biological sciences, clinical chemists and laboratory physicians, and their principal staff.

May this book also contribute to the expert utilization of the methods of enzymatic analysis developed by *Otto Warburg* everywhere where they are of use. Their fields of application are broad and manifold.

The authors are to be thanked for the thorough and rapid preparation of their manuscripts, my colleagues for much advice and help, and the publishers for their full cooperation.

Tutzing, January 1978   Hans Ulrich Bergmeyer

---

* 2nd edition 1974, Verlag Chemie, Weinheim, and Academic Press, New York.

Contents

Contributors

Anderson, Norman G.
  Molecular Anatomy Program
  Oakridge National Laboratory*
  Oakridge, Tennessee 37830, USA
  and the Molecular Anatomy Institut,
  P.O. Box 117
  Oakridge, Tennessee 37830, USA
  p. 193

Bergmeyer, Hans Ulrich
  Boehringer Mannheim GmbH
  Biochemica Werk Tutzing
  D-8132 Tutzing/Obb.
  p. 1, 13, 40, 56, 83, 99, 109,
  168, 213, 216, 236

Bernt, Erich
  Boehringer Mannheim GmbH
  Werk Penzberg
  D-8122 Penzberg/Obb.
  p. 109, 216

Gawehn, Karlfried
  Boehringer Mannheim GmbH
  Biochemica Werk Tutzing
  D-8132 Tutzing/Obb.
  p. 109

Graßl, Marianne
  Boehringer Mannheim GmbH
  Biochemica Werk Tutzing
  D-8132 Tutzing/Obb.
  p. 216

Hagen, Alexander
  Boehringer Mannheim GmbH
  Biochemica Werk Tutzing
  D-8132 Tutzing/Obb.
  p. 202

Lowry, Oliver H.
  Washington University
  School of Medicine
  Department of Pharmacology
  St. Louis, Missouri 63110, USA
  p. 86

Michal, Gerhard
  Boehringer Mannheim GmbH
  Biochemica Werk Tutzing
  D-8132 Tutzing/Obb.
  p. 29, 88, 109, 216

Möllering, Hans
  Boehringer Mannheim GmbH
  Biochemica Werk Tutzing
  D-8132 Tutzing/Obb.
  p. 88

Moss, Donald W.
  Royal Postgraduate Medical School
  University of London
  Hammersmith Hospital
  London W 12
  p. 6

Netheler, Heinrich
  Eppendorf Gerätebau
  Netheler & Hinz GmbH
  Barkhausenweg 1
  D-2000 Hamburg 63
  p. 134, 175

Newsholme, Eric A.
  Department of Biochemistry,
  Souths Parks Road
  Oxford, England
  p. 202

---

* Operated for the U.S. Atomic Energy Commission by Union Carbide Corporation.

Passonneau, Janet V.

Section on Cellular Neurochemistry
Bethesda, Maryland 20014, USA
p. 86

Schuler, Peter

Boehringer Mannheim GmbH
Biochemica Werk Tutzing
D-8132 Tutzing/Obb.
p. 152, 155, 163, 168

Schuurs, Antonius H. W. M.

Organon Scientific Development Group
Oss, Holland
p. 93

Stähler, Fritz

Boehringer Mannheim GmbH
Biochemica Werk Tutzing
D-8132 Tutzing/Obb.
p. 219

Völkert, Emil

Boehringer Mannheim GmbH
Sandhofer Straße
D-6800 Mannheim 31
p. 119

Wahlefeld, August Wilhelm

Boehringer Mannheim GmbH
Biochemica Werk Tutzing
D-8132 Tutzing/Obb.
p. 88

van Weemen, Bauke Klaas

Organon Scientific Development Group
Oss, Holland
p. 93

Ziegenhorn, Joachim

Boehringer Mannheim GmbH
Biochemica Werk Tutzing
D-8132 Tutzing/Obb.
p. 79, 81, 175

Abbreviations
Symbols and Units

m	Meter	m
mm	Millimeter	10^{-3} m
nm	Nanometer	10^{-9} m
s	Second	
min	Minute	
h	Hour	
kg	Kilogram	kg
g	Gram	g
mg	Milligram	10^{-3} g
µg	Mikrogram	10^{-6} g
ng	Nanogram	10^{-9} g
l	Liter	l
ml	Milliliter	10^{-3} l
µl	Microliter	10^{-6} l
t	Reaction time	s
Δt	Interval between measurements	s
T	Temperature	°C, K
K	Kelvin	K
R	Gas constant	J/mol K
V	Volume (usually volume of assay mixture)	l
v	Volume (usually volume of sample in assay mixture)	l
v	Reaction rate*	mol/s
v_0	Reaction rate* at t = 0 (theoretical)	mol/s
v_i	Reaction rate*, initial, at t = 0 (in practice)	mol/s
V	Maximum reaction rate*	mol/s
k	Rate constant**	
K_m	Michaelis constant	mol/l
K_I	Inhibitor constant	mol/l
$[A]_0, [B]_0$, or a, b, resp.	Initial concentration of starting substance A, B at time t = 0	mol/l
$[A], [B]$	Concentration of starting substance A, B at time t	mol/l
x	Concentration of reaction product at time t	mol/l
$\xi_{cat.}$	Catalyzed reaction rate	mol/s
z	Catalytic activity	kat

---

* Only for enzymatic reactions. The rate of reactions not catalyzed enzymatically are expressed in mol/l × s (cf. also p. 56).
** Units: for zero-order reactions mol/l × s, for first-order reactions s^{-1}, for second-order reactions l/mol × s.

b	Catalytic activity concentration	kat/l
kat	Katal	mol/s
U	International enzyme unit	μmol/min
	Specific catalytic activity	kat/kg
	Molar catalytic activity	kat/mol
MW	Weight of one mole, millimole, resp.	g/mol, mg/mmol
c	Substance concentration	mol/l, g/l
% (v/v)	Percent, volume related to volume	
% (v/w)	Percent, volume related to weight	
% (w/v)	Percent, weight related to volume	
% (w/w)	Percent, weight related to weight	
d	Path length, light path	mm
Ci	Curie $\cong 3.7 \times 10^{10}$ s^{-1}	s^{-1}
cpm	Counts per minute	min^{-1}
ε	Absorption coefficient*	$l \times mol^{-1} \times mm^{-1}$
A	Absorbance	1
ΔA	Absorbance change	1
I	Luminous flux	lm
$\bar{x}$	Mean value	
s	Standard deviation	
CV	Coefficient of variation	%
log	Logarithm	
lg	Logarithm to the base 10	
ln	Logarithm to the base e	
S	Electrical conductance, Siemens	$S(1/\Omega)$
ϱ	Specific electrical resistance	$\Omega m\,(\Omega m^2/m)$
$\varkappa$	Electrical conductivity, $\dfrac{1}{\varrho}$	$S/m\,(m/\Omega m^2)$
Λ	Equivalent conductivity	$S\,m^2/mol$
ΔH	Enthalpy of the reaction	

---

* The unit for ε follows from the *Lambert-Beer* law and the units used for the light path and the concentration of the solution. In international usage, the concentration is expressed in mol/l and the light path in cm, and the unit for ε is accordingly $1/(mol/l) \times cm = l \times mol^{-1} \times cm^{-1}$.
According to the SI-system, the unit of concentration is mol/m^3, and of light path m, which leads to a unit of $1/(mol/m^3) \times m = m^2/mol$ for ε. The discussion concerning the units of concentration and absorption coefficient has not yet ceased. With regard to the field of clinical chemistry in particular, the non-coherent derived unit mol/l has been fixed as the unit of concentration.
For practical reasons, we shall use mol/l as the unit of concentration and mm for the light path in this book; ε is therefore expressed in $l \times mol^{-1} \times mm^{-1}$.

Abbreviations for Chemical and Biochemical Compounds

Ac	Acetate
Ac-P	Acetyl phosphate
ADH	Alcohol dehydrogenase
ADP	Adenosine-5'-diphosphate
AK	Acetate kinase
ALD	Fructose-1,6-diphosphate aldolase
ALT (GPT)	Alanine aminotransferase (glutamate-pyrurate transaminase)
AMP	Adenosine-5'-monophosphate
APAD	Acetylpyridine-adenine dinucleotide
APADH	Acetylpyridine-adenine dinucleotide, reduced
AST (GOT)	Aspartate aminotransferase (glutamate-oxaloacetate transaminase)
ATP	Adenosine-5'-triphosphate
CK	Creatine kinase
CL	Citrate lyase
CoA, CoA-SH	Coenzyme A
CS	Citrate synthase
Cyt-c	Cytochrome c
DAP	Dihydroxyacetone phosphate
DNA	Deoxyribonucleic acid
FAD	Flavin-adenine dinucleotide
F-1-P	D-Fructose-1-phosphate
F-1,6-P_2	D-Fructose-1,6-diphosphate
F-6-P	D-Fructose-6-phosphate
F-6-PK	Fructose-6-phosphate kinase
GAP	D-Glyceraldehyde-3-phosphate
GDH	L-Glycerol-3-phosphate dehydrogenase
GlDH	L-Glutamate dehydrogenase
GOD	Glucose oxidase
GOT (AST)	Glutamate-oxaloacetate transaminase (aspartate aminotransferase)
G-1-P	D-Glucose-1-phosphate
G-6-P	D-Glucose-6-phosphate
G6P-DH	Glucose-6-phosphate dehydrogenase
GPT (ALT)	Glutamate-pyruvate transaminase (alanine aminotransferase)
GSH	Glutathione
HCG	Chorionic gonadotropin
HPL	Lactogenic placental hormone
HK	Hexokinase
INT	2-(p-Iodophenyl)-3-(p-nitrophenyl)-5-phenyltetrazolium chloride
LDH	L-Lactate dehydrogenase
MDH	L-Malate dehydrogenase
MTT	3-(4',5'-dimethylthiazolyl-2-)-2,4-diphenyl-tetrazolium bromide
NAC	N-Acetylcysteine
NAD	Nicotinamide-adenine dinucleotide

NADH	Nicotinamide-adenine dinucleotide, reduced
NADP	Nicotinamide-adenine dinucleotide phosphate
NADPH	Nicotinamide-adenine dinucleotide phosphate, reduced
NBT	Nitro-BT-tetrazolium salt, 2,2′-di-p-nitrophenyl-5,5′-diphenyl-3,3′-(-dimethoxy-4,4′-diphenylene)-ditetrazolium chloride
NT	2,2′-p-Diphenylene-3,3′,5,5′-tetraphenyl-ditetrazolium chloride (Neotetrazolium chloride)
OA	Oxaloacetate
OxoG	2-Oxoglutaric acid
PEP	Phosphoenol pyruvate
3-PG	3-Phosphoglycerate, D-glycerate-3-phosphate
6-PG	6-Phosphogluconate, D-gluconate-6-phosphate
PGI	Phosphoglucose-isomerase
PGK	3-Phosphoglycerate kinase
PGluM	Phosphoglucomutase
1,3-PGP	D-Glycerate-1,3-diphosphate, 1,3-Diphosphoglycerate
P_i	Inorganic phosphate
PK	Pyruvate kinase
PMS	Phenazine methosulphate
PTA	Phosphotransacetylase
TIM	Triosephosphate isomerase
TNBT	2,2′-Di(p-nitrophenyl)-5,5′-diphenyl-3,3′-(3,3′-dimethoxy, 4,4′-diphenylene)-ditetrazolium chloride
TSH	Thyreotropic hormone
TT	2,3,5-Triphenyl-tetrazolium chloride

Introduction

Terminology, Importance, and Limits of Enzymatic Analysis

Hans Ulrich Bergmeyer

Introduction; Terminology

Enzymatic analysis is a branch of analytical chemistry and by no means a new field. It began in 1845, when *G. Osann*[1] in Würzburg (Germany) detected H_2O_2 with peroxidase. In 1851, *C.F. Schönbein*[2] stated that the minimum concentration detectable was $1 : 2,000,000$. In the 1880's, enzymes were used in food chemistry[3] to determine carbohydrates.

However, it is only since the discovery of the hydrogen-transferring enzymes and the corresponding coenzymes in 1935 by *Otto Warburg*[4,5] that enzymatic analyses based on the absorption of light by the hydrogenated pyridine coenzymes have been performed to a relatively large extent. These methods have found wider application only since the Second World War, when reliable optical measuring instruments became commercially available. Another step in this development was the measurement of the fluorescence of these coenzymes[6,7]; this increased the sensitivity of the determinations by two to three powers of ten. In the last few years, the techniques of measurement have been refined and largely mechanized.

Enzymes are biological catalysts, proteins with functional groups where the exchange or transfer of matter takes place. Analysis with the aid of enzymes presupposes that metabolic reactions that take place in the living cell can be transferred to the test-tube. This is in fact possible, as *E. Buchner*[8] already showed for the case of yeast press juice about 75 years ago: alcoholic fermentation can be performed not only with intact cells, but also with the juice alone.

If the enzymes are available as pure reagents, the metabolic reactions catalyzed by them can be used to keep track of the substances transformed in these reactions analytically. If, for example, in the cell the enzyme lactate dehydrogenase maintains the redox equilibrium between pyruvic acid and lactic acid, it is possible to use the same enzyme for the conversion of pyruvic acid into lactic acid and vice versa (by hydrogenation or dehydrogenation, respectively) *in vitro* and to determine their concentrations on the basis of easily-measurable reactants.

The substances to be analyzed can, of course, only be substrates of enzymes or they must, as effectors of enzymes, influence an enzyme-catalyzed reaction in some way such that the magnitude of the effect depends on the concentration. Essentially, then, it will be the natural substances which can be determined with the aid of enzymes. Such compounds are generally difficult to analyze by chemical methods.

The measurement of the utilization of a substance of interest by living cells (e.g. microorganisms) is not part of enzymatic analysis; this is the field of microbiological determinations. The particular value of analysis with enzymes resides in the possibility of specifically determining individual substances in a mixture. This eliminates the need for separation procedures, which are usually laborious and often associated with large losses. The cost of the analysis is low.

Enzyme-catalyzed reactions take place at atmospheric pressure, moderate temperatures, and near-neutral pH. Often, it is only these mild reaction conditions that make the determination of labile substances possible in the first place.

Enzymatic analysis therefore means *analysis with the aid of enzymes*.

It has also become customary to include the determination of the catalytic activity of enzymes in animal organs, biological fluids, plants, nutrient media, foodstuffs, etc., in the term "enzymatic analysis". The catalytic activity of enzymes in body fluids or samples of tissue obtained by biopsy is measured in the clinical laboratory in particular; valuable diagnostic or prognostic conclusions can be drawn from pathologically altered values, as compared with the values in healthy subjects.

Enzymatic analysis therefore also means the determination of the catalytic activity of enzymes as a characteristic of the functional state of their carrier or their organ of origin, respectively.

Enzymatic analysis has recently found a quite different field of application in the detection of enzymatically "inert" substances that are present in particularly low concentrations in animal tissues or body fluids such as blood plasma. Today it is possible to bind enzymes covalently to molecules of very different structures in such a way that the catalytic activity of the bound enzyme is retained. Consequently, such substances are "enzyme-labelled". By making use of the specificity of antigen-antibody reactions or of specific receptor proteins, very sensitive detection processes can be devised which are entirely on a par with radioligand techniques (e.g. the radio-immunoassays, cf. "Principle of Enzyme Immunoassays", p. 93). By means of such enzyme immunoassays, enzymatically "inert" active proteins can be determined on the basis of the measured catalytic activity of the bound enzyme. This branch of analytical immunology is also included in "enzymatic analysis".

Definition of the term "enzymatic analysis":
- *Determination of the concentrations of substances with the aid of enzymes*
- *Determination of the catalytic activities of enzymes in biological materials*
- *Determination of the concentrations of substances with the aid of enzyme-labelled reagents.*

The Importance of Enzymatic Analysis

The importance of enzymatic analysis in its various fields of application is manifold. It will be treated below only on a keyword basis.

Biochemistry and organic chemistry

The importance of enzymatic analysis for biochemistry has been strikingly characterized by *B. Hess*[9]: "Die Biochemie der Enzyme ist die Mutter der enzymatischen Methoden. Dabei leisten neue Methoden nicht nur wesentliche Beiträge zur Entwicklung und Förderung der angewandten enzymatischen Biochemie, sondern auch, und schließlich in weit größerem Umfang, rückgekoppelt zur Entwicklung der Biochemie selbst." ["The biochemistry of enzymes is the mother of enzymatic methods. At the same time, new methods make a substantial contribution not only to the development and advance of applied enzymatic biochemistry but also, and in the final account to a far greater extent, by a feedback mechanism to the development of biochemistry itself."].

In organic chemistry, it is the simple acids in particular that are difficult to determine: e.g. formate, oxalate, acetate, but also malate, succinate, and tartrate. On the other hand, their enzymatic analysis is largely unproblematic. For example, *H. Fasold*[10] determines acetyl groups in proteins enzymatically as acetate after hydrolysis. In sugar chemistry, enzymatic analysis will probably be the method of choice.

Food chemistry

Here enzymes are being used to an increasing extent for the determination of carbohydrates (mono-, di-, and polysaccharides in the presence of each other), organic acids (such as citrate, isocitrate, malate, D- and L-lactate), alcohols (such as ethanol, glycerol, and sorbitol), nitrogen compounds, etc., in beverages, baked products, chocolate, sugar, and sugar confectionery. For meat products there is the determination of, for example, pyrophosphate, creatine and creatinine, as well as gluconate, and for egg-containing products and fats, the determination of cholesterol. The number of parameters that can be determined is increasing steadily.

The chemistry of cosmetics

The foodstuffs legislation of many countries also includes cosmetics. Again, the determination of such substances as glycerol, glucose, fructose, cholesterol, lactate, citrate, and ethanol in skin creams or face lotions, etc., by means of enzymatic analysis has many advantages.

Botany and agricultural chemistry

Enzymatic methods are becoming more and more widely used for the investigation of the physiology of plant metabolism in the normal state, in parasitic and nonparasitic plant diseases, and under stress, and for evaluation of the quality of plant products with respect to their suitability for storage and technological processing. This also applies to the investigation of soil biology and the characterization of its biological activity.

Microbiology

Enzymatic analysis is used for monitoring the growth and metabolism of microorganisms. In the cultivation of microorganisms as raw materials for the production of enzymes, the amount of substrate in the nutrient medium is determined in relation to the amount of enzyme in the microorganism (e.g. glycerol in the cultivation of *Candida mycoderma* for the production of glycerol kinase[11]). In fermentation processes in the foodstuffs sector, faulty fermentation can readily be discovered by determining certain parameters, (e.g. in the manufacture of sauerkraut or milk products by determining D- and L-lactate and acetate).

The latest developments have made it possible to follow fermentation processes continuously by enzymatic analysis. For this purpose monitors are used that operate with carrier-fixed enzymes (see p. 168).

Pharmacology

Enzymatic methods are being used increasingly in biochemical pharmacology. *Summ* and *Christ*[12] have investigated the different inhibitory effects of various tetracycline derivatives in systems of cell-free protein biosynthesis. With this experimental arrangement it is possible to screen various antineoplastic agents for their action on tissue samples.

Digoxin in the blood of patients[14] is determined by the enzyme immunoassay method[13] (see p. 97).

Clinical chemistry

For the whole of human (and, to an increasing extent, also veterinary) medicine, enzymology and hence enzymatic analysis have become so important as a diagnostic aid and in the monitoring of diseases during treatment that this activity is now a large specialty by itself (see for example[15, 16]). This is the domain of the determination of the catalytic activities of enzymes (amino transferases, creatine kinase, alkaline phosphatase, etc.). The classical metabolites determinable by enzymatic analysis are glucose, triglycerides, cholesterol, uric acid, urea, and many others. Here, too, the parameters of thyroid gland function, steroid hormones, insulin, immunoglobulins, viral antigens, etc., are determined by means of enzyme immunoassays.

Limits of Enzymatic Analysis

As stated above, analysis with the aid of enzymes is limited to their substrates or to substances which affect enzyme reactions positively or negatively. No limits are set to the measurement of the catalytic activities of enzymes. The determination of enzymatically "inert" active substances on the basis of the catalytic activities of "marker" enzymes is in such a state of flux at the present time that the limits of this field of application cannot yet be estimated.

Methodological limits

The sensitivity of enzymatic analyses is high. Micromolar amounts in the assay sample can be determined by photometry, and nanomolar amounts[17] in catalytic assays. With the aid of fluorimetry, the sensitivity becomes greater by two to three powers of ten. If the methods of "enzymatic cycling" (see p. 85) are used, as little as 1×10^{-16} mol of substance in the assay sample can be determined quantitatively. The accuracy of enzymatic determinations is high because of the generally marked specificity of the enzymes. The precision of enzymatic analyses depends on the complexity of the assay system. Metabolites can be determined with greater precision by endpoint procedures than the catalytic activities of enzymes. If errors due to the measuring and reagent-dispensing apparatus are minimized, coefficients of variation of 1% and less are readily attainable in metabolite assays. The precision of the determination of the catalytic activity of an enzyme has a coefficient of variation of 2 to 4% in the case of simple reactions, and higher in the case of coupled or multiply-coupled reactions (in routine clinical chemistry, for example, $CV = 6\%$ for the enzyme creatine kinase).

As for all analytical methods, there are also limits to enzymatic analysis when it is transferred to automatic analyzers. Frequently, such instruments do not permit the simultaneous determination of one or more blank values, and it is often impossible to let a certain preliminary reaction take place. Occasionally, moreover, the method has to be modified; for example, the reaction is started with a reagent different from that used in the manual technique. However, these difficulties can generally be eliminated by a suitable modification of the procedure.

Economic limits

The term "highly purified enzymes as reagents" is still associated with the idea of "expensive reagents". It is overlooked that only microgram or, at the most, milligram amounts of enzymes are used for an analysis. Nevertheless, for some analyses of interest in food chemistry, for example, the costs of the reagents for the enzymatic procedure are generally higher than for the conventional one. At the same time, in contrast to enzymatic analysis, the total cost of a chemical analysis is generally substantially higher than the cost of the reagents.

In particular, economic considerations must also take the time involved into account. The separate budgeting of reagents and personnel, still customary in most government and municipal laboratories, has often stood in the path of the introduction of rational methods.

A comparison of the expenses for some analyses of interest in food chemistry *(G. Michal[+])* shows how economical enzymatic analyses can be (Table 1). Similar results are obtained for the determination of malate, lactate, cholesterol, etc.

Table 1. Comparison of the costs of chemical and enzymatic methods of analysis in food chemistry (Figures in DM).
(The total cost for one hour's work has been deliberately set low at DM 10.–)

	chemical method	enzymatic method
	Glucose acc. to *Luff & Schoorl*[18] *	Glucose + Fructose with HK, PGI, G6P-DH[19] *
Reagents	0.84	2.64
Working time	10.50	1.00
Total	11.34	3.64
	Citrate in wine, pentabromoacetone[18] **	Citrate in wine with CL, MDH, LDH[20] **
Reagents	1.22	2.76
Working time	24.00	1.00
Total	25.22	3.76

   * 5 simultaneous determinations + 2 blanks (chemical method) or 1 blank (enzymatic method), technician time for preparation of the samples not included.
  ** 5 simultaneous determinations + 1 blank in each case, including technician time for preparation of the samples.

The great advantage of enzymatic analyses, namely their specificity and ease of execution, has not been taken into account in the above comparison. For example, D- and L-lactate can be determined specifically by the enzymatic assay, which is impossible by chemical methods. Thus, in enzymatic analyses the multiplicity of chemical operations disappears, particularly in the preparation of samples. The technique of measurement is largely standard; it can be mastered by semiskilled personnel.

Thus, methods of enzymatic analysis are advantageous from economic points of views as well.

References

1 Osann, G. (1845) *Poggendorfs Ann.* **67**, 372.
2 Schönbein, C.F. (1851) *J. prakt. Chem.* (1) **53**, 69.
3 Stetter, H. (1951) *Enzymatische Analyse*, Verlag Chemie, Weinheim/Bergstr.

[+] Unpublished.

4 Warburg, O., Christian, W. & Griese, A. (1935) *Biochem. Z.* **282**, 157.
5 Warburg, O. (1948) *Wasserstoffübertragende Fermente*, Verlag Dr. W. Saenger, Berlin.
6 Kaplan, N.O., Colowick, S.P. & Parnes, C.C. (1951) *J. biol. Chem.* **191**, 461.
7 Lowry, O.H., Robert, N.R., Kapphahn, J.L. & Lewis, C. (1956) *Feder. Proc.* **15**, 304.
8 Buchner, E. (1903) in *Die Zymasegärung* (Buchner, E., Buchner, H. & Hahn, M., eds.) Verlag R. Oldenbourg, München & Berlin.
9 Hess, B. (1974) in *Methods of Enzymatic Analysis* (Bergmeyer, H.U., ed.) p. 3, Verlag Chemie, Weinheim & Academic Press, New York & London.
10 Fasold, H. (1974) in *Methods of Enzymatic Analysis* (Bergmeyer, H.U., ed.) p. 1640, Verlag Chemie, Weinheim & Academic Press, New York & London.
11 Holz, G. (1974) in *Methods of Enzymatic Analysis* (Bergmeyer, H.U., ed.) p. 87, Verlag Chemie, Weinheim & Academic Press, New York & London.
12 Summ, H.D. & Christ, D. (1967) *Arzneimittelforschung* **17**, 1186.
13 Scharpe, S.L., Cooreman, W.M., Blomme, W.J. & Laekemann, G.M. (1976) *Clin. Chem.* **22**, 733.
14 Smith, T.W. & Haber, E. (1973) in *Progress in Cardiology* (Yu, P.N. & Goodwin, J.F. eds.) **2**, 49, Lea & Febiger, Philadelphia.
15 Schmidt, E. & Schmidt, F.W. (1974) in *Methods of Enzymatic Analysis* (Bergmeyer, H.U., ed.) p. 6, Verlag Chemie, Weinheim & Academic Press, New York & London.
16 Schmidt, E. & Schmidt, F.W. (1972) *Selecta* **31**, 2782.
17 Lowry, O.H. (1973), *Accounts of Clinical Research* **6**, 289.
18 Diemair, W. (1972) *Laboratoriumsbuch für den Lebensmittelchemiker*, pp. 21 & 516. Liedl, G., München.
19 Bergmeyer, H.U., Bernt, E., Schmidt, F. & Stork, H. (1974) in *Methods of Enzymatic Analysis* (Bergmeyer, H.U., ed.) p. 1196, Verlag Chemie, Weinheim & Academic Press, New York & London.
20 Dagley, S. (1974) in *Methods of Enzymatic Analysis* (Bergmeyer, H.U., ed.) p. 1562, Verlag Chemie, Weinheim & Academic Press, New York & London.

Nomenclature and Units in Enzymology

Donald W. Moss

Introduction

Enzymes are proteins with catalytic activity because of their powers of specific activation of their substrates[1]. This definition, now generally accepted in biochemistry, conveys much information about the nature and properties of enzymes. It also indicates areas in which definitions are required to ensure uniformity of understanding amongst enzymologists. For example, it introduces the concept of "catalytic activity", i.e. the power of an enzyme molecule to transform large numbers of molecules of its substrate while itself emerging unchanged at the end of each reaction cycle, which forms the basis of almost all measurements in enzymology. Formal definitions of this concept and of the units in which results of measurements are expressed are needed, therefore.

The reference to specific activation of the substrate expresses the idea that, for each enzyme, only a single type of chemical reaction (e.g. saponification of esters) is catalyzed – in many cases restricted even further to a unique substrate.

It was quickly recognized in the early development of enzymology that the specificity of enzymes provides a convenient system for classifying and naming them, according to the substrate upon which each one acts. Extended to include the type of reaction catalyzed as well as the nature of the substrate acted upon, this system remains the foundation of enzyme nomenclature.

Classification of Enzymes according to the *Enzyme Commission*

As enzymology has developed it has become increasingly clear that a particular type of biological reaction may be catalyzed by several different enzymes. These functionally similar enzymes may be distinct with regard to other properties which may be characteristic of the type of cell, or even of the subcellular component, from which the respective enzymes originate: it might be said that nature has solved the problem of catalyzing a particular reaction in several different ways. For example, aspartate aminotransferase exist in both the mitochondria and cytoplasm of cells, but these catalytically similar enzymes are, in fact, distinct proteins with different structures. Thus, an enzyme cannot be identified unequivocally merely by describing the nature of the reaction which it catalyzes.

Classification and numbering

By 1955, when nearly 1000 enzymes had been discovered, the *International Union of Biochemistry* (IUB) decided that the naming of enzymes could no longer be left to the initiative of individual scientists. The possibilities of confusion or misunderstanding were too great in the absence of accepted rules of classification and nomenclature, while some older coinages such as "Zwischen-ferment" or "diaphorase" were insufficiently descriptive for modern needs. A *Commission on Enzymes* was therefore set up, which produced an interim report in 1958 and a final report[2] in 1961. The report of the *Commission on Enzymes* received a general welcome from biochemists, thus demonstrating its timeliness, and, with some later modifications of detail[3,4], it has become accepted as the foundation of classification and nomenclature in enzymology.

The *Enzyme Commission* divided enzymes into six main classes according to the general nature of the reactions which they catalyze:

1. Oxidoreductases
2. Transferases
3. Hydrolases
4. Lyases (enzymes which remove groups from their substrates, not by hydrolysis, leaving double bonds, or which add groups to double bonds)
5. Isomerases
6. Ligases (synthetases: enzymes which join together two molecules while at the same time breaking a pyrophosphate bond in a nucleoside triphosphate)

Within each class are subclasses which further define the nature of the reaction, e.g., by specifying the donor in oxidation-reduction reactions, or the nature of the group which is transferred by enzymes of the transferase class. For each subclass, a number of sub-subclasses have been defined: e.g., the class of hydrolases has a subclass of enzymes which act on ester linkages. This subclass comprises six sub-subclasses, each made up of enzymes which catalyze the hydrolysis of a particular type of ester bond, such as carboxylic esters.

Each known enzyme has been given a place in the hierarchy of classes, subclasses and sub-subclasses. Its place in the scheme is designated by a number, unique to that enzyme, within the appropriate sub-subclass. The numbering scheme allows for the insertion of newly recognized subclasses, sub-subclasses and enzymes.

A systematic and descriptive nomenclature is an essential part of the *Enzyme Commission's* proposals. Although the termination "-ase" is retained to indicate the enzymic nature of each catalyst, the formal name of each enzyme is based on the equation of the overall observed chemical change, and not merely on the name of a single substrate.

The method of use of the enzyme classification can be seen by considering the example of a well-known enzyme. Creatine kinase of muscle catalyzes the reaction

$$ATP + creatine \rightleftharpoons ADP + creatine\ phosphate$$

Its systematic name is therefore ATP: creatine phosphotransferase and its system number is

EC 2. 7. 3. 2

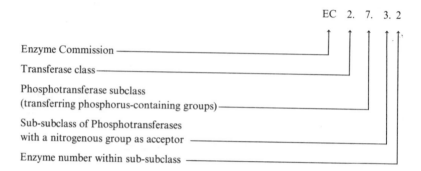

Enzyme Commission ——————————————————————

Transferase class ——————————————————————

Phosphotransferase subclass
(transferring phosphorus-containing groups) ——————————

Sub-subclass of Phosphotransferases
with a nitrogenous group as acceptor ——————————

Enzyme number within sub-subclass ——————————

Trivial names and abbreviations for enzymes

The systematic name and number identify an enzyme unequivocally, e.g., when it is first mentioned in a scientific paper. However, subsequent references to the same enzyme can make use of its mostly shorter trivial name. The trivial names recommended by the *Enzyme Commission* generally follow the well-established practice of adding "-ase" to the name of the substrate, as in amylase, or to words which describe the nature of the reaction too, such as alcohol dehydrogenase. However, in a few cases the *Enzyme Commission* preferred a more descriptive trivial name such as "urate oxidase" to an older but rather uninformative name such as "uricase".

When particular enzymes are referred to repeatedly in scientific papers, or when large numbers of results of enzyme assays are reported daily, as is the case in clinical laboratories, it becomes very convenient to use abbreviations for common enzyme names. Since so much data-processing in clinical laboratories is now carried out by computers, any system of abbreviations should use as few letters as possible in order to economize on space in the computer's memory and in print-out time. It is not easy to devise two- or three-letter codes for enzymes which are free from ambiguity. Furthermore, abbreviations which are logical in one language may not be so in another, in which the order of words in the name of the enzyme may be different. Nevertheless, lists of abbreviations for use in clinical enzymology have been suggested[5].

It must be emphasized that all such lists are unofficial. If abbreviations are used, either in publications or within laboratories, their meanings should be clearly defined.

Quantities and Units in Enzymology

The most distinctive property of any enzyme is its power to catalyze the transformation of its substrate. Measurement of this ability is the basis of most quantitative studies in enzymology. It involves determination of the increase in the rate of the specific chemical reaction produced by a sample of the enzyme under study above that which would be observed if the enzyme were not present; i.e., the rate of reaction which is attributable to catalysis by the enzyme.

Catalyzed rate of reaction

The catalytic activity of an enzyme is only manifested under appropriate conditions, when its substrate and any specific cofactors are present and within fairly narrow limits of pH, etc. The observed effect of an enzyme in a given assay system is therefore defined as the *catalyzed rate of reaction*, which is the rate of conversion of the substrate that is attributable to catalysis by the enzyme. This kind of quantity is *extensive*, i.e., addition of more enzyme produces an increased rate (unless some other factor in the assay system becomes limiting), and it is *derived*, in the sense that it can be expressed in terms of other, more *basic kinds of quantities*. In the *Système International d'Unités* (SI), *amount of substance* is a basic kind of quantity expressed in moles and the *unit of time*, also a basic kind of quantity, is the second. Thus the catalyzed rate of reaction has the dimensions $N \times T^{-1}$ and its unit is the *mole per second* (mol $\times$ s^{-1}). It has been given the symbol ξ_{cat}.

Catalytic activity (or ability)

In most cases, the enzymologist wishes to go beyond the catalyzed rate of reaction observed in his assay system and to relate the value so obtained to some property of the original system containing the enzyme, such as a sample of blood serum or an extract of tissue. The way in which this relationship between the observed effect and the original system should be defined has given rise to much philosophical debate. This may be summarized briefly as follows.

The catalyzed rate of reaction observed when the original system is introduced into the assay mixture reflects the number of active enzyme molecules which the system contains. The *Enzyme Commission* originally defined a unit of enzyme as that *amount* which would catalyze the transformation of 1 μmole of substrate per minute under standard conditions[2]. This quantity was later given the name "*International Unit*" (I.U.).

The word "amount" was also used in a similar way by the *Expert Panel on Quantities and Units* (EPQU) of IFCC and the *Commission on Quantities and Units in Clinical Chemistry* (CQUCC) of IUPAC, who defined the base unit *katal* as the catalytic amount of any enzyme which catalyzes a reaction rate of 1 mole per second in an assay system[6].

However, the word "amount" carries a strong connotation of "amount of substance", whereas the intention in definitions with respect to enzymes is to refer to the catalytic property of these substances. Therefore, many enzymologists remained dissatisfied with the idea of an amount of enzyme, preferring the well-established term "catalytic (or enzymic) activity". Alternative positions derived from the use of either "amount" or "activity" have been published[7].

The term activity also has its critics, mainly on the grounds that this word is used in other senses in physical chemistry. Alternatives to either amount or activity have been sought, therefore. One possible solution is to use the word "ability": this expresses the potential or latent nature of the activity of the enzyme in its original system, which is only expressed in catalysis in a suitable assay medium. However, it is not certain that enzymologists are willing to relinquish the term activity.

Catalytic activity is therefore used here, with the understanding that the word *ability* may be substituted for *activity*.

Catalytic activity is a property of a system which contains a catalyst and it corresponds to the catalyzed rate of reaction produced when all or part of the system is introduced into a specified assay system. The unit of catalytic activity is the *katal* (symbol kat) and is that catalytic activity which produces a catalyzed rate of reaction of 1 mole per second in an assay system.

Catalytic activity is an extensive kind of quantity, its symbol is z and its dimensions Z. It functions as a basic kind of quantity and its unit, the katal, as a base unit. However, neither is included amongst the base quantities and units of SI.

It should be noted that one katal of catalytic activity always corresponds to the transformation of 1 mole of substrate per second: this relationship is not dependent on the assay conditions. However, the number of katals of activity present in a given enzyme sample will be different when measured in different assay systems, i.e., it is method-dependent.

The protracted discussions about quantities and units in enzymology seem to many enzymologists to be unrelated to the practical problems of enzyme assay. Nevertheless, the conceptual distinction between the observed phenomenon, namely the catalyzed rate of reaction, and the property of the system which gives rise to it is a useful one, especially when derived quantities such as *concentrations of catalytic activity* have to be considered.

Other derived kinds of quantities in enzymology

The clinical enzymologist in particular usually wishes to express his results as the concentration of the enzyme in the serum or plasma of the patient under study. He therefore requires the derived kind of quantity *catalytic activity concentration*. This is defined as the catalytic activity of the enzyme divided by the volume of the system. The system in this case refers to the original sample containing the enzyme, not to the assay mixture. The symbol of catalytic activity concentration is b and its dimensions are $Z \times L^{-3}$. The unit of catalytic activity concentration is the *katal per liter* (kat $\times$ l^{-1}), and decimal multiples and submultiples of this unit are constructed in the usual way. In clinical enzymology the submultiples µkat $\times$ l^{-1} (10^{-6} kat $\times$ l^{-1}) and nkat $\times$ l^{-1} (10^{-9} kat $\times$ l^{-1}) are most generally useful.

Another useful derived kind of quantity in enzymology is *specific catalytic activity*. "Specific" has the meaning "divided by mass". In enzymology, the mass of protein in the system is usually chosen as the divisor, so that specific catalytic activity (dimensions $Z \times M^{-1}$) is the catalytic activity divided by the mass of protein. Its unit is the *katal per kilogram of protein* (kat $\times$ kg^{-1}) or appropriate multiples of this (e.g. µkat $\times$ mg^{-1}).

When an enzyme has been obtained in a pure state, solutions of it can be prepared which are of known molar concentration with respect to enzyme. Thus, the catalytic activity can be related to the amount of substance (i.e. enzyme) present in the solution. Therefore, *molar catalytic activity* is derived by dividing the catalytic activity of the system by the amount of enzyme substance (expressed in moles) that it contains. The dimensions of molar catalytic activity are $Z \times N^{-1}$ and its unit is the *katal per mole of enzyme* (kat $\times$ mol^{-1}).

The concept of *molar catalytic activity* has previously been called "molecular activity", while the term "turnover number" has often been used in a similar sense in the older literature. Turnover number has also been used to describe the number of substrate molecules transformed in unit time by each active center in the enzyme molecule. If each molecule of enzyme contains only one active center, the *catalytic center activity* is equal to the *molar catalytic* activity. If each molecule of enzyme has n active centers, catalytic center activity equals molar activity divided by n.

Summary

The various kinds of quantities which are mainly useful in enzymology and their dimensions and units are summarized in Table 1. Together they form a system which is coherent with SI and, although details are still under discussion, they are likely to receive general acceptance in the future.

Table 1. Kinds of quantities and units in enzymology.

Kind of quantity	Status	Symbol	Dimensions	Unit
Catalyzed rate o reaction	Derived, extensive	ξ_{cat}	$N \times T^{-1}$	$mol \times s^{-1}$
Catalytic activity*	Functionally basic, extensive	z	Z	katal: that catalytic activity which corresponds to a catalyzed rate of reaction of 1 mole per second in an assay system (symbol: kat).
Catalytic activity* concentration	Derived	b	$Z \times L^{-3}$	$kat \times l^{-1}$
Specific catalytic activity*	Derived		$Z \times M^{-1}$	$kat \times kg^{-1}$
Molar catalytic activity	Derived		$Z \times N^{-1}$	$kat \times mol^{-1}$

* Alternatively "ability".

References

1 Dixon, M. & Webb, E.C., eds. (1964) *Enzymes*, 2nd ed., p. 5, Longmans, Green & Co., London.
2 *Report of the Commission on Enzymes of the International Union of Biochemistry* (1961) Pergamon Press Ltd., Oxford.
3 *Enzyme Nomenclature*. Recommendations (1972) of the Commission on Biochemical Nomenclature on the Nomenclature and Classification of Enzymes together with their Units and the Symbols of Enzyme Kinetics. Prepared by the Commission on Biochemical Nomenclature and approved by I.U.P.A.C. and I.U.B. (1975) Elsevier, Amsterdam.
4 Commission on Biochemical Nomenclature (1972). – Enzyme Nomenclature: Recommendations (1972) of the International Union of Pure and Applied Chemistry and the International Union of Biochemistry. Supplement 1. Corrections and Additions (1975). *Biochim. Biophys. Acta* (1976) **429**, 1.
5 Baron, D.N., Moss, D.W., Walker, P.G. & Wilkinson, J.H. (1975) *J. Clin. Path.* **28**, 592.
6 I.U.P.A.C. and I.F.C.C. Quantities and Units in Clinical Chemistry. Recommendation 1973. *Pure appl. Chem.* (1974) **37**, 519.
7 IFCC Committee on Standards, Expert Panel on Enzymes. Provisional Recommendation (1974) on IFCC Methods for the Measurement of Catalytic Concentration of Enzymes. *Clin. chim. Acta* (1975) **61**, F 11.

Theoretical Principles

Enzymatic analyses are simple to perform. Nevertheless, the reactions in question obey definite physicochemical laws, and the development of procedures of enzymatic analysis must take these laws into account. In the following, reaction mechanisms are treated only to the extent that is necessary for practical unterstanding.

Reaction Kinetics

Hans Ulrich Bergmeyer

Enzymes are catalysts. This means that they considerably increase the rates of reactions. To determine the catalytic activities of enzymes, then, it is necessary to measure the rates of chemical reactions. These are subject to definite laws.

These laws must be known in order to calculate, or even to estimate, such parameters as the reaction time or the maximum possible rate of conversion of substrate.

Fundamentals of Reaction Kinetics

The rate of a reaction is measured in terms of the quantity(ies) of substance(s) being converted or the quantity(ies) of product(s) being formed per unit of time. The parameter to be measured is therefore conversion of substance per unit of time.

Classical reaction kinetics of homogeneous systems makes use of the orders of reaction and formulae described below (cf.[1-4]). For simpler systems, derivation of the reaction rate in terms of the decrease of substance is preferred; for more complicated systems, the formulae become simpler if based on product increase. Different symbols are used for concentration in the literature. In the following, the initial concentration of the starting substance is designated by $[A]_0$, for example, but by "a" when the concentration "x" of the product also appears.

$[A]_0, [B]_0$ or a, b	Initial concentration of starting substance
$[A], [B]$	Concentration of starting substance at time t
x	Concentration of reaction product at time t
k	Rate constant ($k_1, k_2 \ldots$ for the forward reaction; $k_{-1}, k_{-2} \ldots$ for the reverse reaction)
t	Reaction time
$-d[A]/dt$	Rate of decrease of the starting substance
dx/dt	Rate of increase of the reaction product.

The different orders of reaction are:

Zero order (1) $$-\frac{d[A]}{dt} = k_1 \qquad\qquad dx/dt = k_1$$

Examples: Particularly heterogeneous catalysis (dx/dt is independent of the concentration).

First order

$A \to B$ (2) $-\dfrac{d[A]}{dt} = k_1[A]$ $dx/dt = k_1(a - x)$

or (3) $t = \dfrac{1}{k} \times \ln \dfrac{[A]_0}{[A]}$ $t = \dfrac{1}{k_1} \times \ln \dfrac{a}{a - x}$

$A \to B + C$ (4) $[A] = [A]_0 \times e^{-k_1 t}$ $x = a(1 - e^{-k_1 t})$

Examples: Decay of radioactive elements; thermal decomposition of organic compounds. An example of a pseudo-unimolecular reaction is the hydrolysis of esters in acid media (H_2O concentration constant), mutarotation of glucose.

Second order

$A + B \to C + D$ (5) $-\dfrac{d[A]}{dt} = k_1[A] \times [B]$ $dx/dt = k_1(a - x)(b - x)$

(6) $t = \dfrac{1}{k_1} \times \dfrac{1}{[A]_0 - [B]_0} \times \ln \dfrac{[B]_0 \times [A]}{[A]_0 \times [B]}$ $t = \dfrac{1}{k_1} \times \dfrac{1}{a - b} \times \ln \dfrac{b(a - x)}{a(b - x)}$

(7) $x = \dfrac{ab(1 - e^{-k_1 t(a - b)})}{a - be^{-k_1 t(a - b)}}$

Examples: Hydrolysis of esters in alkaline media ($R_1 - COO - R_2$ and OH^- are reactants).

if a = b, then (8) $-\dfrac{d[A]}{dt} = k_1[A]^2$ $dx/dt = k_1(a - x)^2$

(9) $t = \dfrac{1}{k_1}\left(\dfrac{1}{[A]} - \dfrac{1}{[A]_0}\right)$ $t = \dfrac{1}{k_1} \times \dfrac{x}{a(a - x)}$

(10) $[A] = \dfrac{[A]_0}{[A]_0 k_1 t + 1}$ $x = ak_1 t(a - x)$

The reaction curve of a zero-order reaction is linear; that of a first-order reaction can be represented as a straight line if plotted semilogarithmically according to equation (3), i.e. $\dfrac{a}{a - x}$ (or $[A]_0/[A]$) is plotted along the logarithmically scaled ordinate and the time t along the linearly scaled abscissa. Second-order reactions can be linearized by plotting $1/[A]$ against t (cf. 3).
The rate constant "k" is dimensionless for reactions of zero order. For first-order reactions, the dimension is s^{-1}, for second-order reactions $(mol/l)^{-1} \times s^{-1}$.
In biochemistry, the relationships are normally more complex. The reaction product is usually the parameter measured.

Equilibrium reactions are very common:

$A \underset{k_{-1}}{\overset{k_1}{\rightleftharpoons}} B + C$ initially let

b = c = 0 (11) $dx/dt = k_1(a - x) - k_{-1}x^2$
b ≠ c ≠ 0 (12) $dx/dt = k_1(a - x) - k_{-1}(b + x)(c + x)$

$$A + B \underset{k_{-1}}{\overset{k_1}{\rightleftharpoons}} C \qquad \text{initially let}$$

$$\begin{aligned} c &= 0 \\ a &= b \end{aligned} \qquad (13) \quad dx/dt = k_1(a - x)^2 - k_{-1}x$$

$$\begin{aligned} c &= 0 \\ a &\neq b \end{aligned} \qquad (14) \quad dx/dt = k_1(a - x)(b - x) - k_{-1}x$$

$$A + B \underset{k_{-1}}{\overset{k_1}{\rightleftharpoons}} C + D \qquad \text{initially let}$$

$$\begin{aligned} c &= d = 0 \\ a &= b \end{aligned} \qquad (15) \quad dx/dt = k_1(a - x)^2 - k_{-1}x^2$$

$$\begin{aligned} c &= d = 0 \\ a &\neq b \end{aligned} \qquad (16) \quad dx/dt = k_1(a - x)(b - x) - k_{-1}x^2$$

$$\begin{aligned} c &\neq d \neq 0 \\ a &= b \end{aligned} \qquad (17) \quad dx/dt = k_1(a - x)^2 - k_{-1}(c + x)(d + x)$$

This list could be expanded indefinitely, e.g. to the effect that in the reaction sequences so common in biochemistry, the product C reacts further with another substrate E to form the product F to be measured:

$$A + B \underset{k_{-1}}{\overset{k_1}{\rightleftharpoons}} C + D$$

$$C + E \underset{k_{-2}}{\overset{k_2}{\rightleftharpoons}} F + G$$

Here again we generally find the variations $a \neq b$ and $c \neq e$. All these reactions can be formulated mathematically. In the more complicated metabolic pathways with equilibrium steps, however, it is no longer possible mathematically to solve such equations explicithy for x or t. Such complicated reactions can often be simplified in practice. With a large excess of one reactant (e.g. $b \gg a$), second-order reactions become first-order (pseudo-unimolecular reactions). In catalytic (e.g. enzymatic) reactions, the values of k can be modified by an increase in the quantity of catalyst, so that e.g. $k_2 \gg k_1$, with the result that only the rate-determining first step is evident. Coupled reactions can often be modified in this way until they can be described by the simple sequence

$$A \overset{k_1}{\longrightarrow} B \overset{k_2}{\longrightarrow} C$$

where the individual steps may again be first- or even zero-order.
The course of the reaction curves for A, B, and C is shown schematically in Figure 1 (p. 16). The sum of the concentrations $a + b + c$ at any time is constant (cf.[2,3]).
In the ideal case, curve a (decrease in the concentration of A) is a mirror image of curve c (increase in the concentration of C). For this to occur, however, B must be converted in the second reaction step as quickly as it is formed $[b = 0]$; otherwise one obtains lag phases (curve c_1), in which B accumulates (curve b). In this connection, the family of curves in Figure 2 (p. 16) will now be explained in more detail.
If a value of 1×10^{-2} be chosen for k_2 and values from ∞ to 1×10^{-3} for k_1, the family of curves shown is obtained for a constant initial concentration $a = 200$. (Dimensions are of no interest here.) It can be seen that a curve of the type for a first-order reaction is obtained for $k_1 = \infty$ (curve a), and that e.g. for curve e with $k_1 = 1.2 \times 10^{-2}$ (i.e. k_1 of the same order of magnitude

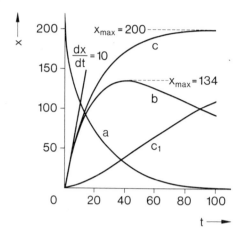

Fig. 1. $a = 200$; $b = c = 0$; $k_1 = 5 \times 10^{-2}$
Curve c: $k_2 = \infty$,   parameter : c
Curve b_1 : $k_2 = 10^{-2}$, parameter : b
Curve c_1 : $k_2 = 10^{-2}$, parameter : c

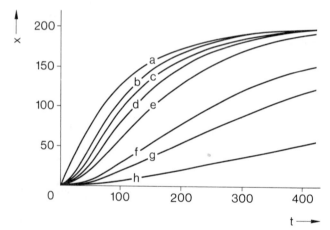

Fig. 2. $A \xrightarrow{k_1} B \xrightarrow{k_2} C$.
$a = 200$; $b = c = 0$; $k_2 = 10^{-2}$.
For curves a to h $k_1 = \infty$ to
10^{-3}

as k_2) a distinct lag phase occurs. This is understandable, since the rate constants k show how rapidly the individual reaction steps can proceed in principle. However, the effective rate is dependent on the substance concentration. As long as the quantity of product B produced in the first reaction step is still relatively small, the second reaction step will proceed relatively slowly. Only with the accumulation of sufficient B does the second reaction step become faster. The curves all have an inflection point.

A decisive factor for all the calculations is whether B or C is the parameter.

Incorrect values would result from the use of the apparently linear part of the curve near the inflection point for determination of the rate. The slope at the point of inflection is always less than the slope of the curve c at the origin 0 (Fig. 1).

If one considers the formation of B, the same data give the reaction course represented by curve b in Figure 1. Curves b and c_1 are both valid for the ratio $k_1 : k_2 = 5 : 1$ (i.e. for comparable rate constants for the reaction steps). Curve b is typical of the determination of the intermediate product B, which accumulates for a time.

If the difference between the two reaction constants is not sufficiently large, then, one obtains the curves b and c_1. This is often the case in biological systems.

With the aid of suitable mathematical expressions, and if the kinetic data are known, it is possible to calculate the time at which the maximum of curve b will be reached, so that the reaction may be stopped in due time, if necessary or desired.

For two coupled first-order reactions, the initial concentration of the substance to be converted is:

(18) $$[A]_0 = [C] + [B] + [C]; \qquad [C] = [A]_0 \times e^{-kt}$$

(19) $$d[B]/dt = k_2[B]$$

(20) $$d[B]/dt = -d[A]/dt - d[C]/dt$$

It follows that:

(21) $$[B] = \frac{[A]_0 k_1}{k_2 - k_1} \times (e^{-k_1 t} - e^{-k_2 t})$$

(22) $$d[B]/dt = \frac{[A]_0 k_1}{k_2 - k_1} \times (k_2 e^{-k_2 t} - k_1 e^{-k_1 t})$$

[B] has reached the maximum when the rate $d[B]/dt$ is no longer positive but is not yet negative, i.e. when it is exactly zero. If the right-hand side of eqn. (22) is equated to 0, one obtains:

(23) $$k_1 e^{-k_1 t} = k_2 e^{-k_2 t}$$

(24) $$t_{max} = \frac{\ln k_1/k_2}{k_1 - k_2}$$

This is also the equation for the time at which the point of inflection of curve c_1 is reached. The same expression is found for $t_{infl.}$ as for t_{max} from corresponding equations for $d[C]/dt$ (in this case the concentration of the end product C is measured) if the change in the reaction rate with time is equated to 0. This is obvious, for the maximum of curve b naturally coincides with the point of inflection of curve c_1.

To calculate the maximum concentration [B], it is only necessary to substitute the expression for t_{max} from eqn. (24) for t in equation (21).

Kinetics of Enzyme-Catalyzed Reactions

Enzymes accelerate the reaction of their substrates or permit reactions that would not otherwise occur. The co-operation of another substance with the enzyme may be necessary for the reaction of a substrate. One-substrate, two-substrate, and three-substrate reactions are possible (corresponding to unimolecular, bimolecular, and trimolecular reactions: first-, second-, and third-order reactions). Water is disregarded as a reactant since it has a constant, very high concentration (55.6 mol/l).

Example of a one-substrate reaction:

$$\text{oxaloacetate} \longrightarrow \text{pyruvate} + CO_2$$

Example of a two-substrate reaction:

$$\text{D-glucose} + \text{ATP} \longrightarrow \text{D-glucose-6-phosphate} + \text{ADP}$$

It will be shown later that enzymatic reactions can also be zero-order under certain conditions.

Simple Enzymatic Reactions

One-substrate Reactions

Every enzymatic reaction proceeds in several steps. If the enzyme reacts with only one substrate, the mechanism can be represented as follows[4]:

$$S + E \underset{k_{-1}}{\overset{k_1}{\rightleftharpoons}} ES \overset{k_2}{\longrightarrow} E + P$$

The enzyme E reacts with the substrate S to give an intermediate enzyme-substrate complex ES. The reaction proceeds within this complex, and the latter then decomposes into the enzyme and the reaction product P. A number of simplifications are possible in the formulation of the mathematical expression for the rate of transformation of S in this reaction chain. For example, the enzyme concentration is normally very much lower than the substrate concentration, and the same is true of the concentration of the enzyme-substrate complex. If the first step in this reaction sequence is fast and the enzyme-substrate complex decomposes irreversibly, the following expression in the notation of chemical reaction kinetics (cf.[4]) is valid for this reaction sequence:

$$(25) \qquad dx/dt = k_2 \times e \; \frac{(a - x)}{(a - x) + \dfrac{k_{-1} + k_2}{k_1}}$$

In this expression, a is the initial concentration of the substance to be converted
  x is the quantity of substance converted
  k is the rate constant of the reaction
  e is the enzyme concentration
  dx/dt is the rate of increase in the concentration of the reaction product.

Using square brackets to denote the concentrations of the enzyme and the substrate, and substituting[5] $(k_{-1} + k_2)/k_1 = K_m$, one obtains the *Michaelis-Menten* equation[6] for the reaction rate*:

$$(26) \qquad v = k \; \frac{[E] \times [S]}{[S] + K_m}$$

(cf. also p. 29), where k is the rate constant of the decomposition reaction and K_m is the *Michaelis* constant. This *Michaelis-Menten* equation can be used for the majority of enzyme-catalyzed one-substrate reactions. It follows directly from eqn. (26) that the values of [S] and K_m determine

---

* In enzyme-catalyzed reactions, the reaction rate is denoted by v. Subscripts indicate the point in time to which the reaction rate v refers. The *initial rate* of a reaction is of particular interest. Instead of the theoretical value v_0, however, v_i is measured in practice. Efforts must always be made to ensure that v_i deviates from v_0 as little as possible.

the rate of the reaction and its type. With an excess of substrate, so that $[S] \gg K_m$ and K_m is therefore negligible in relation to $[S]$, one obtains

(27) $$v = k[E] = V$$

i.e. a zero-order reaction. The (maximum) rate, according to eqn. (1), is independent of the (high) substrate concentration, and depends only on the constant enzyme concentration.
If $[S] = K_m$, then

(28) $$v = k[E]/2 = \frac{V}{2}$$

The *Michaelis* constant K_m is thus equivalent to the substrate concentration at which the enzyme reaction proceeds at half of its maximum rate.
If the substrate concentration is very much smaller than the *Michaelis* constant, i.e. if $[S] \ll K_m$, then $[S]$ disappears from the denominator and

(29) $$v = k\frac{[E]}{K_m} \times [S] = \frac{V}{K_m} \times [S] = k' \times [S] \,.$$

This is a first-order reaction. From the point of view of reaction kinetics, it must be treated in the same way as an uncatalyzed reaction. The term V/K_m corresponds to the rate constant k in eqn. (2). The rate is directly proportional to the substrate concentration.

Two-substrate reactions

In enzyme reactions with two substrates, the binding of the substrates to the enzyme (p. 18) may be effected in different ways. To catalyze the reaction, either ternary enzyme-substrate complexes (enzyme + two substrates) or only binary complexes (enzyme + first substrate and enzyme + second substrate) are necessary (ping-pong mechanism); see[7.8].
Ternary enzyme-substrate complexes can form in two different ways. Either the substrates add to the enzyme nonselectively *(random order)*, or in a definite sequence such that the binary complex ES_1 must be formed first, this alone being capable of joining with S_2 to form the ternary complex ES_1S_2 *(compulsory order, ordered mechanism)*.

Ordered mechanism *(compulsory order)*:

$$E + S_1 \rightleftharpoons ES_1$$
$$ES_1 + S_2 \rightleftharpoons ES_1S_2$$

Here S_1 is the "leading" substrate. S_2 can be bound only if the complex ES_1 has already been formed. Many pyridine-coenzyme-dependent dehydrogenases function by this scheme with, for example, NAD as the "leading" substrate: the primary complex ES_1 is E-NAD$^+$.

Random order mechanism:

$$E + S_1 \rightleftharpoons ES_1$$
$$ES_1 + S_2 \rightleftharpoons ES_1S_2$$

or

$$E + S_2 \rightleftharpoons ES_2$$
$$ES_2 + S_1 \rightleftharpoons ES_1S_2$$

The two mechanisms are equivalent, and complex formation may follow either route:

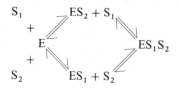

An example of this random mechanism is what happens with the enzyme molecule creatine kinase:

$$\text{creatinine} + \text{ATP} \rightleftharpoons \text{creatine phosphate} + \text{ADP}$$

The two substrates are bound to the active center of the enzyme molecule in any sequence to form the ternary complex, and phosphate is transferred. Both products are then liberated.

Ping-pong mechanism:
Binary enzyme-substrate complexes catalyze two-substrate reactions – without formation of the ternary complex – by the following mechanism (here, in general, we are dealing with reactions in which functional groups are transferred).
A substrate is bound to the enzyme (ES_1) and reacts with a change in the enzyme (the prosthetic group) to give the product P_1, which is liberated. The altered enzyme F binds the second substrate S_2 to form FS_2, the reaction $FS_2 \rightarrow EP_2$ takes place (with regeneration of the E-form of the enzyme in the complex EP_2), and the product P_2 is liberated. E is now available for a new reaction cycle.
This mechanism at the enzyme molecule is known as the ping-pong (Bi-Bi) mechanism. An example is the transfer of amino groups as by aspartate aminotransferase[9-11].

$$\text{aspartate} + \text{2-oxoglutarate} \rightleftharpoons \text{oxaloacetate} + \text{glutamate}.$$

The enzyme requires pyridoxal phosphate as coenzyme. The reaction proceeds as follows:

aspartate   Oxac   Oxoglut   Glut

E $\longrightarrow$ E-Asp $\longrightarrow$ F-Oxac $\longrightarrow$ F $\longrightarrow$ F-Oxoglut $\longrightarrow$ E-Glut $\longrightarrow$ E

E represents the pyridoxal form,
F represents the pyridoxamine form of the enzyme.

In this case aspartate is the "leading" substrate. The changes in the enzyme molecule are effected by the alternating transfer of the very firmly bound prosthetic group.

$$\text{pyridoxal phosphate} \rightleftharpoons \text{pyridoxamine phosphate}$$

Other mechanisms are possible. The formulae for the rate of two-substrate reactions are more complicated than those for one-substrate reactions (cf. Table 1, p. 22).
On the assumption that the transformation of the ternary enzyme-substrate complex ES_1S_2 into the reaction products takes place relatively slowly and the individual enzyme-substrate com-

plexes form rapidly, the following equation, analogous to eqn. (26), is obtained for the reaction rate:

(30)
$$v = \frac{V \times [S_1] \times [S_2]}{[S_1] \times [S_2] + (K_m)_{S_1} \times [S_2] + (K_m)_{S_2} \times [S_1] + (K_m)_{S_1 S_2}}$$

$$= \frac{1}{1 + \dfrac{(K_m)_{S_1}}{[S_1]} + \dfrac{(K_m)_{S_2}}{[S_2]} + \dfrac{(K_m)_{S_1 S_2}}{[S_1] \times [S_2]}} \, .$$

Provided that the binding of one substrate does not affect that of the other (which, however, does take place in the case of allosteric enzymes), and that furthermore each substrate combines strictly only with its binding site, and if in the formation of the ternary complex ES_1S_2 the substrates are bound to the enzyme in a definite sequence *(ordered mechanism)*, $(K_m)_{S_1 S_2}$ will be equal to $(K_m)_{S_1} \times (K_m)_{S_2}$:

(31)
$$v = \frac{1}{1 + \dfrac{(K_m)_{S_1}}{[S_1]} + \dfrac{(K_m)_{S_2}}{[S_2]} + \dfrac{(K_m)_{S_1}}{[S_1]} \times \dfrac{(K_m)_{S_2}}{[S_2]}} \times V$$

If the two-substrate reaction is a primary reaction in which the substrate concentrations are high compared to their K_m values, the expression $(K_m)_{S_1} \times (K_m)_{S_2}/[S_1] \times [S_2]$ is negligibly small and can be omitted.

If no ternary-enzyme substrate complex is formed, but the enzyme acts as a transfer agent *(ping-pong mechanism)*, the term containing $(K_m)_{S_1 S_2}$ is absent.

For such cases, the following simplified rate equation applies:

(32)
$$v = \frac{1}{1 + \dfrac{(K_m)_{S_1}}{[S_1]} + \dfrac{(K_m)_{S_2}}{[S_2]}} \times V$$

The boundary conditions for eqns. (30) and (32) are given in Table 1.

In certain cases, enzyme reactions with two substrates can be treated as single-substrate reactions, and reactions with three substrates as two-substrate reactions.

Examples:

a) lactose + H_2O → D-galactose + D-glucose

b) D-glucose + O_2 + H_2O → δ-gluconolactone + H_2O_2

c) pyruvate + NADH + H^+ → L-lactate + NAD^+

In two-substrate reactions with water as the second substrate – as in eqn. (a) –, the condition $[S_2] \gg (K_m)_{S_2}$ is certainly always satisfied, since $[S_2] = 55.6$ mol/l. $(K_m)_{H_2O}$ will probably be very small in comparison to $[S_2]$, although this value cannot be determined but only estimated indirectly. The third and fourth addends in the denominator of eqn. (30) disappear; the rate equation for a single-substrate reaction applies. By analogy, eqn. (b) must be treated according to the laws govering two-substrate reactions.

If H^+ is a reactant – as in eqn. (c) – the concentration is about 1×10^{-6} mol/l to 1×10^{-8} mol/l at measurements near the neutral point. An estimate of the ratio $[S]:K_m$ is difficult, since there

Table 1. Comparison of equations for One-Substrate and Two-Substrate Reactions.

Conditions	One-Substrate Reaction $S \xrightarrow{E} P$	Two-Substrate Reaction $S_1 + S_2 \xrightarrow{E} P_1 + P_2$	
General Equation	(26a) $v = \dfrac{V \times [S]}{[S] + K_m}$ $= \dfrac{1}{1 + \dfrac{K_m}{[S]}} \times V$	(30) $v = \dfrac{V \times [S_1] \times [S_2]}{[S_1] \times [S_2] + (K_m)_{S_1} \times [S_2] + (K_m)_{S_2} \times [S_1] + (K_m)_{S_1 S_2}}$ $= \dfrac{1}{1 + \dfrac{(K_m)_{S_1}}{[S_1]} + \dfrac{(K_m)_{S_2}}{[S_2]} + \dfrac{(K_m)_{S_1 S_2}}{[S_1] \times [S_2]}} \times V$	
Two-Substrate-Reaction: Condition a*	—	(31) $v = \dfrac{1}{1 + \dfrac{(K_m)_{S_1}}{[S_1]} + \dfrac{(K_m)_{S_2}}{[S_2]} + \dfrac{(K_m)_{S_1}}{[S_1]} \times \dfrac{(K_m)_{S_2}}{[S_2]}} \times V$	
Two-Substrate-Reaction: Condition b**	—	(32) $v = \dfrac{1}{1 + \dfrac{(K_m)_{S_1}}{[S_1]} + \dfrac{(K_m)_{S_2}}{[S_2]}} \times V$	
$[S_1] \gg (K_m)_{S_1}$	(27) $v = V$	(33) $v = \dfrac{[S_2]}{[S_2] + (K_m)_{S_2}} \times V = \dfrac{1}{1 + \dfrac{(K_m)_{S_2}}{[S_2]}} \times V$	
$[S_1] = (K_m)_{S_1}$	(28) $v = V/2$	(34) $v = \dfrac{1}{2 + \dfrac{(K_m)_{S_2}}{[S_2]} + \dfrac{(K_m)_{S_1 S_2}}{[S_1] \times [S_2]}} \times V$	
		(35) $v = \dfrac{1}{2\left(1 + \dfrac{(K_m)_{S_2}}{[S_2]}\right)} \times V$	(acc. to eqn. (31))
		(36) $v = \dfrac{1}{2 + \dfrac{(K_m)_{S_2}}{[S_2]}} \times V$	(acc. to eqn. (32))
$S_1 \ll (K_m)_{S_1}$	(29) $v = \dfrac{V}{K_m} \times [S_1]$	(37) $v = \dfrac{[S_1]}{(K_m)_{S_1} + \dfrac{(K_m)_{S_1 S_2}}{[S_2]}} \times V$	(acc. to eqn. (30))
		(38) $v = \dfrac{[S_1]}{(K_m)_{S_1}\left(1 + \dfrac{(K_m)_{S_2}}{[S_2]}\right)} \times V$	(acc. to eqn. (31))
		(29) $v = \dfrac{V}{(K_m)_{S_1}} \times [S_1]$	(acc. to eqn. (32))
$[S_1] \ll (K_m)_{S_1}$ $[S_2] \gg (K_m)_{S_2}$	—	(29) $v = \dfrac{V}{(K_m)_{S_1}} \times [S_1]$	
$[S_1] \gg (K_m)_{S_1}$ $[S_2] \gg (K_m)_{S_2}$	—	(27) $v = V$	

* a) Each substrate combines only with its binding site in the enzyme. The binding of one substrate does not affect the binding of the other.
** b) Ping-pong bi-bi-mechanism (cf. pp. 20 and 61).

are not data available on the K_m value of an enzyme in relation to its "substrate" H^+. Nevertheless, this value can be determined approximately or estimated.

It is well known that if, when $[S_1] \gg (K_m)_{S_1}$ and $[S_2] \gg (K_m)_{S_2}$ the pH-dependence of a reaction such as that given in eqn. (c) be measured, a curve (ordinate v_i; abscissa pH) with an optimum will be obtained. If the value pairs $(v_i, [H^+])$ corresponding to the value pairs (v_i, pH) from the "alkaline side" of this curve are plotted according to *Lineweaver* and *Burk*, $(K_m)_{H^+}$ can be determined. To estimate the order of magnitude of $(K_m)_{H^+}$, it is also sufficient to obtain the pH-value corresponding to $V/2$. In general, it is found that with a broad pH-optimum, $V/2$ is at least two pH-units greater than the pH-optimum. This means that at the pH-optimum, $[H^+]$ is at least two powers of ten larger than $(K_m)_{H^+}$. In such cases, the resulting deviation of v_i from V is less than 1%.

In buffered solutions, $[H^+]$ is constant. In any case, deviations of v_i from V (e.g. at a very narrow pH-optimum) appear in the rate equation as constants. Thus, in all reactions with H^+ as reactant this "substrate" can be neglected in the kinetics of the reactions.

Reduced pyridine coenzymes as substrates can give rise to difficulties in measurement, since their absorption of light limits the concentration that can be used. In the case of eqn. (c) with $(K_m)_{S_2}$ of the order of magnitude of 10^{-5} mol/l for lactate dehydrogenase in the presence of NADH, the coenzyme can be used only in a concentration of the order of 10^{-4} mol/l (absorbance of NADH at 339 nm being 0.630). Here $(K_m)_{S_2}/[S_2] \cong 0.1$. The deviation from the ideal case $1 + K_m/[S] = 1$ is therefore 10%. Thus, although the Michaelis constants of dehydrogenases in reactions involving pyridine coenzymes are generally small, the ratio $K_m/[S]$ must always be checked for systems containing NAD(P)H.

Thus, although enzymatic reactions with two substrates can often be set up experimentally in such a way that the laws for one-substrate reactions can be applied, it is also often necessary to take both substrates into account.

If inhibitors are involved in the enzyme reaction, the additional term $(1 + I/K_I)$ always appears in the rate equations as a factor modifying K_m, V, or both, depending on the type of inhibition (cf. pp. 35–40).

Coupled enzyme reactions

One-substrate reactions

The coupling of enzyme reactions for practical purposes is described on pp. 69–78. By the careful choice of measurement conditions, one will always try to keep the order of the reactions in the individual steps as low as possible.

In the determination of the catalytic activities of enzymes, the first step is frequently of zero order on account of a high substrate concentration. In order to keep the concentration of P_1 in the sequence

$$S \xrightarrow{E_{prim.}} P_1 \xrightarrow{E_{ind.}} P_2$$

small (which is desirable for both rapid conversion in endpoint determinations and for determinations of the catalytic activity of $E_{prim.}$ in order to keep the lag phase as small as possible), the rates of the partial steps of such reactions must come into equilibrium very rapidly. The effective rate $(v_{eff.})_{ind.}$ of the indicator reaction must be equal to the maximum rate $V_{prim.}$ of the primary reaction.

(39)
$$V_{\text{prim.}} = (V_{\text{eff.}})_{\text{ind.}} = \frac{V_{\text{ind.}} \times [P_1]}{(K_m)_{P_1} + [P_1]}$$

The only variable that can be freely chosen, V_{ind}, must be made large. Since $V = k[E]$, one can only add a large amount of the enzyme E_{ind}. $[P_1]$ must be as small as possible. According to eqn. (23) on p. 71, $[P_1]$ can be kept small only when the one variable that can be freely chosen – V_{ind} – is large.

(40)
$$[P_1] = (K_m)_{P_1} \times \frac{V_{\text{prim.}}}{V_{\text{ind.}} - V_{\text{prim.}}}$$

It is not always possible to the conditions of measurement in such a way that a linear conversion is obtained. The first step of the sequence may proceed between the boundary conditions of enzymatic reactions, namely between zero order (with $v_i = V$) and first order ($v_i = V[S]$), the indicator reaction being of zero, first, or fractional order. The situation may be reversed. Both reactions may be of zero order. In the most unfavorable case, the primary and indicator reactions are both first-order.

In principle, nine combinations are possible. The most important will be considered briefly below. The question is always the same: how large must $V_{\text{ind.}}$ be, compared to $V_{\text{prim.}}$, in order that the primary reaction may be measured correctly?

1. Primary reaction and indicator reaction of fractional order:

$$(v_i)_{\text{prim.}} = \frac{V_{\text{prim.}}}{[S_1] + (K_m)_{S_1}} \times [S_1]$$

$$(v_{\text{eff.}})_{\text{ind.}} = \frac{V_{\text{ind.}}}{[P_1] + (K_m)_{P_1}} \times [P_1]$$

In the steady state, $(v_i)_{\text{prim.}} = (v_{\text{eff.}})_{\text{ind.}}$;
i.e.

$$V_{\text{ind.}} = \frac{[P_1] + (K_m)_{P_1}}{[S_1] + (K_m)_{S_1}} \times \frac{[S_1]}{[P_1]} \times V_{\text{prim.}}$$

or

$$\frac{V_{\text{ind.}}}{[P_1] + (K_m)_{P_1}} = \frac{[S_1]}{[P_1]} \times \frac{V_{\text{prim.}}}{[S_1] + (K_m)_{S_1}}$$

$$\frac{V_{\text{ind.}}}{1 + \dfrac{(K_m)_{P_1}}{[P_1]}} = \frac{V_{\text{prim.}}}{1 + \dfrac{(K_m)_{S_1}}{[S_1]}}$$

2. Primary reaction of fractional order, indicator reaction of zero order:

$$(v_i)_{\text{prim.}} = \frac{V_{\text{prim.}}}{[S_1] + (K_m)_{S_1}} \times [S_1]$$

$$(v_{\text{eff.}})_{\text{ind.}} = V_{\text{ind.}}$$

In the steady state, $(v_i)_{\text{prim.}} = (v_{\text{eff.}})_{\text{ind.}}$;
i.e.

$$V_{\text{ind.}} = \frac{V_{\text{prim.}}}{[S_1] + (K_m)_{S_1}} \times [S_1] = \frac{1}{1 + \dfrac{(K_m)_{S_1}}{[S_1]}} \times V_{\text{prim.}}$$

The value of $1/\{1 + (K_m)_{S_1}/[S_1]\}$ shows what the ratio of $V_{ind.}$ to $V_{prim.}$ must be for a steady state to be achieved.

3. Primary reaction of zero order, indicator reaction of fractional order:

$$(v_i)_{prim.} = V_{prim.}$$

$$(v_{eff.})_{ind.} = \frac{V_{ind.}}{[P_1] + (K_m)_{P_1}} \times [P_1]$$

In the steady state, $(v_i)_{prim.} = (v_{eff.})_{ind.}$;
i.e.

$$V_{ind.} = \frac{[P_1] + (K_m)_{P_1}}{[P_1]} \times V_{prim.} = \left(1 + \frac{(K_m)_{P_1}}{[P_1]}\right) \times V_{prim.}$$

or

$$\frac{V_{ind.}}{[P_1] + (K_m)_{P_1}} = \frac{1}{[P_1]} \times V_{prim.}$$

4. Primary and indicator reactions both of first order:

$$(v_i)_{prim.} = \frac{V_{prim.}}{(K_m)_{S_1}} \times [S_1]$$

$$(v_{eff.})_{ind.} = \frac{V_{ind.}}{(K_m)_{P_1}} \times [P_1]$$

$$V_{ind.} = \frac{(K_m)_{P_1}}{[P_1]} \times \frac{[S_1]}{(K_m)_{S_1}} \times V_{prim.}$$

or

$$\frac{V_{ind.}}{(K_m)_{P_1}} = \frac{[S_1]}{[P_1]} \times \frac{V_{prim.}}{(K_m)_{S_1}}$$

5. Primary and indicator reactions both of zero order:

$$(v_i)_{prim.} = V_{prim.}$$

$$(v_{eff.})_{ind.} = V_{ind.}$$

In the steady state, $(v_i)_{prim.} = (v_{eff.})_{ind.}$;
i.e.

$$V_{ind.} = V_{prim.}$$

Conclusions:

It follows from case (5) that in the ideal situation of two coupled reactions of zero order, the catalytic activity of the indicator enzyme may be equal to that of the primary enzyme. Where there is only slight deviation from zero order, the two are of the same order of magnitude.

It follows from case (2) that $V_{ind.}$ can be calculated directly from given data if the indicator reaction proceeds as a zero-order reaction. The over-all reaction is then represented by a straight line (zero order) as long as $(v_i)_{eff.} = V_{ind.} = const. \times V_{prim.}$, i.e. as long as $1 + (K_m)_{S_1}/[S_1]$ is practically constant. This is the case when the value of $(K_m)_{S_1}/[S_1]$ is small compared to 1, i.e. $[S_1] > (K_m)_{S_1}$.

Example:

$[S_1] = 1 \times 10^{-3}$ mol/l; $(K_m)_{s_1} = 1 \times 10^{-4}$ mol/l. Let 0.1 $[S_1]$ react in the course of the reaction. The value of $1 + (K_m)_{s_1}/[S_1]$ changes from $1 + 0.1 = 1.1$ to $1 + 0.111 = 1.111$, i.e. by 1.1%.

It is therefore sufficient that $[S_1] \approx 10(K_m)_{s_1}$ in the primary reaction for an approximately linear over-all reaction to be achieved in this case. It is then only necessary that $V_{ind.} \approx 0.9 V_{prim.}$. The conditions with $[S_1] \leq (K_m)_{s_1}$ are not realistic, since then $(v_i)_{prim.}$ would deviate too greatly from $V_{prim.}$ and the primary reaction would be measured incorrectly.

It follows from case (3) that the ratio $V_{ind.} : V_{prim.}$ cannot be calculated directly. The variable $[P_1]$ can be considered only in relation to other known parameters (see p. 71–75). However, $[P_1]$ can be specified beforehand as a parameter for the lag phase of the reaction. The smaller $[P_1]$ must be in order to keep the lag phase of the over-all reaction as small as possible, the greater does the expression $1 + (K_m)_{P_1}/[P_1]$ become. In any case, $V_{ind.}$ must be greater than $V_{prim.}$. In contrast to case (2) however, $1 + (K_m)_{P_1}/[P_1]$ is a constant, since $[P_1]$ is constant when the reaction has reached the steady state. The over-all reaction is therefore linear.

In case (1) the situation is similar to that in case (3). In the steady state, $1 + (K_m)_{P_1}/[P_1]$ is constant. As stated above for case (2), the expression $1 + (K_m)_{s_1}/[S_1]$ is also practically constant, provided that only a small fraction of the excess of substrate S_1 is converted. Consequently, $V_{ind.} \cong$ const. $\times V_{prim.}$, i.e. the reaction is approximately linear.

Case (4) is the most unfavorable. Both the primary and indicator reactions must be treated as uncatalyzed first-order reactions. If the calculation is performed according to the laws of chemical reaction kinetics (see p. 14, 17 and Fig. 2), one must set $k_1 = V_{prim.}/(K_m)_{prim.}$ and $k_2 = V_{ind.}/(K_m)_{P_1}$. The rate of coupled reactions at any time t (cf.[3]) is given by:

(41)
$$v = [A]k_1 \left[e^{-k_1 t} + \frac{1}{k_1 - k_2}(k_1 e^{-k_1 t} - k_2 e^{-k_2 t}) \right];$$

$[A]$ is the substrate concentration at time t.

To obtain $v_{infl.}$, i.e. the rate at the inflection point of the curve of the coupled reaction, t in eqn. (41) must be replaced by

$$t_{infl.} = \frac{\ln(k_1/k_2)}{k_1 - k_2}$$

in accordance with eqn. (24) on p. 17.

Numerical example:

Let $k_1 : k_2 = 1 : 10$. The expression in round brackets in eqn. (41) can then be disregarded. One then has

$$v_{infl.} \approx [A]k_1 \times e^{-k_1 t_{infl.}} \approx [A]k_1 \times e^{-k_1 \times \frac{\ln(k_1/k_2)}{k_1 - k_2}}$$

$$v_{infl.} \approx [A]k_1 \times e^{-0.256} \approx 0.774[A]k_1 \approx 0.774 \times V.$$

Provided that $k_2 = 10 k_1$, then, the slope at the point of inflection represents a rate approximately 23% lower than the preceding reaction step actually has at $t = 0$. The same calculation for $k_2 = 100 k_1$ gives an error of 4%, and for $k_2 = 1000 k_1$ an error of 0.7%. A rough calculation shows that $k = V/K_m$ of the indicator reaction must be at least 100 times greater than $k = V/K_m$ of the primary reaction.

This limiting value $k_2 \geq 100\,k_1$ or $V_{\text{ind.}}/(K_m)_{P_1} \geq 100\,(V_{\text{prim.}}/(K_m)_{S_1})$ represents the most unfavorable ratio of the catalytic activities of the indicator and primary enzymes. It can be much smaller in all the other cases discussed above.

Two-substrate reactions

In principle, the same conditions obtain for coupled two-substrate reactions. In the case of two-substrate indicator reactions, simplified according to eqn.(31), we have for the steady state with $[P_1]$ constant.

$$(v_{\text{eff.}})_{\text{ind.}} = \frac{V_{\text{ind.}}}{1 + \dfrac{(K_m)_{P_1}}{[P_1]} + \dfrac{(K_m)_{S_3}}{[S_3]}} = \frac{V_{\text{ind.}}}{(1 + Q) + \dfrac{(K_m)_{S_3}}{[S_3]}}$$

$$= \frac{V_{\text{ind.}}}{(1 + Q)\times[S_3] + (K_m)_{S_3}} \times [S_3],$$

where $(1 + Q)\times[S_3] \gg (K_m)_{S_3}$ in almost all cases, so that $(K_m)_{S_3}$ can be neglected and

$$(v_{\text{eff.}})_{\text{ind.}} = \frac{1}{1 + Q} \times V_{\text{ind.}}.$$

Thus, the indicator reaction can be taken as zero-order. The situation for two-substrate reactions corresponding to case (2) above still remains to be discussed.

Two-substrate primary reaction of fractional or 1st order
Zero-order Indicator reaction:

$$(v_i)_{\text{prim.}} = \frac{V_{\text{prim.}}}{1 + \dfrac{(K_m)_{S_1}}{[S_1]} + \dfrac{(K_m)_{S_2}}{[S_2]}}$$

$$(v_{\text{eff.}})_{\text{ind.}} = \frac{1}{1 + Q} \times V_{\text{ind.}}$$

The following conditions for the primary reaction may be considered:

a)
$$[S_1] \approx (K_m)_{S_1}$$
$$[S_2] \gg (K_m)_{S_2} \qquad \text{or vice versa.}$$

The primary reaction must then be treated as a one-substrate reaction.

$$V_{\text{ind.}} = (1 + Q)\times \frac{1}{1 + \dfrac{(K_m)_{S_1}}{[S_1]}} \times V_{\text{prim.}}$$

Here, according to p. 26, the expression $1 + (K_m)_{S_1}/[S_1]$ can be taken as constant at the start of the reaction in most cases. As long as this condition is satisfied, the course of the reaction is linear.

b)
$$[S_1] \ll (K_m)_{S_1}$$
$$[S_2] \gg (K_m)_{S_2}, \qquad \text{or vice versa.}$$

Then

$$(v_i)_{prim.} = \frac{V_{prim.}}{(K_m)_{S_1}} \times [S_1]$$

$$(v_{eff.})_{ind.} = \frac{1}{1 + Q} \times V_{ind.}$$

The primary reaction proceeds as an uncatalyzed first-order reaction.

$$V_{ind.} = (1 + Q) \times \frac{[S_1]}{(K_m)_{S_1}} \times V_{prim.}$$

The over-all reaction is curvilinear like a first-order reaction. However, this case is hardly encountered, since in general the catalytic activity of the primary enzyme is to be measured under optimized conditions and therefore the concentration of one substrate will be kept much smaller than the corresponding K_m value only in exceptional cases, e.g. for technical reasons.

The above examples serve to explain the well-known fact that it is nearly always possible to achieve a linear or approximately linear reaction course, even for coupled reactions. The rule of thumb used previously, *viz.*, that the values of the quotients V/K_m for the indicator and primary reactions should be in the ratio of 100 : 1 insofar as possible, provides a safety margin. It applies only in the unlikely case of two coupled reactions of first order. In all other cases, the ratio $V_{ind.}/V_{prim.}$ is much smaller than 100.

References

1 Aebi, H. (1964) in *Biochemisches Taschenbuch* (Rauen, H.M., ed.) part II, p. 159 ff., Springer-Verlag, Berlin, Göttingen, Heidelberg
2 Bergmeyer, H.U. (1973) *Dechema-Monographien*. Vol. **71**, p. 277, Verlag Chemie, Weinheim
3 Bergmeyer, H.U. (1953) *Biochem. Z.* **324**, 408.
4 Lumper, L. (1964) in *Handbuch der physiologisch- und pathologisch-chemischen Analyse* (Hoppe-Seyler, E.F.I. & Thierfelder, H., eds.), 10. edn., Vol. VI A, p. 17, Springer-Verlag, Berlin, Göttingen, Heidelberg.
5 Brigg, G.E. & Haldane, J.B.S. (1925) *Biochem. J.* **19**, 338.
6 Michaelis, L. & Menten, M.L. (1913) *Biochem. Z.* **49**, 333.
7 Fromm, H.J. (1961) *Biochim. biophys. Acta.* **52**, 199.
8 Lehninger, A.L. (1975) *Biochemistry*, 2nd edition, p. 202, Worth Publishers, Inc., New York.
9 Menson, C.P. & Cleland, W.W. (1964) *Biochemistry* **3**, 338.
10 Velick, S.F. & Vavra, J. (1962) *J. biol. Chem.* **237**, 2109.
11 Cleland, W.W. (1963) *Biochim. Biophys. Acta* **67**, 104.

Determination of Michaelis Constants and Inhibitor Constants

Gerhard Michal

Michaelis Constants

Theory

Michaelis and *Menten*[1] defined the fundamental quantity of enzyme kinetics as the dissociation constant of the enzyme-substrate complex ES formed from the enzyme E and the substrate S.

$$(1) \qquad K_S = \frac{[E] \times [S]}{[ES]}$$

From this equation, an expression for the reaction rate can be derived (see below).
For one-substrate reactions, the *steady-state* derivation* according to *Briggs* and *Haldane*[2] from

$$(2) \qquad S + E \underset{k_{-1}}{\overset{k_1}{\rightleftharpoons}} ES \xrightarrow{k_2} E + P$$

gives the expression

$$(3) \qquad K_m = \frac{k_{-1} + k_2}{k_1} .$$

K_m is the Michaelis constant. It expresses the substrate concentration at which the reaction rate** has half of its maximum value[3] (cf. pp. 18, 30). From eqn. (3) the reaction rate is

$$(4) \qquad v = \frac{V \times [S]}{[S] + K_m} = \frac{V}{1 + K_m/[S]}$$

This expression formally agrees with the result of the derivation according to *Michaelis* and *Menten*[1], and becomes identical with the latter ($K_m = K_S$) when the formation of the enzyme-substrate complex is fast in comparison with the reaction rate. K_m can be easily determined under standardized conditions (see below).

The situation is much more complicated in the case of two-substrate (and three-substrate) reactions. In the general case *(random order)*, the *steady-state* derivation gives expressions of higher order that are difficult to comprehend[4]. Provided that the transformation of the ternary enzyme-substrate complex into the reaction products is relatively slow and that the individual enzyme-substrate complexes are formed rapidly, the result can be simplified. The following form is then obtained[5] (cf. p. 21)

$$(5) \qquad v = \frac{V}{1 + \dfrac{(K_m)_{S_1}}{[S_1]} + \dfrac{(K_m)_{S_2}}{[S_2]} + \dfrac{(K_m)_{S_1 S_2}}{[S_1] \times [S_2]}}$$

---

* On the assumption that there is only one kinetically active intermediate complex and that the reverse reaction has not yet started.
** For definition of the initial reaction rate v_0 or v_i, see foot-note on p. 18.

A similar form (under the same condition) can also be obtained by derivation according to the principles of *Michaelis* and *Menten*[6]. In this case the Michaelis constants (K_m) are replaced by dissociation constants (K_S), which are assigned to the following reactions[7]: $(K_S)_{S_1}$ to the reaction $ES_1 S_2 \rightleftharpoons ES_2 + S_1$; $(K_S)_{S_2}$ to the reaction $ES_1 S_2 \rightleftharpoons ES_1 + S_2$; $(K_S)_{S_1 S_2}$ to the identical product of either the dissociation constants $(K_S')_{S_1}$ (reaction $ES_1 \rightleftharpoons E + S_1$) and $(K_S)_{S_2}$ (reaction $ES_1 S_2 \rightleftharpoons ES_1 + S_2$) or the dissociation constants $(K_S')_{S_2}$ (reaction $ES_2 \rightleftharpoons E + S_2$) and $(K_S)_{S_1}$ (reaction $ES_1 S_2 \rightleftharpoons ES_2 + S_1$).

As long as the binding of one substrate does not influence that of the other (such an effect does occur with allosteric enzymes) and each substrate combines only with its own binding site, the reactions $ES_1 S_2 \rightleftharpoons S_1 + ES_2$ and $ES_1 \rightleftharpoons S_1 + E$, for example, give the same dissociation constant, and $(K_S)_{S_1 S_2} = (K_S)_{S_1} \times (K_S)_{S_2}$.

Eqn. (5) is valid even if the substrates are bound to the enzyme in a definite sequence in the formation of the ternary complex *(ordered mechanism*[8]*)*. If no ternary complex is formed, the enzyme acting instead as a transfer agent *(ping-pong* mechanism)[8], the term containing $(K_m)_{S_1 S_2}$ in eqn. (5) disappears.

The determination of K_m for two-substrate reactions (on the assumption that the formation of the enzyme-substrate complexes is fast in comparison with the reaction rate) is described on p. 32 ff.

K_m is by no means an absolute constant, but depends on pH, temperature, effectors, buffer, etc. The reaction conditions should therefore always be specified in connection with the K_m values. The initial reaction rates must always be used in the determination of K_m, because of the known dependence of the reaction rate on the substrate concentration (which decreases in the course of the reaction). Reverse reactions and any product inhibition thus become ineffective, which is the basic assumption here.

Determination of K_m in One-Substrate Reactions

a) If V can be easily determined and if the reaction rate is measured at various substrate concentrations, v_i may simply be plotted against [S] (Fig. 1). The concentration for $v_i = V/2$ is easy to determine. According to eqn. (4), $V/2$ is reached at the concentration $[S] = K_m$.

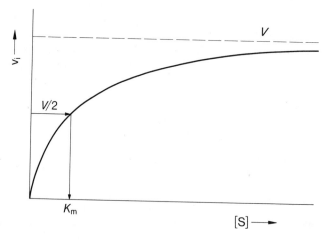

Fig. 1. Determination of K_m via $V_m/2$.

b) The most commonly used method is that of *Lineweaver* and *Burk*[9]. The reciprocal form of eqn. (4) is

(6)
$$\frac{1}{v} = \frac{K_m}{V} \times \frac{1}{[S]} + \frac{1}{V}.$$

This is the equation of a straight line (1/v plotted against 1/[S]), corresponding to

$$y = ax + b.$$

Insertion of $y = 0$ gives $ax = -b$, $-x = b/a$. In this case: for $1/v_i = 0$ (intercept on the abscissa), $-[S] = K_m$. If $x = 0$, then $y = b$. In this case: for $1/[S] = 0$ (intercept on the ordinate), $1/v_i = 1/V$ (Fig. 2).

Both important characteristics of an enzyme are thus obtained in a single operation. Fewer measurements are required than in method a). Deviations from linearity, i.e. from normal kinetics, are readily apparent. These include inhibition by excess substrate[10], negative cooperativity (concave curvature from above), and positive cooperativity (convex curvature from above).

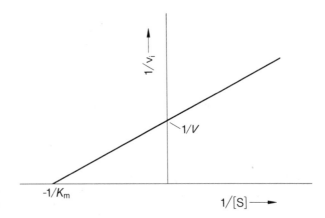

Fig. 2. Determination of K_m according to *Lineweaver* and *Burk*.

c) A linear curve can also be obtained by the method of *Hofstee*[11] (Fig. 3). From eqn. (4) it follows that

$$v[S] + vK_m = V \times [S]; \quad v + \frac{V}{[S]} \times K_m = V \quad \text{and hence}$$

(7)
$$v = -K_m \times \frac{V}{[S]} + V.$$

This is the equation of a descending straight line (v plotted against v/[S]) corresponding to

$$y = -ax + b.$$

Insertion of $y = 0$ gives $ax = b$, $x = b/a$. In this case: for $v_i = 0$ (intercept on the abscissa), $v_i/[S] = V/K_m$. If $x = 0$, then $y = b$. In this case: for $v_i/[S] = 0$ (intercept on the ordinate), $v_i = V$. The author[11] regards the uniform distribution of the experimental points as offering special advantages; this has been denied by *Dixon* and *Webb*[12]. Deviations from normal kinetics can also be easily seen, see e.g.[13].

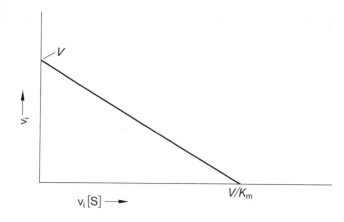

Fig. 3. Determination of K_m according to *Hofstee*[11]. K_m is the ratio of the intercepts on the ordinate and on the abscissa.

d) A possibility for statistical evaluation using the method of least squares has been described by *Wilkinson*[14].

Determination of K_m in Two-Substrate Reactions

a) If the concentration of the substrate S_1 is much greater than $(K_m)_{S_1}$, eqn. (5) can be reduced (cf. p. 22) to:

(8)
$$v = \frac{V}{1 + (K_m)_{S_2}/[S_2]}$$

One thus obtains an equation that formally corresponds to that of a one-substrate reaction and gives $(K_m)_{S_2}$ on evaluation by methods (a) to (d) above. $(K_m)_{S_1}$ can be determined by repetition of the procedure with high concentrations of the other substrate.

Example: K_m *of Alcohol Dehydrogenase from Yeast (EC 1.1.1.1), for Ethanol*

Reaction: ethanol + NAD$^+$ → acetaldehyde + NADH + H$^+$.

The acetaldehyde formed is trapped with semicarbazide. The second substrate NAD is present in a concentration corresponding to 27 times the $(K_m)_{NAD}$ (measured[15] at pH 7.15).

Concentrations in assay mixture: glycine/pyrophosphate buffer, pH 9.0 (0.1 mol/l)
　　　　　　　　　　　　　　　semicarbazide (75 mmol/l)
　　　　　　　　　　　　　　　NAD (2 mmol/l)
　　　　　　　　　　　　　　　glutathione (1 mmol/l)
　　　　　　　　　　　　　　　0.16 µg enzyme protein/assay mixture
　　　　　　　　　　　　　　　various ethanol concentrations (see below).

Wavelength Hg 365 nm, light path 1 cm, final volume 3.02 ml, temperature 25°C.
Activity data are given for the complete assay mixture, calculation of the enzyme activity in accordance with eqn. (7) on p. 238.

Ethanol concentrations [S]		$\dfrac{1}{[S]}$	$\dfrac{\Delta A/\Delta t}{\text{min}^{-1}}$	U	1/U
µmol/assay	mmol/l				
1770	586	0.00171	0.067	0.0595	16.8
177	58.6	0.0171	0.061	0.0541	18.5
35.3	11.7	0.0855	0.040	0.0355	28.2
17.7	5.86	0.171	0.029	0.0256	39.0
11.60	3.84	0.260	0.024	0.0211	47.5

Figure 4 shows a graph of the measurements.

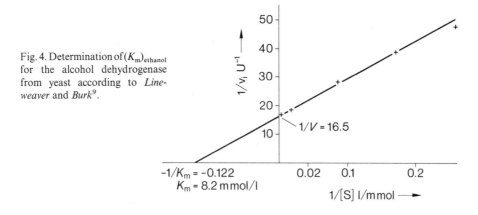

Fig. 4. Determination of $(K_m)_{ethanol}$ for the alcohol dehydrogenase from yeast according to *Lineweaver* and *Burk*[9].

Result:

$$-\frac{1}{K_m} = -0.122 \ \text{l/mmol}; \quad K_m = 8.2 \ \text{mmol/l}$$

$$\frac{1}{V} = 16.5 \ \text{U}^{-1}; \quad V = 0.061 \ \text{U (for 0.16 µg)} \quad \text{or} \quad 381 \ \text{U/mg}$$

Extensive studies by *Wratten* and *Cleland*[15] showed that eqn. (5) is valid for the enzyme (ordered bi-bi mechanism). They found a value of 13 mmol/l for $(K_m)_{ethanol}$ at a pH of 7.15.

The determination of $(K_m)_{S_1 S_2}$ (the last constant in the denominator of eqn.(5)) is easy if one can assume that $K_m = K_S$ (see above, p. 29). The constant can then be broken down into $(K_m)_{S_1 S_2} = (K'_S)_{S_1} \times (K_S)_{S_2}$ or into $(K_m)_{S_1 S_2} = (K'_S)_{S_2} \times (K_S)_{S_1}$. For low concentrations of S_1, eqn.(5) can then be transformed into

(9)

$$v = \frac{\dfrac{V[S_1]}{(K_S)_{S_1}}}{1 + \dfrac{(K'_S)_{S_2}}{[S_2]}}$$

If $[S_1]$ is kept low and constant for a series of measurements and only $[S_2]$ is varied, the numerator in eqn. (9) becomes a constant. The equation is then formally equivalent to eqn. (4), and by the procedures for the determination of K_m (p. 30ff.) it gives the value of $(K'_S)_{S_2}$.

Similarly, with low constant concentrations of S_2 and variation of the concentration of S_1, one obtains $(K_s')_{S_1} \times (K_m)_{S_1 S_2}$ can be calculated as $(K_s')_{S_1} \times (K_s)_{S_2}$ or as $(K_s')_{S_2} \times (K_s)_{S_1}$.

b) If it is difficult to achieve the high concentrations of one of the substrates required according to eqn. (7) for method (a), the method of *Florini* and *Vestling*[16] can be used. It is again assumed that $K_m = K_s$.

$[S_1]$ is kept constant and $[S_2]$ is varied, and the results are plotted reciprocally according to *Lineweaver* and *Burk*[9]. However, the intercept on the ordinate does not correspond to $1/V$, but depends on $[S_1]$ (no substrate saturation!). From the reciprocal form of eqn. (5), for $1/[S_2] = 0$, one obtains the following expression for the intercept on the ordinate:

$$(10) \qquad \frac{1}{(v_i)_{S_1}} = \frac{1}{V} \times \left(1 + \frac{(K_m)_{S_1}}{[S_1]} \right)$$

This measurement is repeated with other constant concentrations of S_1, and $1/(v_i)_{S_1}$ is determined in each case (Fig. 5a). These values are plotted against the corresponding values of $1/[S_1]$

Fig. 5a and 5b. Determination of the dissociation constants of the enzyme-substrate complexes of a two-substrate reaction according to *Florini* and *Vestling*[16].

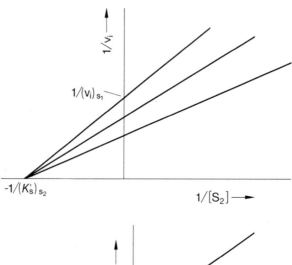

First step (Fig. 5a): Determination of the relative maximum reaction rates with constant $[S_1]$ and varying $[S_2]$. Each concentration of S_1 gives a straight line. If a ternary complex is formed, these lines intersect at a point, the abscissa value of which corresponds to $-1/(K_s')_{S_2}$.

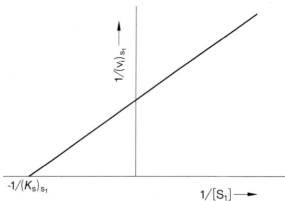

Second step (Fig. 5b): The relative maximum reaction rates $1/(v_i)_{S_1}$ found in the first step are plotted as a function of the reciprocal substrate concentration $(1/[S_1])$. The straight line intersects the abscissa at $-1/[S_1] = -1/(K_s)_{S_1}$. The other two dissociation constants $(K_s')_{S_1}$ and $(K_s)_{S_1}$ are obtained in a similar manner by keeping $[S_2]$ constant and varying $[S_1]$ in the measurements.

(Fig. 5b). The result is a straight line that cuts the abscissa at $1/[S_1] = -1/(K_m)_{s_1}$. Similarly, repetition of the measurement with constant values of $[S_2]$ gives $(K_m)_{s_2}$.

If the reaction mechanism involves formation of a ternary complex, the straight lines in Figure 5a (derived for various constant values of $[S_1]$) meet at a point (on, above, or below the abscissa according to *Frieden*[17]) whose abscissa value is $1/[S_2] = -1/(K'_s)_{s_2} = -(K_s)_{s_1}/(K_m)_{s_1 s_2}$. If one also wishes to determine $(K'_s)_{s_1}$, the same operation is repeated, and $1/v_i$ is plotted against $1/[S_1]$ at various constant values of $[S_2]$. The complex quantity $(K_m)_{s_1 s_2}$ can be calculated by multiplication of either $(K'_s)_{s_1}$ by $(K_s)_{s_2}$, or $(K'_s)_{s_2}$ by $(K_s)_{s_1}$.

Inhibitor Constants

Theory of Reversible Inhibition

Inhibitors can influence the enzymatic reaction in such a way that either K_m is apparently increased or V is apparently decreased, or that both parameters are apparently changed. The first case is known as competitive inhibition, and the second as non-competitive inhibition*[5]. Of the third (mixed) type, the special case in which K_m and V are apparently equally changed is known as "uncompetitive inhibition". The formulae contain an additional term $(1 + [I]/K_I)$, where $[I]$ is the inhibitor concentration and K_I, as a measure of the inhibiting effect, is known as the inhibitor constant. It corresponds[3] to the dissociation constant of the enzyme-inhibitor complex $EI \rightleftharpoons E + I$.

Competitive inhibition is interpreted as competition between the substrate and the inhibitor for the (reactive) enzyme; it is represented (for one-substrate reactions) by the formula

(11)
$$v = \frac{V[S]}{[S] + K_m\left(1 + \frac{[I]}{K_I}\right)}$$

or reciprocally

(12)
$$\frac{1}{v} = \frac{K_m\left(1 + \frac{[I]}{K_I}\right)}{V \times [S]} + \frac{1}{V}$$

This can be derived both by the *steady-state* theory[5] and (with K_S instead of K_m) according to *Michaelis* and *Menten*[1]. For multi-substrate reactions, each term of the denominator of eqn. (5) that corresponds to an enzyme species capable of reacting with the inhibitor must be multiplied

by the expression $\left(1 + \frac{[I]}{K_I}\right)$.

Non-competitive inhibition has been interpreted for one-substrate reactions as interference with the conversion of the enzyme-substrate complex into the reaction products, while the formation of the complex is not affected[5]. The quantity of active enzyme present is thus apparently less, and this is expressed in a decrease in V. According to the *Michaelis-Menten* principles, it is possible to obtain the following equation

(13)
$$v = \frac{V[S]/(1 + [I]/K_I)}{[S] + K_S}$$

---

* *Cleland*[18] uses other definitions. His formulae are therefore different, particularly in the case of non-competitive inhibition.

or reciprocally

(14)
$$\frac{1}{v} = \frac{K_S}{V[S]}\left(1 + \frac{[I]}{K_1}\right) + \frac{1}{V}\left(1 + \frac{[I]}{K_1}\right).$$

For mixed types, in which K_m and V are affected, a combination of the above mechanisms must be assumed. The special case* of "uncompetitive inhibition" is open to several mechanistic interpretations[5,19]; for one-substrate reactions it can be represented by

(15)
$$v = \frac{\dfrac{V[S]}{1 + [I]/K_1}}{\dfrac{K_m}{1 + [I]/K_1} + [S]}$$

or reciprocally

(16)
$$\frac{1}{v} = \frac{K_m}{V[S]} + \frac{1 + [I]/K_1}{V}$$

Other cases, such as allosteric inhibition, partly competitive inhibition, or partly non-competitive inhibition, will not be discussed here.

Determination of the Type of Inhibition and the Value of K_I in One-Substrate Reactions

In principle, all the methods (a) to (d) mentioned on p. 30–32 can be used to determine the type of inhibition and the value of K_1. However, only two of these methods are widely used; these are discussed below. For detailed descriptions, see[5,20,21].

a) If $1/v_i$ is plotted against $1/[S]$ according to *Lineweaver* and *Burk* (see p. 33), one obtains a straight line for each (constant) inhibitor concentration. These straight lines generally have different slopes for different (constant) inhibitor concentrations. In the case of competitive inhibition, they intersect on the ordinate, while in the case of non-competitive inhibition they intersect on the negative abscissa. In mixed types of inhibition, the point of intersection lies in the second quadrant; the special case of uncompetitive inhibition revealed by parallel lines (Fig. 6a–c). The intercepts on the axes can be easily derived from eqns. (12), (14), and (16), and are as follows (unchanged terms are not mentioned):

Competitive inhibition:

Intercept on the abscissa $\qquad \dfrac{1}{[S]} = -\dfrac{1}{K_m(1 + [I]/K_1)}$

Non-competitive inhibition:

Intercept on the ordinate $\qquad \dfrac{1}{v} = \dfrac{1 + [I]/K_1}{V}$

Uncompetitive inhibition:

Intercept on the abscissa $\qquad \dfrac{1}{[S]} = -\dfrac{1 + [I]/K_1}{K_m}$

Intercept on the ordinate $\qquad \dfrac{1}{v} = \dfrac{1 + [I]/K_1}{V}$

---

* Rare in one-substrate reactions, more common in multi-substrate reactions.

Fig. 6a–6c. *Lineweaver-Burk* plots of inhibited enzyme reactions.

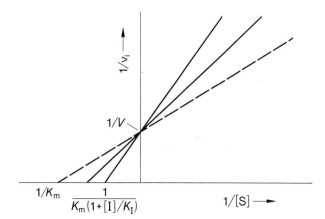

Fig. 6a. Competitive inhibition.

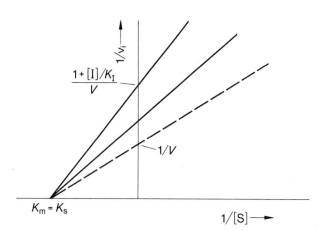

Fig. 6b. Non-competitive inhibition.

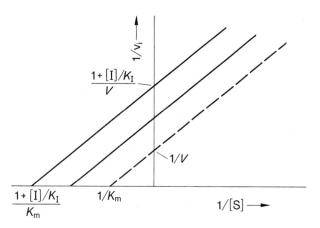

Fig. 6c. Uncompetitive inhibition. The straight line for the uninhibited enzyme reaction is shown broken. The expressions for the intercepts on the coordinates are indicated (see text).

Fig. 7a–7c. *Dixon* plots[22] of inhibited enzyme reactions.

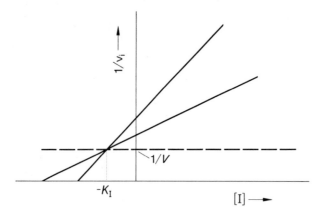

Fig. 7a. Competitive inhibition.

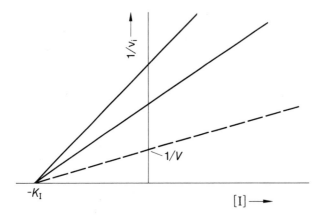

Fig. 7b. Non-competitive inhibition.

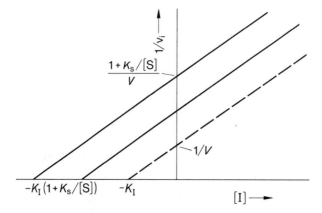

Fig. 7c. Uncompetitive inhibition. The broken straight lines indicate a large excess of substrate. The expressions for the intercepts on the coordinates are indicated (see text).

K_I can be calculated by insertion of the known quantities $1/[S]$ or $1/v$, K_m or V, and $[I]$.

b) A more convenient method is that described by *Dixon*[22]. With $[S]$ constant, v_i is measured with varying $[I]$, and $1/v_i$ is plotted against $[I]$. In all the types of inhibition mentioned, a straight line is obtained for each substrate concentration. These lines intersect in the second quadrant at an ordinate value of $1/V$ in the case of competitive inhibition, and on the negative abscissa in the case of noncompetitive inhibition, whereas in uncompetitive inhibition they are again parallel (Fig. 7 a–c). The negative abscissa value of the intersection points for competitive and non-competitive inhibition corresponds to K_I. For this point, eqns. (12) and (14) must become independent of $[S]$; this is achieved by the condition that $[I] = -K_I$.

If the type of inhibition is known, the evaluation can be further simplified by simply plotting a straight line for one substrate concentration and various inhibitor concentrations, and then plotting $1/v_i$ against $[I]$ according to *Dixon*. In the case of competitive inhibition, the intersection of this straight line with the horizontal line through $1/v_i = 1/V$ ist determined. In the case of non-competitive inhibition, the intercept on the abscissa is determined. These values correspond to $-K_I$.

In other types of inhibition, which are not discussed in detail here, curved lines may be obtained, according to Dixon. The reader must be referred here to more comprehensive articles[5,18,20,23].

Treatment of Inhibited Two-Substrate Reactions

Kinetic derivations for inhibited two-substrate reactions are usually very complex. The result of graphic representation depends both on the type of the uninhibited reaction and on the attack mechanism of the inhibitor. It also depends on which substrate concentration is kept constant in the measurement and which is varied. For example *Cleland*[23] showed for an inhibitor with competitive behaviour towards one substrate that the graph of its reaction with other substrate can indicate very different types of inhibition.

For *Lineweaver-Burk* plots, *Cleland*[23] stated rules that allow a certain differentiation of the reaction mechanisms. An interpretation of K_I values for two-substrate reactions is possible only with this information. In this connection, the reader must be referred to the original publication.

References

1 Michaelis, L. & Menten, M.L. (1913) *Biochem. Z.* **49**, 333.
2 Briggs, G.E. & Haldane, J.B.S. (1925) *Biochem. J.* **19**, 338.
3 *Enzyme Nomenclature*, Recommendations (1964) of the IUB, Elsevier Publishing Company, Amsterdam, London, New York 1973, p. 29.
4 King, E.L. & Altman, C. (1956) *J. phys. Chem.* **60**, 1375.
5 Dixon, M. & Webb, E.C. (1964) *Enzymes*, 2nd edition, Longmans, London.
6 Haldane, J.B.S. (1930) *Enzymes*, Longmans, London.
7 Alberty, R.A. (1953) *J. Am. Chem. Soc.* **75**, 1928.
8 Cleland, W.W. (1963) *Biochim. Biophys. Acta* **67**, 104.
9 Lineweaver, H. & Burk, D. (1934) *J. Chem. Soc.* **56**, 658.
10 Hakala, M.T., Glajd, A.J. & Schwert, G.W. (1956) *J. biol. Chem.* **221**, 191.
11 Hofstee, B.H.J. (1959) *Nature* **184**, 1296.
12 Dixon, M. & Webb, E.C. (1959) *Nature* **184**, 1298.
13 Beavo, J.A., Hardman, J.G. & Sutherland, E.W. (1971) *J. biol. Chem.* **246**, 3841.
14 Wilkinson, G.N. (1961) *Biochem. J.* **80**, 324.
15 Wratten, C.C. & Cleland, W.W. (1963) *Biochemistry* **2**, 935.
16 Florini, J.R. & Vestling, C.S. (1957) *Biochim. Biophys. Acta* **25**, 575.

17 Frieden, C. (1957) *J. Amer. Soc.* **79**, 1849.
18 Cleland, W.W. (1963) *Biochim. Biophys. Acta* **67**, 173.
19 Friedenwald, J.S. & Maengwyn-Davies, G.D. (1954) in *A Symposium on the Mechanism of Enzyme Action* (McElroy, W.D. & Glass, B., eds.) Johns Hopkins Press, Baltimore.
20 Webb, J.L. (1963) *Enzyme and Metabolic Inhibitors*, Vol. I, Academic Press, New York & London.
21 Cleland, W.W. (1970) in *The Enzymes* (Boyer, P.D., ed.) Vol. II, Academic Press, New York & London, p. 1.
22 Dixon, M. (1953) *Biochem. J.* **55**, 170.
23 Cleland, W.W. (1963) *Biochim. biophys. Acta* **67**, 188.

Determination of Substance Concentration of Metabolites (End-Point Methods)

Hans Ulrich Bergmeyer

If a substance takes part in an enzymatic reaction, this reaction can be used for the quantitative determination of the substance by physical, chemical or enzymatic analysis of the product or of the unreacted starting material after the completion of the enzyme-catalyzed reaction.

If the conversion of the substrate is practically complete, the enzymatic analysis is simple, and the result can easily be calculated with the aid of the known physical constants of the substrate (e.g. the absorption coefficient in the case light-absorbing substances).

Simple End-Point Methods

Basis

Let us suppose that we wish to determine a substance S, which is completely converted into the product P in an enzymatic reaction S → P, where P is chemically and physically different from S. If S, unlike P, has a characteristic light absorption, then S can be determined directly even in the presence of other absorbing substances, by letting the enzymatic reaction take place in the spectrophotometer cuvette. The absorbance decreases by an amount corresponding to the quantity of S converted.

> *Example:* Determination of uric acid ($\varepsilon_{293\,nm} = 12.6 \times 10^2\,1 \times mol^{-1} \times mm^{-1}$) with urate oxidase.
>
> $$uric\ acid + O_2 + 2\,H_2O \rightarrow allantoin + H_2O_2 + CO_2$$

Conversely, P may absorb light while S does not.

> *Example:* Determination of CoA with phosphotransacetylase; the reaction product acetyl-CoA absorbs light at 233 nm ($\varepsilon = 4.44 \times 10^2\,1 \times mol^{-1} \times mm^{-1}$).
>
> $$CoA-SH + CH_3CO-OPO_3H_2 \underset{}{\overset{PTA}{\rightleftharpoons}} CoA-S-COCH_3 + H_3PO_4$$

Another possibility is that P possesses acidic properties. In this case it may be titrated or determined by manometric measurement of the liberation of CO_2 from bicarbonate buffer. Various measuring techniques can be used. The technique naturally does not affect the principles of enzymatic analysis. The examples given below refer to absorption spectrophotometers since, next to fluorimetry, spectrophotometric methods of measurement are by far the most strongly favoured at present. The most widely used enzymatic reactions are those with NAD*-dependent and NADP*-dependent dehydrogenases.

General equation:

$$S_1 + \text{coenzyme}^+ \rightarrow P_1 + \text{coenzyme H} + H^+$$

$$\text{or} \quad S_2 + \text{coenzyme H} + H^+ \rightarrow P_2 + \text{coenzyme}^+$$

Examples:

$$\text{ethanol} + NAD^+ \rightarrow \text{acetaldehyde} + NADH + H^+$$

$$\text{or} \quad \text{pyruvate} + NADH + H^+ \rightarrow \text{lactate} + NAD^+$$

The pyridine coenzymes absorb light at 260 nm, and in the reduced state they have an additional absorbance peak at 339 nm (see Fig. 1). By monitoring the absorbance at 339 nm, the enzymatic

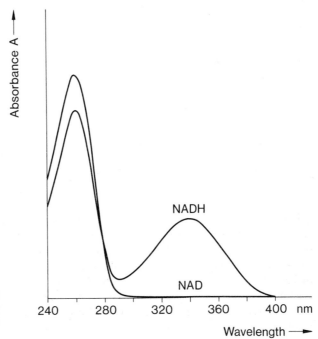

Fig. 1. Absorbance of NAD and NADP as a function of wavelength. NADP and NADPH have the same curves.

conversion of the substrate S_1 or S_2 can be followed directly in the photometer cuvette without intervention in the chemical process. Regardless of whether NAD accepts hydrogen from the substrate as in the above example of the oxidation of ethanol, or whether NADH donates hydro-

---

* NAD = nicotinamide-adenine dinucleotide. NADP = nicotinamide-adenine dinucleotide phosphate.

gen as in the reduction of pyruvate to lactate, the considerations that apply are the same. The
quantity measured is the absorbance change ΔA.

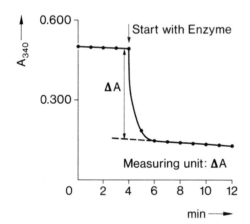

β-Nicotinamide-adenide dinucleotide (phosphate)

The course of the reaction in an assay by the end-point method (decrease in the concentration
of NADH) is shown schematically in Fig. 2.

Fig. 2. Enzymatic determination of a substrate by
the end-point method (schematic).

All enzymatic reactions involving coenzymes are two-substrate reactions. However, two-substrate
reactions can be treated kinetically as one-substrate reactions (cf. eqn. (33) in Table 1, p. 22) if
one of the substrates is present in a very high concentration in relation to its Michaelis constant.
These conditions are also desirable for end-point determinations with coenzymes, simply because
of the righer reaction rate. If NAD(P)H is the second substrate, however, the degree to which its
concentration can be increased is limited by its absorbance. On the basis of experience, relatively
large quantities of enzyme are used with relatively little substrate, so that the reaction proceeds
rapidly to completion. The value should thus be easily readable (neither too low or too high).

In general, the following questions must be considered in designing an enzymatic assay:

Is the action of the enzyme specific?
Is the affinity of the enzyme for its substrate sufficiently high (sufficiently small K_m)?
Is the enzyme sufficiently active?
Is the equilibrium of the reaction favourable?
Can complete conversion of the substrate be achieved in an acceptable time?

Some of these questions can be answered with the aid of data from the literature. Measurement and calculation are necessary for the others.

If the reaction equilibrium lies almost entirely on the product side, the calculation of the reaction time or of the catalytic activity of the enzyme to be used is relatively simple.

With smaller concentrations of substrate in the assay, depending on the K_m of the substance to be determined, we may have $[S] \cong K_m$, $[S] < K_m$, or $[S] \ll K_m$. However, in any case by the end of the reaction at the latest, $[S] \ll K_m$. The reaction then takes place according to the laws for first-order reactions. The conversion curve approaches the end point asymptotically.

Example:

If in the final phase of the reaction $[S_1] = 0.01 (K_m)_{S_1}$, then $v_i \cong 0.01 V$. This means that the enzyme now reacts with only 1% of its declared maximum catalytic activity (see p. 71). Since V is proportional to the enzyme concentration, for complete conversion in reasonable time (especially for the small residual concentrations of the order of 10^{-7} to 10^{-6} mol/l), relatively large amounts of enzyme must be used.

In the large part of the reaction time that is of interest here, the laws for first-order reactions are approximately valid for calculating the end point. Consequently, according to eqn. (29) on p. 22, the quotient V/K_m is decisive. V is nothing other than the catalytic activity of the enzyme used in the assay, expressed in units (U) or katals (kat) (see p. 19). With these quantities it is possible to estimate whether a substance in a particular (e.g. physiological) concentration will react to completion in a reasonable time with a given enzyme.

Examples:

Let a one-substrate reaction run "practically to completion", e.g. to 99%. Let the concentration of the substrate in the assay be $[S]_0 = 5 \times 10^{-5}$ mol/l, and at the end of the reaction, therefore, $[S]_t = 5 \times 10^{-7}$ mol/l. Let $K_m = 7 \times 10^{-4}$ mol/l. Consequently, even at the beginning $[S]_0 = 0.07 K_m$, and according to eqn. (26a) on p. 22, $v_i = V[S]/1.07 K_m$. This corresponds to an uncatalyzed reaction of the first order, so that eqn. (2) on p. 14 applies. In this equation, k must be replaced by $V/1.07 K_m$. The catalytic activity of the enzyme is put in place of V. K_m is expressed in mol/l or 10^3 μmol/ml. Consequently,

$$\frac{V}{K_m} = \frac{V}{1.07 \times 7 \times 10^{-1}} = 1.335 \, V \, (\mu mol/min)/(\mu mol/ml)$$

Expressing the catalytic activity per unit volume yields k = 1.335 V/V min^{-1}, so that for 1 U of enzyme per ml of the assay mixture, k = 1.335 min^{-1}. The reaction time is therefore given by eqn. (3) on p. 14 as

$$t = \frac{2.3}{k} \times lg \frac{a}{a-x} = \frac{2.3}{1.335} \times lg \frac{5 \times 10^{-5}}{5 \times 10^{-7}} = \frac{2.3}{1.335} \times lg \, 10^2 = \frac{2.3}{1.395} \times 2 = 3.4 \, min.$$

For a two-substrate reaction, let the following be given: $[S_1]_0 = 5 \times 10^{-5}$ mol/l, $[S_2]_0 = 1 \times 10^{-1}$ mol/l, $(K_m)_{S_1} = 7 \times 10^{-4}$ mol/l, $(K_m)_{S_2} = 1 \times 10^{-3}$ mol/l. Again 99% conversion of S_1 is to be achieved. In the simplified reaction equation for a two-substrate reaction that can be used for a rough calculation (see p. 21),

$$v = \frac{V}{1 + \frac{(K_m)_{S_1}}{[S_1]} + \frac{(K_m)_{S_2}}{[S_2]}}$$

then, $(K_m)_{S_2}/[S_2] = 0.01$, i.e. is negligible, and as above $v_i = V[S_1]/1.07 (K_m)_{S_1}$.

Thus, to determine the concentrations of substrates in two-substrate reactions, the second substrate must be present in a very high concentration in relation to its Michaelis constant.

Since 99% conversion of the substrate in the formula for uncatalyzed reactions of the first order always leads to the factor $\lg 10^2 = 2$, V/K_m should have a value of the order of 1 ml/min, if the reaction time is to be only a few minutes. *Examples* are shown in Table 1.

Table 1. Examples of practicable catalytic concentrations for end-point methods with given K_m values.

Substrate	Enzyme*	K_m (mol/l)	$V/K_m = 1$ ml/min is given by
ADP	Adenylate kinase	1.6×10^{-3} (30 °C)	1600 U/l
Glucose	Hexokinase	1.0×10^{-4} (30 °C)	100 U/l
Glycerol	Glycerol kinase	5.0×10^{-5} (25 °C)	50 U/l
Uric acid	Urate oxidase	1.7×10^{-5} (20 °C)	17 U/l
Fumarate	Fumarase	1.7×10^{-6} (21 °C)	1.7 U/l

Under these conditions, therefore, the reaction time is independent of the initial concentration of the substrate to be used, provided that the latter is small in relation to K_m. The time required to achieve 99.9% conversion is only 1.5 times this value ($\lg 10^3 = 3$ compared with $\lg 10^2 = 2$).

Measurements using Displacement of Reaction Equilibrium

Enzymatic reactions are equilibrium reactions. If the conversion is incomplete because of an unfavourable equilibrium, a determination is often possible only with the aid of special experimental techniques. If the equilibrium cannot be displaced far enough in favour of the product, calibration curves must be constructed for fixed assay conditions.

Influencing the Equilibrium

1. Increase of substrate concentration, variation of pH, trapping agent: displacement of the equilibrium by high substance concentration of substrate or cofactor, increase of hydrogen ion concentration (within reasonable limits) in reactions starting with reduced coenzymes. Use of alkaline medium with proton-donating reactions, and especially of trapping agents, e.g. when ketones and aldehydes are reaction products. The most common trapping agents are semicarbazide and hydrazine.

Less well known is the fact that occasionally ketone trapping agents can inhibit the catalyzing enzyme, as in the case of 3-hydroxybutyrate dehydrogenase[1]. In the determination of 3-hydroxybutyrate, a minimum of trapping agent (or none at all) should be used; the coenzyme concentration and alkaline medium alone should be sufficient. Semicarbazide and hydrazine react slowly with NAD to form a compound that absorbs in the long-wave UV and surpasses the absorption of NADH.

2. NAD-analogues: a second possibility is the use of NAD-analogues as coenzymes, e.g. acetyl-pyridine-adenine dinucleotide (APAD)[2]. The higher redox potential (NAD/NADH $= -320$ mV;

---

* Adenylate kinase, ATP: AMP phosphotransferase, EC 2.7.4.3.
  Hexokinase, ATP: D-hexose 6-phosphotransferase, EC 2.7.1.1.
  Glycerol kinase, ATP: glycerol 3-phosphotransferase, EC 2.7.1.30.
  Urate oxidase, Urate: oxygen oxidoreductase, EC 1.7.3.3.
  Fumarase, L-Malate hydro-lyase, EC 4.2.1.2.

APAD/APADH $= -248\,\text{mV}$) displaces the equilibrium, and this facilitates the determination of the reduced substrates[3], as is shown by the equilibrium constants in Table 2.

Table 2. Equilibrium constants K of enzymatic reactions (25 °C) acc. to *Holzer*[3].

Reaction*	NAD	APAD
Ethanol $\xrightarrow{\text{ADH}}$ Acetaldehyde	1.0×10^{-11}	1.09×10^{-9}
Glutamate $\xrightarrow{\text{GLDH}}$ 2-Oxoglutarate $+\,NH_3$	7.2×10^{-14}	1.58×10^{-12}
Malate $\xrightarrow{\text{MDH}}$ Oxaloacetate	1.6×10^{-12}	1.00×10^{-10}
Lactate $\xrightarrow{\text{LDH}}$ Pyruvate	2.5×10^{-12}	5.65×10^{-10}

3. Substitution of other reactants: The use of different coenzymes is not the only means of displacing the equilibrium. For example, in the determination of glyceraldehyde-3-phosphate with glyceraldehyde-3-phosphate dehydrogenase (EC 1.2.1.12) in accordance with the equation:

$$\text{glyceraldehyde-3-P} + NAD^+ + P_i \rightarrow \text{1,3-phosphoglycerate-P} + NADH + H^+$$

arsenate may be used instead of phosphate[4]. The 3-phosphoglycerate-1-arsenate formed is labile and decomposes immediately to 3-phosphoglycerate and arsenate. Since the concentration of 1,3-phosphoglycerate-phosphate thus remains at zero, the reaction proceeds to completion.

Regenerating Systems

Another possibility for measurements based on displacement of the equilibrium is the use of "regenerating systems". The determination of glutamate, e.g. with glutamate dehydrogenase (GlDH) proceeds very well without the use of trapping agent at pH 7.6 if the reaction product NADH is continually removed from the equilibrium and simultaneously converted to NAD by lactate dehydrogenase and pyruvate. Thus the effect of NAD on the equilibrium is kept constant[5].

$$\text{glutamate} + NAD^+ + H_2O \xrightarrow{\text{GlDH}} \text{2-oxoglutarate} + NADH + H^+ + NH_3$$

lactate $\xleftarrow{\hspace{2cm}\text{LDH}\hspace{2cm}}$ pyruvate

With a rapid LDH reaction, a cycle is started in which NADH is converted to NAD, and this is continually reduced to NADH in the primary reaction until all the glutamate has reacted. Then the reaction is stopped by destruction of the enzymes and the amount of 2-oxoglutarate formed is determined via reversal of the first reaction by addition of NADH and GlDH.

These "regenerating systems" are particularly important for reactions in which a reaction product inhibits the enzyme catalyzing the reaction. For example, this is often the case with ADP formed

---

* Enzymes
  ADH, Alcohol: NAD oxidoreductase (EC. 1.1.1.1).
  GlDH, L-Glutamate: NAD(P) oxidoreductase (deaminating) (EC 1.4.1.3).
  MDH, L-Malate: NAD oxidoreductase (EC 1.1.1.37).
  LDH, L-Lactate: NAD oxidoreductase (EC 1.1.1.27).

from ATP after phosphorylation in reactions catalyzed by kinases. In this case, the enzyme inhibition by the reaction product can very easily be eliminated by inclusion of the pyruvate kinase reaction. Pyruvate kinase and phosphoenolpyruvate are added as a "regenerating system" to the assay mixture to initiate an ATP/ADP cycle analogous to the NAD/NADH cycle described above.

Specificity of Enzyme Reactions

Enzymes, because of their specificity, allow the quantitative determination of a compound in a mixture (e.g. tissue extract) containing numerous substances of similar chemical structure. *Otto Warburg* termed enzymes the most specific reagents known.

However, apart from those enzymes which are absolutely specific and those with specificity for a group of compounds, there are some enzymes which are unspecific; these react with substances other than "the substrate" at slower rates. As enzymes can be isolated in a high state of purity, it is easy to distinguish whether an enzyme is contaminated by other enzymes or whether it reacts with several substrates. The following distinction has proven useful:

Contaminating activities: An enzyme is contaminated by other enzymes.

Side activities: An enzyme reacts with compounds other than its true substrate.

Just as contaminants (e.g. of 0.1%) in the enzymes used can interfere with enzymatic analysis, so also can side activities of this order of magnitude. The use of impure enzymes can be avoided, but this is not always possible in the case of unspecific enzymes. However, by coupling with a specific enzyme it is possible to make the analysis specific (see p. 48).

Measurements with Aid of Coupled Reactions

If none of the reactants or products of an enzymatic reaction lends itself readily to physical or chemical measurements, it is often possible to determine one of these components enzymatically. This considerably increases the number of substances that can be determined enzymatically.

The reaction in which the substance to be determined is transformed is known as the *auxiliary reaction*, while the reaction used for the actual measurement is called the *indicator reaction*. Both reactions can generally be carried out in a single assay mixture (coupled reactions). If a product of the auxiliary reaction is measured in the indicator reaction, one speaks of a *succeeding indicator reaction*. This is the more common sequence. However, it is also possible for the indicator reaction to yield a necessary substance that reacts stoichiometrically with the substance to be analyzed in the auxiliary reaction; this is known as a *preceding indicator reaction*[6].

If S_1 is the substance to be analyzed, the two cases can be represented schematically as follows.

Succeeding indicator reaction:

$$S_1 + S_2 \xrightarrow{\text{Auxiliary enzyme, } E_{\text{aux.}}} P_1 + P_2$$

$$P_1 + S_3 \xrightarrow{\text{Indicator enzyme, } E_{\text{ind.}}} P_3 + P_4$$

A physical or chemical property of S_2, S_3, P_3, or P_4 is measured.

Preceding indicator reaction:

$$M + N \xrightarrow{\text{Auxiliary enzyme, } E_{aux.}} O + S_2$$

$$S_1 + S_2 \xrightarrow{\text{Indicator enzyme, } E_{ind.}} P_1 + P_2$$

A physical or chemical property of M, N, or O is measured.

Succeeding Indicator Reactions

The function of the auxiliary enzyme is to "bring" the substance to be analyzed into the indicator reaction, which can be measured.

An example is the determination of glucose.

Auxiliary reaction   Indicator reaction

$$\text{glucose} + \text{ATP} \xrightarrow{\text{HK}} \text{ADP} + \text{G-6-P} \qquad \text{G-6-P} + \text{NADP}^+ \xrightarrow{\text{G6P-DH}} \text{6-PG} + \text{NADPH} + \text{H}^+$$

In the auxiliary reaction*, glucose is phosphorylated by ATP to glucose-6-phosphate, and this is the substrate of the NADP-dependent indicator reaction**. The enzymatic determination of G-6-P by the end-point method is a quantitative method for glucose, since the auxiliary enzyme hexokinase quantitatively converts glucose into G-6-P.

Several auxiliary reactions may also be carried out in succession, e.g. in the sequence

$$\text{Sucrose} \rightarrow \text{glucose} \rightarrow \text{G-6-P} \rightarrow \text{6-PG}$$

If different auxiliary reactions give the same reaction product (e.g. in the analysis of sugars), only one indicator reaction is required:

$$\text{Maltose} \rightarrow \boxed{\text{Glucose}} + \boxed{\text{Glucose}}$$
$$\text{Lactose} \rightarrow \boxed{\text{Glucose}} + \text{Galactose}$$
$$\text{Sucrose} \rightarrow \boxed{\text{Glucose}} + \text{Fructose}$$
$$\boxed{\text{Glucose}} + \text{ATP} \rightarrow \boxed{\text{G-6-P}} + \text{ADP}$$
$$\text{G-1-P} \rightarrow \boxed{\text{G-6-P}}$$
$$\text{Fructose} + \text{ATP} \rightarrow \text{ADP} + \text{F-6-P} \rightarrow \boxed{\text{G-6-P}}$$
$$\boxed{\text{G-6-P} + \text{NADP}^+ \rightarrow \text{6-PG} + \text{NADPH} + \text{H}^+}$$

All the reactions shown here finally yield glucose or glucose-6-phosphate, and therefore all of these compounds can be determined by the glucose-6-phosphate-dehydrogenase indicator reaction. These assay methods are attracting great interest in the analysis of foods[7].

Since the assay mixture may already contain compounds that react in the indicator reaction, this reaction is run first. After the indicator reaction has run to completion, the first auxiliary enzyme is added. The determination is thus started "backwards". The principle of the successive addition

---

* Auxiliary enzyme: hexokinase, HK (ATP: D-hexose 6-phosphotransferase, EC 2.7.1.1).

** Indicator enzyme: glucose-6-phosphate dehydrogenase, G6P-DH (D-Glucose-6-phosphate: NADP 1-oxidoreductase, EC 1.1.1.49).

of enzymes can be used for the determination of several substances in the same sample. Several auxiliary reactions are carried out successively as a "chain". One substrate reacts in each of these reactions.

Figure 3 shows a diagram for the determination of 8 substances.

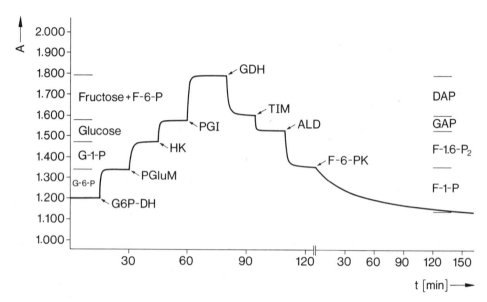

Fig. 3. Determination of a mixture of sugars and sugar phosphates in a single cuvette[8].

When several enzymatic reactions are coupled, a favourable equilibrium is necessary (with or without the aid of special techniques) only for the succeeding indicator reaction. For the auxiliary reactions, it suffices if their equilibrium constants are not as large as the reciprocal of the equilibrium constant of the indicator reaction, as they would otherwise compensate the "suction" of the indicator enzyme.

Coupled reactions also offer advantages with regard to specificity. Whereas the specificity of direct end-point determinations naturally depends on a single enzyme, the specificity of a reaction sequence depends on the most specific enzyme.

> *Examples:* Hexokinase catalyzes the phosphorylation not only of glucose but also – for example – of fructose by ATP. The glucose determination is made specific only by glucose-6-phosphate dehydrogenase, which is specific for G-6-P (not F-6-P). Sorbitol can be determined in the presence of glycerol with the non-specific enzyme polyol dehydrogenase because the reaction product – fructose – can be determined specifically.

The side activities of some enzymes can also be used for the determination of substrates for which there is otherwise no suitable or easily isolable enzyme. For example, *Michal* et al.[9] used the side activity of fructose-6-phosphate kinase with respect to fructose-1-phosphate for the determination of the latter. The determination is made specific for F-1-P by allowing the F-6-P in the sample to react in another way (with PGI via G-6-P) prior to addition of the enzyme.

The reaction times for end-point determinations (cf. also[10]) comprising several steps are generally somewhat longer than in one-step reactions. For the sequence

$$S \xrightarrow{\text{Auxiliary enzyme, } E_{\text{aux.}}} P_1 \xrightarrow{\text{Indicator enzyme, } E_{\text{ind.}}} P_2$$

the indicator reaction generally behaves as a zero-order reaction (see p. 28). If there are two substrates, and $[S_2]_0 \gg (K_m)_{S_2}$, one will always try to treat the auxiliary reaction as a one-substrate reaction. Depending on the size of $[S_1]_0$ in relation to $(K_m)_{S_1}$, it behaves initially in accordance with eqns. (26a) and (29) on p. 22. For most of the time that it takes approach the end point, it can be regarded as a first-order reaction when $[S_1] \ll (K_m)_{S_1}$. To calculate the reaction time for practically complete (e.g. 99%) conversion in analogy with the example on p. 43, the first requirement is that the indicator reaction does not affect the auxiliary reaction, so that, for example, there is no lag phase. This means that the steady state (where the rates of auxiliary and indicator reactions are equal) must be reached rapidly (see p. 23). This must be ascertained along the lines of the calculation of the catalytic activity of the indicator enzyme on p. 70. The reaction time is then calculated as on p. 43.

Example:

Coupled reaction; auxiliary reaction: two substrates; indicator reaction: NADH-dependent (two substrates). The reaction time is to be calculated for 99% conversion of S_1.
Let $[S_1]_0 = 5 \times 10^{-5}$ mol/l, $[S_1]_t = 5 \times 10^{-7}$ mol/l, $(K_m)_{S_1} = 7 \times 10^{-4}$ mol/l. $[S_2]_0 = 1 \times 10^{-1}$ mol/l, $(K_m)_{S_2} = 1 \times 10^{-4}$ mol/l. Hence, even at the beginning, $[S_1]_0 \ll (K_m)_{S_1}$ and $[S_2]_0 \gg (K_m)_{S_2}$, and eqns. (33) and (29) on p. 22 apply. The auxiliary reaction proceeds as a first-order reaction.
In the indicator reaction, for NADH as the second substrate $[S_3]_0 = 1 \times 10^{-4}$ mol/l, $(K_m)_{S_3} = 1 \times 10^{-5}$ mol/l. According to p. 27, in the steady state the concentration of the first substrate $[P_1]$ is constant and therefore the expression $1 + (K_m)_{P_1}/[P_1]$ in eqn. (32) on p. 22 is also a constant. Consequently, the indicator reaction behaves according to eqn. (26a) on p. 22. If $[P_1]$ is kept very low at $10^{-2}(K_m)_{P_1}$ (very short lag phase of the reaction), $(1 + (K_m)_{P_1}/[P_1]) \times [S_3] = 101 \times 10^{-4} \cong 1 \times 10^{-2} \gg (K_m)_{S_3} = 1 \times 10^{-5}$ mol/l, and the indicator reaction is of zero order (see p. 73).
To calculate the required catalytic activity of the indicator enzyme, the following expression from p. 24 applies (primary reaction is identical with auxiliary reaction):

$$V_{\text{ind.}} = \frac{V_{\text{aux.}}}{[S_1] + (K_m)_{S_1}} \times [S_1]$$

With the known values of $[S_1]_0$ and $(K_m)_{S_1}$, then, the value of $V_{\text{ind.}}$ in this case must be at least

$$V_{\text{ind.}} = \frac{5 \times 10^{-5}}{7.5 \times 10^{-4}} \times V_{\text{aux.}} = 0.07 \, V_{\text{aux.}}$$

If this is ensured, the reaction time for 99% conversion is calculated as shown on p. 43, by means of the expression

$$k = \frac{V_{\text{aux.}}}{(K_m)_{S_1}} = \frac{V_{\text{aux.}}}{1.07 \times 7 \times 10^{-1}} = 1.335 \, V_{\text{aux.}} \, (\mu\text{mol/min})/(\mu\text{mol/ml}),$$

and given a catalytic activity of, for example, 1 U of auxiliary enzyme per ml,

$$t = \frac{2.3}{k} \times \lg \frac{[S_1]_0}{[S_1]_t} = \frac{2.3}{1.335} \times \lg 10^2 = 1.72 \times 2 = 3.4 \text{ min}.$$

If the sequence contains several auxiliary reactions, care must again be taken to achieve the smallest possible lag-phase for the over-all reaction. The conditions for this are described on p. 73. In general, the catalytic activity of the second, third, ... auxiliary enzyme may be of the same order of magnitude as that of the indicator enzyme. Even reactions running through several steps can be made to proceed relatively rapidly. Only rarely are long reaction times unavoidable.

Preceding Indicator Reactions

The preceding indicator reaction is used in cases where a succeeding indicator reaction cannot be used or where one reactant is so labile that it is preferable to produce it in the course of the determination.

Applications

Preliminary reactions for the production of unavailable or unstable reactants are known.

> *Example:* Formation of oxaloacetate from stable aspartate and 2-oxoglutarate with aspartate amino-transferase* to provide the (unstable) substrate for malate dehydrogenase**, whose catalytic activity is to be determined.
>
> $$\text{aspartate} + \text{2-oxoglutarate} \xrightleftharpoons{\text{AST}} \text{oxaloacetate} + \text{glutamate}$$
>
> $$\text{oxaloacetate} + \text{NADH} + \text{H}^+ \xrightleftharpoons{\text{MDH}} \text{malate} + \text{NAD}^+$$

With a sufficient excess of catalytic activity of AST, the MDH reaction is rate-determining and can be measured correctly.

If, however, the preceding reaction is also an indicator reaction, problems arise.

> *Examples:*
>
> *Bücher*[11] was the first to use this measuring principle for the determination of the catalytic activity of phosphoglycerate kinase:
>
> $$\text{GAP} + \text{NAD}^+ + \text{P}_i \xrightleftharpoons{\text{GAPDH}^x} \text{1,3-PGP} + \text{NADH} + \text{H}^+$$
>
> $$\text{ADP} + \text{1,3-PGP} \xrightleftharpoons{\text{PGK}^{xx}} \text{3-PG} + \text{ATP}$$

The preliminary reaction not only produces the unstable substrate 1,3-PGP, but also functions as the indicator reaction, since as 1,3-PGP is consumed in the main reaction, and equal quantity is produced in the preliminary reaction with simultaneous formation of NADH. The same situation is found in the determination of the catalytic activity of citrate synthase and in the determination of acetyl-CoA by the same reaction sequence[12]:

$$\text{malate} + \text{NAD}^+ \xrightleftharpoons{\text{MDH}} \text{oxaloacetate} + \text{NADH} + \text{H}^+$$

$$\text{acetyl-CoA} + \text{oxaloacetate} \xrightleftharpoons{\text{CS}\dagger} \text{citrate} + \text{CoA-SH}$$

---

  * L-Aspartate: 2-oxoglutarate aminotransferase (EC 2.6.1.1).
 ** L-Malate: NAD oxidoreductase (EC 1.1.1.37).
  x Glyceraldehyde phosphate dehydrogenase, GAPDH (D-Glyceraldehyde-3-phosphate: NAD oxido-reductase phosphorylating (EC 1.2.1.12).
 xx Phosphoglycerate kinase, PGK (ATP: 3-phospho-D-glycerate 1-phosphotransferase, EC 2.7.2.3).
  † Citrate synthase, CS, "condensing enzyme" (Citrate oxaloacetate-lyase, EC 4.1.3.7).

The calculation of the results of the end-point method with a preceding indicator reaction for the determination of acetate[6] and of acetylphosphate[12] was desribed in detail for the first time in 1965/66. The previously incorrect calculation in the determination of acetyl-CoA had also been pointed out by *Pearson*[13] in 1965. The acetate determination was probably the first determination of this type to be carried out on biological material.

Special Aspects and Calculation

Using the determination of acetate as an example, the following illustrates details of the reactions involved in an assay with a preceding indicator reaction.

(a) $$\text{Ac} + \text{ATP} \xrightarrow{\text{AK*}} \text{Ac} \sim \text{P} + \text{ADP}$$

(b) $$\text{Ac} \sim \text{P} + \text{CoA-SH} \xrightarrow{\text{PTA**}} \text{Ac-S-CoA} + \text{P}_i$$

(c) $$\text{Ac-S-CoA} + \text{OA} + \text{H}_2\text{O} \xrightarrow{\text{CS}} \text{citrate} + \text{CoA-SH}$$

To provide OA and to act as *preceding* indicator reaction:

(d) $$\text{malate} + \text{NAD}^+ \xrightarrow{\text{MDH}} \text{OA} + \text{NADH} + \text{H}^+$$

The oxoaloacetate required in reaction (c) is produced in reaction (d). This is also the indicator reaction. As oxaloacetate is consumed by reaction with acetate in accordance with eqn. (c), the equilibrium of reaction (d) is adjusted with formation of NADH which can be determined from the absorbance change at 339 (Hg 334, Hg 365) nm. The overall formula

(e) $$\text{acetate} + \text{ATP} + \text{NAD}^+ + \text{malate} \rightarrow \text{citrate} + \text{ADP} + \text{NADH} + \text{H}^+ + \text{P}_i$$

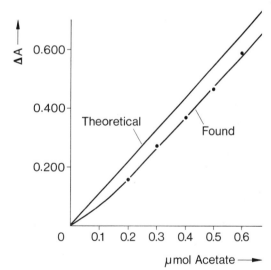

Fig. 4. Experimental values for the acetate determination after conventional evaluation. Without taking into account the displacement of the MDH equilibrium it was assumed that $\Delta A_{365} = A_2 - A_1$. The experimental values are corrected for the acetate content of the reagents. Assay conditions: 365 nm; pH 8.0; final volume 3 ml; 25 °C.

---

* Acetate kinase, AK (ATP: acetate phosphotransferase, EC 2.7.2.1).
** Phosphotransacetylase, PTA (Acetyl-CoA: orthophosphate acetyltransferase, EC 2.3.1.8).

suggests that the quantity of acetate transformed will be directly proportional to the increase in absorbance due to NADH. The acetate conversion in accordance with eqns. (a)–(c) is in fact directly proportional to the consumption of oxaloacetate (OA). However, this is not directly proportional to the increase in the NADH concentration; the values found are too low (Fig. 4, p. 51), since the increase in the NADH absorbance, according to the law of mass action, results from the restoration of the equilibrium of reaction (d) as a consequence of the consumption of oxaloacetate.

By how much the NADH measurements are too low can be shown in model experiments. If increasing amounts of NADH (of known absorbance) are added to a mixture in which the MDH equilibrium has been attained and which has an NADH absorbance A_1, the theoretical increase in absorbance should be as shown in Figure 5. However, in practice the increase is too small; the dotted curve agrees with that in Figure 6, p. 53, which results from the acetate conversion when µmol acetate are expressed in terms of the absorbance of NADH. The differences δA between the measured values and the theoretical values are plotted in the lower half of Fig. 5 (right-hand ordinate). The result is a curve which corresponds to the oxaloacetate content of the system.

At different pH values, curves are obtained whose starting points (intercepts with the ordinate) correspond to the K' values for the MDH equilibrium (Fig. 7, p. 54).

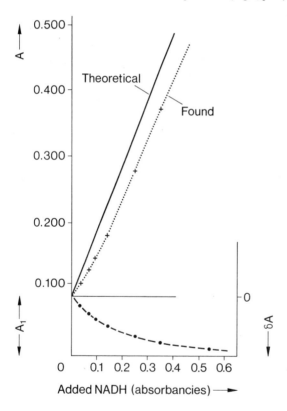

Fig. 5. Model experiment on the displacement of the MDH equilibrium by addition of NADH. Defined amounts of NADH were added to a system where the MDH equilibrium was already attained. Conditions of assay: 365 nm; pH 8.0; final volume 3 ml; 29°C. Differences δ A between the measured values and the theoretical values are plotted in the lower half (right-hand ordinate). The dotted curve corresponds to the oxaloacetate concentration of the assay system.

In the undisturbed equilibrium at time t_1 (Fig. 6, p. 53), the NADH concentration (absorbance A_1) is given by the equilibrium constant:

(1)
$$\frac{K}{[H^+]} \equiv K' = \frac{[OA] \times [NADH]}{[malate] \times [NAD^+]} = \frac{[NADH]^2}{[malate] \times [NAD^+]}$$

$$= \frac{[NADH]^2}{([malate]_0 - [NADH]_1) \times ([NAD^+]_0 - [NADH]_1)}$$

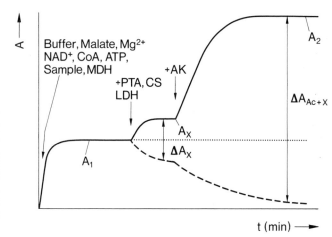

Fig. 6. Schematic representation of the enzymatic determination of acetate (or acetyl phosphate or acetyl-CoA). ΔA_x corresponds to the acetyl phosphate, acetyl-CoA and lactate content of the sample. It also includes the slight absorption due to the enzymes PTA, CS and LDH.

The concentrations of OA and NADH are the same at equilibrium. From the A_1 values at various pH values a K of 9.92×10^{-13} (see Table 3) is obtained. The increase in absorbance from A_1 to A_2 cannot, contrary to usual practice, serve as a measure of the conversion of acetate, because the NADH concentration in the MDH equilibrium at time t_1 does *not* remain constant, due to simultaneous the removal of oxaloacetate. *Bücher*[11, 14, 15] first noted this effect in 1947 in the determination of the activity of phosphoglycerate kinase with a preceding indicator reaction and published the calculations.

Table 3. Equilibrium constants of the MDH reaction, L-malate, 10 mmol/l, NAD, 1 mmol/l, triethanolamine buffer, 150 mmol/l; 25 °C.

pH	$[H^+]$	Absorbance A_1 339 nm	Hg 365 nm	$K' \equiv K/[H^+]$ from measured values*	K from measured values	K' calculated from mean K
7.37	4.27×10^{-8}	0.096	0.051	2.32×10^{-5}	9.906×10^{-13}	2.32×10^{-5}
7.54	2.88×10^{-8}	0.115	0.061	3.34×10^{-5}	9.619×10^{-13}	3.44×10^{-5}
7.68	2.09×10^{-8}	0.134	0.071	4.55×10^{-5}	9.499×10^{-13}	4.75×10^{-5}
7.76	1.74×10^{-8}	0.153	0.081	5.95×10^{-5}	10.344×10^{-13}	5.70×10^{-5}
7.87	1.35×10^{-8}	0.170	0.090	7.36×10^{-5}	9.936×10^{-13}	7.35×10^{-5}
7.99	1.02×10^{-8}	0.195	0.103	9.71×10^{-5}	9.899×10^{-13}	9.73×10^{-5}
8.09	8.13×10^{-9}	0.220	0.116	1.24×10^{-4}	10.081×10^{-13}	1.22×10^{-4}
8.19	6.46×10^{-9}	0.246	0.130	1.56×10^{-4}	10.077×10^{-13}	1.54×10^{-4}

Mean: 9.920×10^{-13}

* Mean values of measurements at 339 mn and Hg 365 nm.

What is required is the absorbance change due to NADH corresponding to the acetate concentration present. It can be calculated from the decrease in oxaloacetate concentration, which is directly proportional to the conversion of acetate. At time t_2 this is given by:

$$(2) \qquad [OA]_2 = K' \times \frac{[malate]_2 \times [NAD^+]_2}{[NADH]_2} =$$

$$= K' \times \frac{([malate]_0 - [NADH]_2) \times ([NAD^+]_0 - [NADH]_2)}{[NADH]_2}$$

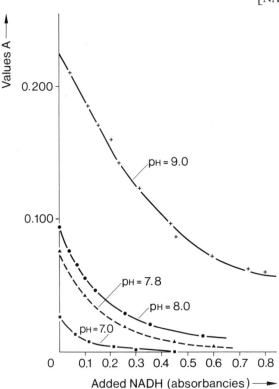

Fig. 7. Displacement of the MDH equilibrium by addition of NADH at different pH values. The curves correspond to the K values in Table 3, p. 53.

According to Figs. 5 and 6, the conversion of acetate can be represented by the effect that it produces: OA decrease + NADH increase.

$$(3) \qquad \Delta[Acetate] = [NADH]_2 - [OA]_2$$

Substituting equation (2) into equation (3) yields

$$(4) \qquad \Delta[acetate] = [NADH]_2 - K' \times \frac{([malate]_0 - [NADH]_2) \times ([NAD^+]_0 - [NADH]_2)}{[NADH]_2}$$

Generally $[NADH]_2 \ll [malate]_0$, therefore

$$(5) \qquad \Delta[acetate] = [NADH]_2 - K' \times \frac{[malate]_0}{[NADH]_2} \times ([NAD^+]_0 - [NADH]_2)$$

If all concentrations are expressed as NADH absorbances and $[\text{malate}]_0$ is 10 mmol/l and $[\text{NAD}^+]_0$ is 1 mmol/l, the absorbances at 339 nm are 63 and 6.3 respectively, and at Hg 365 nm 34 and 3.4 respectively.

Therefore, for measurements at 339 nm:

$$(6) \qquad \Delta A_{\text{acetate}} = A_2 - K' \times \frac{63}{A_2} \times (6.3 - A_2)$$

and for measurements at Hg 365 nm:

$$(7) \qquad \Delta A_{\text{acetate}} = A_2 - K' \times \frac{34}{A_2} \times (3.4 - A_2)$$

According to equation (1) the K' values can be expressed in terms of absorbance; e.g. for 339 nm:

$$K' = \frac{A_1^2}{63 \times (6.3 - A_1)}.$$

It follows that for measurements at 339 nm:

$$(8) \qquad \Delta A_{\text{acetate}} = A_2 - \frac{A_1^2 \times (6.3 - A_2)}{A_2 \times (6.3 - A_1)}$$

and for measurements at Hg 365 nm:

$$(9) \qquad \Delta A_{\text{acetate}} = A_2 - \frac{A_1^2 \times (3.4 - A_2)}{A_2 \times (3.4 - A_1)}$$

When A_2 is large, the term to be subtracted can be neglected; for small values of A_2 the ratios $(6.3 - A_2)/(6.3 - A_1)$ and $(3.4 - A_2)/(3.4 - A_1)$ will not deviate from 1 by more than 1–2%; therefore

$$(10) \qquad \Delta A_{\text{acetate}} = A_2 - \frac{A_1^2}{A_2}$$

can be used.

Since eqns. (6) and (7) are tied by K' to the accurate maintenance of a particular pH, eqns. (8) and (9) or (10) can always be used for the calculation. Measurement of A_1 serves, at a given pH, to simultaneously check on the concentrations of L-malate and NAD^+, and in assays on biological material to check whether the sample contains interfering compounds. The correct values for A_1 for the pH-range 7.37–8.19 can be obtained from Table 3; if necessary, other values can be obtained by interpolation.

The calculations for other systems are similar. A prerequisite for assays based on this principle is that the equilibrium of the indicator reaction lie more on the side of the starting material, but that of the overall reaction more on the side of the end products. Extreme care must be taken to ensure that no interfering side reactions remove the products of the indicator reaction, examples of such reactions in the present case being the decomposition of oxaloacetate to pyruvate (giving artificially high results) and the reoxidation of NADH by NADH-oxidase (giving artificially low results). Since both the product of the indicator reaction (in this case oxaloacetate) and the substrate to be determined (in this case acetate or acetyl-CoA) are present only in low concentrations, the kinetics are necessarily unfavourable, and large quantities of enzyme must be used.

References

1 Bergmeyer, H.U. & Bernt, E. (1965) *Enzymol. Biol. Clin.* **5**, 65.
2 Kaplan, N.O., Ciotti, M.M. & Stolzenbach, F.E. (1956) *J. biol. Chem.* **221**, 833.
3 Holzer, H. & Söling, H.D. (1962) *Biochem. Z.* **336**, 201.
4 Negelein, E. & Brömel, H. (1939) *Biochem. Z.* **301**, 135.
5 Bergmeyer, H.U. & Czok, R. (1963) in *Methods of Enzymatic Analysis* (Bergmeyer, H.U., ed.) 1st edn., p. 388, Verlag Chemie, Weinheim and Academic Press, New York.
6 Bergmeyer, H.U. & Möllering, H. (1966) *Biochem. Z.* **344**, 167.
7 Bergmeyer, H.U. (1964) *Mitt. Bl. der GDCh-Fachgr. Lebensm.-Chem. gerichtl. Chem.* **18**, 129.
8 Möllering, H. & Michal, G. (1968) unpublished.
9 Michal, G., Möllering, H. & Gruber, W. (1968) *Enzymol. Biol. Chem.* **9**, 154.
10 Bergmeyer, H.U. (1973) *Dechema-Monographien*, Vol. **71**, p. 277, Verlag Chemie, Weinheim.
11 Bücher, Th. (1947) *Biochim. Biophys. Acta* **1**, 292.
12 Buckel, W. & Eggerer, H. (1965) *Biochem. Z.* **343**, 29.
13 Pearson, D.J. (1965) *Biochem. J.* **95**, 23c.
14 Bücher, Th. (1955) in *Methods in Enzymology* (Colowick, S.P. & Kaplan, N.O., eds.) Vol. **I**, p. 415, Academic Press, New York.
15 Bücher, Th., Luh, W. & Pette, D. (1964) in *Handbuch der physiologisch- und pathologisch-chemischen Analyse* (Hoppe-Seyler/Thierfelder, eds.) Vol. **6**, part A, p. 292, Springer-Verlag, Berlin, Göttingen, Heidelberg.

Determination of the Catalytic Activity of Enzymes

Hans Ulrich Bergmeyer

The catalytic activity of an enzyme is measured in terms of the rate of the reaction catalyzed. The reaction rate has until now been expressed in units* of μmol/min. According to the SI-system (see p. 9) the unit is mol/s and this kind of quantity is called a katal (kat)[1-3]. 1 U $\cong$ 16.67 × 10^{-9} kat = 16.67 nkat.

This unit does not agree with the definition of the reaction rate in classical reaction kinetics, where the measured magnitude is the change in *concentration* per unit time; here, it is the change in *amount* per unit time. Since in practice, e.g. in photometric determinations, one always measures time-dependent changes in concentration (mol/l · s from $\Delta A/\Delta t$), the change in amount per unit time (mol/s) can be obtained via the volume, in order to obtain U or kat (cf. p. 238).

The reaction conditions for measurement of the catalytic activities of enzymes should be optimal, so that the maximum possible rate of reaction is measured. This requirement is fundamental to the definition of the kind of quantity[1,2]. The optimum reaction conditions refer to the type of the buffer and its concentration, the pH, cofactors, activators, and substrate concentration(s).

Factors Affecting Catalytic Activity

Only optimum conditions for the individual methods of measuring the catalytic activities of enzymes make the results of measurement comparable. For some years, attempts have been made on the national and international levels to standardize these methods for the field of clinical chemistry (cf.[4-8]); for this purpose, optimum experimental conditions must be worked out. In

---

* international unit U.

all attempts to make the conditions of measurement optimal, the procedure must remain practicable. The term "optimized methods" has been coined for methods which take both aspects into account[4,7].

In contrast to the determination of the substance concentration of substrates (where the accuracy of the results of a method can be checked by comparison with a weighed-out standard), standardization in the determination of the catalytic activities of enzymes can be achieved only on the basis of defined conditions of measurement. The weighing out of a crystalline enzyme with a definite catalytic activity would by no means lead to identical, accurate results under different conditions of measurement.

Standardizing the conditions of measurement means taking a multiplicity of factors into account. The basis is the measurement temperature.

Temperature

Like all chemical reactions, enzyme-catalyzed reactions are sensitive to temperature changes. The temperature coefficient of the reaction rate can be as large as 10% per degree or more (cf.[9]). This means that for a temperature rise of 1°C, the value found for the catalytic activity of an enzyme is about 10% too high. The temperature dependence of chemical reactions can be formulated mathematically. It was found empirically that a linear relation generally exists between the logarithm of the rate constant k and the reciprocal of the absolute temperature T (see Fig. 1):

$$(1) \qquad \qquad \log k = a - \frac{b}{T}$$

(a and b are constant for a given reaction).

This equation was interpreted theoretically by S. Arrhenius[10].

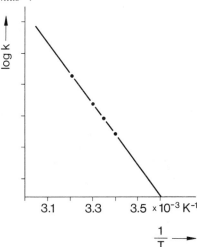

Fig. 1. Linear relationship between the logarithm of the rate constant and the reciprocal of the absolute temperature.

In the case of enzyme reactions, the rate constant k of eqn. (1) corresponds to the expression $k[E] = V$, according to eqn. (26) on p. 18. By means of an *Arrhenius* plot (plot of $\log V$ against $1/T$; cf.[11]), one can determine for a given enzyme reaction whether, for example, the effective enzyme concentration changes with a deviation from linearity at elevated temperatures. Such measurements have been performed by G. Szasz[12,13].

For practical laboratory work in any case, the greatest possible constancy of temperature is essential in determinations of catalytic activity.

At what temperature the catalytic activities should be measured is another question. In 1961, the *International Union of Biochemistry* (IUB) recommended 25°C as the measurement temperature[14]. This recommendation was changed to 30°C in 1964[1,2]. Some groups of clinical chemists (cf.[15-17]) are demanding 37°C.

However, the specification of a uniform reaction temperature is of fundamental importance, all the more so in view of the worldwide attempts at optimization and standardization in biochemistry and clinical chemistry. Both technical and physico-chemical reasons speak against 37°C as the measurement temperature[18].

Arguments in favor of the lowest possible measurement temperature are as follows: the smaller difference from room temperature (smaller fluctuations of temperature in the cuvette, faster temperature equilibration, approximation to the calibration temperature of pipettes and other measuring vessels); the often inadequate solubility of substrates (which is sometimes not even sufficient to obtain the higher optimum concentrations at elevated temperatures – cf. also p. 60); the inactivation of enzyme proteins during measurement and preparation, which increases considerably with rising temperature; and finally, the problems with allosteric enzymes. On the other hand, the understandable desire for the greatest possible measured effect in a short time (i.e. high reaction rates) can be satisfied most easily by the highest possible reaction temperature. These opposing arguments point to 25°C (30°C as a maximum) as the most suitable temperature of measurement, particularly since the 37°C that is often demanded for emotional reasons corresponds to "physiological" conditions just as little as do the other parameters in the cuvette.

It is particularly in the use of automatic analyzers that further attempts are always being made to establish a link with measured values at other temperatures by means of conversion factors. Caution is necessary here. For clinical chemistry, such conversion factors must have been derived from a sufficiently large group of subjects, and they must be identical for low and high catalytic activities of an enzyme, i.e. be independent of the organ or cell compartment of origin. It is well known that in the pathologic range in particular, the ratio of the amounts of isoenzymes (e.g. those of lactate dehydrogenase) can be greatly changed. Consequently, not only are the poorly defined optimum substrate, buffer, and pH-conditions for "LDH" upset, but the temperature dependence is decisively determined by the isoenzyme that has been discharged into the serum in increased amounts. Conversion factors *(temperature converting factors)* must therefore be determined carefully for each individual enzyme and their applicability strictly checked (cf.[19]). For use in clinical chemistry, such factors have been determined for the temperatures 25°C, 35°C, and 37°C for the enzymes γ-glutamyl transpeptidase, alkaline phosphatase, creatine kinase, and alanine aminotransferase[19].

International agreement on a measurement temperature would be the simplest basis for an international standardization of methods. The *International Federation of Clinical Chemistry* (IFCC) therefore recommends a temperature of 30°C for the determination of the catalytic activities of enzymes[7].

Buffer and pH-values

All enzymes have an optimum pH-range for their activity. This range is often very narrow. The pH-optimum not only depends on the nature and ionic strength of the buffer, but also generally varies with both temperature and substrate concentration. For example, the pH-optima for alkaline phosphatase at 25°C, 30°C, and 37°C are 10.3, 10.1, and 9.9 respectively[20]. The optimum substrate concentration for p-nitrophenyl phosphate at pH 9.8 is 10 mmol/l, while the corresponding value at pH 10.0 is 25 mmol/l.

In choosing the buffer, care must be taken that the pH-optimum of the reaction is as close as possible to the pK of the buffer. The type of buffer may also affect catalytic activity. Thus, leucine aminopeptidase shows a higher activity in tris buffer than in phosphate buffer[21] at the same pH.

Substance concentration of substrates

According to eqn. (26), p. 18, the rate of an enzyme reaction depends on the substance concentration of the substrates. Coenzymes behave as substrates from the point of view of reaction kinetics. With increasing coenzyme concentration, the rate of the reaction becomes greater until it approaches a limiting value.

If the optimum reaction rate V of an enzyme reaction is to be attained, the Michaelis constant K_m must be negligibly small in comparison with the concentration of the substrate (see p. 19). However, the ideal case in which, in conformance with the equation of *Michaelis* and *Menten*

(2)
$$v = \frac{V \times [S]}{K_m + [S]},$$

$[S] \gg K_m$, so that $v = V$, is probably rare, since practical factors often prevent it.

Example of the practical upper limit of usable substrate concentrations: In the case of aspartate amino-transferase (EC 2.6.1.1), the second substrate 2-oxoglutarate cannot be added in unlimited concentration, since this substance absorbs light to an appreciable extent at 339 nm and since relatively high concentrations of 2-oxoglutarate inhibit the enzyme[22].

One must decide what errors are tolerable if the condition $[S] \gg K_m$ cannot be realized. Small deviations of v_i from V can in general be compensated by greater sophistication of the measurement (several blank values, compensation of the initial absorbance, etc.).

The K_m value measured in the optimum buffer system with all the cofactors and activators is therefore the reference parameter for the substrate concentration.

The practical consequence of eqn. (2) is that

(3)
$$[S] = \frac{v_i}{V - v_i} \times K_m = F \times K_m$$

If, for example, a value of 0.99 V be substituted for v_i (which means a 1% deviation from V) a value of 99 K_m will be obtained for $[S]$. Thus, for 2%, 3%, 4%, and 5% deviations of v_i from V, for example, the substrate concentrations can be calculated as 49 K_m, 32.3 K_m, 24 K_m, and 19 K_m.

For a given value of F, the optimum substrate concentration can be calculated in the same way as the value of F when the substrate concentration is specified. In practice[22], this procedure is frequently limited by the fact that the enzyme is already inhibited by an excess of substrate (or its product) before it is saturated with it. Consequently, the calculated optimum substrate concentrations may be unreal. The values of $[S]$ determined empirically from the measured values of v_i at increasing substrate concentrations should, however, always be compared with those calculated from them. For determination of the optimum substrate concentrations, see p. 61.

As a rule, the substrate optimum depends on the pH and the temperature (see also[23]).

Other parameters

The protein concentration in the assay mixture may decisively influence the stability of the enzymes during preincubation and the (sometimes longer) duration of the assay[18]. The best-known example is the effect of dilution on the catalytic activity of creatine kinase in serum. Highly active sera diluted with physiological saline give excessively high activities. The serum is assumed to contain an inhibitor. The effect is suppressed by dilution with inactivated serum. It is generally advisable when measuring enzyme activities in serum to specify the ratio of the sample volume to the total volume of the assay mixture.

Inhibitors and activators influence the catalytic activity of enzymes. To achieve full CK activity, for example, a sulfhydryl compound must be added to the assay mixture (cf. p.114, Table 5). The fast inactivation of this enzyme is based on the oxidation of the two sulfhydryl groups at the active binding site of the enzyme. These can be reactivated by SH-reagents. Metal ions are also known to be activators of various enzymes. Another example is the activation of glutamate dehydrogenase by ADP. Inhibitors are more common. These may come either from the sample or from the reagents. It is well known that urine contains particularly large quantities of inhibitors, e.g. for LDH. It is still a problem to obtain an NADH preparation that is free from inhibitors after prolonged storage. Dehydrogenases, particularly LDH, are inhibited by inhibitors of this coenzyme. Moreover, organic and inorganic reagents may contain heavy-metal ions, which inhibit most enzymes.

Synthetic substrates are used for a series of hydrolases because the natural substrates are often not precisely definable or because the products obtained by the action of the enzymes on synthetic substrates are easier to measure. The choice of substrate is of decisive importance, since synthetic substrates are hydrolyzed at different rates. The rate of hydrolysis of synthetic substrates is usually one order of magnitude higher than that of the natural substrates.

Example:

β-Galactosidase hydrolyzes the synthetic substrate o-nitrophenyl-β-D-galactoside about 7 times as rapidly, and p-nitrophenyl-β-D-galactoside about 17 times as rapidly, as the natural substrate lactose. The rates are related as $100:13.8:6.5$ and the Michaelis constants are $K_m = 9.5 \times 10^{-4}$ mol/l, $K_m = 4.45 \times 10^{-4}$ mol/l and $K_m = 7.52 \times 10^{-3}$ mol/l.

However, one is not entirely free in choosing the substrate, since concentrations exceeding the solubility of the substrate are frequently necessary in order to attain the optimum enzyme activity.

Example:

The substrate of γ-glutamyl transpeptidase (EC 2.3.2.1), viz., L-γ-glutamyl-p-nitroanilide, can be kept in solution only up to a concentration of 4 mol/l, whereas the optimum substrate concentration would be about 5.5 mol/l at 25°C.

Determination of the Optimum Substance Concentration of Substrates

The empirical determination of the optimum substance concentration of substrates, namely by plotting v_i against increasing concentrations of [S], leads to a relatively arbitrary determination of the optimum value. It is better to determine the K_m value from such curves or their value pairs, calculate according to eqn. (3) on p. 59 with the given value of F, and check whether the calculated value of [S] can be realized in practice.

However, eqn. (3) applies only to one-substrate reactions. In most cases, two-substrate reactions are involved which, however, occasionally or under certain conditions, can be treated as one-substrate reactions (for examples, see p. 21).

Substrate concentrations for two-substrate reactions

The rate equation for two-substrate reactions is

(4)
$$v = \frac{V}{1 + \dfrac{(K_m)_{S_1}}{[S_1]} + \dfrac{(K_m)_{S_2}}{[S_2]} + \dfrac{(K_m)_{S_1 S_2}}{[S_1][S_2]}}$$

Only at values of $(K_m)_{S_1} \ll [S_1]$ and $(K_m)_{S_2} \ll [S_2]$ it is $v = V$. However, this condition usually cannot be met in practice. The deviations from the ideal value are additive. Frequently, for example, a substrate concentration of 100 times the K_m value (corresponding to an error of 1%) cannot be attained simply by reason of solubility limitations.

Example:

Alanine aminotransferase (EC 2.6.1.2). For alanine, K_m is about 22 mmol/l; the optimum concentration of substrate, $100 K_m$, i.e. 2200 mmol/l, is precluded by the solubility of alanine, which is about 800–1000 mmol/l at 30°C.

If in such cases [S₁] for example, is very large compared to [S₂], then [S₁] can be regarded as constant over a certain reaction time. Consequently, in the denominator of eqn. (4) the constant $1 + (K_m)_{S_1}/[S_1] = 1 + Q$ is obtained. Hence, the deviation of v from V thus produced is a constant factor with respect to V. The order of the reaction does not change.

The last term in the denominator of eqn. (4) disappears in enzyme reactions according to the ping-pong bi-bi mechanism (see p. 20).

For such reactions, and also in many other cases (see p. 21), the following relation holds

(5)
$$v = \frac{V}{1 + \dfrac{(K_m)_{S_1}}{[S_1]} + \dfrac{(K_m)_{S_2}}{[S_2]}}$$

The determination of the optimum substrate concentrations with the aid of this simplified equation is explained below.

The Michaelis constants of the enzyme with respect to both substrates are required. These must be determined in the assay system that was set up empirically with respect to buffer, pH, activators, and cofactors.

As is well known, several value pairs of v_i and [S] are required to determine K_m values. In principle, these can be obtained in two ways: by the classical procedure, the initial rate of the reaction is measured in several experiments with different substrate concentrations in each. However, it is also possible (cf.[24,25]) to let the reaction proceed very far in an assay system with a relatively low concentration of substrate. Since $[S] < K_m$, a non-linear conversion curve is obtained (with absorbance of $[S]$ as the ordinate and time as the abscissa). To every value of the ordinate $[S]$ there corresponds a definite tangent to the curve, v_i. However, it is difficult to determine the exakt value of this tangent without a computer and an appropriate program. Consequently, the following is based on the conventional measurement of individual values of v_i at various substrate concentrations. However, even if – to determine $(K_m)_{S_1}$ for example – the concentration of the substrate $[S_2]$ is made very high (which, however, is often not possible for technical reasons), an excessively large error remains. The K_m figures should be determined as accurately as possible. It is therefore appropriate to determine the K_m values not by the *Lineweaver-Burk* method but by the method of *Florini* and *Vestling* (cf. p. 34).

If $(K_m)_{S_1}$ and $(K_m)_{S_2}$ are known, the relationship between the concentrations $[S_1]$ and $[S_2]$ can be investigated. The following equations follow from eqn. (5):

(5a)
$$v/V = \frac{1}{1 + \dfrac{(K_m)_{S_1}}{[S_1]} + \dfrac{(K_m)_{S_2}}{[S_2]}}$$

(5b)
$$\frac{V}{v} - 1 = \frac{V - v_i}{v} = \frac{(K_m)_{S_1}}{[S_1]} + \frac{(K_m)_{S_2}}{[S_2]}$$

or

(6)
$$\frac{(K_m)_{S_1}}{[S_1]} + \frac{(K_m)_{S_2}}{[S_2]} = \frac{1}{F}$$

Consequently,

(7)
$$[S_1] = \frac{(K_m)_{S_1}}{\dfrac{1}{F} - \dfrac{(K_m)_{S_2}}{[S_2]}} \qquad \text{or} \qquad [S_2] = \frac{(K_m)_{S_2}}{\dfrac{1}{F} - \dfrac{(K_m)_{S_1}}{[S_1]}}$$

This is the equation of a hyperbola (cf. Fig. 2).

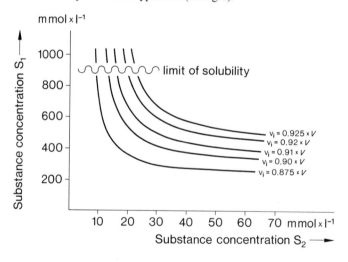

Fig. 2.
Two-substrate reaction. Dependence of the substrate concentrations on one another (schematic). $(K_m)_{S_1} = 33$ mmol/l; $(K_m)_{S_2} = 1$ mmol/l.

For two-substrate reactions, therefore, there is not only one optimum condition with respect to substrate concentrations. On the contrary, according to eqn. (6), the optimum substrate concentrations are variable within certain limits. High values of $[S_1]$ permit lower value of $[S_2]$, and vice versa. This indefinitely large number of value pairs for $[S_1]$ and $[S_2]$ defines a hyperbola whose shape depends on the selected value of F^{26}.

What pair of substrate concentrations should be chosen in practice is, however, still left open by this discovery. The selection can be made from various points of view. For example:

1. That pair which, for a small change in concentration of one substrate produces the smallest change in the concentration of the other substrate (smallest variation).
2. The pair with the lowest concentration of both substrates.
3. The pair that offers the least difficulty in practical performance (e.g. solubility, inhibition by substrates or products).

In general, the third point will be dictated by practical considerations; one will be guided – as far as possible – by points 1 and 2.

The pair of substrate concentrations with the smallest variation

In this case the smallest variation means that a small change in the substrate concentration $[S_1]$ evokes the smallest possible change in the corresponding concentration $[S_2]$, and vice versa. This condition is certainly not represented by any point of the hyperbola that lies near an asymptote; on the contrary, the desired point should lie in its most strongly curved region.

If in eqn. (6) one of the substrate concentrations becomes infinitely large, then

(8 a)
$$[S_2] = F \times (K_m)_{S_2}$$

(8 b)
$$[S_1] = F \times (K_m)_{S_1}$$

For a specified value of F, then, the asymptotes to the hyperbola have the following distances from the axes: from the abscissa, $[S_1] = F \times (K_m)_{S_1}$, and from the ordinate, $[S_2] = F \times (K_m)_{S_2}$. It follows from eqn. (8 a) and (8 b) that

(9)
$$F = \frac{[S_2]}{(K_m)_{S_2}} = \frac{[S_1]}{(K_m)_{S_1}},$$

which means that the points of intersection of the asymptotes to all the hyperbolas lie on a straight line (dotted line in Fig. 3):

(10)
$$[S_1] = \frac{(K_m)_{S_1}}{(K_m)_{S_2}} \times [S_2]$$

with the slope $(K_m)_{S_1}/(K_m)_{S_2}$.

If the hyperbola is now referred to the asymptotes as a system of coordinates, it may be expected that the most strongly curved part of the hyperbola will be at the point where the tangent has a value of -1. The point of smallest variation should be located at this point.

To determine this point mathematically, we need only set the first derivative of eqn. (7) with respect to $[S_2]$ equal to -1.

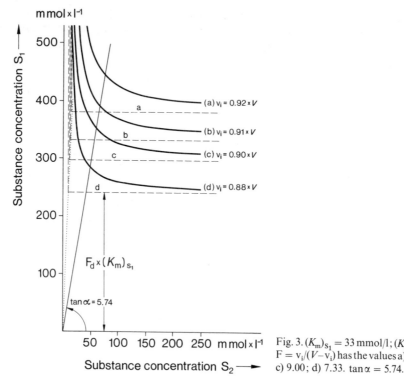

Fig. 3. $(K_m)_{S_1} = 33$ mmol/l; $(K_m)_{S_2} = 1$ mmol/l. $F = v_i/(V - v_i)$ has the values a) 11.50; b) 10.11; c) 9.00; d) 7.33. $\tan \alpha = 5.74$.

(11)
$$[S_1] = \frac{(K_m)_{S_1}}{\dfrac{1}{F} - \dfrac{(K_m)_{S_2}}{[S_2]}} = y = \frac{a}{b - \dfrac{c}{x}} = \frac{ax}{bx - c}$$

$y = [S_1] \quad (K_m)_{S_1} = a$
$x = [S_2] \quad 1/F \quad = b$
$ \quad (K_m)_{S_2} = c$

(12)
$$\frac{dy}{dx} = \frac{a}{bx - c} - \frac{abx}{(bx - c)^2} = -1$$

and
$$x = \frac{1}{b}\left(c \pm \sqrt{a \times c}\right)$$

(13a)
$$[S_2] = F \times \left[(K_m)_{S_2} \pm \sqrt{(K_m)_{S_1} \times (K_m)_{S_2}}\right]$$

or

(13b)
$$[S_1] = F \times \left[(K_m)_{S_1} \pm \sqrt{(K_m)_{S_2} \times (K_m)_{S_1}}\right]$$

Division of eqn. (13b) by eqn. (13a) gives:

(14)
$$[S_1] = \frac{(K_m)_{S_1} \pm \sqrt{(K_m)_{S_1} \times (K_m)_{S_2}}}{(K_m)_{S_2} \pm \sqrt{(K_m)_{S_1} \times (K_m)_{S_2}}} \times [S_2] = \tan \alpha \times [S_2]$$

All points for the pairs of substrate concentrations with the smallest variation lie on a straight line of slope $\tan \alpha$. This line passes through the origin of the coordinate system $[S_1]; [S_2]$.
In Fig. 3, the hyperbolas of Fig. 2 are shown in a system with equally subdivided coordinates. The parameters corresponding to eqns. (8), (10), and (14) are given.
According to eqn. (14), $[S_1] = \tan \alpha \times [S_2]$; therefore the following expressions follow from eqn. (7) for the coordinates of the point with the smallest variation:

(15a)
$$[S_1] = F \times [(K_m)_{s_1} + \tan \alpha \times (K_m)_{s_2}];$$

(15b)
$$[S_2] = F \times \left[\frac{(K_m)_{s_1}}{\tan \alpha} + (K_m)_{s_2}\right].$$

The most economical pair of substrate concentrations

In this case economical means the lowest possible sum of the two substrate concentrations.
If

(16)
$$[S_1] + [S_2] = u,$$

this expression must be minimized. Together with eqn. (7), eqn. (16) gives

(17)
$$u = [S_2] + \frac{(K_m)_{s_1}}{\dfrac{1}{F} - \dfrac{(K_m)_{s_2}}{[S_2]}}.$$

Setting the first derivative of this equation with respect to $[S_2]$ equal to zero gives the same result as eqns. (13a) and (13b). This means that the point on the hyperbola that is most favorable with respect to variation is identical with the point for the lowest possible sum of the concentrations of the two substrates.
Consequently, in practical work it is possible, for a desired value of F, to calculate the optimum and most economical substrate concentrations, which are also those for which a change in one concentration produces the smallest change in the other.

Example:

For technical reasons, $[S_2]$ cannot be greater than 50 mmol/l. No deviation of v_i from V greater than 10% can be tolerated. $v_i = 0.9\,V$ means that $F = 9$. Given the data of Fig. 3, for $[S_2] = 50$ mmol/l eqn. (7) gives $[S_1] = 362.6$ mmol/l. The most economical pair of concentrations (simultaneously the pair with least variation) for $v_i = 0.90\,V$ according to eqns. (15a) and (15b) is $[S_1] = 348.7$ mmol/l and $[S_2] = 60.7$ mmol/l. The following concentrations were chosen: $[S_1] = 400$ mmol/l, $[S_2] = 50$ mmol/l. The deviation of v_i from V is calculated by means of eqn. (5a) as $v_i = 0.907\,V$, i.e. 9.3%.

Substrate concentrations for inhibited reactions

If an inhibitor of the enzyme reaction is present, the mathematical expressions become more or less complicated. They also depend on the type of inhibition (cf. p. 35 and p. 36). The variation of $[S_1]$ with $[S_2]$ changes.

Given, for example, competitive inhibition and a reaction following the ping-pong bi-bi mecha-nism, the following rate equation applies (by analogy with eqn. (11) on p. 35 according to[26]):

(18)
$$v = \frac{V}{1 + \dfrac{(K_m)_{S_1}}{[S_1]} + \dfrac{(K_m)_{S_2}}{[S_2]} + \dfrac{(K_m)_{S_1}}{K_1} \times \dfrac{[I]}{[S_1]}}.$$

This leads by analogy with eqn. (7) to

(19)
$$[S_1] = \frac{(K_m)_{S_1} \times \left(1 + \dfrac{[I]}{K_1}\right)}{\dfrac{1}{F} - \dfrac{(K_m)_{S_2}}{[S_2]}}.$$

In accordance with p. 35, the "inhibition term" $(1 + [I]/K_1)$ is a factor of $(K_m)_{S_1}$. (In noncompetitive and in uncompetitive inhibition, other relationships apply; cf. pp. 35 and 36). The inhibiting effect is the more pronounced the larger $[I]/K_1$ is. If the concentration of the inhibitor is equal to its inhibition constant, the expression in brackets in eqn. (19) becomes equal to 2. The Michaelis constant $(K_m)_{S_1}$ has apparently doubled in value. The concentration of S_1 corresponding to $[S_2]$ must be twice as great to achieve the desired reaction rate. If, for example, $[I]/K_1$ has a value of 0.1, $[S_1]$ must be raised by 10%. From this relation it is possible to calculate the necessary changes in $[S_1]$ for the inhibited reaction, as compared with the noninhibited reaction (for practical applications, cf. also p. 67, 68).

Substrate inhibition

For substrate inhibition, which is often observed, S is identical with I. If the dependence of v_i on $[S]$ is plotted, the curve is found to have a maximum. The following equation corresponds to eqn. (19) for $I = S_2$:

(20)
$$[S_1] = \frac{(K_m)_{S_1} \left(1 + \dfrac{[S_2]}{K_1}\right)}{\dfrac{1}{F} - \dfrac{(K_m)_{S_2}}{[S_2]}}.$$

The activity of a substrate as inhibitor varies with the square of its concentration (eqn. (20)). Consequently, this inhibition is correspondingly greater than product inhibition at the same K_1 values. Eqn. (20) is the equation of a parabola. The curve of the interdependence of the concen-trations therefore passes through a minimum (cf. curves b and c in Figs. 4 and 5, pp. 67 and 68 resp.).

Here other factors limit the choice of the most favorable pair of substrate concentrations. In order to keep the inhibiting effect of the substrate $[S_2]$, i.e. $(1 + [S_2]/K_1)$ small, one is forced to work with the smallest possible values of $[S_2]$. The minimum point of the curve may be regarded as the maximum value. This can easily be calculated: if we set $d[S_1]/d[S_2] = 0$, we obtain from eqn. (20)

(21)
$$[S_2] = F \times (K_m)_{S_2} \pm \sqrt{F^2 \times (K_m)_{S_2}^2 + F \times (K_m)_{S_2} \times K_1}$$

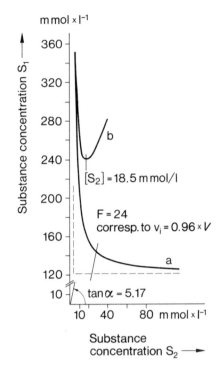

Fig. 4. Aspartate aminotransferase. Dependence of the substrate concentrations on one another. $S_1 = $ L-Aspartate; $S_2 = $ 2-Oxoglutarate. $(K_m)_{S_1} = 5.07$ mmol/l; $(K_m)_{S_2} = 0.19$ mmol/l. $F = 24$ according to $v_i = 0.96\ V$.
a) Calculated with the above figures acc. to eqn. (7).
b) Calculated with the above figures for competitive substrate inihibition by 2-oxoglutarate ($K_1 = 38$ mmol/l) acc. to eqn. (20).

Examples:

a) Aspartate aminotransferase (EC 2.6.1.1); two-substrate reaction; ping-pong bi-bi mechanism[22,27,28]. The second substrate (2-oxoglutarate) inhibits the enzyme competitively[22]. According to[26], eqn. (18) applies.
Data[29]: $(K_m)_{S_1} = 5.07$ mmol/l; $(K_m)_{S_2} = 0.19$ mmol/l. $K_1 = 38$ mmol/l. If $v_i = 0.96\ V$ is tolerated, then $F = 24$.
If, on the basis of eqn. (19), $[S_1]$ is plotted against $[S_2]$, the curve b shown in Fig. 4 is obtained. Taking the curve a of the noninhibited reaction, we find as the theoretically most favorable pair of concentrations $[S_1] = 145.2$ mmol/l and $[S_2] = 28.1$ mmol/l. However simply because of the strong absorption of light by S_2 (2-oxoglutarate), $[S_2]$ should remain distinctly below 20 mmol/l. For the reaction inhibited competitively by S_2, eqn. (21) yields a maximum value (minimum of curve b in Fig. 4) of $[S_2] = 18.5$ mmol/l. A value of $[S_2] = 12$ mmol/l was chosen. The corresponding value of $[S_1]$ in curve (a) is calculated as 196 mol/l and in curve (b) 258 mmol/l. Since the inhibition term $(1 + 12/38) = 1.316$, $[S_1]$ must be increased by this factor.
b) Alanine aminotransferase (EC 2.6.1.2) two-substrate reaction; ping-pong bi-bi mechanism. The second substrate (2-oxoglutarate) does inhibit the enzyme competitively, but much less so than aspartate aminotransferase.
Data[29]: $(K_m)_{S_1} = 21.9$ mmol/l; $(K_m)_{S_2} = 0.67$ mmol/l; $K_1 = 400$ mmol/l (approximate value). If $v_i = 0.91\ V$ is tolerated, then $F = 10.11$.
The variation of $[S_1]$ with $[S_2]$ is shown in Fig. 5, p. 68. The most favorable pair of concentrations would be (from curve a) $[S_1] = 260.2$ mmol/l and $[S_2] = 45.5$ mmol/l. For the inhibited reaction (curve b), the value must be less than the maximum value of $[S_2] = 59.27$ mmol/l. Because of excessive absorption of light, however, $[S_2]$ must be less than 20 mmol/l. With the selected value of $[S_2] = $

15 mmol/l, $[S_1] = 420,2$ mmol/l according to eqn. (20). For the non-inhibited reaction, according to eqn. (7), the value is $[S_1] = 403.8$ mmol/l. At such a low concentration as $[S_2] = 15$ mmol/l, the increase in $[S_1]$ necessary on account of the inhibitor is therefore only 4%.

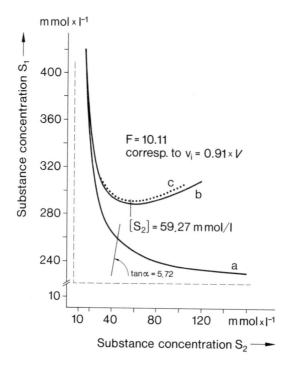

Fig. 5. Alanine aminotransferase. Dependence of the substrate concentrations on one another. $S_1 = $ L-Alanine; $S_2 = $ 2-Oxoglutarate. $(K_m)_{S_1} = 21.9$ mmol/l; $(K_m)_{S_2} = 0.67$ mmol/l. F = 10.11 according to $v_i = 0.91$ V.
a) Calculated with the above figures acc. to eqn. (7).
b) Calculated with the above figures for competitive substrate inhibition by 2-oxoglutarate (K_I about 400 mmol/l) acc. to eqn. (20).
c) Calculated with the above figures for competitive substrate inhibition by 2-oxoglutarate (K_I about 550 mmol/l) acc. to eqn. (20). Also included in the calculation competitive product inhibition by L-glutamate ($K_I = 14$ mmol/l).

Inhibition by the product

For inhibition by the product, which is also frequently observed (for example, in the case of the kinases, which are inhibited by ADP), eqn. (19) applies, provided that the inhibition is competitive. In coupled reactions, a distinction must be made as to whether the inhibiting product reacts further in the indicator reaction or whether it accumulates in the course of the reaction.

In the first situation, in any case, it is important that the concentration of the intermediate product $[P_1]$ in the steady state be small (cf. p. 71). If it is possible to make $[I] \ll K_I$ (in this case $[P_1] \ll K_I$), the expression in parentheses in eqn. (19) assumes the value 1. Inhibition is then without effect.

Example:

Alanine aminotransferase[29]; two-substrate reaction; ping-pong bi-bi mechanism. Inhibition by the product, i.e. pyruvate. If an approximate literature value [30] for the inhibitor constant of $K_1 = 20$ mmol/l is used and, as outlined on p.73, in order of magnitude we put $[P_1] = 0.01$ mmol/l, then $[P_1]/K_1 = 0.005$, i.e. negligible compared to 1. The most favorable pair of substrate concentrations can be determined by means of eqn. (7) or (20).

In the other case, when the inhibiting product P_2 accumulates, $[P_2] = [I]$ becomes larger and the inhibiting effect greater as the reaction proceeds. Frequently it is possible, as in the use of

ATP-regenerating systems for the ADP-inhibition of kinases, to keep $[P_2]$ small by means of a skillful technique and thus prevent inhibition. Depending on the type of inhibition, the calculations involved are fairly complicated; however, rough estimates are possible. Since the initial rate of the reaction is measured in the determination of the catalytic activity of enzymes, the time interval of the measurement is small. Consequently, the inhibiting product cannot attain a high concentration.

Example:

Aspartate and alanine aminotransferases[29]. The reaction product glutamate inhibits competitively; it accumulates. $(K_I)_{AST} \cong 47$ mmol/l; $(K_I)_{ALT} = 14$ mmol/l. If measurements are performed for 5 min with a catalytic activity in the serum of 300 U/l $\cong$ 5000 nkat/l (in the assay system: 25 U/l $\cong$ 417 nkat/l; cf. p. 73), 5×25 µmol/l or 0.125 mmol/l of inhibiting reaction product will be formed. The inhibition term $(1 + [I]/K_I)$ takes on a value of $(1 + 0.125/47) = 1.0027$ for the AST reaction and $(1 + 0.125/14) = 1.0089$ for the ALT reaction. Inhibition by the product becomes evident only after a relatively long reaction time. Consequently, the substrate concentration $[S_1]$ needs to be increased by only 0.27% and 0.89%, respectively (cf. Fig. 5).

Conclusions

In selecting the optimum substrate concentrations, it is decisive whether technical conditions (solubility of the substance, absorption of light, etc.) or the properties of the enzyme (inhibition by substrates or products) determine the choice of the most economical pair of concentrations. For inhibited reactions, one will always keep to that branch of the hyperbola where the curves of the non-inhibited and inhibited reactions are closest to one another. In cases of relatively strong inhibition, this may lead to a considerable deviation from the ideal pair of values, but this must be accepted.

Determination of Optimum Conditions for the Auxiliary and Indicator Reactions in Coupled Enzyme Reactions

The type of buffer, the ionic strength, and the pH as determined for the primary reaction are not necessarily the optimum for the auxiliary and indicator reactions as well. However, this can in general be compensated by the addition of more enzyme. On the other hand, the optimum concentrations of effectors and, where appropriate, coenzymes or second substrates for the auxiliary and indicator reactions must be determined separately (as described on p. 61 ff.).

Below we shall discuss the question of the necessary amount of auxiliary or indicator enzyme. This can be determined empirically on the basis of several experiments with increasing amounts of the enzyme. Calculations with the values of V and K_m appropriate to the measuring system are more accurate (at least for testing empirically determined values).

Coupled one-substrate reactions

The indicator reaction is either a preceding or a succeeding reaction (cf. p. 46). The latter is normally the case. In determinations of catalytic activity, the task of the indicator reaction is to indicate continually the amount of reaction product of the primary reaction. The rate of the coupled over-all reaction is traced on the basis of the increase of the reaction product of the indicator reaction with time.

For the practical performance of rate measurements of coupled reactions, we must know how much indicator enzyme is to be added in order to rapidly establish a steady state in which the two reactions of the sequence proceed at the same rate.

In the simplest case of two coupled one-substrate reactions, let $E_{prim.}$ be the enzyme of unknown activity (primary enzyme) and $E_{ind.}$ the indicator enzyme; then

$$S \xrightarrow{\ E_{prim.}\ } P_1 \xrightarrow{\ E_{ind.}\ } P_2$$

In measurements of catalytic activity, $E_{prim.}$ generally reacts at substrate saturation, and as the reaction proceeds increasing amounts of P_1 are formed. Then, however, the activity of $E_{ind.}$ begins to be effective, and this activity rises with increasing concentrations of P_1 until the two reaction rates become equal (steady state). The lag phase should be as short as possible.

For the primary reaction $S \rightarrow P_1$, $[S] \gg (K_m)_S$, and therefore according to p. 19:

(a) $$v = V = k \times [E_{prim.}].$$

For the indicator reaction $P_1 \rightarrow P_2$, $[P_1]$ is initially zero and rises in the steady state to a constant value between $[P_1] \ll (K_m)_{P_1}$ and $[P_1] \gtrless (K_m)_{P_1}$. The effective rate of the indicator reaction is therefore determined initially by the formula

(b) $$(v_{eff.})_{ind.} = \frac{k \times [E_{ind.}]}{(K_m)_{P_1}} \times [P_1] = \frac{V_{ind.}}{(K_m)_{P_1}} \times [P_1].$$

As the value of $[P_1]$ increases, the effective reaction rate of the indicator reaction tends towards a value between the boundary conditions (a) and (b). The concentration of the intermediate product $[P_1]$ must always be viewed in relation to $(K_m)_{P_1}$. At constant $[E_{ind.}]$, the equation

(c) $$(v_{eff.})_{ind.} = V_{ind.} \times \frac{[P_1]}{[P_1] + (K_m)_{P_1}} = \frac{V_{ind.}}{1 + \dfrac{(K_m)_{P_1}}{[P_1]}}$$

gives, for various values of $(K_m)_{P_1}/[P_1] = Q$, the following relative rates $(v_{eff.})_{ind.}/V_{ind.}$ and deviations from the boundary conditions (a) and (b):

$Q = \dfrac{(K_m)_{P_1}}{[P_1]}$	$\dfrac{(v_{eff.})_{ind.}}{V_{ind.}}$	Deviation from boundary conditions	
100	0.0099	(b)	1%
10	0.091	(b)	9%
1	0.5	(a), (b)	50%
0.1	0.91	(a)	9%
0.01	0.99	(a)	1%

As soon as the steady state has been reached, $(v_{eff.})_{ind.} = V_{ind.}$. The smaller the required constant concentration of the substrate $[P_1]$ is in relation to the Michaelis constant of $E_{ind.}$, the earlier will the steady state be reached. According to eqn. (b), the smallest possible value of $[P_1]/(K_m)_{P_1}$ is achieved only by high values of $V_{ind.}$.

A massive excess of the enzyme $E_{ind.}$ is particularly important since the system approaches the steady state only asymptotically, but substrate saturation for $E_{prim.}$ exists only for a limited time because of the decreasing concentration $[S]$.

Example:

If an enzyme sequence contains $E_{ind.}$ with $(K_m)_{P_1} = 10^{-5}$ mmol/l and a catalytic activity of 1 U or 16.67 nkat, the enzyme displays an effective catalytic activity of 0.091 U (1.517 nkat) at a concentration $[P_1] = 10^{-6}$ mmol/l, and an effective activity of 0.0099 U (0.165 nkat) at a concentration $[P_1] = 10^{-7}$ mmol/l. Consequently, 10 times (in the second case, 100 times) the amount of enzyme $E_{ind.}$ must be added in order to keep $V_{prim.} = (v_{eff.})_{ind.}$ and therefore to measure correctly the rate of the primary reaction catalyzed by $E_{prim.}$

There are thus two mutually oposite effects: the larger $[P_1]$ is, the more nearly does the behavior of the indicator reaction approach case (a) and the smaller the excess of the enzyme $E_{ind.}$ necessary to maintain $(v_{eff.})_{ind.} = V_{prim.}$. On the other hand, $[P_1]$ should be as small as possible in order to avoid lag phases in the coupled reaction. However, according to eqn. (b), small values of $[P_1]$ require correspondingly high values of $E_{ind.}$ or $V_{ind.}/(K_m)_{P_1}$. As is well known, for reactions according to eqn. (b), the expression $V_{ind.}/(K_m)_{P_1}$ corresponds to the rate constant of non-catalyzed first-order reactions (cf. p. 19).
The concentration of $[P_1]$, considered in the above example as the substrate for the indicator enzyme, can be calculated. In the steady state we have:

$$(22) \qquad (v_{eff.})_{ind.} = V_{prim.} = \frac{V_{ind.} \times [P_1]}{[P_1] + (K_m)_{P_1}} = \frac{V_{ind.}}{1 + \dfrac{(K_m)_{P_1}}{[P_1]}}$$

and

$$(23) \qquad [P_1] = (K_m)_{P_1} \times \frac{V_{prim.}}{V_{ind.} - V_{prim.}}$$

If the prior condition that $(K_m)_{P_1}/[P_1] = Q$ shall have a given value be imposed, then

$$(24) \qquad V_{ind.} = (1 + Q) \times V_{prim.}$$

In the steady state, $[P_1]$ is constant. Consequently, according to eqn. (22) we have for the indicator reaction

$$(v_{eff.})_{ind.} = \frac{1}{1 + Q} \times V_{ind.}$$

which means that the indicator reaction proceeds as a zero-order reaction.
$[P_1]$ is an expression for the magnitude of the lag phase of the coupled reaction (cf. Fig. 2 on p. 16) and should therefore be as small as possible.

The auxiliary reaction in the system

$$S \xrightarrow{E_{prim.}} P_1 \xrightarrow{E_{aux.}} P_2 \xrightarrow{E_{ind.}} P_3$$

is to be treated as an indicator reaction. However, its product P_2 is not a measured parameter; rather, it becomes the substrate of the indicator reaction. Both concentrations, $[P_1]$ and $[P_2]$, should be kept as small as possible in order to avoid lag phases in the reaction. In order for the steady state of equal partial rates

$$V_{prim.} = (v_{eff.})_{aux.} = (v_{eff.})_{ind.}$$

to be attained, we must have for the auxiliary reaction

$$(v_{eff.})_{aux.} = V_{aux.} \times \frac{[P_1]}{[P_1] + (K_m)_{P_1}} = V_{prim.}$$

and for the indicator reaction

$$(v_{\text{eff.}})_{\text{ind.}} = V_{\text{ind.}} \times \frac{[P_2]}{[P_2] + (K_m)_{P_2}} = V_{\text{prim.}}$$

Then

$$V_{\text{ind.}} \times \frac{[P_2]}{[P_2] + (K_m)_{P_2}} = V_{\text{aux.}} \times \frac{[P_1]}{[P_1] + (K_m)_{P_1}}$$

(25) $$V_{\text{ind.}} = V_{\text{aux.}} \times \frac{[P_1]}{[P_1] + (K_m)_{P_1}} \times \frac{[P_2] + (K_m)_{P_2}}{[P_2]}$$

If very small values of $[P]/(K_m)_P$, e.g. 0.001 mmol/l, are required for the auxiliary and the indicator reactions, then

$$V_{\text{ind.}} = V_{\text{aux.}}$$

Coupled two-substrate reactions

The rate of two-substrate reactions is given by eqn.(4), p. 61 and eqn.(5), p. 29. Not always can the v_i of the primary reaction be measured under ideal conditions, viz., that $[S_1]$ and $[S_2]$ are infinitely large compared to their Michaelis constants. Certain deviations of v_i from V must be tolerated (cf. p.59).

Similarly, for two-substrate indicator reactions, frequent deviations from the ideal case where $[S] \gg K_m$ must be expected. This is the case, for example, in coenzyme-dependent dehydrogenase reactions when the concentration of NAD(P)H cannot be made sufficiently large in comparison with $(K_m)_{\text{NAD(P)H}}$ because of its excessive absorbance (cf. p.73).

In the coupled reaction

$$S_1 + S_2 \xrightarrow{E_{\text{prim.}}} P_1 + U$$

$$P_1 + S_3 \xrightarrow{E_{\text{ind.}}} P_2 + W$$

the rate of the indicator reaction in the simplest case is given, according to eqn. (5), by the formula:

$$(v_{\text{eff.}})_{\text{ind.}} = \frac{V_{\text{ind.}}}{1 + \dfrac{(K_m)_{P_1}}{[P_1]} + \dfrac{(K_m)_{S_3}}{[S_3]}}$$

In the steady state, $(v_{\text{eff.}})_{\text{ind.}} = V_{\text{prim.}}$ and $Q = (K_m)_{P_1}/[P_1]$ is a constant. From this it follows that

(26) $$(v_{\text{eff.}})_{\text{ind.}} = \frac{V_{\text{ind.}} \times [S_3]}{(1 + Q) \times [S_3] + (K_m)_{S_3}} = V_{\text{prim.}}$$

This is the equation of a one-substrate reaction. If it be assumed that, in addition, $(K_m)_{P_1}/[P_1] = Q$ must have a particular value (cf. p.71), then $(1 + Q) \times [S_3] \gg (K_m)_{S_3}$. Eqn. (26) then becomes

$$(v_{\text{eff.}})_{\text{ind.}} = V_{\text{prim.}} = \frac{1}{(1 + Q)} \times V_{\text{ind.}}$$

or

$$V_{\text{ind.}} = (1 + Q) \times V_{\text{prim.}}$$

This is the same result as for the one-substrate indicator reaction; cf. eqn. (24).

It is hardly to be expected that the condition $(1 + Q) \times [S_3] \gg (K_m)_{S_3}$ should not be satisfied.

Corresponding considerations apply to two-substrate auxiliary reactions. Here again – as stated on p. 72 – $V_{aux.}$ is generally of the same order of magnitude as $V_{ind.}$

Examples:

a) Determination[30] of the catalytic activity of alanine aminotransferase (EC 2.6.1.2) with lactate dehydrogenase (EC 1.1.1.27) as indicator enzyme.

$$\text{alanine} + \text{2-oxoglutarate} \underset{}{\overset{\text{ALT}}{\rightleftharpoons}} \text{pyruvate} + \text{glutamate}$$

$$\text{pyruvate} + \text{NADH} + \text{H}^+ \xrightarrow{\text{LDH}} \text{lactate} + \text{NAD}^+$$

$$\text{in general:} \qquad S_1 + S_2 \underset{}{\overset{E_{prim.}}{\rightleftharpoons}} P_1 + P_2$$

$$P_1 + S_3 \xrightarrow{E_{ind.}} P_3 + P_4$$

The product P_1 formed in this two-substrate reaction reacts further with a second substrate S_3 in another two-substrate reaction. The maximum rate of the first step is to be measured correctly.

The substance concentration of the substrate of the primary reaction was selected in accordance with p. 67: alanine, $[S_1] = 420$ mmol/l, 2-oxoglutarate, $[S_2] = 15$ mmol/l. The Michaelis constants – determined in the measurement system for ALT – are $(K_m)_{S_1} = 21.9$ mmol/l and $(K_m)_{S_2} = 0.67$ mmol/l. K_1 for 2-oxoglutarate: 400 mmol/l. With these values, $(v_i)_{prim.} = 0.091 \, V_{prim.}$, i.e. a 9% deviation from the maximum rate of the primary reaction is tolerated (cf. p. 59).

In the indicator reaction, the concentration of NADH $[S_3] = 0.18$ mmol/l. $(K_m)_{NADH} \cong 0.01$ mmol/l. The condition $[S_3] \gg (K_m)_{NADH}$ is therefore not satisfied. $(K_m)_{P_1} = 0.16$ mmol/l.

If the indicator reaction is designed for a maximum catalytic activity of ALT in the serum of 300 U/l $\triangleq$ 5000 nkat/l (corresponding to 417 nkat/l in the test system), then

$$(v_i)_{prim.} = 0.91 \, V_{prim.} = 0.91 \times 417 \times 10^{-6} \, \text{mmol/s}.$$

and the requisite catalytic activity of the indicator enzyme is given by the expression (cf. eqn. 24):

$$V_{ind.} = (1 + Q) \times 379 \times 10^{-6} \, \text{mmol/s}.$$

Eqn. (26) requires that the condition $(1 + Q) \times [S_3] \gg (K_m)_{S_3}$ be satisfied. In the expression $Q = (K_m)_{P_1}/[P_1]$, $[P_1]$ should be $= 0.005$ mmol/l, corresponding to a lag phase of the coupled reaction of $\Delta A = 0.032$ at 339 nm.

For $(K_m)_{P_1} = 0.16$ mmol/l, $Q = 32$. Then $(1 + Q) \times [S_3] = 33 \times 0.18 = 3.94$ mmol/l, which is much larger than $(K_m)_{S_3} = 0.01$ mmol/l.

For $1 + Q = 33$, $V_{ind.} = 33 \times 379 \times 10^{-4} = 12{,}507 \times 10^{-6}$ mmol/s.

The catalytic concentration of the indicator enzyme is

$$b = 12.5 \, \mu\text{kat/l} \, (750 \, \text{U/l}).$$

Under these conditions, the indicator reaction and therefore the coupled over-all reaction in the steady state follow zero-order kinetics.

b) Determination of the catalytic activity of creatine kinase:

$$\text{(a)} \qquad \text{creatine phosphate} + \text{ADP} \underset{}{\overset{\text{CK}*}{\rightleftharpoons}} \text{ATP} + \text{creatine}$$

$$\text{(b)} \qquad \text{ATP} + \text{glucose} \underset{}{\overset{\text{HK}**}{\rightleftharpoons}} \text{glucose-6-P} + \text{ADP}$$

$$\text{(c)} \qquad \text{glucose-6-P} + \text{NADP}^+ \underset{}{\overset{\text{G6P DH}***}{\rightleftharpoons}} \text{gluconate-6-P} + \text{NADPH} + \text{H}^+$$

---

* Creatine kinase, CK (ATP: creatine N-phosphotransferase, EC 2.7.3.2).
** Hexokinase, HK (ATP: D-hexose-6-phosphotransferase, EC 2.7.1.1).
*** Glucose-6-phosphate dehydrogenase, G6P-DH (D-Glucose-6-phosphate: NADP 1-oxidoreductase, EC 1.1.1.49).

in general:

$$S_1 + S_2 \xrightarrow{\text{E}_{\text{prim.}}} P_1 + U$$

$$P_1 + S_3 \xrightarrow{\text{E}_{\text{aux.}}} P_2 + S_2$$

$$P_2 + S_4 \xrightarrow{\text{E}_{\text{ind.}}} P_3 + W$$

For the following calculation, complete reactivation of the CK by SH-reagents is assumed, and, similarly, complete activation of the HK by magnesium ions. Interfering reactions due to other enzymes present in the sample (e.g. adenylate kinase) and their inhibition has been left out of consideration. Any inhibition by substrates or products has likewise been ignored.

According to the data of G. *Szasz* et al.[31], for a concentration of creatine phosphate $[S_1]$ of 30 mmol/l, the corresponding Michaelis constant $(K_m)_{S_1} = 1.17$ mmol/l. The concentration of the second substrate, ADP, is $[S_2] = 2$ mmol/l, and the corresponding Michaelis constant $(K_m)_{S_2} = 0.099$ mmol/l. The substance concentration [ADP] is relatively low, since higher concentrations do not lead to an increase but to a fall in the catalytic activity. However, [ADP] is kept constant by rephosphorylation according to reaction (b). Thus, the primary reaction (a) behaves as a single-substrate reaction. With these data, according to eqn. (5a) on p. 62.

$$(v_i)_{\text{prim.}} = 0.92 \, V_{\text{prim.}}$$

i.e., an 8% deviation from the maximum rate of the primary reaction (due to an insufficiently high concentration of the substrate, because a higher one is impracticable) is tolerated. The deviation from a reaction of zero-order kinetics is equally large.

In the auxiliary reaction the concentration of glucose $[S_3] = 20$ mmol/l and in the indicator reaction the concentration of NADP $[S_4] = 2$ mmol/l. The corresponding Michaelis constants were not measured; approximate literature figures are adequate for the following calculations. These constants are $(K_m)_{S_3} \cong 0.1$ mmol/l and $(K_m)_{S_4} \cong 0.06$ mmol/l. The same applies to the Michaelis constants of the intermediate products P_1 (ATP) and P_2 (glucose-6-phosphate): $(K_m)_{P_1} \cong 0.2$ mmol/l, $(K_m)_{P_2} \cong 0.3$ mmol/l.

In the steady state, $[P_1]$ and $[P_2]$ may be regarded as constant; they should be small.

The primary reaction should be designed for a maximum catalytic activity of CK in serum of 300 U/l (5000 nkat/l). This corresponds to 111 U/l or 1852 nkat/l in the assay system. The following relationship should therefore hold:

$$(v_i)_{\text{prim.}} = 0.92 \, V_{\text{prim.}} = (v_{\text{eff.}})_{\text{aux.}} = (v_{\text{eff.}})_{\text{ind.}} = 0.92 \times 1852 \text{ nmol/s}.$$

According to Eq. (26), the relations $(1 + Q_1) \times [S_3] \gg (K_m)_{S_3}$ and $(1 + Q_2) \times [S_4] \gg (K_m)_{S_4}$ should hold for both the auxiliary and the indicator reactions. Moreover (see the alanine aminotransferase example, p. 73), $[P_1] + [P_2]$ should be so small that the shortest possible lag phase occurs in the reaction. If $[P_1] + [P_2] = 0.01$ mmol/l is tolerated, which for measurements at 339 nm corresponds to an absorbance change of 0.063, then

$$Q_1 = (K_m)_{P_1}/[P_1]; \qquad Q_2 = (K_m)_{P_2}/[P_2]$$

become approximately

$$Q_1 = (K_m)_{P_1}/0.005 = 0.2/0.005 = 40$$
$$Q_2 = (K_m)_{P_2}/0.005 = 0.3/0.005 = 60$$

Consequently,

$$(1 + Q_1) \times [S_3] = 40 \times 20 = 800 \text{ mmol/l}.$$
i.e. very large compared to $(K_m)_{S_3} = 0.1$ mmol/l.

and

$$(1 + Q_2) \times [S_4] = 60 \times 2 = 120 \text{ mmol/l},$$
i.e. very large compared to $(K_m)_{S_4} = 0.06$ mmol/l.

The two-substrate reactions of the auxiliary and the indicator enzyme consequently proceed according to eqn. (26) as zero-order reactions. For the conditions specified and the numerical values used,

$$V_{aux.} = (1 + Q_1) \times 0.92 \times V_{prim.} = 41 \times 1704 = 69{,}864 \text{ nmol/s}$$
$$V_{ind.} = (1 + Q_2) \times 0.92 \times V_{prim.} = 60 \times 1704 = 103{,}944 \text{ nmol/s}$$

This means that the following catalytic concentrations must be used:
in the auxiliary reaction
for hexokinase $b = 70 \, \mu kat/l$
                                                                    (4550 U/l)

in the indicator reaction
for glucose-6-phosphate dehydrogenase $b = 104 \, \mu kat/l$
                                                                    (6200 U/l).

Under these conditions, the three-step coupled reaction proceeds linearly after a lag phase of $\Delta A = 0.063$.

In general, for the correct measurement of enzyme activities in coupled assays, the reaction curves should have only negligibly small lag phases. Each tangent at a point of inflection is smaller than the tangent to the ideal conversion curve at the origin (cf. Fig. 1, p. 16).
The primary reaction must always be rate-limiting. For all auxiliary reactions and for the indicator reaction the rate constant k must be very much greater than that of the primary reaction. In enzyme reactions, k corresponds to the expressions V (in zero-order reactions), V/K_m (in first-order reactions), and, for fractional orders between these limits, to $V/[S] + K_m$ (one-substrate reactions) and $V/[S_1] \times [S_2] + (K_m)_{s_1} \times [S_2] + (K_m)_{s_2} \times [S_1]$ (two-substrate reactions) respectively.
If the conditions outlined above can be fulfilled, even four-step coupled assays are possible.

Example:

The determination of the catalytic activity of F-6-PK (fructose-6-phosphate kinase; ATP: D-fructose-6-phosphate 1-phosphotransferase, (EC 2.7.1.1)) from muscle[32,33].

$$\text{F-6-P} + \text{ATP} \xrightarrow{\text{F-6-PK}} \text{F-1,6-P}_2 + \text{ADP}$$

$$\text{F-1,6-P}_2 + \xrightarrow{\text{ALD*}} \text{GAP} + \text{DAP}$$

$$\text{GAP} \xrightarrow{\text{TIM**}} \text{DAP}$$

$$\text{DAP} + \text{NADH} + \text{H}^+ \xrightarrow{\text{GDH***}} \text{Gly-3-P} + \text{NAD}^+.$$

It must be borne in mind, especially in multistep coupled assays, that the concentrations of the intermediate products behave additively as regards the development of lag phases. The sum $[P_1] + \cdots [P_x]$ should always be distinctly smaller than $^1/_{10}$ of the lowest concentration of a substrate that is consumed in the sequence.

---

   * F-1.6-P$_2$ aldolase, ALD (Fructose-1.6-biphosphate D-glyceraldehyde-3-phosphate-lyase, EC 4.1.2.13).
  ** Triosephosphate isomerase, TIM (D-Glyceraldehyde-3-phosphate ketol-isomerase, EC 5.3.1.1).
*** Glycerol-3-phosphate dehydrogenase GDH (sn-Glycerol-3-phosphate: NAD 2-oxidoreductase, EC 1.1.1.8).

Some Measuring Techniques

In contrast to the determination of a substrate, the reactions involved in the measurement of the catalytic activity of an enzyme must (apart from a few exceptions) proceed so slowly that only a small proportion of the substrate has been converted by the end of the measurement. The enzyme sample to be investigated is diluted appropriately. The substrate must be pure. Contamination with substrates of other enzymes leads to errors.

Example:

To measure the catalytic activity of malate dehydrogenase* in serum, the oxaloacetate used must be free from its decarboxylation product, pyruvate. Otherwise, the decrease in the NADH absorbance would simultaneously include that catalytic activity of the lactate dehydrogenase also present in the serum.

Since the sample must not de deproteinized, all the enzymes contained in it are active and react with their substrates if these are present in the sample or the reagents. This can interfere substantially with the measurement.

In the photometric methods, the change in the concentration with time (reaction rate) is directly proportional to the change in the absorbance with time. The unit of measurement is therefore $\Delta A/\Delta t$. Fig. 6 shows graphically the course of the reaction in the determination of the catalytic activity of an enzyme. After a certain preliminary reaction**, the actual measurement of the reaction is generally started with substrate. The example shown relates to a zero-order reaction giving a linear plot.

Normally, relatively fast reactions are measured optically at intervals of 30 s or 60 s with a total measuring time of 150 to 300 seconds. For low reactions, measurement intervals of 300, 600, or even 1200 s and more may be used. Often, only two measurements are taken when the

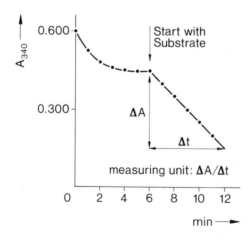

Fig. 6. Determination of the catalytic activity of an enzyme (schematic).

---

* L-Malate: NAD^+ oxidoreductase, EC 1.1.1.37.
** In the photometric measurement of dehydrogenase reactions in serum for example, a distinct decrease in absorbance is observed immediately after the addition of NADH. This is mainly due to the reduction of serum pyruvate by lactate dehydrogenase present in the serum. The actual measurement is started only after this reaction has come to the end.

reaction follows linear kinetics; one then speaks of "two-point methods" as opposed to "continuous monitoring" at small time intervals.

If the plot of the reaction is curved, the measurement intervals should be small. It is w r o n g to take only two pairs of values (at the beginning and after a relatively long incubation time). Unfortunately, the course of the reaction cannot always be monitored continuously, as is possible on the basis of the absorbance changes that accompany dehydrogenase reactions. Only by the continual removal and analysis of samples, involving great expenditure in time and effort, is it possible to obtain reaction curves for such methods. The simple method of determining the amount of substrate converted after a fixed time must lead to erroneous results (cf.[34]), since the curvature of the reaction curve depends on several factors, including the substrate concentration.

In the case of curved reaction plots, the definition of the catalytic activity is based on the initial rate v_i. (It should be noted, however, that for measurements with fast recording photometers, the "initial rate" v_i as determined by the normal measuring technique is reached only after a few tens or hundreds of milliseconds. This was pointed out in 1960 by *B. Chance*.[35]) To determine the correct value for v_i, a tangent is drawn to the reaction curve at the point t = 0. This gives the correct value $\Delta A/\Delta t$.

For the practical determination of catalytic activities even from curved reaction plots, the determination of v_i, i.e. construction of the tangent to the curve at time 0, is occasionally omitted. In 1953, *Bücher*[34] introduced the so-called "flying-start" assay. Fig. 7, which is taken from his original publication, shows that with non-linear reaction plots of the LDH reaction, the stopwatch is started only after there has been an absorbance increase of 0.030 due to NADH formation, after which the time required for a further absorbance increase of 0.100 is measured.

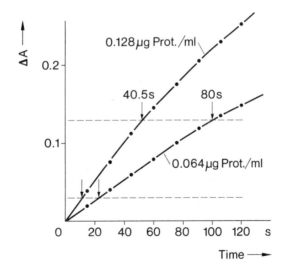

Fig. 7. Determination of the catalytic activity of lactate dehydrogenase with a "flying start" acc. to *Bücher*[36].

This procedure does not yield the maximum values, but the measured values are nonetheless approximately proportional to the amount of enzyme because in all enzyme reactions (carried out under the same conditions) the enzyme concentration [E] is proportional to the reaction rate v_i, and by definition the latter is inversely proportional to the reaction time for a small conversion of substrate to product.

If enzyme units are determined from curved plots on this basis, their recalculation into international units or katals (μmol/min or nmol/s for v_i) leads to only approximate values.

References

1 *Enzyme Nomenclature*, Recommendations 1964 of the International Union of Biochemistry (1963), Elsevier Publ. Comp. Amsterdam. London, New York.
2 Florkin, M. & Stotz, E. H. (1965) in *Comprehensive Biochemistry*, Vol. 13, 2. edn., Elsevier Publ. Comp. Amsterdam, London, New York.
3 IUPAC and IFCC: Quantities and Units in Clinical Chemistry. Recommendation 1973 (1974) *Pure appl. Chem.* **37**, 519.
4 Deutsche Ges. f. Klinische Chemie, Enzymkommission (1970) *J. Clin. Chem. Clin. Biochem.*, **8**, 658.
5 Empfehlungen der Deutschen Gesellschaft für Klinische Chemie (1972) *J. Clin. Chem. Clin. Biochem.* **10**, 182.
6 Scandinavian Committee on Enzymes: „Recommended Methods for the Determination for Enzymes in Blood" (1974) *Scand. J. Clin. Lab. Invest.* **22**, 291–306.
7 IFCC Commission on Standards, Expert Panel on Enzymes. Provisional Recommendation (1974) on IFCC Methods for the Measurement of Catalytic Concentration of Enzymes. Part 1. General Considerations (1975) *Clin. chim. Acta* **61**, F 11.
8 IFCC Commission on Standards, Expert Panel on Enzymes. Provisional Recommendation (1975) on IFCC Methods for the Measurement of Catalytic Concentration of Enzymes. Part 2. IFCC Method for Aspartate Aminotransferase (1976) *Clin. chim. Acta* **70**, F 19.
9 Netter, H. (1959) *Theoretische Biochemie*, p. 554ff., Springer-Verlag, Berlin, Göttingen, Heidelberg.
10 Arrhenius, S. (1889) *Z. physik. Chem.* **4**, 226.
11 Dixon, M. & Webb, E. C. (1964) in *Enzymes*, 2. edn., p. 160, Longmans, Green & Co. Ltd., London.
12 Szasz, G. (1969) *Clin. Chem.* **15**, 124.
13 Szasz, G. (1972) Lecture 8. Int. Kongr. Klin. Chem. Copenhagen, Abstracts of Papers 23.12.
14 Report of the Commission on Enzymes (1961) I.U.B. Symposium Series, Vol. **20**, Pergamon Press, London.
15 King, J. (10. Oct. 1972) 2ème Colloque Automation et Biologie Prospektive, Round Table-Discussion, Pont-à-Mousson, France.
16 Frei, J. (10. Oct. 1972) 2ème Colloque Automation et Biologie Prospective, Round Table-Discussion, Pont-à-Mousson, France.
17 Roth, M. (1972) *Clin. Chem.* **18**, 739.
18 Bergmeyer, H. U. (1973) *J. Clin. Chem. Clin. Biochem.* **11**, 39.
19 Stähler, F., Gruber, W., Stolz, M. & Kessler, A. (1976) 2nd European Congress Clin. Chem., Prague.
20 Bowers, G. N. & McComb, R. B. (1966) *Clin. Chem.* **12**, 70.
21 Szasz, G. (1973) Lecture Symp. The Optimisation and Standardisation of Enzyme Assays, *Ass. Clin. Biochemists*, Engl.
22 Henson, C. P. & Cleland, W. W. (1964) *Biochemistry* **3**, 338.
23 King, J. (1967) *Clin. Biochem.* **1**, 42.
24 Markus, M., Hess, B., Ottaway, J. H. & Cornish-Bowden, A. (1976) FEBS-Letters **63**, 225.
25 Markus, M. & Plesser, Th. (1976) 10th Intern. Congress of Biochemistry, Abstracts p. 399, 07-5-133.
26 London, J. W., Shaw, L. M., Fetterolf, D. & Garfinkel, D. (1975) *Clin. Chem.* **21**, 1939.
27 Cleland, W. W. (1970) in *The Enzymes* (Boyer, P. D., ed.), Vol. **2**, p. 1ff., Academic Press, New York u. London.
28 Cleland, W. W. (1963) *Biochim. Biophys. Acta* **67**, 104–137.
29 Bergmeyer, H. U. (1977) *J. Clin. Chem. Clin. Biochem.* **15**, 405.
30 Saier, M. H. & Jenkins, W. T. (1967) *J. biol. Chem.* **242**, 91.
31 Szasz, G., Gruber, W. & Bernt, E. (1976) *Clin. Chem.* **22**, 650.
32 Racker, E. (1947) *J. biol. Chem.* **167**, 843.
33 Passonneau, J. V. & Lowry, O. H. (1962) *Biochem. Biophys. Res. Comm.* **7**, 10.
34 Bergmeyer, H. U. (1952) *Biochem. Z.* **325**, 163.
35 Chance, B. (1960) *J. biol. Chem.* **235**, 2440.
36 Beisenherz, G., Boltze, H. J., Bücher, Th., Czok, R., Garbade, K. H., Meyer-Arendt, E. & Pfleiderer, G. (1953) *Z. Naturforsch.* **8b**, 555.

Determination of the Substance Concentration of Metabolites
(Kinetic Methods)

In the kinetic methods for the determination of substance concentrations, the parameter measured is the reaction rate. Depending on the type of reaction, the consequences for the practical performance of the determination are different.

Fundamentals of Reaction kinetics

Joachim Ziegenhorn

Zero-order reactions

The rate of zero- or pseudo-zero-order reactions is, by definition, independent of the concentration of the substance being converted (cf. p. 13), and therefore cannot be used to measure this concentration.

However, methods have been described in which linearized concentration/time curves (i.e. pseudo-zero-order reactions) have been used for an approximately quantitative determination of the reacting substance[1-5]. The evaluation in this case entails drawing the tangent to the concentration/time curve and determining the approximate value of the reaction rate from the angle between this tangent and the time axis. The error in these methods depends on the size of the concentration change of the substance during the measurement; the smaller the concentration change of the substance, the smaller the error[1,6]. In practice, this means extremely short measurement times and high demands on the resolution of the measuring apparatus. Very low substance concentrations can be determined accurately by means of pseudo-zero-order reactions if the principle of "catalytic assay" is used (cf. p. 83).

First-order reactions

First- or pseudo-first-order reactions are by far the most important for the kinetic determination of substance concentrations[6-13]. In the simplest case of such reactions – an irreversible process – the following rate equation applies[6] (cf. also p. 14):

$$(1) \qquad -\frac{d[A]}{dt} = k[A] = k[A]_0 e^{-kt}$$

From this we obtain, by integration and rearrangement:

$$(2) \qquad [A]_0 = -\frac{\Delta[A]}{e^{-kt_1} - e^{-kt_2}}$$

where

$[A]$ = concentration of the substance converted at time t
$[A]_0$ = initial concentration of the substance converted
$\Delta[A]$ = change in the concentration of the substance converted during the time interval
$\qquad \Delta t = t_2 - t_1$
k = rate constant.

It follows from eqn. (2) that the change $\Delta[A]$ in the concentration of the substance converted in a time interval Δt of any magnitude is directly proportional to the initial concentration $[A]_0$ if, for a given rate constant k, the measurement times t_1 and t_2 are kept constant. Such conditions are particularly easy to maintain, as regards measurement technique, with automatic analyzers, for which the so-called "fixed-time" procedures are therefore especially suitable. The method can be applied not only to simple, but also to complex pseudo-first-order reactions (reversible reactions, coupled reactions)[6,7,10-12]. Only a single standard is necessary for calibration, which is always required.

Eqn. (2) applies both to enzymatic and to non-enzymatic reactions. It follows from the Michaelis-Menten theory for enzymatic one-substrate reactions that they obey pseudo-first-order kinetics if $[S] \ll K_m$ (cf. p. 19). The following equation then holds:

$$(3) \qquad\qquad v = -\frac{d[S]}{dt} = \frac{V}{K_m} \cdot [S] = k' \cdot [S]$$

Reactions with several substrates can usually be set up as one-substrate reactions with sufficient accuracy (cf. p. 21, 23). Coenzymes behave kinetically as substrates.

For eqn. (3) to be satisfied, i.e. for v to be directly proportional to $[S]$, the value of $[S]/K_m$ must generally be smaller than 0.2, and if possible smaller than 0.05[6,7,13].

It follows from the above considerations for the kinetic determination of substrate concentrations that – in contrast to end-point methods – enzymes with the highest possible Michaelis constants are required. Since for practical reasons (dilution of the sample should be avoided) the upper limit for the substrate concentration in the assay has generally been fixed, it is only thus that sufficiently small values of $[S]/K_m$ can be attained and relatively high substrate concentrations measured. Such enzymes are available in many cases[7,8,11,12]. If the Michaelis constants are too low for the kinetic procedure, K_m can be apparently increased by the addition of a competitive inhibitor[3,4,10] (cf. eqn. 11, p. 35).

Second-order reactions

In the case of second-order reactions, there is no linear relationship between the reaction rate and the concentration of the substance being converted. Calibration curves must generally be used in these cases. This greatly limits the practical applications of such reactions in the kinetic determination of substance concentrations. Since the measured value always changes in direct proportion to the catalytic activity of the enzyme, a new calibration curve must be constructed for each series of measurements, and this requires that the substance concentration be close to the value expected from the analysis.

Conclusions

Since the rate of an enzyme-catalyzed reaction, like that of any chemical reaction, depends on the reaction conditions, the experimental conditions must be held constant in kinetic methods for the determination of substance concentrations. This can be done particularly easily with automatic analyzers. The kinetic assays are therefore of great importance for the automated laboratory. They allow a drastic reduction of the time required per analysis and therefore contribute to the efficient use of automatic analyzers. Moreover, they are generally less sensitive to interference (e.g. turbidity, intrinsic colour of the sample) than end-point methods. Consequently, sample blanks can usually be omitted.

References

1 Faust, U., Keller, H. & Becker, J. (1973) *Chem. Rundschau* **26**, 24.
2 Hewitt, T.E. & Pardue, H.L. (1973) *Clin. Chem.* **19**, 1128.
3 Müller-Matthesius, R. (1975) *J. Clin. Chem. Clin. Biochem.* **13**, 169.
4 Müller-Matthesius, R. (1975) *J. Clin. Chem. Clin. Biochem.* **13**, 187.
5 Keller, H. & Wolf, V. (1976) *J. Clin. Chem. Clin. Biochem.* **14**, 27.
6 Ingle, J.D. & Crouch, S.R. (1971) *Anal. Chem.* **43**, 697.
7 Tiffany, T.O., Jansen, J.M., Burtis, C.A., Overton, J.B. & Scott, C.D. (1972) *Clin. Chem.* **18**, 829.
8 Haeckel, R. & Mathias, D. (1974) *J. Clin. Chem. Clin. Biochem.* **12**, 515.
9 Ziegenhorn, J. (1975) *J. Clin. Chem. Clin. Biochem.* **13**, 109.
10 Ziegenhorn, J. (1975) *Clin. Chem.* **21**, 1627.
11 Römer, P. & Ziegenhorn, J. (1975) in *Organisation des laboratoires et interprétation des résultats, Biologie prospective* (Siest, G., ed.), pp. 241–246, L'Expansion Scientifique Française, Paris.
12 Ziegenhorn, J., Neumann, U., Hagen, A., Bablok, W. & Stinshoff, K. (1977) *J. Clin. Chem. Clin. Biochem.* **15**, 13.
13 Tiffany, T.O., Burtis, C.A., Mailen, I.C. & Thacker, L.H. (1973) *Anal. Chem.* **45**, 1716.

Kinetic Assays

Joachim Ziegenhorn

Typical examples of the kinetic determination of substance concentrations in the automated clinical chemistry laboratory are the analyses of glucose and glycerol or triglycerides in serum.

Glucose can be determined as follows by means of glucose oxidase and *Trinder*'s color reaction[1]:

(1) α-D-glucopyranose + $H_2O \rightleftharpoons$ al-D-glucose $\cdots$ $H_2O \rightleftharpoons$ β-D-glucopyranose + H_2O
         (36%)   (<0,1%)   (64%)

(2) β-D-glucopyranose + H_2O + O_2 $\xrightarrow{\text{glucose oxidase}}$ D-glucono-δ-lactone + H_2O_2

(3) $2H_2O_2$ + phenol + 4-aminophenazone $\xrightarrow{\text{peroxidase}}$ 4-(p-benzoquinone-mono-imino)-phenazone + $4H_2O$

Although glucose oxidase oxidizes only the β-form of glucose[2], the total amount of glucose present in the solution as a mixture of isomers can be determined. The α- and β-forms of glucose undergo spontaneous interconversion by mutarotation (eqn. (1)[3]). By choosing appropriate conditions of measurement[4], one can ensure that the rate of the over-all reaction will be determined first by the conversion of the β-glucose already present in the solution by glucose oxidase, and then by the subsequent production of the β-form by mutarotation of the α-form. Since the Michaelis constant of glucose oxidase, with a value[2] of 7×10^{-2} mol/l, is always substantially greater than the glucose concentrations encountered in assay mixtures in practice (about 8×10^{-6} mol/l to 5×10^{-4} mol/l), the oxidation of glucose by glucose oxidase obeys pseudo-first-order kinetics with respect to β-glucose[4]. The kinetics of mutarotation are of the same order[3]. This is because here only the concentration of the glucose isomer changes, while the concentration of water as reactant remains practically constant. This results in a sequence of coupled reactions that are pseudo-first-order in glucose concentration, and to which one can therefore apply the principle of the kinetic "fixed-time" measurement to determine the glucose concentration[4]. The parameter measured in this method is the change in the absorbance of the dye formed during a fixed-time interval (e.g. the change in absorbance between the 35th and 125th seconds after the start)[4].

The characteristic features of the use of a competitive inhibitor in the kinetic analysis of substance concentrations may be illustrated by taking the determination of glycerol and triglycerides as an example.

The determination of glycerol is based on the following sequence of coupled reactions[5]:

(4) $\text{glycerol} + \text{ATP} \xrightleftharpoons{\text{glycerol kinase}} \text{glycerol-3-phosphate} + \text{ADP}$

(5) $\text{ADP} + \text{PEP} \xrightleftharpoons{\text{pyruvate kinase}} \text{ATP} + \text{pyruvate}$

(6) $\text{pyruvate} + \text{NADH} + \text{H}^+ \xrightleftharpoons{\text{lactate dehydrogenase}} \text{L-lactate} + \text{NAD}^+.$

When supplemented by a (enzymatic) hydrolysis step, the system can also be used for the determination of triglycerides[5].

The Michaelis constants of the enzymes involved[2] are between 6.0×10^{-5} and 3.0×10^{-4} mol/l, and the glycerol concentrations encountered in the assay mixture in practice lie between about 7×10^{-6} and 2×10^{-4} mol/l. In the most favorable case, this gives values of 2×10^{-2} to 0.7 for $[S]/K_m$, and therefore eqn. (3) (cf. p. 80) has only limited validity. Consequently, only comparatively low glycerol or triglyceride concentrations could be determined with this system. However, the concentration range can be considerably extended by artificially increasing the limiting Michaelis constant, which may be done by using more ATP in the assay mixture[6].

ATP inhibits pyruvate kinase competitively with respect to ADP. The expression $K_m(1 + [I]/K_I)$ may in these circumstances assume a value of 6×10^{-3} mol/l, for example[6] (cf. p. 66). This means an apparent increase by a factor of 20 for the Michaelis constant[2] of ADP (3×10^{-4} mol/l). The ratio $[S]/K_m(1 + [I]/K_I)$ therefore becomes 1×10^{-3} to 3×10^{-2}. Under these conditions, the auxiliary reaction with pyruvate kinase follows pseudo-first-order kinetics with respect to ADP

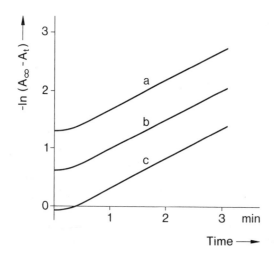

Fig. 1. Time course of the determination of glycerol. A_t: Absorbance at time t; A_∞: Absorbance at the end of the reaction. Initial concentration of glycerol in the assay system[6]: curve a = 43 µmol/l; curve b = 87 µmol/l; curve c = 172 µmol/l. Wavelength: Hg 334 nm.

over a wide range of concentrations, and as a result of the inhibition by ATP, it is also the rate-determining step of the over-all reaction. This circumstance and the stoichiometry of the reaction sequence mean that the indicator reaction also obeys pseudo-first order kinetics. Consequently, the kinetic "fixed-time" procedure can be used for the determination of glycerol concentrations[6]. The parameter measured is the change in the NADH-absorbance during a fixed time interval.

Fig. 1 shows the time course of a glycerol determination. As can be seen, a first-order or pseudo-first-order reaction (straight sections of the curves) sets in after a short induction phase.

For kinetic assays for the determination of cholesterol[9], uric acid[7,10], and urea[7,8,11], reference may be made to the original literature.

References

1 Trinder, P. (1969) *Ann. Clin. Biochem.* **6**, 24.
2 Bergmeyer, H. U., Gawehn, K. & Grassl, M. (1974) in *Methods of Enzymatic Analysis* (Bergmeyer, H. U., ed.) 2nd ed., pp. 425–522, Verlag Chemie, Weinheim & Academic Press, New York.
3 Pigman, W. & Anet, E. F. L. J. (1972) in *The Carbohydrates Chemistry and Biochemistry* (Pigman, W. & Horton, D., eds.) Vol. IA, pp. 165–194, Academic Press, New York, London.
4 Ziegenhorn, J., Neumann, U., Hagen, A., Bablok, W. & Stinshoff, K. (1977) *J. Clin. Chem. Clin. Biochem.* **15**, 13.
5 Wahlefeld, A. W. (1974) in *Methods of Enzymatic Analysis* (Bergmeyer, H. U., ed.) 2nd ed. pp. 1878–1882, Verlag Chemie, Weinheim & Academie Press, New York.
6 Ziegenhorn, J. (1975) *Clin. Chem.* **21**, 1627.
7 Tiffany, T. O., Jansen, J. M., Burtis, C. A., Overton, J. B. & Scott, C. D. (1972) *Clin. Chem.* **18**, 829.
8 Haeckel, R. & Mathias, D. (1974) *J. Clin. Chem. Clin. Biochem.* **12**, 515.
9 Ziegenhorn, J. (1975) *J. Clin. Chem. Clin. Biochem.* **13**, 109.
10 Müller-Matthesius, R. (1975) *J. Clin. Chem. Clin. Biochem.* **13**, 169.
11 Römer, P. & Ziegenhorn, J. (1975) in *Organisation des laboratoires et interprétation des résultats, Biologie prospective* (Siest, G., ed.), pp. 241–246, L'Expansion Scientifique Française, Paris.

Catalytic Assays

Hans Ulrich Bergmeyer

Very small quantities of substrate that satisfy the second boundary condition of the *Michaelis-Menten* equation (cf. p. 18) cannot always be determined directly by simple kinetic methods. They are often consumed so quickly that the reaction rate cannot be measured. However, their concentration can be kept constant by a regenerating reaction. The substrate then behaves as an intermediate catalyst that is not consumed; this is the basis of the term "catalytic assay".

As early as 1935, the "hydrogen-transferring coferment" nicotinamide-adenine dinucleotide phosphate was determined in Dahlem[1] by its catalytic activity.

The "catalytic assay" method has proved effective for the determination of coenzyme A, e.g. in yeast cells according to *Michal* and *Bergmeyer*[2].

The (very low) CoA concentration remains constant, as can be seen from the reaction scheme. The assay mixture contains acetylphosphate, malate, NAD, and the enzymes* PTA, CS, and

---

* PTA, phosphotransacetylase, Acetyl-CoA: orthophosphate acetyltransferase (EC 2.3.1.8).
  CS, citrate synthase, Citrate oxaloacetate-lyase, (EC 4.1.3.7)
  MDH, malate dehydrogenase, L-Malate: NAD oxidoreductase (EC 1.1.1.37).

MDH. Acetylphosphate acetylates CoA; acetyl-S-CoA reacts with oxaloacetate and water to form citrate (with regeneration of CoA). Oxaloacetate is formed from malate by oxidation. This is accompanied by an increase in the formation of NADH from NAD. This reaction is also a preceding indicator reaction. The parameter is $\Delta A/\Delta t$. The concentrations that can be determined in the sample are in the nanomole range.

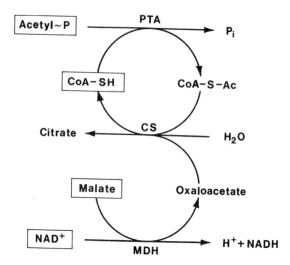

The catalytic assay principle has also been used in particular for the measurement of small concentrations of the coenzymes NAD and NADP by *Hastings* et al.[3] in 1941, by *Anfinsen*[4] in 1944, and by *Glock* and *McLean*[5] in 1955.

Since the rate of the reaction cannot be measured directly by the increase in absorbance at 340 nm with time in a cycle of the oxidized and reduced forms of the coenzyme, *Glock* and *McLean*[5] used the cytochrome-reductase reaction as an indicator and also as a regenerating system. Determination of about 0.1 μg (2×10^{-10} mol) NAD:

(1) $$NAD^+ + \text{ethanol} \xrightarrow{\text{ADH*}} \text{acetaldehyde} + NADH + H^+$$

(2) $$NADH + H^+ + 2\,Cytc^{3+} \xrightarrow{\text{reductase**}} 2\,Cytc^{2+} + NAD^+ + 2H^+$$

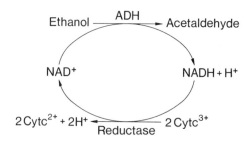

---

* ADH, alcohol dehydrogenase, Alcohol: NAD oxidoreductase (EC 1.1.1.1).
** Cytochrome reductase, NADH: (acceptor) oxidoreductase (EC 1.6.99.3).

The measure of the reaction is the increase in absorbance of the reduced cyctochrome c (Cyt c^{2+}) at 550 nm with time.

The method is applicable to numerous other coenzymes and metabolites. *Examples:* determination of flavin-adenine dinucleotide with apo-D-amino-acid oxidase[6]; flavin mononucleotide with lactate oxidase[7]; determination of thiamine pyrophosphate with apo-pyruvate decarboxylase[8].

Catalytic assays without coupled indicator reactions are particularly sensitive methods of analysis. According to *Lowry*[9], the regenerating system is allowed to cycle for a defined time (e.g. 30 min), then the reaction is stopped by destruction of all enzymes and coenzymes and the most easily determined product is measured in a separate assay (*enzymatic cycling*, cf. p. 86).

Example:

$$(3) \quad NADPH + H^+ + \text{2-oxoglutarate} + NH_3 \xrightarrow{\text{GlDH*}} NADP^+ + \text{glutamate} + H_2O$$

$$NADP^+ + \text{G-6-P} \xrightarrow{\text{G6P-DH**}} NADPH + H^+ + \text{6-PG}$$

Reaction products are glutamate and 6-phosphogluconate, of which 6-phosphogluconate is the easier to determine spectrophotometrically in a assay by the end-point method using 6-phosphogluconate dehydrogenase and NADP.

In 30 min under defined conditions, 5000–10000 molecules of NADPH react, compared to 1 molecule in the end-point method! In the above mentioned separate assay the product is again a pyridine nucleotide, so that a sample of the assay mixture can be used to repeat the *enzymatic cycling*, with a resulting increase in sensitivity of 10^6 to 10^8. End-point methods allow, at 339 nm in a 1-cm cuvette, the accurate determination of about 10^{-2} µmol/ml. With *enzymatic cycling* this is increased to 10^{-8} to 10^{-10} µmol/ml, i.e. a solution of 10^{-11} to 10^{-13} mol/l. If, like *Lowry*, one uses fluorescence measurement of the pyridine nucleotides, the sensitivity is increased by two or three orders of magnitude, giving an accurate measurement of concentrations as low as 10^{-13} µmol/ml or 10^{-16} mol/l.

These methods permit measurements in the submicro range, e.g. metabolite assays in individual, isolated cells. For the kinetics, see p. 86.

---

  * GlDH, glutamate dehydrogenase, L-Glutamate: NAD(P) oxidoreductase, deaminating, (EC 1.4.1.3).
 ** G6P-DH, glucose-6-phosphate dehydrogenase, D-Glucose-6-phosphate: NADP 1-oxidoreductase (EC 1.1.1.49).

Determination of Concentrations by Measurement of Activation or Inhibition of Enzymes

If the substance to be determined does not react in a manner that can be detected, but does change the activity of an added enzyme, the concentration can be measured by the degree of activation or inhibition. *Examples:* determination of magnesium[10] by activation of isocitrate dehydrogenase; heparin[11] by inhibition of ribonuclease or pyruvate kinase; insecticides by inhibition of cholinesterase[12] or carbonic anhydrase[13].

Here again, a calibration curve must be constructed with standard substances under fixed conditions. This curve is frequently non-linear, but can often be linearized. In the determination of parathion by inhibition of cholinesterase, for example, a straight calibration line is obtained if the degree of inhibition is plotted on a logarithmic scale against the concentration on a linear scale.

References

1 Warburg, O., Christian, W. & Griese, A. (1935) *Biochem. Z.* **282**, 157.
2 Michal, G. & Bergmeyer, H. U. (1974) in *Methods of Enzymatic Analysis* (Bergmeyer, H. U., ed.) 2nd ed. p. 1975, Verlag Chemie, Weinheim & Academic Press, New York.
3 Jandorf, B., Klemperer, F. W. & Hastings, A. B. (1941) *J. biol. Chem.* **138**, 311.
4 Anfinsen, G. B. (1944) *J. biol. Chem.* **152**, 285.
5 Glock, G. E. & McLean, P. (1955) *Biochem. J.* **61**, 381.
6 Friedmann, H. C. (1974) in *Methods of Enzymatic Analysis* (Bergmeyer, H. U., ed.) 2nd ed. p. 2182, Verlag Chemie, Weinheim & Academic Press, New York.
7 Friedmann, H. C. (1974) in *Methods of Enzymatic Analysis* (Bergmeyer, H. U., ed.) 2nd ed. p. 2179, Verlag Chemie, Weinheim & Academic Press, New York.
8 Ullrich, J. (1974) in *Methods of Enzymatic Analysis* (Bergmeyer, H. U., ed.) 2nd ed. p. 2186, Verlag Chemie, Weinheim & Academic Press, New York.
9 Lowry, O. H., Passonneau, J. V., Schulz, D. W. & Rock, K. M. (1962) *J. biol. Chem.* **236**, 2746.
10 Baum, P. & Czok, R. (1959) *Biochem. Z.* **332**, 121.
11 Zöllner, N. & Kaiser, W. (1974) in *Methods of Enzymatic Analysis* (Bergmeyer, H. U., ed.) 2nd ed. p. 1151 Verlag Chemie, Weinheim & Academic Press, New York.
12 Giang, P. A. (1974) in *Methods of Enzymatic Analysis* (Bergmeyer, H. U., ed.) 2nd ed. p. 2249, Verlag Chemie, Weinheim & Academic Press, New York.
13 Keller, H. (1952) *Naturwiss.* **39**, 109.

Kinetics of "Enzymatic Cycling"

Janet V. Passonneau and Oliver H. Lowry

A "cycling system" contains two enzymes that catalyze two linked reactions of the following type:

(1)
$$A + S_1 \xrightarrow{\text{enzyme 1}} B + P_1$$

(2)
$$B + S \xrightarrow{\text{enzyme 2}} A + P_2$$

Overall reaction

(3)
$$S_1 + S_2 \longrightarrow P_1 + P_2$$

A may be a coenzyme that is oxidized or reduced to B; it may also be a second substrate of enzyme 1 that is converted into a second product B. With relatively high activities of both enzymes and large quantities of substrates S_1 and S_2, a small quantity of A (or B) can "catalyze" the formation of large quantities of the products P_1 and P_2. If either P_1 or P_2 is measured in a suitable second analysis step, the system acts as a chemical amplifier in the determination of A (or B).

There are many pairs of enzymes that can be coupled with each other in this way (for examples, see[1,2]). The possibility of using such an enzymatic cycle for analysis depends a) on the molar catalytic activity of each enzyme towards the "catalytically" active substance, b) on the extent to which the reaction is influenced by accumulation of the end products, and c) on the ease with which the end product or end products can be measured.

During the cycling, the concentration of the substance to be measured must be distinctly lower than its Michaelis constant K_m, so that the reaction rates are proportional to the quantities of substance to be determined. The decisive kinetic factor for each enzyme is its apparent first-order rate constant $k = V/K_m$ (V is the reaction rate at saturation with A or B). When the steady state is reached, the rate of formation of B [eqn. (1)] is equal to the rate of regeneration of A [eqn. (2)], i.e. $k_1[A] = k_2[B]$. The general rate constant for the overall reaction is

$$k = \frac{k_1 \times k_2}{k_1 + k_2}$$

Derivation: In the state of dynamic equlibrium, we have

$$k([A] + [B]) = k_1[A]$$

$$k = \frac{k_1[A]}{[A] + [B]}$$

With

$$[B] = \frac{k_1}{k_2}[A]$$

one obtains

$$k = \frac{k_1[A]}{[A] + \dfrac{k_1}{k_2}[A]} = \frac{k_1 \times k_2}{k_1 + k_2}$$

For example, if k_1 is kept constant at 100/min and given k_2 values of 50/min, 100/min, and 200/min, the corresponding cycling rates are 33/min, 50/min, and 67/min respectively, i.e. 2000/hr, 3000/hr, and 4000/hr.

One might have expected that when both enzyme activities are increased, the cycling rate would increase in proportion. This is true at medium, but not at high catalytic activities of the enzymes. The quantities of enzyme used in a "cycling system" are often so large that its molar concentration considerably exceeds that of the substance to be masured. In this case, the reaction rate of the system as a whole is determined by the molar catalytic activities of the enzymes in question, and is independent of the quantity of enzyme.

References

1 Passonneau, J.V. & Lowry, O.H. (1974) in *Methods of Enzymatic Analysis* (Bergmeyer, H.U., ed.) 2nd ed., pp. 2059–2072, Verlag Chemie, Weinheim & Academic Press, New York.
2 Änggård, E. & Samuelsson, B. (1974) in *Methods of Enzymatic Analysis* (Bergmeyer, H.U., ed.) 2nd ed., pp. 1877–1885, Verlag Chemie, Weinheim & Academic Press, New York.

Visualization of NAD(P)-Dependent Reactions

Hans Möllering, August W. Wahlefeld and Gerhard Michal

In enzymatic analysis, reactions in which NAD or NADP is the coenzyme are generally followed spectro-photometrically. Reduction of NAD(P) or oxidation of NAD(P)H leads to a change in the light absorption in the UV region with a maximum at 339 nm.

For a variety of reasons, however, it may be desirable to follow NAD(P)-dependent reactions in the visible region of the spectrum. To allow this, dehydrogenase reactions of this kind must be coupled with suitable redox dye reactions (conversion reactions).

Reaction of nicotinamide coenzymes with dyes can generally be achieved only indirectly (for exceptions see below). Enzymes of the respiratory chain or diaphorase*, which bring about the reoxidation of NADH or NADPH, are therefore often used. The hydrogen transport is diverted at suitable points to dyes, in which it produces colour changes. The first practical application of this principle was the *Thunberg* technique[1] with methylene blue. However, this had certain disadvantages: it was necessary to work under vacuum, since the leuco dye is autoxidizable, and it was necessary to determine the end point of a decolorization. A search for other dyes led to the use of hexacyanoferrate(III), MnO_2, quinones, etc., and the natural cytochrome c (survey, see[2]).

The greatest progress in this direction resulted from the use of tetrazolium salts (*Kuhn* and *Jerchel*[3]). These colourless or weakly coloured compounds, which have been known as a class for a long time[4], are converted into intensely coloured formazans by reduction under mild conditions. Particular advantages over the *Thunberg* technique are the increase in colour during the reaction, the irreversibility of the reduction under biological conditions[5], and the fact that oxygen has little influence on the reactions. Only tetrazolium salts will be discussed here; for other compounds, the reader is referred to the original literature or to reviews[1,2,6,7].

Tetrazolium Salts and their Reduction

The tetrazolium salts used in biochemistry are generally 2,3,5-aryl-substituted derivatives of 1,2,3,4-tetrazole, and thus have a quaternary nitrogen. In addition to these monotetrazolium compounds there are also ditetrazolium compounds, in which two tetrazolium rings are linked by an aromatic grouping, e.g. of the biphenyl type. For synthesis and chemistry, see[5,8] (X = Cl, Br).

Monotetrazolium salts   Ditetrazolium salts

They are generally white or light yellow water-soluble compounds. Irreversible[5] reduction can be achieved very easily and at neutral pH by transfer of hydrogen to give formazans.

---

* Reduced NAD: lipoamide oxidoreductase, EC 1.6.4.3.

These formazans[9] are deeply coloured, sparingly water-soluble compounds that dissolve well in organic solvents. Monoformazans are yellow to red, while diformazans are mostly blue to black. For the mechanism of the reduction, see[10].

The redox potential for the conversion of the tetrazolium salts into the corresponding formazans can be determined only by special procedures owing to the irreversibility of the reaction; large discrepancies exist in the literature data[11, 12].

Table 1 shows the tetrazolium salts most often used in biochemistry, together with their redox potentials.

NAD(P)H cannot reduce TT*, and reduces NBT, TNBT, INT, and MTT to only a small extent[18]. An auxiliary reaction must be inserted. With the enzymes of the respiratory chain that are often used for this purpose, the precise point of attack for the diversion of hydrogen cannot yet be specified for all tetrazolium salts, but the first four compounds of Table 1 act before the antimycin block, and NT and TT after it[18-20]. INT, NBT, etc., can react directly with diaphorase[21, 22], and thus directly with a flavoprotein:

$$NADH + H^+ + \text{diaphorase-FAD} \rightarrow NAD^+ + \text{diaphorase-FADH}_2$$

$$\text{diaphorase-FADH}_2 + \text{tetrazolium salt}^+ \rightarrow \text{diaphorase-FAD} + \text{formazan} + H^+$$

Whereas diaphorase form heart muscle reacts only with NADH, the enzyme from *Clostridium kluyveri* reacts with both NADPH and NADH.

Diaphorase can oxidize NADH at a small rate (about 5% of maximal activity[21]) with atmospheric oxygen. In the presence of NAD, 1.6 mmol/l, (usual concentration in enzymatic reactions), this side reaction is suppressed to such a degree that the hydrogen is quantitatively transferred to the tetrazolium salt[21].

The hydrogen of reduced nicotinamide coenzymes can also be transferred non-enzymatically to tetrazolium salts in the presence of 5-methylphenazinium methyl sulphate (phenazine methosulphate, PMS)[23-25].

Formazan   Tetrazolium salt$^+$

This reaction follows a course analogous to that of the well-known hydrogen transfer from flavin enzymes to PMS followed by further reaction[26, 27]. For the mechanism of the PMS reduction, see[28, 29]. PMS is autoxidizable, but the hydrogen is transferred to any suitable acceptors that are present (tetrazolium salts or other dyes). Moreover, PMS is sensitive to light. This difficulty can be overcome by the use of Meldola Blue (Fast New Blue 3R, 8-dimethylamino-2,3-benzophenoxazine)[30]. This is practically insensitive to light, and is even somewhat superior to PMS with regard to the rate of transfer[21].

---

* Abbreviations: see Table 1. PMS = 5-methylphenazinium methyl sulphate.

Table 1. Tetrazolium salts commonly used in biochemistry.

Abbreviation	Name	Structural formula	E' for reduction[14] [mV]
MTT	3-(4′,5′-dimethyl-thiazol-2-yl)-2,4-diphenyltetra-zolium bromide[14]		+110
INT	2-(p-iodophenyl)-3-(p-nitrophenyl)-5-phenyltetra-zolium chloride[14]		+90
TNBT	2,2′,5,5′-tetra-(p-nitrophenyl)-3,3′-(3,3′-dimethoxy-4,4′-diphenylene)di-tetrazolium chloride[15]		
NBT	2,2′-di-(p-nitro-phenyl)-5,5′-di-phenyl-3,3′-(3,3′-dimethoxy-4,4′-di-phenylene)ditetra-zolium chloride[15]		+50
NT	2,2′-p-diphenylene-3,3′,5,5′-tetra-phenylditetra-zolium chloride (neotetrazolium chloride)[16]		+170
TT	2,3,5-triphenyl-tetrazolium chloride[4]		+460 (or +240[17]; +83[11])

NADH   NAD$^+$

(CH$_3$)$_2$N$^+$ N   O

Formazan   Tetrazolium salt$^+$

The reduction of the tetrazolium salts MTT, INT, TNBT, and NBT is not affected by oxygen[31], whereas interference occurs in the case of the long-known compounds with higher redox potentials, such as NT and TT[2,19]. Once formed, the formazan is always stable to O$_2$. Tetrazolium salts can undergo disproportionation on exposure to light. In the case of triphenyltetrazolium chloride, for example, 2,3-diphenylene-5-phenyltetrazolium chloride is formed as well as formazan[32]. Exposure to strong light must therefore be avoided in optical measurements. Tetrazolium salt solutions (and particularly PMS solutions) must be protected from light during storage.

Application to Enzymatic Reactions

Following the course of enzymatic reactions in the visible region (instead of in the UV) is of the greatest importance in histochemistry (for the localization of catalytic activities of enzymes in tissue) and in practical enzyme analysis (measurements with simple instruments, visualization of the reactions).

The histochemical application has been described by numerous authors [2,5−7,12,18,20]. It will therefore be discussed only superficially. For qualitative determination, thin sections of tissue are incubated with tetrazolium salts in the presence of stabilizers (e.g. polyvinyl alcohol), buffer, substrate, and possibly electron carriers such as PMS (concerning their action, see[18,33,34]) and the formazan precipitates are investigated histologically. Quantitative measurements can be carried out after elution of the formazan with organic solvents.

In practical enzymatic analysis, both concentrations of substrates and of catalytic activities of enzymes in solutions can be determined by the tetrazolium salt method. The sparing solubility of the formazan, which is advantageous in histochemical reaction, is overcome here by the addition of suitable solubilizing agents (Triton, gelatine, etc.).

In principle, all dehydrogenase reactions with formation of NADH or NADPH can be visualized. Reactions that proceed with consumption of NADH or NADPH can be carried out as multipoint measurements if necessary (samples are taken at certain times, the enzyme reaction is stopped, and the NADH or NADPH still present is determined), but this is complicated. Moreover, flavin-dependent dehydrogenases (e.g. succinate dehydrogenase[35]) or oxidases (e.g. xanthine oxidase[36] and glucose oxidase[37]) can also be determined in this way. Though relatively fast reactions occur in these cases even in the absence of carriers such as PMS, the reaction rate can be further increased by the carriers.

A certain disadvantage of these reactions is the fact that many SH-compounds (e.g. cysteine, glutathione) and other reducing agents (e.g. ascorbic acid) can also reduce tetrazolium salts to formazans non-enzymatically, which results in artifacts. This difficulty can be eliminated – for example, by oxidizing the interfering substances with H$_2$O$_2$ in an alkaline medium or by running a sample blank (without diaphorase or NAD).

It is particularly advantageous to couple NAD(P)-dependent dehydrogenase reactions with the reduction of tetrazolium salts, where the equilibrium position of the dehydrogenase reaction is unfavourable. Because of the continuous reoxidation of the reduced coenzyme, short reaction times and complete reaction are achieved under simple conditions. Examples are the determination of lactate, ethanol, and glutamate, in which we have found[21] that the reaction time is decreased by a factor of five on average.

The relatively high absorption coefficients of the formazans increase the sensitivity of the determination methods. For example, the formazan produced from INT has an $\varepsilon_{492\,nm}$ of approx. $1.94\ l \times mmol^{-1} \times mm^{-1}$, and the formazan from MTT an $\varepsilon_{578\,nm}$ of approx. $1.30\ l \times mmol^{-1} \times mm^{-1}$. The sensitivity is increased by a factor of about 5 with respect to the measurement of the absorption of NADH or NADPH at 365 nm, and by a factor of about 2.5 with respect to measurement at 339 or 334 nm.

The absorbances and therefore the absorption coefficients depend greatly on the reaction conditions (e.g. pH, addition of detergents, etc.).

Different commercial tetrazolium salts occasionally do not give formazans of the same colour intensity. The following calibration is therefore recommended (according to[38]) for absolute measurements. A suitable known (optically verified) quantity of NADH is used instead of substrate in the determination and the resulting colour intensity of the formazan is determined. The quantity of formazan is equivalent to the quantity of NADH used, and the absorption coefficient of the formazan can therefore be calculated.

References

1 Thunberg, T. (1917) Scand. Arch. Physiol. **35**, 163.
2 Franke, W. (1955) in Handbuch der physiologisch- und pathologisch-chemischen Analyse (Hoppe-Seyler/Thierfelder, eds.) 10th edition, Vol. 2, p. 311, Springer Verlag, Berlin, Göttingen, Heidelberg.
3 Kuhn, R. & Jerchel, D. (1941) Ber. dtsch. Chem. Ges. **74**, 941.
4 Pechmann, H. V. & Runge, P. (1894) Ber. dtsch. Chem. Ges. **27**, 2920.
5 Ried, W. (1952) Angew. Chem. **64**, 391.
6 Duspiva, F. (1963) in Methods of Enzymatic Analysis (Bergmeyer, H. U., ed.) 1st edition, p. 920, Verlag Chemie, Weinheim and Academic Press, New York & London.
7 Gomori, G. (1953) Microscopic Histochemistry, 2nd impression, p. 150, University of Chicago Press.
8 Nineham, A. W. (1955) Chem. Reviews **55**, 355.
9 Pechmann, H. V. (1892) Ber. dtsch. Chem. Ges. **25**, 3175.
10 Eadie, M. J., Tyrer, J. H., Kukums, J. R. & Hooper, W. D. (1970) Histochemie **21**, 170.
11 Jerchel, D. & Moehle, W. (1944) Ber. dtsch. Chem. Ges. **77**, 591.
12 Pearse, A. G. E. (1960) Histochemistry, Theoretical and Applied, 2nd edition, J. A. Churchill, London.
13 Beyer, H. & Pyl, T. (1954) Chem. Ber. **87**, 1505.
14 Fox, S. W. & Atkinson, E. H. (1950) J. Am. Chem. Soc. **72**, 3629.
15 Tsou, K. C., Cheng, C. S., Nachlas, M. M. & Seligman, A. M. (1956) J. Am. Chem. Soc. **78**, 6139.
16 Wedekind, E. (1896) Ber. dtsch. Chem. Ges. **29**, 1846.
17 Ried, W. & Wilk, M. (1953) Ann. **581**, 49.
18 Altman, F. P. (1972) An Introduction to the Use of Tetrazolium Salts in Quantitative Enzyme Cytochemistry, Koch-Light Laboratories, Colnbrook, Bucksh.
19 Nachlas, M. M., Margulies, S. I. & Seligman, A. M. (1960) J. biol. Chem. **235**, 2739
20 Burstone, M. S. (1962) Enzyme Histochemistry and Its Application in the Study of Neoplasms, p. 470 ff., Academic Press, New York & London.
21 Möllering, H., Wahlefeld, A. W. & Michal, G., unpublished.
22 Koudstaal, J. & Hardonk, M. J. (1969) Histochemie **20**, 68.
23 Sowerby, J. M. & Ottaway, J. H. (1961) Biochem. J. **79**, 21 P.
24 Blanchaer, M. C., van Wijhe, M. & Mezersky, D. (1963) J. Histochem. Cytochem. **11**, 500.
25 Pallini, V., Pompucci, G. & Martelli, P. (1963) Boll. Soc. Ital. Biol. Sper. **39**, 236.

26 Dickens, F. & McIlwain, H. (1938) *Biochem. J.* **32,** 1615.
27 Singer, T.P. & Kearny, E.B. (1957) in *Methods of Biochemical Analysis* (Glick, D., ed.) Vol. IV, p. 307, Interscience Publishers, New York.
28 King, T.E. (1963) *J. biol. Chem.* **238,** 4032.
29 Zaugg, W.S. (1964) *J. biol. Chem.* **239,** 3964.
30 Boehringer Mannheim GmbH, German Patent P 1 959 410.
31 Altman, F.P. (1970) *Histochemie* **22,** 256.
32 Hausser, I., Jerchel, D. & Kuhn, R. (1948) *Ber. dtsch. Chem. Ges.* **82,** 195.
33 Altman, F.P. (1969) *Biochem. J.* **114,** 13 P.
34 Altman, F.P. (1971) *Biochem. J.* **125,** 21 P.
35 Nachlas, M.M., Margulies, S.I. & Seligman, A.M. (1960) *J. biol. Chem.* **235,** 499.
36 Fried, R. (1966) *Anal. Biochem.* **16,** 427.
37 Reiß, J. (1966) *Histochemie* **7,** 202.
38 Möllering, H., Wahlefeld, A.W. & Michal, G. (1974) in *Methods of Enzymatic Analysis* (Bergmeyer, H.U., ed.) 2nd edition, pp. 136–144, Verlag Chemie, Weinheim and Academic Press, New York & London.
39 Whitaker, J.F. (1969) *Clin. Acta* **24,** 23.

Principles of Enzyme-Immunoassays

Bauke K. van Weemen and Anton H.W.M. Schuurs

Introduction

Since enzymes are often detectable with great ease and in very small amounts, they can conveniently be used as labels in immunological reactions.

Initially, enzyme-labelled antibodies and antigens were used for identification and localization of the corresponding antigens and antibodies in histological preparations and for identification of precipitation lines on immunodiffusion and immunoelectrophoresis plates[1-3]. Later, it was realized that enzyme labels also have a potential for use in quantitative detection methods, analogous to radioimmunoassays (RIA), while a number of the disadvantages of radioimmunoassays can be avoided[4,5]. Such methods are now known as "enzyme-immunoassay" (EIA)[4] or "enzyme-linked immunosorbent assay" (ELISA)[5].

Several variations of the technique have been described since then. A physical phase-separation is an essential part of all of them, except the so-called "enzyme-multiplied immunoassay technique" (EMIT)[6]. Because it requires no phase-separation, this latter technique has also been called "homogeneous enzyme-immunoassay"[6], as opposed to the other, "heterogeneous" enzyme-immunoassay variations.

Heterogeneous Enzyme-Immunoassays (EIA/ELISA)

Principles

Several types of heterogeneous enzyme-immunoassay have been described:

Competitive methods

a) with enzyme-labelled antigen. This method is analogous to the classical radioimmuno-assay:

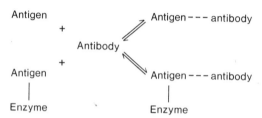

When preselected amounts of antibody and enzyme-labelled antigen are brought together with a sample containing antigen, the distribution of the enzyme label over the fractions of free and antibody-bound antigen is a measure of the amount of antigen that was present in the sample. The assay can be run either in one single step or in sequential incubation steps. In practice, the catalytic activity of the enzyme in either the free or the antibody-bound labelled antigen is measured after these two fractions have been separated. Several methods for achieving this separation are available; it is most conveniently performed by using in-solubilized antibodies.

Assays based on this method have been developed for several proteins, such as immuno-globulins G[5,7] and E[8], α-fetoprotein[9], insulin[10,42], human chorionic gonadotropin (HCG)[4], human placental lactogen (HPL)[11] and thyroid-stimulating hormone (TSH)[12], and for steroid hormones, such as estrogens[11,13], progesterone[14] and cortisol[15].

b) with enzyme-labelled antibody:

(Solid carrier) ⫮ Antigen   ⫮ Antigen --- antibody enzyme

         +

        Antibody – enzyme

         +

    Antigen   Antigen --- antibody enzyme

When a sample containing antigen is brought together with matching amounts of insolubilized antigen and enzyme-labelled antibody, the catalytic activity of the enzyme that is bound to the solid phase is inversely proportional to the amount of antigen present in the sample.

Assays based on this principle have been described only for proteins, such as HCG[16], HPL[17] and α-fetoprotein[18].

Both competitive methods are in principle applicable to the determination of compounds of any size, including haptens.

Non-competitive methods

a) with enzyme-labelled antibody for antigen detection:

$$\text{Antibody} \quad + \quad \text{Antigen} \quad + \quad \text{Antibody-enzyme}$$

$$\Updownarrow$$

$$\text{Antibody} \text{---} \text{Antigen} \text{---} \text{Antibody-enzyme}$$

When insolubilized antibody is first brought into contact with a sample containing antigen and subsequently with enzyme-labelled antibody, the fraction of catalytic activity of the enzyme bound to the solid phase is directly proportional to the amount of antigen in the sample.
This "sandwich" method can be used only for the detection of relatively large molecules, since these molecules must be able to bind at least two antibody molecules.
Proteins such as α-fetoprotein[19], HCG[16], pregnancy-associated α-macroglobulin[20] and hepatitis-B surface antigen[21] have been determined by this method.

b) with enzyme-labelled anti-immunoglobulin for the detection of specific antibodies:

$$\text{Antigen} \quad + \quad \text{Antibody} \quad + \quad (\text{Anti-immunoglobulin})\text{-enzyme}$$

$$\Updownarrow$$

$$\text{Antigen} \text{---} \text{Antibody} \text{---} (\text{Anti-immunoglobulin})\text{-enzyme}$$

When insolubilized antigen is first brought into contact with a sample containing antibodies (that are immunoglobulins) against that antigen, and subsequently with enzyme-labelled anti-immunoglobulin, the fraction of catalytic activity of the enzyme bound to the solid phase is proportional to the antibody content of the sample.
Antibodies against antigens of any size, including haptens, can be determined in this way.
This method also offers the possibility of establishing the class of immunoglobulins to which the antibodies belong by using enzyme-labelled anti-IgG, anti-IgM, etc.
Among others, antibodies against DNA[22], *Trichinella spiralis*[23], *Salmonella*[24], *Treponema pallidum*[25] and *Rubella* virus[26] have been detected in this way.

Enzyme Conjugates

The choice of the enzyme for labelling is important because it determines both the sensitivity and the practicability of the assay. Several enzymes have been used, of which horse-radish peroxidase (EC 1.11.1.7)[4,7,11,13,17,20,23,25], alkaline phosphatase (EC 3.1.3.1)[5,8,9,24,26] and β-galactosidase (EC 3.2.1.23)[10,14,15] are the most popular. They are detected photometrically or fluorometrically by means of two-point methods.
The conjugates have been prepared in several ways, depending on the enzyme as well as on the compound to be coupled. When an enzyme is to be coupled to another protein molecule, glutaraldehyde[27,28], sodium periodate[29, 42] and *N,N'-o*-phenylenedimaleimide[10] have proven to be useful coupling agents. When a smaller molecule, containing an amino or carboxyl group, is to be coupled to the enzyme, mixed anhydride methods[13,15] and carbodiimide methods[14] are

efficient and convenient. The same methods have already been used extensively for preparing hapten-protein complexes for immunization purposes[30]. Little attention has been paid to the enzymatic properties of the conjugates, apart from the degree to which the catalytic activity of the enzymes is preserved after the coupling. Only in one instance was it reported that K_m and V of β-galactosidase were hardly affected when up to 10 steroid molecules were coupled to one enzyme molecule[15]. The stability of many enzyme conjugates, prepared from small as well as large molecules, has been reported to be good (months to years)[5,7,9,12,14,18,19]; this has also been the experience in our laboratory.

Special characteristics of the methods

Performance of the assays is relatively simple, but requires a number of manipulations and takes at least several hours. Complete automation has not yet been realized, but partial mechanization has led to a set-up where 4000 samples can be assayed in one day[23].

Sensitivities in the radioimmunoassay-range have been reported in some assays[5,14,18,19,21], but in other instances, the radioimmunoassay was superior in this respect[9,12]. Generally speaking, nanogram to picogram amounts of antigens, haptens, or antibodies can be determined, depending on the nature of the substances to be determined and the choice of assay conditions and enzyme label. Accuracy and precision of enzyme-immunoassays were reported to be similar to those of radioimmunoassays[4,11,12,14,18,19,42].

Homogeneous Enzyme-Immunoassays (EMIT)

Principles

Assays based on EMIT are competitive:

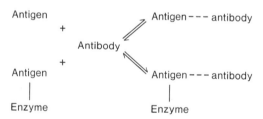

The principal feature of EMIT is that the activity of the enzyme label in the antibody–antigen-enzyme complex is either inhibited[6,32] or stimulated[31], compared with the activity in the free antigen-enzyme conjugate. This makes a phase-separation superfluous, which, of course, simplifies the assay performance. One simply mixes the antigen-containing sample with preselected amounts of antibody and antigen-enzyme.

The catalytic activity of the enzyme measured in this mixture is then either directly or inversely proportional to the antigen content of the sample.

The mechanisms of enzyme inhibition or stimulation by antibodies cannot easily be explained. Steric hindrance is an acceptable explanation for the inhibition phenomenon when lysozyme is used[6]. The inhibition of malate dehydrogenase might involve conformational changes induced by antibody binding to an "active" site, or prevention of conformational changes necessary for catalytic activity[32]. No explanation for the stimulation phenomenon has been offered. EMIT has been applied to the determination of small molecules, such as opiates[6,33], barbiturates[34], diphenylhydantoin[35], digoxin[36] and thyroxine[31].

The technique does not seem to be suitable for the detection of larger molecules, possibly because coupling of such a molecule to the enzyme might result in immediate enzyme inactivation.

Enzyme Conjugates

Whereas any enzyme can in principle be used for EIA/ELISA, this does not hold true for EMIT. The use of lysozyme (EC 3.2.1.17)[6,33,34], malate dehydrogenase (EC 1.1.1.37)[31,32], glucose-6-phosphate dehydrogenase (EC 1.1.1.49)[35,36] and horse-radish peroxidase (EC 1.11.1.7)[37] has been described in the literature. In our assay systems, the latter enzyme was not suitable for the homogeneous technique[42]. In the EMIT technique, the catalytic activity of the enzyme conjugates is determined photometrically by continual measurement, except for the digoxin assay, where the two-point method is used.

The conjugates used were prepared by mixed anhydride reactions or by acetimidate-linking[32]. It was found that coupling of morphine to the sulfhydryl groups of malate dehydrogenase gave conjugates which could not be used for EMIT[32].

The K_m of malate dehydrogenase was found to remain fairly constant after morphine residues were attached to the molecule[32].

Special characteristics of the methods

The present EMIT assays can be performed in less than 5 minutes, with the exception of the digoxin assay, which takes between 30 and 60 minutes[36]. The performance is very simple, and has been automated[38]. The sensitivity of EMIT is in the microgram range, except for the more elaborate digoxin assay, the sensitivity of which is about 1 ng/ml[36]. Precision values similar to those of RIA have been reported[35], but considerably larger variation coefficients have also been found[39].

Conclusion

By using enzymes as labels for immunological reactants, the sensitivities of enzymatic and immunological reactions can be combined while retaining the specificity of the immunological reaction. The resulting assay methods often compete with the radioimmunoassay in sensitivity, while offering advantages in practicability as far as speed, safety, and economy are concerned. Extensive reviews of enzyme-immunoassay[40,43] and coupling methods[41] have recently been published.

References

1 Nakane, P.K. & Pierce, G.B. (1966) *J. Histochem. Cytochem.* **14**, 929.
2 Avrameas, S. & Uriel, J. (1966) *C.R. Acad. Sci.*, Ser. D **262**, 2543.
3 Nakane, P.K. & Pierce, G.B. (1967) *J. Cell Biol.* **33**, 307.
4 van Weemen, B.K. & Schuurs, A.H.W.M. U.S. Patent 3,654,090 (filed 1968); *FEBS Letters* (1971) **15**, 232.

5 Engvall, E. & Perlmann, P. (1971) *Immunochemistry* **8**, 871.
6 Rubenstein, K.E., Schneider, R.S. & Ullman, E.F. (1972) *Biochem. Biophys. Res. Comm.* **47**, 846.
7 Avrameas, S. & Guilbert, B. (1972) *Biochimie* **54**, 837.
8 Hoffman, D.R. (1973) *J. Allergy Clin. Immunol.* **51**, 303.
9 Belanger, L., Hamel, D., Dufour, D. & Pouliot, M. (1976) *Clin. Chem.* **22**, 198.
10 Kato, K., Hamaguchi, Y., Fukui, H. & Ishikawa, E. (1975) *J. Biochem.* **78**, 235.
11 van Hell, H., Bosch, A.M.G., Brands, J.A.M., van Weemen, B.K. & Schuurs, A.H.W.M. (1976) *Z. Anal. Chem.* **279**, 143.
12 Miyai, K., Ishibashi, K. & Kumahara, Y. (1976) *Clin. Chim. Acta* **67**, 263.
13 van Weemen, B.K. & Schuurs, A.H.W.M. (1975) *Immunochemistry* **12**, 667.
14 Dray, F., Andrieu, J.M. & Renaud, R. (1975) *Biochim. Biophys. Acta* **403**, 131.
15 Comoglio, S. & Celada, F. (1976) *J. Immunol. Meth.* **10**, 161.
16 van Weemen, B.K. & Schuurs, A.H.W.M. (1974) *FEBS Letters* **43**, 215.
17 Barbour, H.M. (1976) *J. Immunol. Meth.* **11**, 15.
18 Maiolini, R., Ferrua, B. & Masseyeff, R. (1975) *J. Immunol. Meth.* **6**, 355.
19 Maiolini, R. & Masseyeff, R. (1975) *J. Immunol. Meth.* **8**, 223.
20 Stimson, W.H. & Sinclair, J.M. (1974) *FEBS Letters* **47**, 190.
21 Wolters, G., Kuijpers, L., Kačaki, J. & Schuurs, A. (1976) *J. Clin. Pathol.* **29**, 873.
22 Pesce, A.J., Mendoza, N., Boreisha, I., Gaizutis, M.A. & Pollak, V.E. (1974) *Clin. Chem.* **20**, 353.
23 Ruitenberg, E.J., Steerenberg, P.A., Brosi, B.J.M. & Buys, J. (1974) *Bull. W.H.O.* **51**, 108.
24 Carlsson, H.E., Lindberg, A.A. & Hammarström, S. (1972) *Infect. Immun.* **6**, 703.
25 Veldkamp, J. & Visser, A.M. (1975) *Brit. J. Vener. Dis.* **51**, 227.
26 Voller, A. & Bidwell, D.E. (1975) *Br. J. Exp. Pathol.* **56**, 338.
27 Avrameas, S. (1969) *Immunochemistry* **6**, 43.
28 Avrameas, S. & Ternynck, T. (1971) *Immunochemistry* **8**, 1175.
29 Nakane, P.K. & Kawaoi, A. (1974) *J. Histochem. Cytochem.* **22**, 1084.
30 Erlanger, B.F., Borek, F., Beiser, S.M. & Lieberman, S. (1959) *J. Biol. Chem.* **234**, 1090.
31 Ullman, E.F., Blakemore, J., Leute, R.K., Eimstad, W. & Jaklitsch, A. (1975) *Clin. Chem.* **21**, 1011.
32 Rowley, G.L., Rubenstein, K.E., Huisjen, J. & Ullman, E.F. (1975) *J. Biol. Chem.* **250**, 3759.
33 Schneider, R.S., Lindquist, P., Tong-in Wong, E., Rubenstein, K.E. & Ullman, E.F. (1973) *Clin. Chem.* **19**, 821.
34 Walberg, C.B. (1974) *Clin. Chem.* **20**, 305.
35 Booker, H.E. & Darcey, B.A. (1975) *Clin. Chem.* **21**, 1766
36 Chang, J.J., Crowl, C.P. & Schneider, R.S. (1975) *Clin. Chem.* **21**, 967.
37 Lee, L.M.Y. & Kenney, M.A. (1975) *Clin. Chem.* **21**, 967.
38 Broughton, A. & Ross, D.L. (1975) *Clin. Chem.* **21**, 186.
39 Oellerich, M., Haeckel, R. & Külpmann, W.R. (1976) *Z. Anal. Chem.* **279**, 132.
40 Wisdom, G.B. (1976) *Clin. Chem.* **22**, 1243.
41 Kennedy, J.H., Kricka, L.J. & Wilding, P. (1976) *Clin. Chim. Acta* **70**, 1.
42 Kleinhammer, G., Lenz, H., Linke, R. & Gruber, W. (1976) *Z. Anal. Chem.* **279**, 195.
43 Voller, A., Bidwell, D.E. & Bartlett, A. (1976) *Bull. W.H.O.* **53**, 3418.

Handling of Biochemical Reagents and Samples

In enzymatic analysis, high-molecular-weight, specifically-acting proteins – namely enzymes – serve as analytical reagents. Numerous enzymes of high purity and stability are at present available commercially. Their stability is generally good. It has also become possible to stabilize an increasing number of very sensitive enzymes. Solutions of coenzymes or metabolites are often more labile than enzyme solutions or suspensions. Other analytical reagents (e.g. very dilute NaOH, thiosulfate solutions, etc., for titrations) also decompose easily but, like biochemical reagents, are absolutely reliable when handled correctly. Knowledge of the essential properties of these compounds is a prerequisite for their correct handling.

Reagents for Enzymatic Analysis

Hans Ulrich Bergmeyer

Analysts in general are not nearly as familiar with the biochemicals involved in enzymatic analysis as they are with inorganic reagents, for instance. Learning is made difficult by the number and diversity of the names of substances, abbreviations, and definitions of quality. These concepts are in need of further elucidation.

Nomenclature, Abbreviations, and Standardization

The nomenclature, and particularly the abbreviations, for biochemical substances still have a historical basis, though considerable progress has been made internationally in recent years towards the establishment of uniform and correct nomenclature.

In order to standardize these reagents[1], the Committee on Biological Chemistry, Division of Chemistry and Chemical Technology, National Academy of Sciences – National Research Council (USA) started in 1955 to collect standard values for biochemical compounds[2,3].

Nomenclature and Abbreviations

Recommendations for nomenclature and corresponding abbreviations for complicated biochemical substances have now been made by the Commission on Biochemical Nomenclature (International Union of Pure and Applied Chemistry (IUPAC) – International Union of Biochemistry (IUB))[4-8]. In the field of enzymes in particular, a systematic arrangement and an internationally recognized nomenclature was essential. Such a nomenclature has been in existence since 1964[9,10], was greatly extended in 1972[11], and was completed and revised[12] in 1975 (cf. p. 7). Abbreviated enzyme names are thus made unambiguous by the addition of the Enzyme Commission's classification number (EC no.). See also on p. 242f.

The abbreviations for phosphorylated biochemical substances are less straightforward. Adenosine-5'-triphosphoric acid, for example, contains four dissociable hydrogen atoms. The salts are therefore represented by $ATP-NaH_3$ to $ATP-Na_4$.

In formulas, either the state of dissociation is given, e.g. ATP^{4-}, or generally ATP. This denotes adenosine-5'-triphosphoric acid or triphosphate, the degree of dissociation of the salt being ignored.

The abbreviations NAD^+, NADH, $NADP^+$, and NADPH have become accepted for the pyridine coenzymes. In these abbreviations, H means that the pyridine ring is hydrogenated in position 4, and has nothing to do with the state of dissociation of the pyrophosphate residue in the molecule. The disodium salt, e.g. of the dibasic acid NADH, is represented by the abbreviation $NADH-Na_2$.

Standardization

Standardization is the establishment of criteria for the quality of substances or processes. Concerning the "quality" of substances, see p. 101 ff.

Because of the great importance of standardization in clinical chemistry, national and international commissions in this field as well as in biochemistry (IUB) and chemistry (IUPAC) are particularly closely concerned with these questions (*International Federation of Clinical Chemistry, IFCC; National Committee for Clinical Laboratory Standards, USA, NCCLS; German, Scandinavian, French Societies of Chemical Chemistry*, and others). Whereas the efforts of clinical chemistry are largely directed towards standardization of assay methods, we are interested here exclusively in the standardization of biochemical substances.

The standardization of enzymes is particularly difficult (cf. p. 103 f.); among other things, it calls for standardized methods for the measurement of the activity at a specified temperature. The standardization of coenzymes and metabolites, on the other hand, is comparatively simple.

The most important point in the standardization of these substances is the correct and comprehensive specification of contents and purities (cf. pp. 103–106). The main criterion in the standardization of enzymes is their specific catalytic activity (cf. p. 103).

Efforts have extended in recent years to the unification of all parameters according to the international system (cf. *D. Moss*, p. 9), which is essentially characterized by the fundamental units meter, kilogram, second, and mole. The consistent application of these units (cf.[13]) leads to the volume units m^3 and liter, and in chemistry to mol/l, mol/kg, kg/l, kg/kg, l/l, and for the unit of time to seconds (s) instead of minutes (min).

This leads to a new unit for reaction rates, i.e. mol/s instaed of µmol/min. 1 µmol/min = 16.67 × 10^{-9} mol/s = 16.67 nmol/s. The international unit, U, is replaced by the katal (kat). It remains to be seen how quickly this new unit will become accepted. It is used in the present edition of this book along with the one used hitherto.

Quality Requirements

Enzymatic analysis is concerned mainly with biological material, the substances to be analyzed generally being natural products. The samples contain a large number of chemically very similar substances. The reagents used for the analysis must therefore ensure that the analysis is specific and that the many other substances present in the sample do not interfere. The quality requirements for the reagents used must consequently be high.

Reagents for enzymatic analysis are mainly buffers, inorganic cations and anions, and natural products, in particular enzymes, coenzymes, and metabolites; organic substrates are also used for the determination of enzyme activities.

The Concept of Quality[14,15]

Difficulties are occasionally encountered in defining the purity even of buffers and organic substrates. For example, p-nitrophenyl phosphate, the substrate of alkaline phosphatase, should contain only very small quantities of p-nitrophenol. It is much more difficult, however, to define and adhere to purity criteria for enzymes and coenzymes. The quality requirements for the reagents used in enzymatic analysis, particularly the natural products mentioned, comprise the following:

- purity
- activity
- stability
- type of preparation
- packaging.

The problems start with the definition of *purity*. It would generally be sufficient to adhere to the principle "as pure as necessary, not as pure as possible". However, this principle cannot be used, since a method, together with the reagents that it involves, must be capable of being applied to a wide range of test materials, and since no one can predict what possibly interfering substances are present in the reagent. Purity is thus a relative concept.

The *activity*, particularly the catalytic activity of enzymes, should remain constant over a reasonable period, and should be high enough for enzymatic reactions to proceed in an acceptable time.

The *stability* of the reagent should refer both to the pure substance used and to the solution of the substance. In both cases, the substance must not change during storage.

The *type of preparation* should be application-oriented. It should not cause difficulties in the assay, e.g. because of very viscous solutions, hygroscopic lyophilisates, or reagent tablets that dissolve too slowly. Chemical reaction steps (e.g. the conversion of an insoluble barium salt into the sodium salt) should be avoided.

The *packaging material* usually receives too little attention. Bottles, stoppers, and foil wrappers may release substances that inactivate their contents, or they may be made in such a way that the contents are damaged by access of atmospheric moisture or atmospheric oxygen.

None of the five points mentioned can be considered in isolation. For example, the problem of moisture-permeable stoppers in reagent bottles reflects both on stability and on purity. Absorption of water by NADH, for example, leads to inhibitor formation. The same is true of "type of preparation". The light-sensitive silver-barium salt of phosphoenolpyruvic acid decomposes under the influence of light when colourless glass bottles are used, and problems of stability and purity thus arise.

The quality requirements for the reagents form a complex system of interdependent parameters. The number of factors that influence quality can be limited if (expressed mathematically) the parameters "type of preparation" and "packaging" are kept constant. One can then say that quality is a function of *purity, activity,* and *stability*:

$$quality = f \ (purity, \ activity, \ and \ stability)$$

However, these three concepts again form a trilateral function among themselves:

$$\text{Purity}$$
$$\nearrow \quad \nwarrow$$
$$Activity \longleftrightarrow Stability$$

i.e. purity depends on stability and activity, stability depends on purity and activity, and activity depends on purity and stability. These three concepts must be considered together.

The Individual Quality Requirements

Type of Preparation

The fundamental requirements for an application-oriented type of preparation are maximum simplicity of use of the reagent and a guarantee of the highest possible quality.

Simplicity of use: Soluble alkali metal salts are obviously easier to use than sparingly soluble barium salts. Until recently it was usual to prepare sugar phophates, for example, as barium salts, which had to be converted into the desired alkali metal salt before use. A crystalline substance can be weighed out more easily than a hygroscopic lyophilisate. Preweighed reagent tablets (e.g. p-nitrophenyl phosphate as the substrate for alkaline phosphatase) save weighing out the substrate, but they must dissolve quickly.

Manipulation of the substance before use, e.g. dialysis of enzyme suspensions, should be avoided. This dialysis is necessary when ammonium ions interfere with the determination. Example: Determination of the catalytic activities of the aminotransferases in serum; if the serum contained glutamate dehydrogenase, this would react with the oxoglutarate used and the ammonium ions of the enzyme suspension. In this case the indicator enzymes malate dehydrogenase and lactate dehydrogenase are used as a solution in 50% glycerol.

Guarantee of Quality: This concept is again closely connected with the simplicity of use, and also with stability and activity. An enzyme solution is easier to use than a suspension. Solutions containing preservatives save daily preparation of fresh solutions, and guarantee constant quality for periods of days or weeks. However, preservatives are permissible only if they have no effect on the catalytic activity of either the dissolved enzyme or the enzyme to be determined. Example: Enzyme solutions in 50% glycerol guarantee not only satisfactory determination of the catalytic activities of the aminotransferases but also lasting quality of the indicator enzymes.

Or: The use of CoA preparations in the form of the lithium salt instead of as the free acid offers greater stability and hence satisfactory quality for a longer time.

Packaging

The best of reagents will deteriorate in time if poorly packaged. Glass that gives off heavy metals leads to inhibition of enzymes. Plastics that release plasticizers are no better. Films and stoppers that are permeable to water vapour allow lyophilisates to absorb water and deliquesce. Example: One of the causes of inhibitor formation in NADH is moisture, cf. Fig. 1.

A satisfactory packaging material is particularly important for mixtures of reagents, which are being increasingly used in clinical chemistry for routine determinations. They usually contain a number of different components. It is therefore necessary to rule out a variety of external influences.

The main criterion must be that no component of the packaging material has any effect on its contents; the package itself must provide effective protection against harmful external influences. Conscientious manufacturers of reagents for enzymatic analysis overcome these problems.

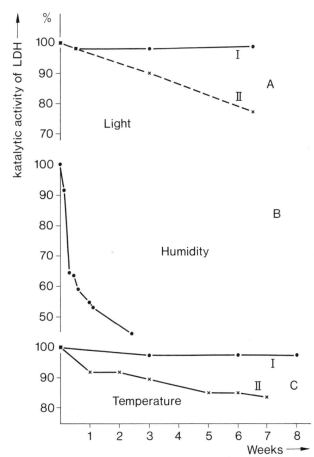

Fig. 1. Stability of NADH preparations (formation of inhibitors as measured by the LDH activity).
A. Effect of light: I dark, II diffuse daylight. Room temperature (ca. 21°C), exclusion of moisture by use of stoppered containers; brown glass (not special glass).
B. Effect of moisture: NADH stored in a thin layer at 22°C in ca. 80% relative humidity. Light excluded.
C. Effect of temperature: I stored at 4°C (refrigerator), II at 33°C. Moisture and light excluded.

It is quite possible to meet the requirements with regard to type of preparation and packaging to such a degree that the reagents are suitable for universal use, or at least for the foreseeable range of applications. Among the various factors that influence quality, therefore, these two can be kept constant. This leaves the parameters *purity*, *stability*, and *activity*.

Purity, Activity, Stability

Enzymes, coenzymes, and metabolites are typical of the reagents used in enzymatic analysis.

Enzymes

The best purity criterion for an enzyme to be used in enzymatic analysis is the specific catalytic activity, with accompanying information on the catalytic activities of contaminating enzyme proteins. These "contaminating activities"* are expressed as percentages of the specific catalytic activity of the enzyme described. The indication of "side activities"* serves to characterize the

---
* Definitions, see p. 46.

enzyme, but provides no further information on its purity. Crystallization is no criterion of purity. It is nonsense, for example, to specify "crystallized 3 times".

The following examples show how seriously contaminating activities can interfere. In the determination of the catalytic activity of pyruvate kinase (PK) in serum, a few thousandths of a percent of pyruvate kinase in the indicator enzyme lactate dehydrogenase (LDH), which is used in excess, lead to errors of more than 5% at normal PK values. A similar situation occurs in the determination of the catalytic activities of the aspartate and alanine aminotransferases[14, 15] (cf. Table 1).

Table 1. Errors due to contaminating activities in indicator enzymes.

Assay	Value measured U/l (nkat/l)	Indicator enzyme and contamination	Error in the value found
PK	12 (200)	LDH (0.006% PK)	5%
AST	7 (117)	MDH (0.03% AST)	6%
ALT	5 (83)	LDH (0.03% ALT)	6%

allowed:	0.001% PK	in LDH
	0.01 % ALT	in LDH
	0.005% AST	in MDH

The number of contaminating activities that must be checked for depends on the expected range of application. A selection is necessary in view of the large number of enzymes known. If intended for a specific purpose, the auxiliary and indicator enzymes must be tested for contaminating activities in the complete assay systems in which they are to be used. Only in this way are the effective figures for interfering catalytic activities obtained. For example, the indicator enzyme LDH for alanine aminotransferase, ALT, must be tested for contaminating activities in the optimized assay system for ALT, including pyroxidal phosphate. In particular, apo-ALT in the LDH is detectable only in the presence of pyridoxal phosphate, which is not ordinarily part of the assay system for LDH. The corresponding remarks apply to creatine kinase (which can be reactivated by SH-reagents) present as an impurity in the auxiliary and indicator enzymes used for its determination.

Freedom from proteases is also important, since these have a decisive influence on the stability of enzyme preparations.

The catalytic activity of enzymes is expressed here in international units[9-11] (units, U, or katals, kat, cf. p. 11). The specific catalytic activity is referred to the mass of protein (U/mg, μkat/mg). Only in exceptional cases (e.g. for some hydrolases) is this definition impracticable. In some cases it is necessary to specify fixed measuring conditions (e.g. the nature and concentration of the substrate); where necessary we then give the definition of other units or the corresponding experimental conditions. The measuring temperature also forms part of a completely defined specific activity of an enzyme, e.g. 400 U/mg (30°C), or 6.7 μkat/mg (30°C).

The stability of enzymes is generally better than of coenzymes. Instability is often due to the growth of micro-organisms that produce proteases. Preservatives may be added to prevent this. However, it is necessary to check whether these inhibit the enzyme and hence interfere with the determination. A stabilizing effect can often be achieved by addition of the substrate or of a homologue (e.g. we stabilize glycerol kinase with 1% (v/v) of ethylene glycol; this is the only way in which stability for well over 1 year can be achieved).

Coenzymes and Metabolites

The concept of "activity" must be understood here as a supplementary criterion of purity. For example, a coenzyme may be chemically almost 100% pure, but it may still inhibit the enzyme-catalyzed system because of practically undetectable traces of heavy metals.

The preparation in a pure form, and hence the characterization of the purity of natural substances used as reagents in enzymatic analysis is also made difficult by the fact that it is often not possible to crystallize them. The use of the melting point as a criterion of purity almost always fails. The isolation methods available at present for preparation of these compounds from biological material frequently yield compounds containing impurities of similar structure or function as well as degradation products.

The purity of coenzymes and substrates is best determined by enzymatic analysis. In practice, only the fraction active in the enzymatic assay is of importance. All other analytical data have only supplementary value.

> *Examples:* It is of little value to determine the purity of a fructose-1,6-diphosphate preparation by its optical rotation, because contamination by other fructose-phosphate esters causes interference. A colorimetric determination of fructose (e.g. with the resorcinol-HCl reaction) is also out of place, because the main contaminants contribute to the colour development. Similarly, the analysis of adenosine-5′-triphosphate by determination of "acid-labile" phosphate is unsatisfactory, because contamination by adenosine-5′-diphosphate leads to values which are too high.

A necessary addition to the results of the enzymatic analysis are details concerning the cation content of the preparation, especially in the case of non-crystalline salts of polybasic acids.

> *Example:* Four sodium salts of fructose-1,6-diphosphoric acid are possible. It is difficult to maintain the conditions of preparation such that only one type of salt is produced. In this case, the data on the degree of purity should most certainly contain the sodium content as well as the percentage of F-1,6-P_2 (free acid) and water content.

The second necessary supplement to the results of the enzymatic analysis is specification of the water content of the preparation. If, apart from the enzymatically active compound and cations, a preparation contains only water, it can be termed "pure". We do not designate a compound containing 90% active material $+10\%$ water as "90% pure"; the substance is pure. On the other hand, the designation "pure" for a non-crystalline preparation is false if its analysis adds up to 100% by including a correction for a fictitious (calculated) water content.

It is misleading to state a definite water content for non-crystalline substances, such as NAD, NADH, NADP, NADPH, alkali salts of some phosphate esters, etc., because this depends on the conditions under which the substance was dried. Even substances which crystallize with water of crystallization, such as adenosine, can lose water on storage, while other compounds are hygroscopic. We do not include the water content in the formulae of non-crystalline preparations (e.g. NAD · $4H_2O$), because such a formula suggests a degree of purity and content of the active substance which is not warranted. The purity of a non-crystalline coenzyme or substrate is therefore given by the sum of the enzymatically active substance, the relevant cation or anion, and water.

Substances that are often used, such as ATP, should also be examined for their ability to function in an assay system that is particularly complicated and hence relatively susceptible to interference. For this purpose we use the creatine kinase reaction, which is particularly sensitive to traces of iron and calcium. Function tests are essential for ready-to-use reagent kits containing many individual components. Purity and activity are best verified here by measurements on standardized control sera with values in the normal and high ranges.

Many examples of the stability of coenzymes and biochemical metabolites have been given above. The trilateral function stability/activity/purity is very clearly evident in the case of NADH. As soon as a hygroscopic NADH lyophilisate absorbs water (possibly deliquesces and turns yellow), not only the purity but also the activity in the enzymatic system is impaired; the stability has been lost.

Ready-to-use reagent compositions

If an analytical procedure is used particularly frequently, it is desirable to premix reagent solutions (reagent mix) in order to cut down on the use of the pipette in the determination. This considerably increases the precision of the procedure. Ready-to-use reagent mixes that, by including many or all of the necessary reagents, simplify their use to the greatest possible extent, satisfy the need for rationalization in routine laboratories in particular. Furthermore, they enable even unskilled personnel to perform enzymatic analyses in a normally equipped laboratory.

In any case, one should only use commercial packages containing reagents of satisfactory quality and, particularly in the determination of the catalytic activity of enzymes, that produce the optimum concentrations in the assay system. All manufacturers of ready-to-use reagent compositions should be urged to accurately specify the concentrations of the solutions contained in them.

In general the reagents and procedures are adapted to a definite material to be investigated (e.g. the serum). If other samples are to be analyzed, one must first check whether reproducible results are obtained with the ready-to-use reagent.

Summary

If care is taken to ensure that no external influences (due to the packaging) adversely affect the quality of biochemical reagents and that the type of preparation has no influence on the quality, but at the same time guarantees maximum simplicity of use of the preparation, the quality of reagents for enzymatic analysis can be defined by the concepts *purity*, *activity*, and *stability*.

There is a another parameter that facilitates routine work and minimizes errors, but in principle is of no relevance to the quality. This is the consistency of the quality of different production lots. The well-known manufacturers take steps to ensure such consistency. If any doubt exists, it is necessary for the investigator himself to check the quality of the reagents in the laboratory before they are used for analysis.

Storage, Stability, and Control of Substances and Solutions

Substances

Enzymes in stabilized aqueous glycerol solution, as suspensions in ammonium sulfate solution, or as lyophilisates should be stored at 0 to $+4°C$, unless other directions are given. When stored under these conditions, the loss of activity, even over some months, is generally minimal. Freezing of crystalline suspensions can frequently lead to a considerable loss of activity. On the other hand, enzyme solutions are generally more stable in the frozen state, particularly if the product is thawed infrequently. Any access of moisture to lyophilized enzymes must be excluded, which means that cold vials of lyophilisate must first be warmed up to room temperature before being opened.

Coenzymes such as NAD(P), NAD(P)H, CoA, and FAD must be stored dry at 0 to +4°C and protected against light. Incorrect storage of NADH, for example, results in the formation of inhibitors of dehydrogenases. This phenomenon is already apparent before any decrease in the NADH content of the preparation can be measured.

Exposure to light, moisture, and – to a lesser extent – temperature are the main factors which cause destruction of NADH. From systematic studies it appears that exposure to atmospheric moisture is the most important factor in the formation of inhibitors in the solid substance (Fig. 1, p. 103). The measured values are referred to a standard LDH preparation, whose activity had been measured with an NADH preparation which could not be purified further (100% activity).

NADH is stable if the following conditions are maintained: absolute exclusion of light and moisture, low temperature (warming to room temperature, up to 33°C, for short periods causes virtually no damage). CoA is oxidized by atmospheric oxygen; moreover, the pyrophosphate bond is easily hydrolyzed. Most coenzymes decompose by hydrolysis, therefore moisture must be excluded. Lyophilized preparations take up water particularly easily, so that they must be stored in a desiccator.

Solutions

Freshly distilled water should be used for the preparation of solutions of biochemical reagents. The term "redistilled water" no longer needs to be stressed. In most cases, it is sufficient to distill deionized water through a glass still in order to remove micro-organisms and substances introduced by the ion-exchange resin. Demineralization and sterilization of tapwater with the aid of membrane filters (e.g. Millipore®) is practicable and economical. It is important that the water be not more than one day old. Special care is required with commercial so-called "sterile aqua dest."; it often contains reducing compounds. Compounds leached from stoppers (usually rubber stoppers) can cause interference in some enzyme reactions. Bottles containing solutions of substrates, coenzymes, or enzymes should therefore be stoppered only with reliable rubber stoppers, or preferably with stoppers made of polyethylene or silicone rubber.

Dilute solutions of coenzymes and substrates should always be stored in a refrigerator, not only because of their chemical instability, but also because of the rapid growth of microorganisms; the content of the solutions should be checked every 10 days. Buffer and substrate solutions, especially phosphate, acetate, amino acid, and sugar solutions should be stored in thoroughly clean and sterilized dark bottles with tapered glass stoppers. The daily requirement should be poured out rather than pipetted. Coenzyme solutions, with the exception of NADH and NADPH, are best frozen in small portions so as to avoid excessive freezing and thawing. Solutions of NADH and NADPH are acid-labile; the pH of the solutions should not fall below 7.5. On the other hand, NAD and NADP are alkali-labile. CoA is most stable around pH 4; ATP around pH 9. Sedimented crystals of enzyme suspensions in ammonium sulfate solution should not be resuspended by shaking, but by careful swirling of the vessels.

The high catalytic activity of highly purified enzymes means that only a fraction of a milligram is required to provide excess of enzyme for substrate and coenzyme assays. Hence the volumes of enzyme suspensions are small. To avoid losses due to dilution by water, precipitation of ammonium sulfate crystals, or contamination by microorganisms, the containers should always be kept stoppered.

Diluted enzyme solutions should be made up only with ice-cold "redistilled" water or buffer solution. Since enzymes are unstable in highly diluted solutions, only the volume required for 1–2 hours should be made up.

It is recommended that all the necessary solutions be stored in an ice-bath on the bench during the working period (Fig. 2). Insulated plastic containers with metal racks that take tubes of various sizes are available commercially*.

Fig. 2. Ice bath for biochemical reagents.

All reagents required for assays, including stock buffer solutions and redistilled water, should be kept covered; otherwise contamination may occur by airborne bacteria or chemical compounds. This can result in interferences such as displacement of the pH of buffer solutions by absorbed carbon dioxide, the inactivation of enzymes in dilute solution by proteases from microorganisms, or the falsification of the results of ethanol determinations by traces of alcohol in the laboratory atmosphere.

Control of Reagents

It is recommended that the activities of the enzymes used and the concentrations of coenzyme and substrate solutions be checked before starting a series of measurements. The correct functioning of a complete assay system for an end-point determination can be tested by adding a trace of the pure substance being measured to the cuvette after the end-point has been reached. A renewed reaction should occur immediately.

Similarly, if there is no reaction in a determination of enzyme activity, a small amount of the pure enzyme should be added to test whether the assay system is in order.

---

* e.g. from Fritz Kniese, Marburg-Marbach, W. Germany.

References

1 Carter, H.E., Edsall, J.T., Weinhouse, S., Neurath, H., Schales, O. & Smythe, C.V. (1956) *Science* **123**, 54.
2 *Publication 719 of the National Academy of Sciences* – National Research Council; Washington D.C., USA, 1960.
3 *Specifications and Criteria for Biochemical Compounds*, Publication 1344, National Academy of Sciences, National Research Council, Washington, D.C., USA, 1967.
4 *J. biol. Chem.* (1966) **241**, 527.
5 *Biochemistry* (1966) **5**, 1445.
6 *Arch. Biochem. Biophys.* (1966) **115**, 1.
7 *Virology* (1966) **29**, 480.
8 *Hoppe-Seyler's Z. Physiol. Chem.* (1967) **348**, 245.
9 *Enzyme Nomenclature*, Recommendations (1964) of the International Union of Biochemistry. – Elsevier Publ. Comp. Amsterdam, London, New York 1965.
10 Florkin, M. & Stotz, E.H. (1965) *Comprehensive Biochemistry*, Vol. 13, 2nd ed. Elsevier Publ. Comp. Amsterdam, London, New York.
11 *Enzyme Nomenclature*, Recommendations (1972) of the IUPAC and IUB, Elsevier Scient. Publ. Comp., Amsterdam, 1973.
12 Commission on Biochemical Nomenclature (1972). Enzyme Nomenclature: Recommendations (1972) of the International Union of Pure and Applied Chemistry and the International Union of Biochemistry. Supplement 1. Corrections and Additions (1975). *Biochim. biophys. Acta* (1976) **429**, 1.
13 Dybkaer, R. & Jørgensen, K. (1967) *Quantities and Units in Clinical Chemistry*, Munksgaard, Kopenhagen.
14 Bergmeyer, H.U., 8th Int. Congr. Clin. Chemistry, Copenhagen, June 1972. Abstracts of papers 12.2.
15 Bergmeyer, H.U. (1972) *Chem. Rundschau* **25**, Nr. 28.

The Sample

Hans Ulrich Bergmeyer, Erich Bernt, Karlfried Gawehn, and Gerhard Michal

Metabolites and enzymes exist in the organism in a dynamic steady state and they adapt to changes in the environment, although at different rates. Such a change occurs when a sample is collected for biochemical analysis, and it is therefore to be expected that the concentration in the sample alters with time. The collection of the sample and its storage must therefore be carried out in such a way that the state of the tissue is fixed at the moment of collection of the sample.

Sample Collection

The methods chosen for the collection of the sample should stop metabolic processes very rapidly and give the greatest possible protection to the substances to be determined. Blood is allowed to flow directly from the cannula into ice-cold perchloric acid, while for tissue samples the "frozen-stop" or "freeze-stop" technique is the method of choice. Despite strict observance of correct techniques, however, experimental results for biological material are not always reproducible. The quantitative and topographic compositions of some cells and tissues exhibit significant variations with the time of day and even with the time of year; sexual and racial differences have also been observed, as well as relationship with body weight (refer e.g. to[1-6]). This is true both of metabolites (e.g. glycogen) and of catalytic activities of enzymes (e.g. esterases, aminotransferases).

According to *Tarnowski* et al.[7] the physiological metabolite content of the rat liver may be drastically changed both by the degree of excitation of the animal and by the method of killing. The depth and duration of anesthesia and the nature of the anesthetic may falsify the result of the assay[8]. These findings no doubt also apply to other types of animals and other organs. Anoxia of the tissue, even for a short time, causes changes particularly in the concentrations of the energy-rich nucleotides and their degradation products as well as in the concentrations of the redox couples and other labile metabolic intermediates[7]. Instead of collecting the tissue *in situ* with freeze-clamps, the excised organs or even whole animals are still often frozen in liquid nitrogen or liquid air. This method must be avoided if metabolite contents are to be assayed, because the tissue samples are insulated for 30 s or more by the gas envelope of the boiling coolant and thus prevented from freezing completely. Some examples of how values[9] obtained by the frozen-stop technique and by rapid homogenization in perchloric acid alone differ are shown in Table 1. The samples were obtained from canine hearts.

Table 1. Metabolite concentrations in canine hearts (n = 4–5). Deproteinization after "frozen-stop" or by homogenization in ice-cold perchloric acid.

Metabolite	Measured concentration (µmol/g fresh wt.)	
	Frozen-stop method	Homogenization in perchloric acid
ATP	3.20	2.87
ADP	0.87	0.94
AMP	0.15	0.19
Creatine phosphate	3.65	<1.0
F-1,6-P$_2$	0.10	0.15
Glycerol-3-phosphate	0.24	0.47
Lactate	3.04	7.43
2-Oxoglutarate	0.095	0.044

Similar findings are obtained with other metabolites. Very great errors can arise, for example, in the measurement of NAD/NADH ratios, because slow deproteinization results in temporary anoxia with consequent inverse changes in the concentrations of the nucleotides[10]. Naturally the samples must be collected under the proper physiological conditions, otherwise erroneous results are obtained which are independent of the analytical technique. The experimental result can naturally only give the numerical value for what is actually present in the assay material at the time of the analysis. Blood from constricted veins will give false pyruvate values, for example. A case has been reported[11] in which abnormally high blood alcohol values were obtained. The subject was a painter who worked for a long time with paints dissolved in ethyl acetate and inhaled the vapour. Endogenous esterases had liberated ethanol from the ethyl acetate.

There are numerous procedures for obtaining samples suitable for the determination of the catalytic activities of enzymes, but they must be appropriate to the type of sample and the enzyme to be measured (for a review, see *Schmidt*[12]). In the case of tissues, an extraction procedure is required. It should be noted here that too low activities can be obtained, not only with overly mild extracting agents, but also with overly intensive extraction, especially in the case of cytoplasmic enzymes. *Schmidt*[12] considers that inactivating factors released by intensive extraction are responsible for this situation. The optimum conditions for extraction vary with the particular enzyme under study. For other details, see[13].

With growing knowledge of these relationships, there is an increasing awareness of the pressing need to standardize the conditions under which biological samples are collected and/or to state these conditions when the experimental results are reported.

Stability of Metabolites and Enzymes in the Sample

There is no difficulty in the preparation of reliable samples for the analysis of substances which are not metabolized further (e.g. certain inorganic ions or end-products of metabolism, such as bilirubin and creatinine). They are stable indefinitely, if bacterial decomposition is prevented. The behaviour of glucose in blood after collection of the sample is typical of that of the majority of compounds of interest. Immediately after collection of the sample, the physiological regulation of the blood sugar concentration breaks down. The degradation of glucose by the erythrocytes continues, and consequently the glucose content of the sample decreases. Attempts to stop the

Table 2. Stability of metabolites in blood and in deproteinized solutions[11,14].

Metabolite	Material	Storage temperature	% of initial value after day				
			1	2	3	5	8
Glucose	Blood	Room temp.	30	6		0	
		+4°C	80	32		20	
	Blood + HClO$_4$ (not centrifuged)	Room temp.	110*	100		115*	
		+4°C	99	102		108*	
	Blood + HClO$_4$ (supernatant after centrifugation)	Room temp.	99	100		102	
		+4°C	99	100		100	
		−25°C			99		104
	Plasma	Room temp.	99	99	99		97[34]
		+4°C	101	101	98		99[34]
		−20°C	99	101	99		77[34]
Lactate	Blood	Room temp.	341	425			
		+4°C	168	210			
	Blood + HClO$_4$ (supernatant after centrifugation)	Room temp.	99	102	98		
		+4°C	101	105	102		
		−25°C			102		
Pyruvate	Blood	Room temp.	856	1065			
		+4°C	101	155			
	Blood + HClO$_4$ (supernatant after centrifugation, neutralized)	Room temp.	101		95		
		−25°C			96		
ATP	Blood	Room temp.	95	74			
		+4°C	62	50			
	Blood + HClO$_4$ (supernatant after centrifugation	Room temp.	78	62	58		32
		+4°C	93	85	87		76
ADP	Blood	Room temp.	131				
		+4°C	112	100			
	Blood + HClO$_4$ (supernatant after centrifugation, neutralized)	Room temp.	97	100	93		
		+4°C	98	95	92		
AMP	Blood	Room temp.	248				
		+4°C	317	346			
	Blood + HClO$_4$ (supernatant after centrifugation, neutralized)	Room temp.	102	100			
		+4°C	100	100			
2-Oxoglutarate	Blood	Room temp.	135	205			
	Blood + HClO$_4$ (supernatant after centrifugation, neutralized)	Room temp.	80		77		
		+4°C	95	91			

* The increase in glucose is caused by the acid hydrolysis of glucose-containing metabolites of the erythrocytes.

decrease of glucose with fluoride are unsuccessful, because fluoride inhibits glycolysis at the relative late enolase stage. Consequently, glucose can be degraded further to the phosphoglyceric acids and is not analyzed. On the other hand, 1 hr after collection of blood, excessively high lactate values are found due to its formation from blood glucose by the erythrocytes. Generally, these reactions are retarded by storage in a refrigerator, but this is only a help for short periods of storage. For this reason, the determination of glucose or lactate in serum is not practical: the time required to obtain serum is relatively long in comparison to the speed with which the metabolic reactions occur, and therefore reliable results are not obtained. Some examples[11,14] related to these problems are shown in Table 2.

The behaviour of individual metabolites is extremely variable. It may seem paradoxical that, for example, the ATP content of non-deproteinized blood decreases more slowly at room temperature than in a refrigerator. However, ATP is continually regenerated by the glycolysis reactions, and these are significantly slower at $4°C$. At 0 to $+4°C$ the decreased rate of decomposition of ATP is still greater than the rate of regeneration of ATP. Consequently AMP, a decomposition product of ATP, rises more rapidly in a refrigerator than at room temperature, whereas ADP, an intermediate product, changes only slowly. Thus, even for closely related compounds, it is not always possible to draw analogies as to their behaviour.

As a rule, metabolite assays without deproteinization of the sample or some other method of stopping metabolism (e.g. by hemolysis of erythrocytes) do not give reliable results, unless the stability of the metabolites to be measured during the period of storage and under the special conditions used has been firmly established.

If the deproteinized samples must be stored for a long time or be sent by post, the stability of the compounds in solution is of particular importance. In contrast to samples which have not been deproteinized, the problems here are non-enzymatic changes or even bacterial decomposition.

The stability of individual metabolites in solution is very variable. Problems arise if several substances have to be determined in the same sample, and have optimum stabilities at different pH-values. For short periods of storage, deviation from the optimum conditions is usually not serious; to simplify the procedure one makes allowance for this. Longer periods of storage or mailing of samples necessitate a closer look at the situation. A few guide values to stability are

Table 3. Stability of glucose in blood dried on different papers. Values as % of initial values.

Storage time at room temperature (days)	Schleicher & Schuell 2992 untreated	soaked with H_3BO_3	Schleicher & Schuell 597 untreated	soaked with H_3BO_3	Whatman WA-2 (ion-exchange paper)
1	98.1	100.0	83.1	97.2	96.7
2	–	98.5	82.2	90.3	97.9
3	–	96.5	–	–	–
4	98.8	97.0	82.1	87.1	–
6	–	–	78.3	86.6	–
7	96.4	96.0	–	–	–
8	–	–	–	–	99.0
9	–	–	74.5	84.5	–
10	96.9	96.2	65.3	82.7	–
20	–	–	70.6	83.2	–
22	–	–	64.6	81.6	–
24	–	–	64.0	80.1	–

given in Table 2 (p. 111), for further data see[13]. Even under the most favourable conditions it is not always possible to achieve prolonged stability.

A method for the dispatch of blood samples for the analysis of glucose, urea, etc., has been described[15]; the samples are stable for several weeks at room temperature. In this method 0.1 to 0.5 ml blood is air-dried on borate-soaked filter paper. For analysis the sample is extracted with water or dilute perchloric acid. The stability of the samples is improved[16,17] considerably by the use of paper coated with an ion-exchange resin. The stability of glucose on paper under various conditions is shown in Table 3.

A number of factors affect the stability of enzymes during storage: extreme pH-values; heat, but also freezing; organic solvents and detergents; specific enzyme inhibitors and the action of micro-organisms.

Tabelle 4. Stability of enzymes in serum[35].

| Enzyme | Storage at | % of initial value after day | | | | |
		1	2	3	5	7
Alanine aminotransferase	4°C	98	95	90	86	80
(EC 2.6.1.1)	25°C	92	88	83	81	71
Aldolase	4°C	100	100	100	92	88
(EC 4.1.2.13)	25°C	100	100	100	85	80
Amino acid arylamidase	4°C	100	100	100	100	100
(EC 3.4.11.1)	25°C	100	100	100	100	100
α-Amylase	4°C	100	100	100	100	100
(EC 3.2.1.1)	25°C	100	100	100	100	100
Aspartate aminotransferase	4°C	98	95	92	90	88
(EC 2.6.1.1)	25°C	98	94	90	89	87
Cholinesterase	4°C	100	100	100	100	100
(EC 3.1.1.8)	25°C	100	100	100	100	100
Creatine kinase*	4°C	100	100	100	100	100
(EC 2.7.3.2)	25°C	100	100	99	96	94
Glutamate dehydrogenase	4°C	100	98	95	87	74
(EC 1.4.1.2)	25°C	90	88	85	76	70
γ-Glutamyltransferase	4°C	100	100	100	100	100
(EC 2.3.2.2)	25°C	100	100	100	100	100
Lactate dehydrogenase	4°C	100	96	92	91	88
(EC 1.1.1.27)	25°C	100	99	98	90	85
LDH-1-Isoenzyme	4°C	100	100	100	97	95
("α-HBDH")	25°C	100	100	100	100	95
Lipase	4°C	100	100	100	100	100
(EC 3.1.1.3)	25°C	100	100	100	100	100
Phosphatase, alkaline	4°C	100	100	100	100	100
(EC 3.1.3.1)	25°C	100	98	97	94	90
Phosphatase, acid**	4°C	100	100	100	100	100
(EC 3.1.3.2)	25°C	100	100	100	100	100
Sorbitol dehydrogenase	4°C	78	–	62	–	–
(EC 1.1.1.14)	25°C	76	69	42	31	22

When stored at −20°C (in a deep-freeze), most of the enzymes keep for many months. Their stability decreases, however, after thawing.

 * Only after reactivation with reagents containing a thiol (-SH) group
** Only in acidified serum (pH 5.5–6.0)

The effect of detergents on the stability of enzyme solutions should not be underrated. According to *Schmidt*[12], the activity of lactate dehydrogenase in serum falls only to 96% after 48 hr in carefully cleaned containers, but to 62% in vessels containing traces of detergent! Consequently, the extensive use of disposable containers is strongly recommended. An apparent decrease in activity can also occur because the pH-optimum of the enzyme is displaced on storage (analogous to the displacement which occurs *in vivo* when the metabolic state changes)[12]. The catalytic activity of an enzyme is a complex property which depends on numerous incompletely elucidated factors.

In general, pure enzymes are more stable than enzymes in tissue extracts, which often contain agents that decrease the stability. Thus *Schmidt*[12] was able to show that enolase is more stable in a carefully prepared "cytoplasmic extract" than when an extract from mitochondria of the same organ is also present. Because of the great dependence of the stability on the method of extraction, it is not really possible to set up tables giving the stability of enzymes in tissue extracts. However, this is possible for samples, e.g. serum, which can be prepared in a uniform, non-destructive manner.

The most extensive data are available on the stability of enzymes in serum. A selection[35] is given in Table 4 (p. 113).

From these data it can be seen that freezing is not necessarily the best method for prolonged storage. Often storage in a refrigerator is sufficient. Very few methods are available for stabilization of enzymes in the sample. A method worthy of note is the stabilization of prostatic phosphatase with citrate or acetate. The addition of SH-reagents is of help with some enzymes, for example creatine kinase is stabilized and activated by SH-reagents (see Table 5). Progress in this field is necessary, because prolonged storage or mailing of samples is of great importance.

Table 5. Stabilization and reactivation of creatine kinase.

Sample	Temperature	% of initial CK activity after day					
		1	2	3	5	7–8	10
Serum (NAC-activated)[36]	25°C	96	87		82		68
	4°C	96	95		96		101
	−20°C			107			99
Serum (GSH-activated)[36]	25°C	86	82		75		67
	4°C	92	87		88		95
	−20°C			85			109
Serum (GSH-activated)[37]	25°C	85	75	67		27	
	4°C	100	99	100			94
	−20°C			97			97

Treatment of Sample for Enzymatic Analysis

The accurate determination of the protein content is an important point of reference for the characterization of enzyme solutions. On the other hand, the removal of protein from sample solutions is usually necessary in the analysis of biological material. Methods for protein determination and for deproteinization are therefore closely linked with methods of enzymatic analysis. Knowledge of the ammonium sulfate concentration of enzyme solutions is also important for enzymatic analysis (because of possible inhibition by ammonium sulfate) and for the determination of protein. The following is a short review of the well-known methods.

Methods for Determination of Protein

At present, there are several methods for the determination of protein in common use, and they differ from each other in the principle employed. It is therefore not surprising that the results obtained also vary.

Measurement of UV Absorbance

Virtually all proteins contain aromatic amino acids and therefore have an absorption maximum around 280 nm. Accordingly, proteins can be rapidly and easily measured at this wavelength. For certain highly purified proteins the absorption coefficients are known (e.g. for trypsin), but in general the protein content can be calculated from the formula published by *Warburg* and *Christian*[18] and by *Kalckar*[19]. In this case any nucleic acids present, which have high absorption at 260 nm, must be taken into account. For the determination according to the *Warburg-Kalckar* method[20], see[13].

The calculation factors are based on the absorption coefficients found for crystalline enolase and yeast nucleic acid. However, the aromatic amino-acid content varies considerably from protein to protein, and so this method is often subject to a large error. It is effective only as a rapid determination. The presence of other UV-absorbing substances also interferes with the determination.

Determination with Folin-Ciocalteu Reagent

The method, which was first described by *Lowry*[21] and later modified by *Oyama* and *Eagle*[22] and by *Itzhaki* and *Gill*[23], is based on two phenomena: the formation of a coloured copper complex due to the presence of peptide linkages and the reduction of phosphomolybdic-phosphotungstic acid by aromatic amino acids. Since the reagents change somewhat during storage, with the result that the colour intensity is affected, a calibration curve must be constructed for each determination. The absorbance is not exactly proportional to the concentration. This method is time-consuming, but it gives very accurate and reproducible results and is sensitive (about 20 times as sensitive as the UV-method and 100 times as sensitive as the biuret method). Amino acids, phenols, purines, and other substances cause interference, as do concentrated glycerol or ammonium sulfate solutions. This interference can be avoided by prior precipitation with trichloroacetic acid (if necessary in the presence of alcohol). Problems arise with enzymes with particularly low molecular weights (e.g. horse-radish peroxidase) or preparations that cannot be precipitated (e.g. glycoproteins such as invertase). For the determination see[13].

Biuret Method

The principle of this method is the formation of a coloured complex of the copper reagent with peptide bonds; the intensity of the colour can easily be measured photometrically[24,25]. The reagent is available commercially or can be prepared in the laboratory and keeps for several weeks, stoppered, at room temperature. The absorbance of the coloured complex is proportional to the concentration of protein over a relatively wide range. The procedure is rapid and gives very reproducible results, which often agree well with values obtained by the *Lowry*[21] method. The intensity of the colour is affected by various substances such as ammonium ions, glycerol, etc., and it is therefore advisable to precipitate the protein with trichloroacetic acid prior to measurement. With low-molecular-weight enzymes the precipitation can be made more quantitative by boiling the solution or by adding alcohol. If the precipitated enzymes have an intrinsic absorbance at Hg 546 nm, this must be taken into account in the calculations.

The extinction of the coloured complex is dependent on the type of protein, but the variation is smaller than with other methods. The conversion factors for several purified enzymes, whose protein content has been determined by different methods[26], are given in Table 6.

Table 6. Comparison of various methods for determination of protein.

Protein	Biuret factor, referred to $N_{Ki} \times 6.25$	Biuret factor, referred to dry weight	Absorbance at 280 nm (maximum), referred to $N_{Ki} \times 6.25$
Aldolase	16.65	17.9	1.00
Lactate dehydrogenase	17.80	18.1	1.27
Glycerol-3-phosphate dehydrogenase	15.20	18.05	0.82
Pyruvate kinase	17.65	17.4	0.52
Glyceraldehyde-3-phosphate dehydrogenase	16.05	15.7	1.16
Alcohol dehydrogenase (yeast)	17.65	18.25	–
Edestin	19.4	–	0.98
Insulin	19.7	–	0.98
Albumin (human serum)	17.1	–	–
Globulin (human serum)	14.5	–	–
Mean value	17.2	17.5	0.961

If the conditions established by *Beisenherz* et al.[26] are maintained, a factor of 17 is usually valid for calculation of the protein concentration (mg/ml) from the measured absorbance.

For the modified determination according to *Beisenherz* et al.[26] see[13].

Determination of Nitrogen

The determination of nitrogen as a basis for protein content is now no longer of any importance. As routine methods, both the total nitrogen determination of *Kjeldahl* and the amino-nitrogen assay of *van Slyke*[27] are too time-consuming and often require a preliminary treatment of the sample to quantitatively remove other nitrogen-containing impurities. This method also employs an empirical factor to convert the nitrogen content to protein concentration.

Deproteinization

In very many methods it is necessary to deproteinize the sample (blood, serum, plasma, urine, tissue, etc.), because turbidity, precipitation, or colour of the sample can interfere with the method. If the sensitivity of the assay method and the stability of the compound to be determined in the sample allow, deproteinization should be avoided. This saves time, the range of error is smaller, co-precipitation with or absorption on the precipitated protein of the compound to be determined does not occur and the volume displacement effect need not be considered.

Volume Displacement Effect

Van Slyke[28] was the first to note this effect. However, *Bürgi*[29] was the first to consider the theory in detail and propose that it applied to all low-molecular-weight compounds in serum or plasma.

A certain total volume consists to a large extent of fluid volume, and to a lesser extent of the space occupied by the protein molecules. This corresponds to the so-called partial specific volume and is the reciprocal of the specific gravity of the protein, i.e., a characteristic property of each protein. The partial specific volume for plasma proteins is around 0.7–0.75. If a certain volume of plasma is pipetted, this contains a fraction of the volume as protein. After deproteinization, the low-molecular-weight compounds are somewhat more concentrated. The following equation permits calculation of the difference in the concentrations of a substance in plasma and in a protein-free extract:

$$\Delta c = c_1 \left(\frac{100}{100 - V \cdot c_p} - 1 \right)$$

Where

c_1 concentration of substance in plasma
c_2 concentration of substance in protein-free supernatant
Δc the difference $c_2 - c_1$
c_p concentration of protein in g/100 ml
V mean partial specific volume of the proteins.

An experimental value of ca. 5% has been found for serum with regard to the acetate determination[30,31].

Method

Anionic and cationic precipitants are most commonly used for deproteinization. Picric acid, tungstic acid, and metaphosphoric acid belong to the first group, but trichloroacetic acid and perchloric acid are the most common. When perchloric acid is used, the excess can be removed by addition of stoichiometric amounts of KOH, K_2CO_3, $KHCO_3$ or, better still, K_2HPO_4 or K_3PO_4, because potassium perchlorate is but sparingly soluble. The advantage of using K_3PO_4 or K_2HPO_4 is that, depending on the phosphate concentration, the sample solution is already buffered at pH 7–8, so that further addition of buffer and consequent dilution of the sample is unnecessary. However, neutralization with potassium phosphate solutions can be carried out only when ammonium or magnesium ions are omitted from the assay mixture. The precipitation is carried out at room temperature and then the mixture is allowed to stand for 10–20 min in an ice-bath. Filtration is better than centrifugation to remove the potassium perchlorate, because on prolonged centrifugation the mixture warms up and a portion of the perchlorate may redissolve, unless a refrigerated centrifuge is used.

The most important cationic precipitating agents are zinc, cadmium, mercury, uranium, iron, copper, and lead solutions. Often, however, there is an unspecific adsorption of compounds on the precipitate. The use of uranyl acetate in isotonic solution has the advantage that at a suitable concentration it is virtually quantitatively bound to the precipitate and therefore there is no need to remove excess cations after precipitation of the protein (see for example determination of glucose with GOD[32]).

Under certain circumstances deproteinization can be omitted entirely, if protein-containing samples are dialyzed. This technique is used in methods with the Technicon AutoAnalyzer®.

Determination of Ammonium Sulfate

Samples subjected to enzyme isolation and purification procedures contain ammonium sulfate up to a concentration of ca. 3.5 mol/l. This may lead to inhibition of the catalytic activities of the enzymes and may affect the optical measurements, if the assay system contains additional phosphate and magnesium ions. The determination of the ammonium sulfate concentration in aqueous extracts from animal tissues is simple.

The determination is based on the titration of sulfate ions with barium chloride solution[33]; barium ions in excess produce an orange-coloured complex with the indicator alizarin S. This procedure has advantages in routine enzyme isolation and is feasible because animal tissues contain only very small amounts of sulfate.

Phosphate interferes with the determination; if the phosphate concentration is known, the result can be corrected for this value. In most cases the phosphate concentration can be neglected in comparison to the amount of ammonium sulfate present. For the procedure, refer to[13].

References

1 Laudahn, G., Hartmann, E., Rosenfeld, E. M., Weyer, H. & Muth, H.W. (1970) *Klin. Wschr.* **48,** 838.
2 Thefeld, W., Hoffmeister, H., Busch, E.W., Koller, P.U. & Vollmar, J. (1974) *Deutsche Med. Wochenschr.* **99,** 343.
3 Yap, P. (1965) *The cellular Aspects of Biorhythms;* VIIIth Intern. Congr. of Anatomy, Wiesbaden, p.143.
4 Mayersbach, H. v. (1967) *Verh. dtsch. Ges. inn. Med.,* 73.*Kongr.* p.942.
5 Leske, R. & Mayersbach H. v. (1969) *J. Histochem. Cytochem.* **17,** 527.
6 Mayersbach, H. v. (1969) *Hoppe-Seyler's Z. physiol. Chem.* **350,** 1169.
7 Faupel, R.P., Seitz, H.J., Tarnowski, W., Thiemann W. & Weiß, Ch. (1972) *Arch. Biochem. Biophys.* **148,** 509.
8 Seitz, H.J., Faupel, R.P., Kampf, S.C. & Tarnowski, W. (1973) *Arch. Biochem. Biophys.* **158,** 12.
9 Michal, G. & Lamprecht, W. (1961) *Z. physiol. Chem.* **324,** 170.
10 Lamprecht, W., Michal, G. & Naegle, S. (1961) *Klin. Wschr.* **39,** 358.
11 Bergmeyer, H.U., VIth Intern. Congress Clin. Pathology, Oct. 1966, Rom: Relazioni. p.175.
12 Schmidt, E. & Schmidt, F.W. (1963) *Enzymol. biol. Clin.* **3,** 80.
13 Bergmeyer, H.U., Bernt, E., Gawehn, K. & Michal, G. (1974) in *Methods of Enzymatic Analysis* (Bergmeyer, H.U., ed.), p.158, Verlag Chemie, Weinheim, and Academic Press, New York.
14 Michal, G., unpublished.
15 Hochella, N.J. & Hill, J.B. (1967) *Lecture Technicon-Symp.* New York.
16. Schmidt, F.H., unpublished.
17 Knitsch, K.W., unpublished.
18 Warburg, O. & Christian, W. (1941) *Biochem, Z.* **310,** 384.
19 Kalckar, H.M. (1947) *J. biol. Chem.* **167,** 461.
20 Layne, E. (1957), in *Methods of Enzymology* (Colowick, S.P. & Kaplan, N.O., eds.) Academic Press. New York, Vol. III, p.454.
21 Lowry, O.H., Rosebrough, N.J., Farr, A.L. & Randal, R.J. (1951) *J. biol. Chem.* **193,** 265.
22 Oyama, V.J. & Eagle, H. (1956) *Proc. Soc. Exptl. Biol. Med.* **91,** 305.
23 Itzhaki, R.F. & Gill, D.M. (1964) *Anal. Biochem.* **9,** 401.
24 Robinson, H.W. & Hodgen, C.G. (1940) *J. biol. Chem.* **135,** 707.
25 Weichselbaum, T.E. (1946) *Amer. J. Clin. Pathol. Suppl.* **10,** 40.
26 Beisenherz, G., Boltze, H.J., Bücher, Th., Czok, R., Garbade, K.H., Meyer-Arendt, E. & Pfleiderer, G. (1953) *Zeitschr. f. Naturf.* **8b,** 555.
27 van Slyke, D.D. (1929) *J. biol. Chem.* **83,** 425.
28 van Slyke, D.D., Hiller, A. & Berthelsen, K.C. (1927) *J. biol. Chem.* **74,** 659.
29 Bürgi, W., Richterich, R. & Mittelholzer, M.L. (1967) *Klin. Wschr.* **45,** 83.
30 Bergmeyer, H.U. & Möllering, H. (1974) in *Methods of Enzymatic Analysis* (Bergmeyer, H.U., ed.), p.1520, Verlag Chemie, Weinheim, and Academic Press, New York.
31 Bergmeyer, H.U. & Möllering, H. (1966) *Biochem. Z.* **344,** 167.
32 Bergmeyer, H.U. & Bernt, E. (1974) in *Methods of Enzymatic Analysis* (Bergmeyer, H.U., ed.), p.1205, Verlag Chemie, Weinheim, and Academic Press, New York.
33 Bergmeyer, H.U., Holz, G., Kauder, E.M., Möllering, H. & Wieland, O. (1961) *Biochem. Z.* **333,** 471.
34 Hoffmeister, H. & Junge, B. (1970) *J. Clin. Chem. u. Clin. Biochem.* **8,** 613.
35 Schmidt, E. & Schmidt, F.W. (1976) in *Brief Guide to Practical Enzyme Diagnosis.* 2nd ed. p.11, Boehringer Mannheim GmbH, Mannheim.
36 Völkert, E. (1976), unpublished.
37 Szasz, G., Busch, E.W. & Farohs, H.B. (1970) *Dt. med. Wschr.* **95,** 829.

Measuring Techniques and Instruments

For the practical performance of enzymatic analyses, it is indispensable to examine critically the special measuring techniques and the relevant measuring instruments. Analytical chemistry has advanced considerably in recent years, and as part of this progress, instruments and methods were developed further; occasionally, new ones were invented as one development influenced the next. In addition to its special techniques, each branch of analytical chemistry developed its own laboratory apparatus. Knowledge of this is absolutely necessary, not only for practical work in the laboratory, but also for an understanding of the fundamental principles of enzymatic analysis.

In the following, the principles of measurement and the instruments used in enzymatic analysis will only be treated to the extent which is required for an understanding of the field in its entirety. The possibilities of application of the measuring techniques and instruments, as well as their efficiency and limits, will be outlined in the individual chapters.

Volume Measurement

Emil Völkert

Introduction

In analytical chemistry, the exact measurement of sample and reagent volumes is of great importance. Although the determination of mass by weighing is more accurate by about 1–2 powers of ten, the volume is generally measured since the samples under investigation are usually liquid, and volume measurements are both faster and simpler to perform with adequate accuracy.

Errors

Errors in the measurement of sample and reagent volumes contribute to the total error of the analysis. Investigations by a fairly large group within the scope of inter-laboratory trials in clinical chemistry have shown[1] that pipetting and photometric measurements can be performed with approximately the same precision.

Nevertheless, depending on the method of analysis, the deviations and variances of volume measurements have different effects on the analytical results. For error theory, see p. 233.

Systematic errors

If a measured quantity is referred to the result of measurement of a standard solution of known concentration, systematic errors are eliminated. Consequently, in the well-known *continuous-flow* systems (Technicon AutoAnalyzer®, SMA®), for example, peristaltic pumps can be used as dispensing devices. Systematic errors lead to correspondingly incorrect results if the substance concentration is calculated from the measured quantity by means of a characteristic constant (e.g. the absorption coefficient). In this case, the total volume and the sample volume enter into the calculation as a quotient (see p. 237); if the systematic or random errors in the measurement of sample and reagent volumes were equal (in terms of percent), the errors would compensate each other. However, as a rule the volume of the sample is about one to two powers of ten smaller than the total volume, so that the percentage error of the volume measurement is considerably greater here. In measuring small volumes of auxiliary reagents, this contributes only slightly to the total error, but it decisively affects the result when small volumes of the sample itself are measured out.

Random errors

Accordingly, random errors become particularly noticeable when they contribute substantially to falsification of the sample volume or the total volume. These errors are obviously not compensated in relative measurements (reference to standard solutions), but reduce the precision instead.

Calibration

Volume-measuring devices are calibrated either to

> *Int, t.c. = to contain* or to
>
> *Ext, t.d. = to deliver.*

A measuring device (such as a volumetric flask) calibrated as "t.c." contains an accurately defined volume once it has been filled up to the mark. When it is emptied, a residue of liquid always remains behind on the walls of the vessel. If the entire amount of the material is to be used further, this residue must be rinsed out.

In order to keep parallax errors as small as possible, the markings are frequently made in the form of rings. The given volume is contained exactly when the lowest point of the meniscus just touches the upper edge of the marking.

Since the expansion of glass at temperatures of about 20°C is generally slight, and much smaller than the expansion of liquids, the calibration temperature on the apparatus is mainly an aid in correcting errors due to the volume changes of liquids caused by changes in temperature.

In the case of devices calibrated as "t.d.", on the other hand, the volume of liquid delivered between two marks or between a mark and the tip of the vessel is accurately defined. Since this type of calibration must also take into account the residue of fluid remaining on the walls and in the tip, the actual volume contained in the measuring device is always greater than the nominal volume delivered. This factor can effect the accuracy considerably and depends on the viscosity and the surface tension of the liquid being measured. If the viscosity and surface tension are fairly constant, these effects can be taken into account by means of the drainage and waiting times. The drainage time is the time necessary for coherent discharge of the volume; it is predetermined by the shape and size of the outlet orifice. Consequently, one should not, for instance, blow out pipettes (unless expressly specified) or break off their tips in order to shorten the drainage time.

Classification and accuracy

Volume-measuring devices are subdivided into two accuracy classes.

The apparatus of *Class A* has narrower tolerance limits, and consequently relatively long drainage times. In order to preclude parallax errors in reading, all the markings are made in the form of rings or half-rings. On the other hand, volumetric apparatus of *Class B* has considerably shorter drainage times and simpler graduations. The tolerances of this class are twice as large as those of Class A. These devices cannot be calibrated. In order to combine the practical advantages of Class B with the accuracy requirements of Class A, a *Class AS* has been created, which is coming increasingly into use (Table 1).

Table 1. Drainage times and tolerances for volumetric pipettes with one mark.

Nominal volume ml	Class A Drainage time s	Tolerance μl	Class AS Drainage time s	Tolerance μl	Class B Drainage time s	Tolerance μl
0,5	10–20	± 5	4– 8	± 5	4–20	± 10
1	10–20	± 7	5– 9	± 7	5–20	± 15
2	10–25	±10	5– 9	±10	5–25	± 20
5	15–30	±15	7–11	±15	7–30	± 30
10	15–40	±20	8–12	±20	8–40	± 40
20	25–50	±30	9–13	±30	9–50	± 60
25	25–50	±30	10–15	±30	10–50	± 60
50	30–60	±50	13–18	±50	13–60	±100
100	40–60	±80	25–30	±80	25–60	±160

Pipettes of class AS have a waiting time of 15 s. The tips of pipettes of classes A and B are to be touched to the receptacle wall 3 s after coherent delivery has ceased.

The apparatus of Classes A and AS can also be purchased officially calibrated, the price of calibrated apparatus being considerably higher than that of uncalibrated products of the same classes. For work in which larger tolerances can be accepted, the cheaper apparatus of Class B is sufficiently accurate.
Volume-measuring apparatus can be calibrated by the user himself in the laboratory. Pipettes can be filled with liquids and their weight determined by weighing. Photometric calibration is simpler (see p.128).

Obligatory calibration

Most countries have laws concerning the obligatory calibration of measuring apparatus. For example, in the German Federal Republic, a Calibration Act[2] that came into force on July 1, 1970 established a general obligation to calibrate apparatus and devices used medicine and the manufacture and testing of drugs. This relates to measuring devices for the determination of mass, pressure, volume, and density, and also to thermometers.
Excepted form this general obligatory calibration are – inter alia – volume-measuring devices used in quantitative analysis when the accuracy of the results is established by continuous supervision according to the methods of statistical quality control and by inter-laboratory trials. For example, the use of mechanical and completely automatic volume-measuring devices that do not meet official calibration standards is permissible.
Also excepted from the obligation to calibrate are volume-measuring devices, measuring and mixing cylinders, test tubes, centrifuge tubes, beakers, Erlenmeyer flasks, and urine vessels used only for qualitative investigations.

Pipettes

Glass pipettes

The most common types of glass pipette are shown in Fig. 1.
One distinguishes between pipettes with a constant volume (examples a–e in Fig. 1) and those with variable volumes (measuring pipettes, enzyme pipettes). The calibration is another distinguishing feature.

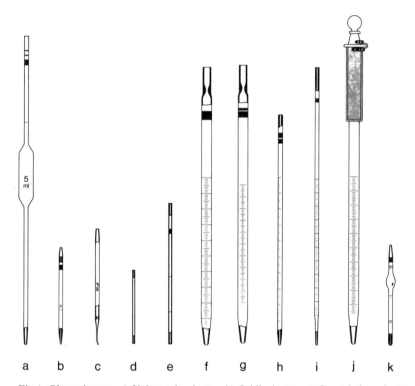

Fig. 1. Glass pipettes: a) Volumetric pipette; b) Sahli pipette; c) Constriction pipette; d) Disposable capillary (end to end); e) Disposable capillary (with ring mark); f) Fully graduated pipette; g) Partly graduated pipette; h) Blood-sugar pipette; i) Enzyme pipette; j) Safety pipette; k) Blood-mixing pipette.

Identification of pipettes. In addition to the name of the manufacturer, the trademark, and the nominal volume, other information is frequently provided, such as the graduation, the class, the reference temperature, the type of calibration, (t.c. or t.d.), waiting time, tolerances, unit symbols, and colour coding. As an example, the coding of an enzyme pipette is shown in Fig. 2.

Types of pipettes

Volumetric pipettes and *measuring pipettes* are generally calibrated for complete drainage. In addition, there are pipettes calibrated as "blow out". Whereas normally the liquid that has

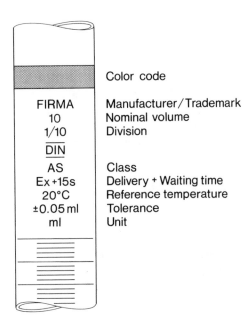

FIRMA	Color code
FIRMA	Manufacturer/Trademark
10	Nominal volume
1/10	Division
DIN	
AS	Class
Ex +15s	Delivery + Waiting time
20°C	Reference temperature
±0.05 ml	Tolerance
ml	Unit

Fig. 2. Specifications on a 10-ml enzyme pipette.

collected in the pipette tip after the prescribed waiting time must remain in the pipette, it must be blown out of pipettes so calibrated.

Enzyme pipettes are measuring pipettes with a narrow tip in which the volume is measured between two marks.

Apparatus that measures the volume by letting the liquid drain down to the tip is easier to handle than enzyme pipettes, but may give lower precision when used with solutions whose viscosity properties are different from those of water.

Constriction pipettes are used particularly for the measurement of small volumes. The liquid is drawn up above a constriction; after the meniscus has positioned itself at the constriction, the liquid is blown out.

Blood-sugar pipettes and *Sahli pipettes* are calibrated to "t.c.", as are capillary pipettes and disposable capillaries. These pipettes must be emptied by repeated flushing (by aspirating and expelling the solution).

Capillary pipettes. Disposable capillary pipettes are cheap and reliable aids, especially for measuring out small volumes. By means of strict in-process control during manufacture, a maximum error of $\pm 1\%$ can be maintained down to 10 μl, and $\pm 2\%$ below this figure. Pipettes with a ring mark (or several ring marks) are also available, as are so-called *end-to-end* capillary pipettes. The former are filled – by capillary action or by suction – up to the mark with the solution to be measured (if necessary, the height of the meniscus is adjusted accurately by wiping the tip with filter paper), and the solution is rinsed out. In the *end-to-end* capillaries, the volume is limited by the two ends of the capillary. They fill automatically and are also emptied by rinsing out. Alternatively, the capillary, together with its contents, is placed into the diluent in the reaction vessel, which is then shaken vigorously. Purchase costs are low for this type of pipette, and no laborious cleaning is necessary.

Technique

Pipettes are calibrated such that the measurement is correct when the solution runs out of the vertically held pipette and down the walls of the receptacle. The necessary waiting times must be observed. Any liquid adhering to the outer surface of the pipette tip is best wiped off beforehand with an absorbent, lint-free material.

Small volumes, particularly those to be admixed to the contents of a cuvette to start an enzymatic reaction, are pipetted onto so-called "cuvette spoons". These are glass or plastic rods, flattened out and bent at the bottom (Figs. 3 and 4). Volumes up to about 0.05 ml (50 µl) can be pipetted onto the flat end.

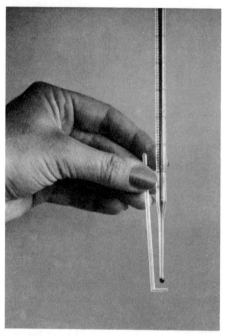

Fig. 3. Glass or plastic rod flattened at one end for mixing small amounts of solutions into assay mixtures.

Fig. 4. Addition of 20 µl of reagent solution to a cuvette.

In multiple determinations, the same pipette can be used repeatedly for the same reagent. Bench-top pipette racks or trays are useful for this purpose (Fig. 5).

Dangerous liquids must not be pipetted by mouth. In clinical chemical laboratories, the possibility of infection must always be borne in mind. Various pipetting aids are available to prevent accidents.

Cleaning

Protein-containing solutions must not be allowed to dry up in pipettes. Until they are cleaned, used pipettes are best placed in plastic cylinders filled with water and a detergent. Practically all

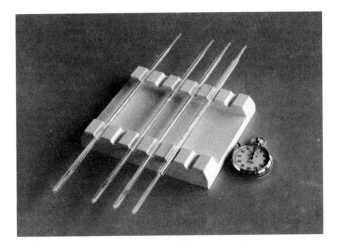

Fig. 5. Pipette tray.

modern laboratory detergents are suitable for cleaning, such as Mucasol (Merz & Co., Frankfurt*; Brand, Wertheim*) or Extran (Merck, Darmstadt*). For reasons of environmental protection the chromate-sulfuric acid mixture should no longer be used. Nitrate-sulfuric acid is necessary only with strongly soiled apparatus. In all cases, thorough rinsing with distilled water to remove all residues of the cleaning agent is important. With correct handling, pipettes can also be cleaned with good results in suitable inserts of automatic laboratory washing machines.

If the glass is of good quality and the workmanship satisfactory, the heating during drying will not affect the apparatus. Nevertheless, pipettes that are to be sterilized at 180°C should first be predried at about 100°C until the water has evaporated, since otherwise the prolonged hydrolytic attack of the hot steam can alter the glass surface. The wetting properties are thereby altered, which leads to deviations from the calibrated value.

Pipette racks, storage vessels, washing apparatus, pipette driers, and pipette stands are marketed by various manufacturers.

Mechanical pipettes

For a long time, the pipetting of extremely small volumes of liquid – from 1 µl to 100 µl – rapidly and without great care and concentration constituted a problem. The absolute accuracy attainable and, in particular, the reproducibility in volume measurements made with the same apparatus, should not be smaller than in the measurement of larger volumes of liquid. Furthermore, errors due to carry-over should be small. This applies equally to measurements using radioactive substances and experiments with enzymes. Possibilities of solving the problems connected with these demands on pipetting technique were already sought before 1957 by *T. Bücher* and *H. Schnitger*. The first plunger pipette was constructed in Marburg *(H. Schnitger[3])*.

The particular feature of this concept is separation of the measuring part (plunger) from the transferring part (tip). The liquid to be dispensed does not come into contact with the pipette part proper.

---

* All in W. Germany.

The volume measured is defined by a mechanical stop that limits the travel of the push-button. In order to expel residues of liquid collecting in the tip, a second stop ("overstroke") is provided.

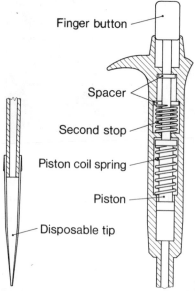

Finger button

Spacer

Second stop

Piston coil spring

Piston

Disposable tip

Fig. 6. Plunger pipette (schematic).

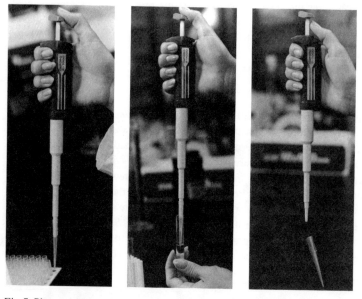

Fig. 7. Plunger pipette with automatic tip ejection (Oxford 7000).

The advantage of such devices is above all their simple operation accompanied by great accuracy[4]. Since suction is mechanical, the dangers due to infectious and other hazardous substances are reduced. On the other hand, the simplicity of the operation must not lead to superficial technique.

Plunger pipettes are widely used, particularly for the routine measurement of volumes in the range from 20 µl to 1000 µl.

Some plunger pipettes provide automatical ejection of the tips (Eppendorf-Pipette 4700, Gilson Pipetman®, Oxford® Sampler P-7000), others are insulated against the heat of the hands (Brand Transferpette®, Eppendorf-Pipette 4700, Oxford Sampler P-7000).

More recent developments include simultaneous parallel pipetting of the same volume with one apparatus (Kemistien Oy, Finland: Finnpipette®) and manually operated mechanical dilutors in pipette form (see p.132) (Gilford, USA: Simplistat®, Gilson, France: Pip dil).

Operation

Before being used, the pipette tips must first be wetted once by suction and expulsion. Although they consist of water-repellent material (polyolefin), this step is necessary in particular with viscous solutions or solutions with different wetting properties towards the plastic[5].

The possibility of errors due to carry-over must be borne in mind when pipetting serum samples. This makes it advisable to use a new tip for each new sample. Suction of liquid into the shaft of the pipette – e.g. by overly rapid aspiration of the solution, formation of foam in pipetting, or by laying down a pipette with a filled tip – must be avoided. Consequently, pipette stands form part of the equipment.

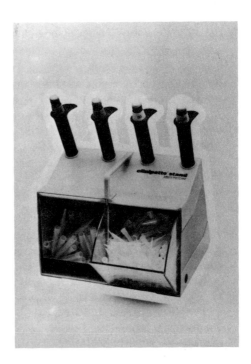

Fig. 8. Pipette stands with storage container for pipette tips (Labora Mannheim).

Aggressive liquids and those of a high vapor pressure should not be measured with plunger pipettes. See Table 2 for data on the stability of plastics.

Table 2. Chemical stability of plastics[6].

	Weak acids	Conc. acids	Weak alkalis	Conc. alkalis	Alcohols	Esters	Ketones	Animal & plant oils	Chlorinated hydrocarbons	Ether
1. Polypropylene	+	+[1]	+	+	+	+	+	O+	−	O
2. Low-pressure polyethylene	+	+[1]	+	+	+	+	+	O	−	O
3. High-pressure polyethylene	+	+[1]	+	+	+	O	+	O	−	O
4. Polyvinyl chloride (PVC)	+	+	+	+	+	−	−	+	−	−
5. Polyamide (Nylon)	O	−	+	O	+	+	O	+	−	+
6. Polymethacrylate (acrylic resins)	+	O	+	O	−	−	−	+	−	−
7. Polytetrafluorethylene	+	+	+	+	+	+	+	+	+	+
8. Urea- and melamine-formaldehyde plastics	O	−	O	−	+	+	+	+	+	+
9. Polystyrene	+[1]	O	+	+	+	−	−	O	−	O

+ stable;   O limited stability;   − unstable;   +[1] unstable to oxidizing acids.

Leaks, either at the seating of the tip or at the plunger seals, become evident in the case of large volumes by a slow running out of the solution.

> Testing for liquid-tight seals: a water-filled transparent plastic tube is mounted on the pipette tip. The height of the meniscus of the solution (a few centimetres below the tip of the pipette) is marked with a felt-tipped pen. On repeated depression of the plunger (including over-strokes), the meniscus must always return to the mark again when the push-button is returned to its initial position.
>
> Alternative: The pipette is immersed in a water-filled test tube. As a result of compression of the air in the pipette, the liquid initially rises somewhat up into the pipette tip. After the plunger has been depressed to the first and second stops, no more liquid must be present or slowly rising up into the tip.

It is advisable to check the accuracy of plunger pipettes routinely at regular intervals (e.g. every 3–6 months), and always when inaccurate measurement is suspected.

> This can be checked by weighing the measured volume of distilled water and making a density correction, or by a photometric technique: the corresponding volume of a $KMnO_4$ solution (about 0.1 mol/l) acidified with H_2SO_4 is taken with an officially calibrated pipette and is made up to the mark with distilled water in a measuring flask of appropriate size; the absorbance is then measured at Hg 546 nm[7]. The procedure is repeated with the pipette to be checked. The deviations between the absorbances should be within $\pm 1\%$. Instead of acidified $KMnO_4$ solutions, a solution of p-nitrophenol at pH 10 may also be used[8].

Various auxiliary equipment is marketed for plunger pipettes: pipette stands, storage containers for tips, tips prearranged in racks, etc.; see Table 3.

Table 3. Plunger pipettes*

Manufacturer	Name	Size**	Notes
Becton, Dickinson Rutherford, N.J., USA	Biopette® Selectapette®	4 Sizes, stepwise adjustment 10–1000 µl	Sales also by Clay Adams and Schwarz/Mann
Biodynamics Indianapolis, Ind., USA	Automatic Pipette	plastic pipette, 4 sizes, metal pipette, 9 sizes, fixed volume	also pipettes for 2 volumes
Brand Wertheim, W. Germany	Transferpette®	8 standard sizes and 20 intermediate, fixed volume 1–1000 µl	Thermal insulation jacket (against heat of hands)
Centaur Chemical Danbury, Conn., USA	Micropipette	21 sizes, fixed volume 5–5000 µl	
Drummond®, Scientific Broomall, Calif., USA	Microdispenser	1 size, stepwise adjustment 1–5 µl	capillary pipette
Eppendorf Gerätebau Hamburg, W. Germany	Pipette 3130	8 standard sizes and 17 intermediate, fixed volume 1–1000 µl	
	Pipette 4700	31 sizes, fixed volume 1–1000 µl	also pipettes for 3 volumes with automatic tip ejection, thermal insulation
Excalibur Laboratories Melbourne, Australia	Varipet®	6 sizes, continuous adjustment 1–1000 µl	
Gilford Instruments Oberlin, Ohio, USA	Simplistat®	Pipette for dilution, 4 different sample volumes, 1.4 ml reagent	takes up sample and flushes with reagent
Gilson Villiers-le-Bel, France	Pipetman® F	26 sizes, fixed volume, 2–1000 µl	readjustable, automatic tip ejection
	Pipetman® P	4 sizes, continuous adjustment, 1–5000 µl	automatic tip ejection
	pip dil	Pipette for dilution 2 models (up to 1 and 5 ml) with variable reagent volume: 5 sizes each with fixed sample volume	automatic tip ejection
Heller Laboratories Santa Rosa, Calif., USA	Mechrolab	4 sizes, fixed volume, 100–1000 µl	available with switch

 * Per October 1976 – no claim that this table is complete is made or implied.
** Many manufacturers offer more sizes on request.

Table 3.

Manufacturer	Name	Size**	Notes
K. Hecht Sondheim/Rhön, W. Germany	Assipette®	25 sizes, fixed volume, 5–1000 µl	
Kemistien Oy, Helsinki, Finnland	Labpipette LP	8 sizes, fixed volume, 5–1000 µl	
	Finnpipette	5 sizes, continuous adjustment, 1–1000 µl	also for multiple pipetting (up to 9 aliquots simultaneously)
Labtronic Zürich/Switzerland	Labtronic® Pipette	9 sizes, fixed volume, 10–1000 µl	
Labora Mannheim, Mannheim, W. Germany	Clinipette®	31 sizes, fixed volume, 1–1000 µl	
	Capilettor®	3 sizes, stepwise adjustment 1– 5 µl 5–25 µl 10–50 µl	capillary pipette, automatic ejection of capillary
Mallinckrodt St. Louis, Mo., USA	Seropette®	3 sizes, fixed volume, 20–100 µl	
Dr. Molter, Heidelberg, W. Germany	Moltronic Mikroliterpipetten-System	10 sizes, fixed volume, 1–1000 µl	pipette 1–5 µl, stepwise adjustment
Medical Laboratory Automation (MLA), Mt. Vernon, N.Y., USA	Fisher – MLA Precision Microliter Pipettingsystem	10 sizes, fixed volume, 10–1000 µl	also available with automatic tip ejection
Oxford Laboratories Foster City, Calif., USA	Oxford® Sampler Macro-set Transferpipette	24 sizes, fixed volume, 10–1000 µl 2 sizes, continuous adjustment 1–10 ml	also pipettes for 2 and 3 volumes
	Ultra-Microsampler	5 sizes, fixed volume, 1–5 µl	capillary tips
	Pipette 7000	15 sizes, fixed volume, 1–1000 µl	automatic tip ejection, thermal insulation
Scientific Manufacturing Industries (SMI), Emeryville, Calif., USA	SMI Micropettor®	9 sizes, stepwise adjustment 1–3000 µl	capillary pipette
	Macro/pettor® (volumes > 1 ml)	41 sizes, fixed volume, 1–3000 µl	capillary pipette
Sherwood Medical Industries St. Louis, Mo., USA	Lancer Precision micropipette	7 sizes, fixed volume, 10–500 µl	
Socorex, Lausanne, Switzerland	Mikroliterpipette	9 sizes, fixed volume, 10–1000 µl	

The various plunger pipettes

Pipettes with a volume > 20 µl

In addition to those with a fixed volume, there are also pipettes which are adjustable in steps (for 2 or 3 volumes), or even continuously. For continuously adjustable pipettes, a check of the accuracy after each adjustment is unconditionally to be recommended. If the same assays are run frequently, plunger pipettes with a fixed volume are better.

Plunger pipettes are available in sizes from 1 µl to 5000 µl. They have become established in the microliter techniques of clinical chemistry, where the use of the 20, 50, 100, 200, 500, and 1000 µl sizes predominantes. Under routine conditions, the relative standard deviations are about 1% for these sizes. Careful technique using water gives considerably better precision, which substantially corresponds to the manufacturers' data. The accuracy of these sizes then also corresponds to the manufacturers' specification ($\pm 1\%$).

Pipettes with a volume < 20 µl

Plunger pipettes with volumes smaller than 20 µl are difficult to handle even in routine operation and require much practice. The *Oxford Ultra Micro-Sampler* is based on the principle of the plunger pipette, but is fitted with special capillary tips. Thus even small volumes (5 µl) can be measured reliably and without prolonged training.

Another group of pipettes also achieves outstanding precision in the range from 1–20 µl. In these pipettes, the liquid is in a glass capillary in direct contact with a plunger of inert material. The accuracy and precision thus attainable are within $\pm 1\%$. These devices (see Fig. 9 for an example) have no dead volume. Consequently, the effects of viscosity are slight and carry-over can be neglected. Serial pipetting is possible without changing the capillary.

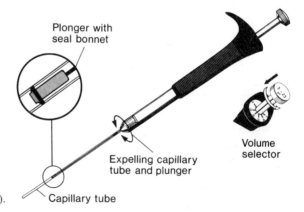

Plonger with
seal bonnet

Expelling capillary
tube and plunger

Volume
selector

Capillary tube

Fig. 9. Capilettor® (Labora Mannheim).

Several products of this type are known. In the *SMI Micropettor®* the volume is adjusted by means of adapters that limit the plunger movement. The *Capilettor®* has 5 fixed volumes; the capillary and plunger can be ejected rapidly and without risk of infection. The insertion and adjustment of the capillary and plunger are simple. A microdispenser for measuring out aliquots of 1–5 µl is also marketed by Drummond® Scientific and Dr. Molter (see Table 3, pp. 129–130).

Mechanical Dispensers

Dispensers

Until recently, relatively large volumes were dispensed with burettes (sometimes with automatic zero-point adjustment) or medial syringes (in some cases with return spring and valve mechanism). Nowadays apparatus made of glass or resistant plastic is used; meters solutions are dispensed by the up-and-down movement of a plunger, the path of the liquid being controlled by valves (Fig. 10). In addition to manually operated dispensers, there are also considerably more expensive motor-driven dispensers available.

Fig. 10. Dispenser. An upward movement of the piston draws the liquid from the storage bottle, the aliquot is dispensed by the downward movement. Liquid flow is automatically controlled by means of valves (Oxford/Labora Mannheim).

In addition to those with fixed volume, dispensers with variable volume are also available. Their accuracy must be checked after each adjustment. The precision of the measurement has a CV $<0.5\%$. There are no maintenance problems, even on prolonged use. For serial dispensing of small volumes (e.g. auxiliary enzymes) with no high demands on accuracy, the Hamilton PB 600 dispenser, an auxiliary apparatus that ejects $1/50$ of the syringe contents at each depression of the knob, is very suitable.

Dilutors

Dilutors (example in Fig. 11) are another step towards greater efficiency and economy in laboratory work. These are a combination of two dispensing units; samples are first drawn in and then forced out together with the diluent. They are usually driven electrically or pneumatically

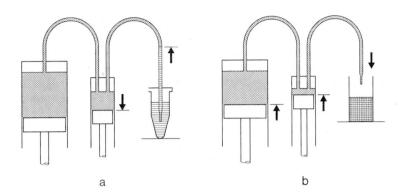

a   b

Fig. 11. Dilutor (Eppendorf). a) In the first stoke, the downward movement of the small sample piston draws in the sample. b) In the subsequent dilution step, the sample is flushed out of the system by the upward movement of both pistons.

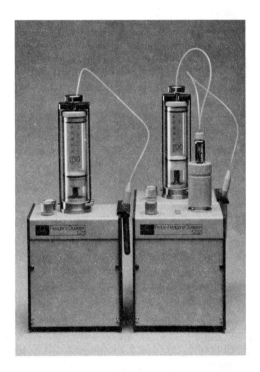

and operate with great precision. Manually operated devices in pipette form have also recently appeared on the market (e.g. Gilford Simplistat®. Gilson pip dil).

There are designs with tips and valves, and systems working on the principle of the valveless plunger burette. These devices can often also be used as dispensers by switching off the sample dispensing unit. Most manufacturers provide a pedal control.

Again, units with fixed adjustment (one pair of volumes) and systems with stepwise or continuously variable volumes are available. In order to keep the carry-over as small as possible, the volume ratio of sample to diluent should be not less than 1 : 4. When the sample is aspirated, it remains in the suction tube and therefore does not enter the sample cylinder. In the subsequent dilution stroke, it is expelled with the larger volume of diluent.

The accuracy of dilutors with continuous volume adjustment must be checked after each adjustment, unless the reproducibility of the adjustment is ensured by special construction features. It is frequently more economical to purchase two or more dilutors or their components (syringes) and leave these unchanged after initial adjustment and checking. Checking can be done by weighing or photometrically (dilution of coloured solutions).

Dilutors are used to prepare samples for measurement and, usually together with dispensers, are integrated components of all fully mechanized discontinuous analysis systems. Since in most cases a change of diluent – frequently necessary with a change or method – is somewhat laborious, they are used mainly for relatively large series.

References

1 Ludewigs, M. & Rotzler, R. (1976) *diagnostic* **9**, 593.
2 Fed. Rep. Germany: An Act concerning Measurement and Calibration (Calibration Act), 11 July 1969. (BGBl. I p. 779).
3 Schnitger, H. (1957) *Deutsches Bundes-Patent* (German Federal Patent), Auslegeschrift 1 090 449 of 6 October 1960.
4 Bechtler, G. (1969) *Ärztl. Lab.* **15**, 86.
5 Zeman, G. H. & Mathewson, N. S. (1974) *Clin. Chem.* **20**, 497.
6 Schramm, W. (1964) *Glas- und Instrum.-Techn.* **8**, 20.
7 Bergmeyer, H. U., Bernt, E., Gawehn, K. & Michal, G. (1974) in *Methods of Enzymatic Analysis* (Bergmeyer, H. U., ed.) 2nd edition, p. 161. Verlag Chemie, Weinheim and Academic Press, New York.
8 Richterich, R. (1971) *Klinische Chemie*, 3. edition, p. 125, S. Karger, Basle.

Absorption Photometry

Heinrich Netheler

In 1936 *O. Warburg*[1] introduced the so-called "optical assay" and with it photometry in the region of ultraviolet radiation. In 1941, *H. H. Cary* and *A. O. Beckman*[2] described the Beckman DU spectrophotometer. In 1948, *Th. Bücher* laid down the requirements for a photometer to be used in enzymatic analysis: Hg spectral lamp as the source of radiation, isolation of the Hg-lines with a coloured glass filter, vacuum cell as photoelectric transducer, direct indication of the absorbance by means of a moving-coil system, ability to register changes in absorbance down to $\Delta A = 1 \times 10^{-3}$.

In 1950 the first apparatus based on this concept (the *Eppendorf* photometer) was introduced for enzyme research[3]. In 1951, the Carl Zeiss PMQ II direct-indicating spectrophotometer improved measuring technique further[4].

In 1952 *B. Chance*[5,6] reported the measurement of fast enzyme reactions by means of periodic switching-over between two wavelengths and recording the difference in absorbance. In 1956, *D. Lübbers*[7] published the first paper on a high-speed recording photometer that permitted optical observation of changes in the spectral absorption curve and later, hooked up to a computer, contributed to the analysis of multicomponent systems.

The first mass-produced recording system based on the compensation principle for analog recording of results was made by Leeds & Northrup, Philadelphia, USA.

With the development of computer technique, digital recording of measurements via the computer print-out was introduced between 1965 and 1970.

The following account is limited to discussing photometry only to the extent that it is important for enzymatic analysis. For more general information, see[8-10].

Theoretical Basis and Terminology

Transmittance and absorbance

The visible distinguishing characteristic of dissolved substances is their colour. Every colour corresponds to a definite range of wavelengths of light. Solutions of substances appear coloured when, because of their chemical structure, they absorb certain fractions of "white" light and are transparent only to radiation corresponding to their colour. The wavelength range known as ultraviolet, from 200 nm to 400 nm, and the visible range from 400 nm to 600 nm, are particularly important in enzymatic analysis.

If light passes through a coloured solution, part of the light is absorbed. The ration I/I_0 of the intensities of transmitted and incident light is a measure of the coloration and therefore of the concentration of the solution. I/I_0 is called the transmittance. A better measure of the absorption of light by a dissolved substance is the absorbance A (also called the extinction or optical density, O.D.). This follows from a closer look at the process of absorption.

Fig. 1 is a schematic diagram of a photometer. It consists of a light source (1), a lens (2) to produce a focused bundle of rays, an optical filter (3) to isolate a definite range of wavelengths, the measurement chamber (4) for the introduction of measurement vessel with a specified path length (which, in the present case, should all contain the substance to be measured at the same

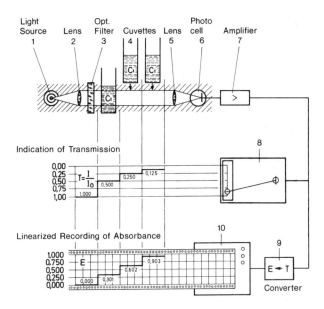

Fig. 1. Schematic diagram of a photometer.

concentration c_1), and a lens (5) to focus the transmitted radiation on the receiver (6). This latter is a photocell, a photoelectric transducer which converts light into an electric current that is then amplified by an amplifier (7) and registered by the indicator (8) as a measure of luminous flux incident on the photocell. A converter is shown at (9), which transforms the output current of the photocell in such a way that the absorbance can be recorded as a function of time on a linear scale (10).

Measurement:

The amplification of the photocurrent is adjusted such that 100 scale divisions of the indicator correspond to a luminous flux $I_0 = 1.00$. The measurement vessel containing the first sample to be measured is placed in the path of the beam. If the concentration c_1 of the absorbing substance has been chosen such that the measured radiation is attenuated to one-half, the indicator (8) will show a luminous flux $I_1 = 0.500$. If sample 2 with the same concentration c_1 is then also inserted into the path of the beam, the emergent luminous flux is again attenuated to one-half, so that $I_2 = 0.250$. Sample 3 (c_1) brings about a further attenuation to one-half, i.e. $I_3 = 0.125$. The same results are obtained if only single measurement vessel containing the substance at the concentrations c_1, $2 \times c_1$, and $3 \times c_1$ are located in the path of the beam.

With linearly rising concentration of the solution, the intensity of the emergent beam of light thus falls off exponentially. Consequently, the transmittance is an inconvenient measure in the case of concentration determinations. For simplicity, therefore, the parameter used is the absorbance, which is linearly proportional to the concentration.

We thus have:

(1)
$$\text{Absorbance } A = \log \frac{1}{\text{transmittance } T} = \log \frac{I_0}{I}.$$

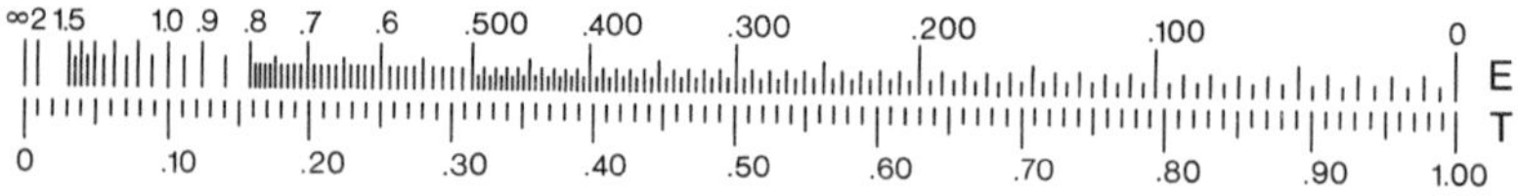

Fig. 2. Photometer scale: graduated logarithmically for absorbance and linearly for transmittance.

Under suitable conditions of measurement the absorbance A is directly proportional to the concentration c of the substance, as illustrated in the following example:

Concentration	$0c_1$	$1c_1$	$2c_1$	$3c_1$
Transmittance I/I_0	$\frac{1}{1}$	$\frac{1}{2}$	$\frac{1}{2 \times 2}$	$\frac{1}{2 \times 2 \times 2}$
Absorbance $\log I_0/I$	$\log 1$ $= 0$	$\log 2$ $= 0.301$	$\log 4$ $= 0.602$	$\log 8$ $= 0.903$

The bottom part of Fig. 1 shows the linearized recording of the absorbance of the measured samples.

The constant by which the substance concentration (mol/l) must be multiplied in order to obtain an absorbance of 1.0 at a fixed wavelength and a path length of 10 mm is called the molar decadic absorption coefficient ε.

Absorption curve and absorption coefficient

The process shown in Fig. 1 for the absorption of light by an absorbing substance in a non-absorbing solvent is based on the *Bouguer-Lambert-Beer* law. This is a limiting law which applies only to highly dilute solutions. In the range of applications considered here, this prerequisite is almost always satisfied.

The *Bouguer-Lambert-Beer* law is:

$$A = \varepsilon \times c \times d,$$

where

A = absorbance   1

c = concentration $mol \times l^{-1}$

d = path length   mm

ε = molar decadic absorption coefficient $l \times mol^{-1} \times mm^{-1}$.

This means that the absorbance is proportional both to the path length d and to the concentration c of the absorbing substance.

The dimensions of ε follow from

$$\varepsilon = \frac{A}{c \times d} \qquad \frac{1}{\dfrac{mol}{l} \times mm} = l \times mol^{-1} \times mm^{-1}.$$

In enzymatic analysis, highly dilute solutions in the mmol/l range are used. The measured absorbances or changes in absorbance are thus less than 1.000. It has therefore proved expedient to read off thousandths of an absorption unit, and to specify $A = x \times 10^{-3}$. Photometers permit readings down to the third decimal place.

The indicator substance most frequently used for photometry in enzymatic analysis is NAD(P)H. There are, however, other substances absorbing in the UV (e.g. nucleotides) and also coloured compounds such as p-nitrophenolate and others. These indicators have absorption maximum at 339 nm (NADH) and 265 nm, at 400 nm, and at other wavelengths. A photometer lamp must therefore emit radiation both in the UV and in the visible region of the spectrum. The sensitivity of the photometric measurement is highest in the wavelength range in which the absorption curve has its maximum. However, for technical reasons it is frequently necessary or desirable to carry out measurements at wavelengths lying outside the maximum of the absorption curve.

Table 1. Molar decadic absorption coefficients ($l \times mol^{-1} \times mm^{-1}$) for β-NADH and β-NADPH (measured in triethanolamine/HCl buffer, 0.1 mol/l; pH = 7.6)[11].

	°C	Hg 334 nm	339 nm	340 nm	339.85 nm[+]	Hg 365 nm
β-NADH	25	6.176×10^2 $6.182 \times 10^{2*}$	no measurement cf. Table 2	$6.317 \times 10^{2++}$ –	6.292×10^2 $6.298 \times 10^{2*}$	3.441×10^2 $3.444 \times 10^{2*}$
β-NADH	30	$6.187 \times 10^{2*}$	–	–	–	$3.427 \times 10^{2*}$
β-NADPH	25	$6.178 \times 10^{2*}$	–	–	–	$3.532 \times 10^{2*}$
β-NADPH	30	$6.186 \times 10^{2*}$	–	–	–	$3.515 \times 10^{2*}$

[+] Checking the photometer revealed 339.85 nm to be correct, instead of 340 nm.

[++] Acc. to[14] in tris buffer, 0.1 mol/l; pH = 7.8.

* Values were not corrected for beam convergence or intrinsic absorbance of the oxidized coenzyme.

In the case of NAD(P)H, measurements are advantageously carried out with spectral-line photometers at Hg 334 nm or at Hg 365 nm (cf. p. 139).

The absorption curves and absorption coefficients may depend on the temperature, pH, and the ionic strength of the solution. The best-investigated cases[11, 12] are NADH and NADPH (Fig. 3). At $\lambda = 334$ nm the temperature dependence of ε is approximately zero. The value of ε falls with rising temperature at wavelengths $\lambda > 334$ nm (including the maximum of the absorption curve) and increases at $\lambda < 334$ nm (Fig. 3); the absorption maximum is shifted accordingly.

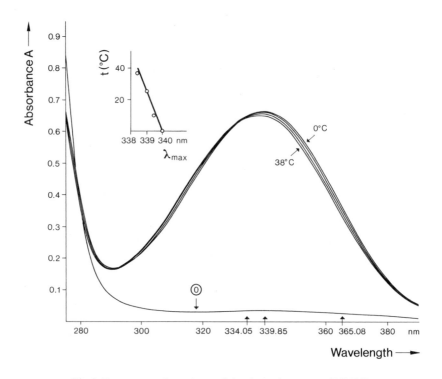

Fig. 3. Temperature dependence of the absorption curve of NADH.

The abovementioned investigations[11, 13] on NAD(P)H show:
- ε is different for NADH and NADPH
- ε is temperature-dependent
- ε depends on the pH and the ionic strength of the solution to be measured
- ε cannot be determined sufficiently accurately at 37°C because of the instability of the coenzyme
- the absorption maximum of NAD(P)H is not located at exactly 340 nm; to a first approximation one can give 339 nm.
- the absorption maximum is temperature-dependent.
- the differences in the value of ε due to the factors mentioned above are smallest by far at Hg 334 nm.

All of the abovementioned influences lead to deviations of the value of ε, not exceeding 0.5%
at Hg 334 nm. Consequently, it is best, since practically independent of the conditions of measurement, to perform measurements at this wavelength. Moreover, the values of ε are identical here
for both coenzymes.

However, the values of ε at 25°C and 30°C at 340 nm (or 339 nm) and Hg 365 nm are also sufficiently close for practical purposes (<1% error at 340 (339) nm; about 2% at Hg 365 nm) and
are independent of the other conditions of measurement. For measurement at Hg 365 nm, however, one must distinguish between the values of ε for NADH and NADPH.

In a routine clinical chemistry laboratory it would not be practical to use the exact values of the
absorption coefficients given above. It would then be necessary, under certain circumstances,
to determine the exact value of ε for each experiment. The figures given in the following table
and recommended for practical purposes in the routine laboratory vary, according to temperature and other measurement conditions, by less than 1 to 2%, which is within the limits of error
attainable for routine enzymatic analyses.

Table 2. Molar decadic absorption coefficients $(l \times mol^{-1} \times mm^{-1})$
for NADH and NADPH at temperatures of 25°C and 30°C[12].

	Hg 334 nm (334.15 nm)	340 nm (339 nm)	Hg 365 nm (365.3 nm)
NADH	6.18×10^2	6.3×10^2	3.4×10^2
NADPH	6.18×10^2	6.3×10^2	3.5×10^2

Light for photometric measurements

Photometers with which narrow wavelength ranges can be isolated and the wavelength of the
light incident on the sample varied continuously over a fairly wide spectral range are called *spectrophotometers*.

For the isolation of narrow wavelength ranges, these instruments make use of wavelength-
dependent diffraction by a grating or refraction by a prism (grating and prism monochroma-
tors).

Quantitative enzymatic analysis demands the determination of absorbance differences at the
optimum wavelength with high precision and accuracy. Special demands are placed on the
measuring apparatus if small changes in the absorbance of the sample solution are to be measured against a high background absorbance.

If measurements of this type are performed with a spectrophotometer, the possibility of selecting
any desired wavelength is generally not utilized. Consequently, photometers that satisfy the
special requirements of enzymatic analysis are generally used. They lack the versatility of a
spectrophotometer, but they are simpler to handle and, for the same precision and accuracy,
are less expensive.

Depending on how the light used for measurement is isolated, two types are distinguished:
spectral-line photometers and *filter-photometers*.

In spectral-line photometers, the light source is a gas-discharge lamp. This emits radiant energy
at wavelengths determined by the atomic structure of the gas it contains. A gas-discharge lamp

containing mercury vapour is used most frequently. The wavelengths emitted by the Hg-lamp
are shown in Fig. 4. For details see[9,15,16].

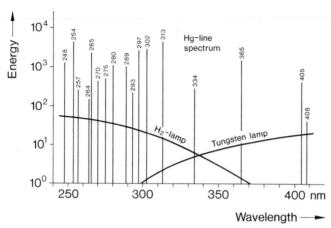

Fig. 4. Emission spectra of
some common sources of light.

The radiation emitted is concentrated in discrete narrow wavelengths range, which appear as
lines on spectral resolution. The spectrum emitted by a gas-discharge lamp is accordingly called
a line spectrum.

The most commonly used wavelengths of the spectral-line photometer equipped with a mercury
lamp are:

Hg 265 nm	Hg 365 nm
Hg 280 nm	Hg 405 nm
Hg 302 nm	Hg 436 nm
Hg 313 nm	Hg 546 nm
Hg 334 nm	Hg 578 nm

Since the energy emitted is concentrated in narrow wavelength ranges, the energy of the individual
lines is greater than when a continuous emitter is used in combination with a narrow-band filter
to isolate the same lines.

The optical filters of a spectral-line photometer must transmit the desired wavelength while
blocking all other radiation.

The mercury vapor lamp has comparatively few lines in the red region of the spectrum; the
following can be used: Hg 623 nm, Hg 691 nm, Hg 1014 nm.

In measurements at Hg 334 nm with the mercury vapor lamp, there is in addition to the line
$\lambda = 334.15$ nm a second line at 335.13 nm. However, this line is so weak that it can be neglected[11].
At Hg 365 nm, there is a group of three lines: $\lambda_1 = 365.01$ nm, $\lambda_2 = 365.48$ nm, and $\lambda_3 = 366.31$ nm.
The energy ratio of these lines depends to a small extent on the vapor pressure in the discharge
tube of the lamp. With the usual lamps, $\lambda = 365.3$ nm can be taken as the maximum-energy
wavelength[11,13].

The filter photometer uses an incandescent lamp (thermal radiator) as the light source. Such a
lamp has a continuous energy spectrum. The spectral energy distribution depends on the tem-

perature of the incandescent filament or strip. The proportion of short-wave radiation increases with rising temperature.

Filter photometers make use of an optical filter to isolate a limited range of wavelengths from the continuous spectrum. The spectral width of the radiation isolated depends on the efficiency of the optical filter. The spectral performance of the apparatus is characterized essentially by the peak widths at half-maximum and at 1%-maximum of the radiation transmitted by the filter. In order to ensure a linear relationship between the substance concentration and the absorbance, the spectral band-widths of energy transmitted by the filter must be narrow in comparison to the absorption curve of the substance being measured. Figs. 5a and 5b show the spectral energy distribution of the light passed by a metal interference filter in comparison with the useful part of the absorption curve of NADH.

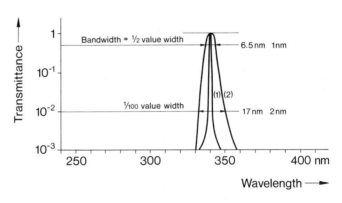

Fig. 5a. Transmission curves of common arrangements for spectral selection (1) Double monochromator MM12 (Zeiss), (2) DEPIL interference filter (Schott).

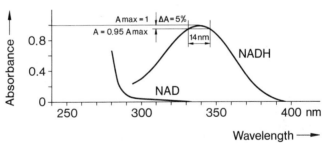

Fig. 5b. Absorption curves of NADH and NAD.

The deviation of a calibration curve from linearity in the case of inadequate filter efficiency increases with the magnitude of the absorbance to be measured. Errors due to inadequate spectral purity of the light used for measurement are most pronounced when small changes in absorbance are measured against high background absorbances.

Whereas in the spectral-line photometer the usable wavelength is determined by the nature of the gas contained in the lamp, the maximum-energy wavelength of the emergent light in a filter photometer with a continuous emitter is determined by the transmission curve of the filter.

If thermal radiators with quartz bulbs are used in conjunction with interference filters of modern design, reliable measurement of the absorption maximum of, for example, NADH at $\lambda = 339$ nm is still possible.

Single-beam technique – Multiple-beam technique

The photometer shown in Fig. 1 uses a single beam. The sample is continuously traversed by the measurement beam and subsequently a reference standard is measured. This is the standard technique in enzymatic analysis.

A double-beam photometer is an apparatus in which the sample and the reference standard are traversed by two different beams, i.e., by a double beam. The double-beam technique is the standard technique when, for example, spectral absorption curves are to be measured, since both the energy of the emitter and the sensitivity of the receiver change with the wavelength. By alternately passing the measuring beam through the sample and the reference standard, it is possible to obtain the ratio of the two luminous fluxes and thus compensate for changes in the photocurrent due to physical factors attendant on a spectral scan.

The procedure in which light of two different wavelengths is alternately passed through a sample has become important in biochemistry. This technique was first used by *B. Chance*[5,6]; it is known as the "split-beam" technique (bichromatic photometry, two-wavelength photometry). The first wavelength is chosen for the optimum absorption conditions of the substance to be measured. The second wavelength is a reference wavelength selected such that it will be absorbed as little as possible while subject to nearly the same interferences as those affecting the first wavelength.

The single-beam technique can be supplemented by a second auxiliary beam. Here, for example, part of the measuring radiation is directed to a second receiver by means of an obliquely arranged quartz plate. The signal of the second receiver serves to compensate for fluctuations in the source of the radiation by modulating the amplification of the received signal. The disadvantage of the various measuring techniques lies in the technological sophistication involved. They offer special advantages for certain problems, but in general, they have not come into wide use in enzymatic analysis in comparison with the single-beam technique.

Cuvette Holders, Cuvettes, Techniques of Measurement, and Evaluation

Cuvette Holders

Correct design of the cuvette holder is an important prerequisite for an efficient technique. The cuvette holder must ensure both reliable and reproducible sample positioning in the path of the beam.

Since enzymatically-catalyzed reactions are highly temperature-dependent ($+5\%$ to $+10\%$ per K), the thermal conductivity from the holder to the cuvette must be good. It must be possible to maintain the holder at any constant temperature between about 25 and 37°C with a precision of ±0.05°C. Temperature is controlled either by means of a system of tubes in the holder through which thermostatted water circulates, or by a built-in electronic regulator with a heating coil.

The sample being analyzed is heated additionally by heat produced in the apparatus, so that cooling is often necessary. Water cooling is the simplest method. A small refrigerating unit is more convenient. Recently, thermoelectric cooling elements (Peltier elements) have also been used[17,18]. These are semiconductors (bismuth telluride Bi_2Te_3) in which a temperature gradient is produced by the passage of current.

Cuvettes and changing cuvette holders

The measurement vessels are cells or cuvettes (from the French: cuvette = small dish).
Many cuvette shapes are in use. For routine applications, the rectangular cells with a path length of 10 mm and external dimensions of $12.5 \times 12.5 \times 45.0 \, mm^3$, developed by Messrs. Beckman in 1946, have come into general use as standard cuvettes (Fig. 6a). To meet the demand for reduction of the sample volume, a semimicro-cuvette has been developed, with the same external dimensions but with the open width reduced from 10 to 4 mm (Fig. 6b). Because of its height of about 45 mm, which is large in comparison with its cross-section, the sample volume can be varied within wide limits. It allows good mixing of the sample. Fig. 6c shows a suction cell. A pump draws air from the right-hand opening; if this is closed by a finger, the cell contents are drawn out.

In addition to rectangular cuvettes, round cuvettes are also used (Fig. 6d). If the photometer slit appears as a linear image coincident with the axis of the cuvette, then the cuvette has the correct path length for the individual rays that make up the beam even when the exit angle of the beam is relatively large. However, their practical use is limited by the fact that the slit image is not a true line, but has a finite size, that the image is displaced along the axis with a change in the wavelength, and that the positioning of holders with several cuvettes must be very accurate, since the cell acts as a cylindrical lens. Round cuvettes must not be moved when series measurements are performed.

If further reduction of the sample volume is required, it is practical to employ a cell with a cylindrical cross-section along the optical axis of the photometer (Fig. 6e). With a diameter of 4 mm and a path length of 10 mm, the cuvette has a volume of 125 µl, so that, including the filling tubes, a total volume of about 200 µl is required.

Cells for very small amounts of substance were first described in 1946 by *Lowry*[19]. His cells had a total volume of 50 µl. Fig. 6f shows a cell designed by *Ullrich* and *Hampel*[20]: with an inside

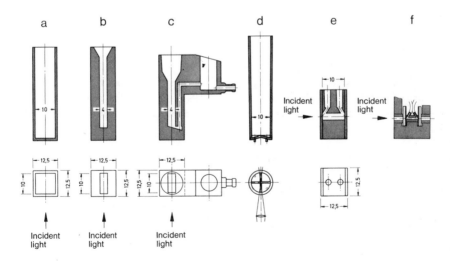

Fig. 6. A typical selection of measuring vessels (cuvettes).

diameter of 0.5 mm, only 3 μl are needed to fill it. (Such cells are filled with piston pipets.) In order to achieve the best possible optical efficiency, planoconvex lenses are used for the cell windows.

The most fundamental characteristic of a cuvette is its accurately defined path length. This is a prerequisite for the accuracy of the measurement. In addition to errors due to excessive tolerances in cuvette manufacture, errors may also arise from inadequacies in the transmission of the beam of light. The width of the beam in the region of the cuvette must be smaller than the inside diameter of the cuvette. The holder must be positioned such that the light passes through the cuvette without touching the side walls. (This is tested by observing the width of the beam inside the cuvette with the aid of a small strip of paper.)

Quartz, glass, and frequently plastic are used as cuvette materials. To facilitate laboratory operations, disposable cuvettes are used more and more. Only quartz cuvettes can be used for measurements at wavelengths below 300 nm. Fig. 7 shows the transmission limits for various materials in the UV.

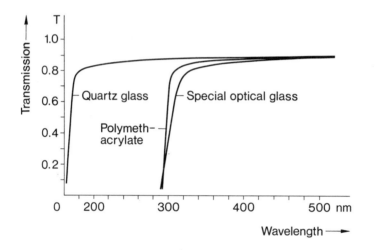

Fig. 7. The limitation of the spectral transmission of cuvettes in the UV region for various materials.

A cuvette containing water or a solvent shows a background absorbance which is due to the fact that part of the radiation incident upon the glass walls is reflected. The magnitude of the fraction reflected depends on the difference between the refractive indices of air, water, and glass. The reflectance is

$$R = \left(\frac{n_2 - n_1}{n_2 + n_1}\right)^2,$$

where n has the value 1.0 for air, 1.5 for glass, and 1.33 for water. The fraction of radiation reflected, R, is 0.04, i.e. about 4%, at each air-to-glass boundary. The part of radiation transmitted is therefore about 96% at each surface. The attenuation of the light beam due to this reflection corresponds to an absorbance of about $A_0 = 20 \times 10^{-3}$ for each interface traversed. The empty cuvette therefore shows a background absorbance of the order of $A_0 = 4 \times 20 \times 10^{-3} = 80 \times 10^{-3}$.

If the cell is filled with water, the reflection losses at the glass-to-water boundaries are less. In the limiting case, when the refractive index of the cuvette contents is equal to that of the cuvette walls, reflection takes place at only two interfaces with a resulting cell blank value $E_0 = 40 \times 10^{-3}$. Photometers are usually provided with holders for several cuvettes. Besides a linear direction of movement (Fig. 8 a), a rotatable arrangement of the cuvettes about the photoelectric receiver is also in common use (Fig. 8 b).

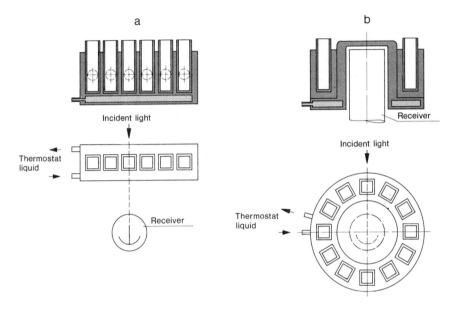

Fig. 8. Cuvette-changing holder; a) direction of linear displacement for a six-cuvette holder, b) circular holder for 12 cuvettes, rotatable about the receiver.

Technique of measurement and evaluation

In the simplest case, the reagents are pipetted into the cuvette, which has been brought to the correct temperature and positioned in the path of the light beam, and, after the cuvette contents have reached the required temperature, the reaction is started by the addition of a small volume of one of the reactants.

The absorbance difference ΔA is read after the reaction has run to completion, or for a predetermined time interval. Recording the absorbance by means of an analog recorder is even simpler.

Recording technique has been greatly improved by the development of efficient recording devices working on the compensation principle and the advent of automatic electronic stepwise attenuation or expansion („stepping“) of the range of measurement. Such apparatus is capable of measuring small absorbance differences against large background absorbances, which is often important. Under certain conditions, it is even possible to record the absorbance to the fourth decimal place.

The precision of the measurement results generally becomes better when the observation time is extended, because the short-term interferences encountered in practice average out and are thus better eliminated. (Such interferences may have various causes: e.g. contamination of the cuvette contents, electronic noise in the photoelectric transducer and the resistors at the amplifier input.) Accordingly, to increase the precision, one sample is observed continuously, or several samples are observed intermittently over a relatively long time.

Fig. 9a shows kinetic recording with continuous, and Fig. 9b with intermittent, observation of several samples over a relatively long time.

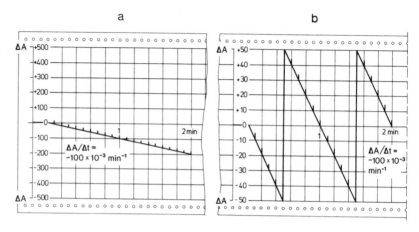

Fig. 9. Record of the determination of a catalytic activity (drawing). a) for measured absorbance range $\Delta A = \pm 500 \times 10^{-3}$, b) for measured absorbance range $\Delta A = \pm 50 \times 10^{-3}$, with automatic "stepping" of the range of measurement; the number of "steps" possible is unlimited.

Expansion of the absorbance scale down to the measurement of $\Delta A = 1 \times 10^{-4}$ makes it possible to lower the detection limits or, in the normal concentration range, to shorten the time of observation. However, the demands on reagent purity and cleanliness of the cuvettes are then increased. Electronic devices offer the possibility of superimposing time-marks (e.g. at intervals of $0.1 \, min = 6 \, sec$), so that the results are independent of the precision of the chart speed.

In routine work, results are being expressed digitally to an increasing extent. Modern instruments offer the possibility of multiplying the measured value ΔA by a factor, so that the substance concentration (mol/l) or catalytic activity concentration (U/l, or kat/l) can be read off directly or printed out.

Because of the better idea it gives of the total course of a reaction, analog recording will retain its importance in the elucidation of interferences, the development of new methods, and the checking of routine methods. In the analysis of large numbers of samples according to a fixed procedure, however, digital expression of the measured value, in conjunction with a check on linearity, is the most practical documentation technique.

Sources of Error and Control Methods

A distinction must be made between random errors and systematic errors (cf. p. 233). Only systematic errors, i.e. errors due to the measurement system, are treated below.

In general, the technical effort rises sharply when the error is reduced from, for example, 1 % to 0.1 %. Consequently, a compromise must always be sought between acceptable technical expenditure and permissible residual errors. In practice, one attempts to reduce the errors below the limit of 1 % of the measured value.

An exhaustive account of the testing of photometers is contained in *Kortüm's* monograph[10]. For descriptions of sources of error, methods of testing, and test substances, see[21-25]. The following account is limited to the requirements of enzymatic analysis.

Sources of error:

– inadequate constancy of the output level
– defect in the measuring circuit of the photometer
– inappropriate spectral energy distribution of the light used for measurement
– inaccuracies in the path length of the cuvette
– deviations and fluctuations of the temperature of measurement
– decomposition of the substrate, induced by the light used for measurement
– light scattering by particles suspended in the cuvette contents

Errors due to inadequate constancy of the output level

A certain constant luminous flux passes through the solution to be measured. The smallest measurable change in the luminous flux is determined by fluctuation of the initial signal in the absence of a cuvette. The accuracy and precision attainable are limited by fluctuations in this signal during the measurement.

If a monotonic drift of the output signal occurs over a relatively long period of time, which usually happens as the result of a temperature dependence of the electronic components, this drift will produce a constant error in the kinetic measurement of a reaction, regardless of the duration of the observation.

Short-lived fluctuations due to voltage jumps in the supply mains are most apparent when the observation time is short. Their effect decreases with longer observation periods.

Another source of perturbations in the constancy of the output level is the after-effect of illumination on the photoelectric transducer. In general, the photocurrent falls off slowly on prolonged illumination. After extinguishment of the source of light and a certain regeneration period, the initial photocurrent is again produced on renewed illumination. In practice, this effect can be kept small, although not completely eliminated, by maintaining a low flux density on the photocathode. Errors of the order of $\Delta A / \Delta t = 1 \times 10^{-3}$ min^{-1} can be demonstrated for all known types of receiver. A basic requirement is that the error due to this drift not be greater than the other types of error mentioned above.

The influence of the photoelectric after-effect that has just been described on the accuracy of the measurement can be taken into account by periodically checking the output level without a sample. The various instruments differ in the frequency with which this check is necessary.

In the case of spectrophotometers the measurement of spectral absorption curves is of prime importance. Here, high-frequency alternate switching of the source beam from one path (in which the beam passes through the substance to be measured) to a second, optically equal path (in which a second cuvette with a blank is measured) is the standard technique.

Defects in the measuring circuit of the photometer

The absorbance shown at the photometer output should correspond to the sample concentration in the beam path in the range of measurement from $A = 0$ to $A = 2$ or $A = 3$.

This is checked most simply by means of gray glass filters of known absorbance. For enzymatic analysis with small absorbance differences against background absorbances of different levels, the photometer is checked by inserting gray glass filters with different absorbances in the path of the beam, reading the absorbance, and then inserting a second gray filter with a lower absorbance in the path of the beam, thus determining the sum of the absorbances of the two filters. If, when the second gray filter is inserted, the measured absorbance difference is constant for different basic absorbances of the first (stronger) gray filter, the photoelectric transducer and the associated electronics are operating correctly.

Inappropriate spectral energy distribution of the light used for measurement

The spectral energy distribution of the measuring radiation must be narrow in comparison to the absorption curve of the substance being measured, so that there is a linear relationship between the concentration and the absorbance.

This is best verified with the substance measured most frequently – NADH. For this test, two cuvettes are used, which can be placed one behind the other or individually in the path of the beam in a similar manner to the test method using gray filters. Cuvette 2 contains a solution of constant concentration, while Cuvette 1 is filled successively with a geometric dilution series of NADH solutions.

Example

Concentration series: 0, 10, 20, 50, 100, 200, 500 μmol/l.

Cuvette 2 is filled with a NADH-solution of fixed concentration such that the absorbance A for a path length of 10 mm is about 200×10^{-3} (30 to 40 μmol/l). In the case of spectrophotometers and filter photometers, the absorbance of cuvette 1, beginning with the concentration 0, is measured at a wavelength of $\lambda = 340$ nm, and in the case of spectral-line photometers at a wavelength of $\lambda = $ Hg 334 nm.

After cuvette 1 has been measured, cuvette 2 is also inserted in the path of the beam, and the sum of absorbances $A_1 + A_2$ of cuvettes 1 and 2 is measured. Cuvette 1 is then filled with the second NADH-solution at 10 μmol/l. The absorbance of cuvette 1 is measured first, as before, and then the absorbance of cuvettes $1 + 2$.

The absorbance of cuvette 2 is plotted along the ordinate and that of cuvette 1 along the abscissa (Fig. 10). When the measurement is repeated several times, the graph gives an idea of the precision and accuracy of the measurement.

If the absorbance of cuvette 2 as measured alone and calculated the difference of the absorbances of the two cuvettes over the entire absorbance range is constant ($A_2 = (A_1 + A_2) - A_1$), the instrument response is linear for NADH over the absorbance range tested at the wavelength under investigation. However, this does not exclude the possibility that all the values are incorrect by a certain factor because of an error in the wavelength calibration of the apparatus.

In the case of the spectrophotometer, the accuracy of the wavelength scale is generally tested with the lines of the built-in deuterium lamp or an Hg-lamp provided for wavelength calibration. The errors that arise in practice from inadequate precision of the wavelength calibration and insuf-

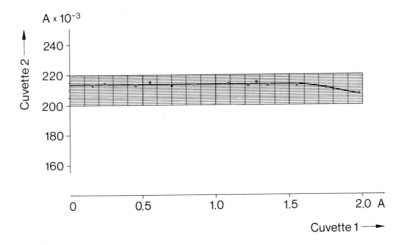

Fig. 10. Testing the accuracy of a photometer with the substance being measured by additive determination of a small absorbance plus an absorbance incremented over the entire range of measurement.

ficient monochromaticity of the light used for measurement in simple spectral photometers have been described by *Rand*[24].

In spectral-line photometers, the Hg-lines (used as calibration standards in spectrophotometers) are the wavelengths of measurement. They are determined by the nature of the gas contained in the lamp. Consequently, with this type of apparatus all that needs to be checked is whether the cut-off filter used satisfactorily filters out the other spectral lines. Changes in the spectral transmission profile of the cut-off filter due to aging or temperature dependence do not affect the wavelength of the measurement radiation in the spectral-line photometer as long as the filter still absorbs the other lines adequately.

The independence of the quality of the measurement radiation from manufacturing tolerances and time-dependent variations of individual components of the instrument is the reason for the widespread use of spectral-line photometers in enzymatic analysis.

In filter photometers with a continuous emitter, on the other hand, a change in the transmission profile of the filter being used leads to a corresponding change in the spectral composition of the measurement radiation, so that the constancy of the filter's transmission profile must be checked in any test of accuracy.

An excessively wide spectral transmission profile of the filter again has the effect of reducing the absorbance range over which the relationship between concentration and absorbance is linear.

Inaccuracies in the path length of the cuvette

Inaccuracies in the path length of the cuvette cause proportional errors in the measurement. In the case of the standard path length of 10 mm, a deviation of 0.1 mm introduces an error of 1%. Consequently, the precision of the cuvette must be such that its path length deviates from the nominal value only by fractions of 0.1 mm, if the total error is to remain below 1%.

Special precision instruments are necessary to check the adherence to this path-length tolerance. It is easiest to test a relatively large number of cuvettes photometrically, if a precision cuvette with the manufacturer's tolerance data is available.

Deviations and fluctuations of the temperature of measurement

In determinations of the catalytic activity of enzymes, the rate of the reaction changes by about 5 to 10% per K in the temperature range from 25 to 30°C. Temperature deviations of ±0.05°C from the specified working temperature therefore produce deviations up to ±0.5% from the correct value. Consequently, checking the correctness of the working temperature and the precision with which it is maintained even during prolonged measurements is particularly important in practice.

The temperature of the liquid in the cuvette is measured with a calibrated thermometer. Electric thermometers have the advantage of a temperature sensor with a small mass, but they are subject to aging phenomena which can give rise to incorrect readings. Consequently, they must be checked against calibrated mercury thermometers at certain intervals.

Restricting temperature fluctuations around the correct value to ±0.1% places high demands on the thermostats, particularly if short-time measurements are not to be exposed to the full amplitude of the temperature fluctuation.

Decomposition of the substrate induced by the light used for measurement

Certain substances decompose on exposure to light. This applies particularly if an Hg-lamp is used and the intensive UV-radiation is transmitted to the substance undergoing measurement via a quartz optical system. To avoid this effect, a cut-off filter must be set up between the cell and the source of the radiation.

Errors due to scattering of light by particles suspended in the cuvette contents

Solid particles scatter the incident light beam. When they are small in comparison to the wavelengths of the incident radiation, they emit uniformly on all sides (*Rayleigh* scattering[9]). Larger particles scatter predominantly in the direction of the primary beam[6] (Fig. 11).

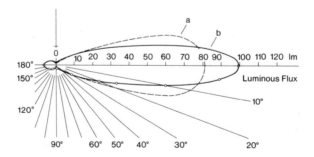

Fig. 11. Direction and extent of the scattering of a diluted serum containing scattering particles: a) dilution with isotonic saline, b) dilution with redist water.

When the exit angle of the optical system is small, only a small part of the scattered radiation is intercepted by the receiver, so that there is an additional loss of light (simulated absorption). As the exit angle of the cuvette image on the receiver becomes larger, the fraction of the scattered light that is intercepted becomes greater, and consequently the effect of scattering on the measured absorbance becomes smaller.

In order to obtain comparable results with different types of instrument, the cross-section of the cuvette that is transilluminated and the exit angle over which the scattered radiation emitted from the cuvette is accepted by the receiver must be specified.

No such specifications have been set up to date, so that at present different types of instrument may give very different measurements on turbid samples.

References

1 Warburg, O. & Christian, W. (1936) *Biochem. Z.* **286,** 81.
2 Cary, H.H. & Beckman, A.O. (1941) *J. opt. Soc. Amer.* **31,** 682.
3 Beisenherz, G., Boltze, H.I., Bücher, Th., Czok, R., Garbade, K.H., Meyer-Arendt, E. & Pfleiderer, G. (1953) *Z. Naturforschg.* **8b,** 555–577.
4 Hoefert, H.I. (1951) *Zeitschr. Glaskunde,* **24,** 63–68.
5 Chance, B. (1942) *The Review of Scientific Instruments,* **13,** 158–161.
6 Chance, B. (1951) *The Review of Scientific Instruments,* **22,** 619–638.
7 Lübbers, D. & Wodick, R. (1972) *Z. Anal. Chem.* **261,**271–280.
8 Physical Science Study Committee, (1974) Physik, Vieweg & Sohn, Braunschweig.
9 Pohl, R.W. (1967) Optik und Atomphysik, 12th edition, Springer Verlag, Berlin.
10 Kortüm, G. (1962) Kolorimetrie, Photometrie und Spektrometrie, 4th edition, Springer Verlag, Berlin.
11 Ziegenhorn, J., Senn, M. & Bücher, Th. (1976) *Clin. Chem.* **22,** 151–160.
12 Bergmeyer, H.U. (1975) *J. Clin. Chem. Clin. Biochem.* **13,** 507–508.
13 Bücher, Th., Lüsch, G. & Krell, H. (1975) in *Quality Control in Clinical Chemistry* (Anido, G., van Kampen, E.J., Rosalki, S.B. & Rubin, M., eds.), p. 301–310. Walter de Gruyter, Berlin, New York.
14 McComb, R.B., Bond, L.W., Burnett, R.W., Keech, R.C. & Bowers,G.N., jr. (1976) *Clin. Chem.* **22,** 141–150.
15 Rössler, F. (1939) *Annalen der Physik,* 5th series, **34,** 1–22.
16 Rössler, F. (1952) *Annalen der Physik,* 6th series, **10,** 177–195.
17 Schirp, W. (1964) *Intern. Zeitschr. Elektrowärme* **22,** 205–214.
18 Rupprecht, J. & Maier, R.G. (1965) *Physica Status solidi* **8,** 3–39.
19 Lowry, O.H. & Bessy, O.A. (1946) *J. Biol. Chem.* **2,** 163, 633.
20 Ullrich, K.I. & Hampel, A. (1959) *Pflügers Archiv* **268,** 177–180.
21 Gottschalk, G. (1976) *Z. Anal. Chem.* **282,** 1–15.
22 Reule, A. (1958) *Applied Opties,* **7,** 1023–1028.
23 Burnet, R.W. (1972) *Journal of Research of the National Bureau of Standards* **76A,** 483–489.
24 Rand, R.N. (1969) *Clin. Chem.* **15,** 839–863.
25 Burke, R.W., Dewdorf, E.R. & Menis, O. (1972) *Journal of Research of National Bureau of Standards,* **76A,** No. 5 & No. 6.
26 Kleine, N., Matthes, M. & Müller, W. (1957) *Klin. Wschr.* **35,** 132–135.

Other Measurement Techniques

Besides photometry, electrochemical techniques (conductometry, potentiometry) and micro-calorimetry have recently been used to an increasing extent for measuring of enzymatic reactions. This is always the case when photometry reaches its limits. For example, it is time-consuming to use dialysis, filtration, or deproteinization in order to prepare for photometric measurement samples that have a marked intrinsic light absorption or that are suspensions (blood, samples in microbiology and food chemistry).

Detectors other than photocells are likewise of interest when none of the participants in the primary enzymatic reaction shows sufficient light absorption and the formation of such products by means of auxiliary reactions poses difficulties. This is the case, for example, with most de-carboxylase reactions. Frequently, as in oxidase reactions, the auxiliary or indicator reactions required for photometry are very complicated, so that detectors that permit a direct measurement of the primary reaction are preferred.

In individual cases, there is a justified hope that measuring systems other than the photometer can be manufactured at less cost in the future.

Conductometry

Peter Schuler

Principles

A detector has the task of measuring continuously a given property of a solution as a physical quantity. If the concentration of a solution constituent that contributes to this physical quantity changes as a result of a chemical reaction, the detector can show this change in concentration. While in photometry the absorption of light is the measured quantity, in conductometry it is the electrical conductance (previously: electrical conductivity). The anions and the cations present in the solution contribute additively to the overall conductance. Enzymatic reactions that lead to a change in the sum of all the ionic mobilities can be measured conductometrically.

The conductance of a solution is the reciprocal of the resistance R between two electrodes of area q immersed in the solution and separated by a distance l:

$$(1) \qquad \frac{1}{R} = \frac{1}{\varrho} \times \frac{q}{l} = \varkappa \times \frac{q}{l} \quad S(\Omega^{-1})$$

Here

$\dfrac{1}{R}$ is the electrical conductance; the unit is the Siemens, S (earlier also called the mho for Ω^{-1})

ϱ specific electrical resistance; unit $\Omega \cdot m$

$\varkappa$ electrical conductivity, $1/\varrho$; unit S/m.

q   area of the electrode, m^2

l   distance between the electrodes, m

The conductivity referred to the concentration c is the equivalent conductivity.

(2) $\Lambda_v = \frac{\varkappa}{c}$ Sm^2/mol

In this equation, c has the dimensions of mol/m^3. In clinical chemistry the preferred unit is mol/l. Consequently,

(2a) $\Lambda_v = \frac{\varkappa}{1000\,c}$ Sm^2/mol

Λ_v decreases with increasing concentration, since the degree of dissociation falls (*Ostwald's* dilution law), and since with increasing density, the ions mutually hinder one another (*Debye-Hueckel-Onsager* theory). We therefore take the "equivalent conductivity at infinite dilution" Λ_0, i.e. the initial slope of the $\varkappa/c$ curve, as the concentration-independent substance constant. Consequently, the measurement must be made in this linear initial region by diluting the samples. In general, the concentration of the ion to be determined must not exceed 100 µmol/l.

If a voltage U is applied to the electrodes, an electric field E is established. The ions in the solution migrate to the cathode or the anode, depending on their charge. The solution containing the ions therefore conducts electric current. The migration velocity w of the ions is determined by the field strength E:

(3) $w = u\,\frac{U}{l} = u \times E$ m/s

The proportionality constant u is called the ionic mobility. It is a substance constant of the ion. An equivalent conductivity λ_0 at infinite dilution for the individual ion can be calculated from it. The relation between the substance concentration to be measured and the measured quantity, e.g. R, is as follows:

(4) $c = \frac{\Delta \varkappa}{\Lambda_0}$ mol/l   with $\varkappa = \frac{1}{R} \times \frac{1}{q}$ S/m

The values of $\varkappa$, Λ_v, Λ_0, and u increase with rising temperature; their temperature coefficient is of the order of 2% per K. To achieve an accuracy of measurement of $\pm1\%$, therefore, the temperature must be kept constant to within ±0.5 K.

Conductometric measurements are usually performed with alternating current, since direct current leads to the formation of electrolysis products at the electrodes. This would quickly lead to polarization of the electrodes, i.e. to the formation of a potential opposed to the original voltage. Polarization potentials can be reduced by increasing the surface area of the electrode (coating with platinum black).

The reaction solutions must be adequately buffered (constant pH). They therefore have a considerable intrinsic conductivity $\varkappa_p$. The electrolyte constituents of the sample cause a further increase in conductivity by $\varkappa_s$ (s for *sample*). $\varkappa_s$ and $\varkappa_p$ are comparable with the reagent blank and sample blank values in photometry. The increase in conductivity due to the enzymatic reactions is relatively small – often only 20% of the total conductivity at the end of the measurement. Such a signal/blank ratio of 1:5 places particular requirements on the noise level and the resolution of the electronic system. To keep $\varkappa_p$ low, buffers of low intrinsic conductivity are used at low concentrations. Tris, imidazole, and Good buffers[1,2] are commonly used.

Applications

The best-investigated reaction at the present time is the enzymatic degradation of urea[1,3-5]:

(5)

$$H_2N-C(=O)-NH_2 + H_2O \xrightarrow{\text{Urease}^*} 2NH_4^+ + CO_3^{2-}$$

Here the conditions are particularly favorable, since an uncharged molecule decomposes completely into ions. The known values of λ_0 for these ions give a theoretical conductivity increase of $\Lambda_0 = 14.28 \times 10^{-3}\,\text{Sm}^2/\text{mol}$ for urea at 25°C. Experimentally, however, a value of $\Lambda_0 = 7.8 \times 10^{-3}\,\text{Sm}^2/\text{mol}$ has been found at 25°C in tris-buffer (5 mmol/l, pH 8), and $\Lambda_0 = 11.2 \times 10^{-3}\,\text{Sm}^2/\text{mol}$ in citrate buffer (2 mmol/l, pH 6.2). Obviously, in different buffers the ions formed undergo different subsequent reactions which lead to a decrease in conductivity yield. A detailed elucidation of the total reaction is still lacking. In view of the linear range of measurement up to 22 µmol/l, the method is nevertheless suitable for the determination of urea in spite of these unanswered questions. At a sample dilution of 1 : 1000, then, the region up to about 22 mmol/l (130 mg/100 ml) is accessible to measurement. This corresponds to the range of linearity required by clinical chemistry.

Meanwhile, a semiautomatic device for the conductometric determination of urea has been put on the market (Beckman BUN-Analyzer)[6-8]. The instrument employs a tris/Hepes** buffer (about 0.08 mmol/l, pH 7.4).

The intrinsic conductivity of the reagent mixture is about $\varkappa = 2.4 \times 10^{-2}\,\text{Sm}^{-1}$. After the addition of 10 µl of the serum sample – due to the electrolyte content of the serum – a conductivity of about $\varkappa = 5 \times 10^{-2}\,\text{Sm}^{-1}$ is obtained. The sample is diluted 1 : 1000; 1 mg of urea/100 ml in the serum therefore corresponds to 0.17 µmol/l in the measuring cell. The linear range of measurement ends at about 25 mmol/l (150 mg/100 ml). The urea concentration is determined completely automatically by a kinetic process (cf. p. 79 ff.): the conductometric sensor continuously reports the conductivity to a computer, which determines the concentration from this via the reaction rate.

Another well-investigated example is the enzymatic hydrolysis of acetylcholine by cholinesterase (ChE***)[9].

(6)

$$H_3C-C(=O)-O-(CH_2)_2-\overset{\oplus}{N}(CH_3)_3 + H_2O \xrightarrow{\text{ChE}} H_3C-C(=O)-O^{\ominus} +H^+ +$$

$$+ HO-(CH_2)_2-\overset{\oplus}{N}(CH_3)_3$$

This reaction starts out with one ion; two ions are formed. Since approximately the same λ_0 values may be taken for acetylcholine and free choline, the expected molar increase in conductivity should correspond to the equivalent conductivity of acetic acid, viz., $\Lambda_0 = 39 \times 10^{-3}\,\text{Sm}^2 \times \text{mol}^{-1}$ (at 25°C), so that the reaction should be satisfactorily accessible to a conductometric measure-

---

   * EC 3.5.1.5.
  ** Hepes = 4-(2-Hydroxyethyl)-1-piperazineethane sulfonic acid.
*** EC 3.1.1.7.

ment. In an experiment using tris-buffer (60 mol/l, pH 8.0), a value of $\Lambda_0 = 6.3 \times 10^{-3}$ Sm^2 per mole of acetylcholine was found; addition of pure acetic acid to the tris-buffer gave an increase in conductivity of $\Lambda_0 = 6.1 \times 10^{-3}$ Sm^2 per mole of acetic acid. This shows that here again, subsequent reactions with the buffer lead to a decrease in conductivity yield.

In contrast to the degradation of urea, it was possible in this case to elucidate the subsequent reactions satisfactorily:

(7)
$$H_3C-C\underset{OH}{\overset{O}{\diagup}} \rightleftharpoons H_3C-C\underset{O^{\ominus}}{\overset{O}{\diagup}} + H^{\oplus}$$

$$H^{\oplus} + \text{Tris} \rightarrow \text{Tris-}H^{\oplus}$$

Given the λ_0 values for the acetate ion (4.08×10^{-3} Sm^2/mol) and for the tris-H$^+$ ion (2.15×10^{-3} Sm^2/mol), the increase in conductivity to be expected for acetylcholine at 25°C is in fact only $\Lambda_0 = 6.23 \times 10^{-3}$ Sm^2/mol, which is in excellent agreement with the experimental result. A value of 10 µmol/l is given for the linear of measurement of the method.

References

1 Good, N.E., Winget, G.D., Winter, W., Conally, T.N., Izawa, S. & Singh, M.M. (1966) *Biochemistry* **5**, 467.
2 Lawrence, A.J. & Moores, G.R. (1972) *Eur. J. Biochem.* **24**, 538.
3 Wei-Tsung Chin & Kroontje, W. (1961) *Anal. Chem.* **33**, 1757.
4 Hanss, M. & Rey, A. (1971) *Biochim. Biophys. Acta* **227**, 630.
5 Hanss, M. & Rey, A. (1971) *Ann. Biol. Clin.* **29**, 323.
6 Paulson, G., Ray, R. & Sternberg, J. (1971) *Clin. Chem.* **17**, 644.
7 Horak, E. & Sundermann, F.W. (1972) *Ann. Clin. Lab. Sci.* **2**, 425.
8 Ziembowicz, R. (1974) *Amer. J. Med. Technol.* **40**, 219.
9 Hanss, M. & Rey, A. (1971) *Biochim. Biophys. Acta* **227**, 618.

Potentiometry and Polarometry

Peter Schuler

Principles

Ions produce concentration-dependent electrochemical potentials at suitable boundary layers in aqueous solutions. Measurement of such potentials permits the determination of the concentration of the ions involved.

Electrode potentials

When a metal rod is immersed in a solution of its own ions, an electrochemical potential difference between the rod and the solution appears spontaneously. Metal ions are formed at the rod surface (oxidation) which pass into solution (solution pressure). The electrons remaining behind give rise to a negative charge on the rod, while correspondingly the solution becomes positively charged. The electric field produced causes back-diffusion of the ions to the metal, where they separate out again as atoms by recombination with electrons (reduction). The equilibrium of the redox process

$$(1) \qquad\qquad Me \rightleftharpoons Me^{n+} + ne^-$$

is reached when solution pressure and back-diffusion compensate one another. The potential difference E then has a constant value which, apart from the temperature and the nature of the metal, depends only on the ion concentration c, or, more precisely, on the activity α of the ions in the solution. It is known as the EMF (electromotive force) of the redox process.

Thus, to establish an equilibrium, ions must – depending on their initial concentration – either be dissolved from the metal surface or separate out upon it. The observed "redox potential" E is the electrochemical work necessary for this purpose, which is accumulated by the metal/solution system. Its magnitude and dependence on equilibrium activity (mol/l) are described by the *Nernst* equation:

$$(2) \qquad\qquad E = E_0 + \frac{R \times T}{n \times F} \ln \alpha \quad V,$$

Here R is the gas constant (8.314 J), T the absolute temperature, F the Faraday constant ($96{,}487$ A $\times$ s $\times$ mol^{-1}), n the number of electrons exchanged per mole, and V the parameter measured in volts. E_0 is the electrode potential at the temperature T for $\alpha = 1$ mol/l; E_0 is called the "normal potential" of the redox reaction.

With the numerical values for R and F, at 25°C (298.15°K) we have

$$(3) \qquad\qquad E = E_0 + \frac{0{,}059}{n} \lg \alpha \quad V.$$

If, in accordance with eqn. (2), the electrode potential changes by 0.059 V for a change in the concentration by one power of ten (concentration decade), we speak of "ideal *Nernst*ian behavior".

Redox potentials do not appear only at the boundary between a solid metal and the solution of its ions. A noble metal (platinum, palladium) rod immersed in a proton-containing solution and swept by gaseous hydrogen can make hydrogen dissolve at its surface. It then behaves like a "hydrogen rod", so that the potential of the redox reaction established at its surface is:

$$(4) \qquad\qquad H_2 \rightleftharpoons 2H^+ + 2e^-.$$

The *Nernst* equation (9) now assumes the following form:

$$(5) \qquad\qquad E = E_0 + \frac{R \times T}{2F} \ln \frac{[\alpha H^+]^2}{P_{H_2}}$$

P_{H_2} is the pressure of gaseous hydrogen sweeping the electrode, i.e. of the oxidized reactant. This quantity appears here but not in eqn. (3), where, because of its constancy, it is included in E_0. In contrast to the first case, here the metal rod is not involved in the redox process but only catalyzes the establishment of its equilibrium.

The electrode/solution arrangement is called a "half-cell". The EMF of a half-cell cannot be measured directly, since potentials can be determined only against a reference potential. Consequently, to measure the EMF of a half-cell a reference electrode is required, which must likewise be immersed in the solution. This gives rise to the complete cell

electrode | electrolyte | reference electrode.

By definition, the values are referred to the normal potential E_0 of the hydrogen electrode, which is taken as zero. The "normal hydrogen electrode" is a platinum rod swept by gaseous hydrogen at a pressure of 1 atm* and immersed in a solution in which the active H^+ concentration corresponds to exactly 1 mol/l. With this experimental set up, the normal potential of a given redox reaction can be measured.

Instead of the normal hydrogen electrode, which is difficult to handle, more convenient reference electrodes are used today, appliing corrections for their potential difference to the hydrogen electrode. The Ag/AgCl and calomel electrodes** are customary; their construction is sufficiently well known[1,2]. Furthermore, the measuring and reference electrodes are often combined in a single shaft (single-rod measuring cells).

Membrane potentials

Redox potentials appear due to electron exchange, while membrane potentials arise by a fundamentally different mechanism. A potential difference can be assigned to a difference in activity between two solutions of the same ion that is given by the *Nernst* equation:

$$(6) \qquad E = \frac{R \times T}{F} \times \ln \frac{\alpha_1}{\alpha_2}$$

To measure the potential, the solutions must be separated by a membrane which "responds" to the ion concerned. Individual potentials then arise at the membrane/solution interface, which are recorded by "tapping electrodes" – usually reference electrodes. Altogether the complete cell consists of the following partial potentials:

$$\text{Electrode 1} \mid \text{Solution 1} \mid \text{Membrane} \mid \text{Solution 2} \mid \text{Electrode 2}$$

| Electrode potential 1 | Membrane potential 1 | Membrane potential 2 | Electrode potential 2 |

The longest-known is the glass pH-electrode[3-5] (Fig. 1), consisting of a glass rod with a thin-walled (about 50 µm) bulb of special glass at the lower end of the membrane. This contains an

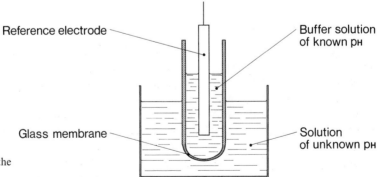

Reference electrode

Buffer solution of known pH

Glass membrane

Solution of unknown pH

Fig. 1. Principle of the glass pH-electrode.

---

* In SI-units: ca. 1×10^5 Pa (Pascals).
** In English-language literature "vs. S.C.E." means "versus Saturated Calomel Electrode".

Ag/AgCl tapping electrode in a buffer solution, usually standard acetate buffer. Before the first use, the glass membrane must be allowed to swell for some time in dilute acid solution, whereby sodium ions are replaced by protons in the outer glass layer:

(7) $-Si-ONa + H_2O \rightleftharpoons -Si-OH + NaOH.$

This results in formation of a substantially protonated swollen layer about 5–100 nm thick, the proton solution pressure of which comes into equilibrium with the H^+ activity.

In analogy with the processes at the metal rod/solution interface (cf. p. 155) a membrane potential arises (Fig. 2). When the electrode is immersed in a solution to be investigated, the potential assumes the value characteristic for its H^+ activity. The potential of the outer swollen layer is opposed by a corresponding one at the inner surface of the membrane; the electrical connection is established by cation (Na^+) conductivity in the glass

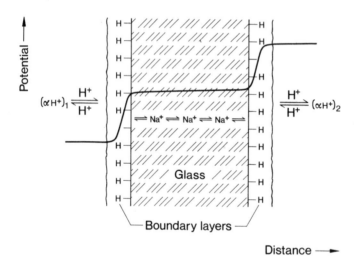

Fig. 2. Build-up of the glass membrane potential.

A good glass electrode shows *Nernst*ian behavior with respect to the H^+ activity up to a pH of about 10. In more alkaline solutions, the protons of the swollen layer are increasingly replaced by alkali-metal ions. Consequently, the proton solution pressure decreases and the electrode gives an artificially low pH (alkaline error). At very low H^+ activities the membrane no longer responds to protons at all, but does manifest *Nernst*ian behavior with respect to alkali-metal ions. This effect can be enhanced still further by addition of Al_2O_3 to the glass of the electrode[4].

A membrane can therefore exhibit *selective* behaviour towards a given ion, depending on its chemical composition, pretreatment, and the experimental conditions. Thus, the F^- activity of a solution can be determined selectively with a lanthanum fluoride membrane. In this way we arrive at *ion-specific electrodes*[6–8], whose preferential response to a given ionic species is expressed by the selectivity constant or cross-sensitivity. A special role is played by Na^+-, K^+-, Ca^{++}-, and NH_4^+-sensitive electrodes.

Applications

Glass pH-electrode

Proton-transfer reactions can be measured by the change in pH. However, it is often advantageous to keep the pH constant by counter-titration and to measure the consumption of acid or base necessary. Here, the glass electrode controls an automatic titrator. Details of this "pH-stat" technique have been described by *Th. Bücher*[9].

Example:

Determination of the catalytic activity of lipase in serum:

(8) $triglyceride + H_2O \xrightarrow{\text{lipase}*} diglyceride + fatty\ acid$.

The substrate is usually olive oil. About 5 ml of the substrate solution is treated with 100 to 500 μl of the lipase-containing sample solution and is automatically titrated with NaOH (10 mmol/l) to maintain pH constancy. A recorder plots the consumption of NaOH versus time. The slope of the curve obtained is a measure of the catalytic activity of the lipase.

Air-gap electrode[11−13]

By means of this interesting application of the glass-pH electrode (Fig. 3), reactions that yield acids or bases can be measured if the product can be driven out of the aqueous phase as a gas.

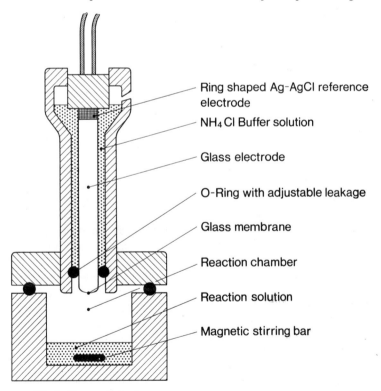

Ring shaped Ag–AgCl reference electrode

NH₄Cl Buffer solution

Glass electrode

O-Ring with adjustable leakage

Glass membrane

Reaction chamber

Reaction solution

Magnetic stirring bar

* EC 3.1.1.3.   Fig. 3. Air-gap electrode.

The advantage of the method is that the sensitive electrode does not come into contact with the reaction solution. The glass electrode is located in the air space of a sealed reaction chamber. The gas expelled comes into contact with the membrane here. The change in pH at the membrane is a measure of the amount of substrate degraded enzymatically. To ensure permanent wetting of the membrane with the electrolyte solution of the Ag/AgCl reference electrode, the shaft of the electrode contains a hydrophilized O-ring seal with a certain leakage rate.

Examples:

1. Enzymatic decarboxylation of amino acids[14]:

(9) $$\text{amino acid} \xrightarrow[\text{decarboxylase*}]{\text{amino acid}} \text{amine} + CO_2$$

(10) $$CO_2 + H_2O \rightleftharpoons HCO_3^- + H^+$$

Incubation at pH 5.2; CO_2 escapes. The pH is measured.

2. Decomposition of urea[12].
   According to the equations

(11) $$\text{urea} + H_2O + OH^- \xrightarrow{\text{urease**}} HCO_3^- + 2\,NH_3$$

(12) $$NH_3 + H_2O \rightleftharpoons NH_4^+ + OH^-$$

a compromise pH where NH_4^+ is sufficiently converted into NH_3 and the catalytic activity of the urease is still great enough cannot exist. Consequently, the determination is performed in two steps (hydrolysis of the urea at pH 7, expulsion of NH_3 by addition of NaOH).

Oxygen-sensitive electrode

There is no metal at whose surface the redox equilibrium according to eqn. (13) becomes established as reversibly and reproducibly as the H_2/H^+ equilibrium at a platinum rod[15] (cf. p. 156, eqn. 4).

(13) $$O_2 + 4H^+ + 4e \rightleftharpoons 2H_2O$$

However, it is possible to reduce oxygen at a platinum or gold surface in accordance with eqn. (13) if this has previously been polarized cathodically. For this purpose an external potential (polarization potential) is applied between it and a reference electrode (Fig. 4). When oxygen reacts at the polarized electrode, electrons are required (depolarization), and to supply them a current must flow. Accordingly, the parameter measured is the current response by which the system attempts to re-establish the initial potential between the polarized electrode and the reference electrode. As of a polarization potential of -0.6 V, this signal is proportional to the partial pressure of oxygen.

In contrast to true potentiometric processes, the O_2-sensitive electrode operates with simultaneous consumption of the substance to be determined – i.e., it operates polarometrically[1] (principle of the polarograph). The signal is stable only if the electrode is always supplied with fresh solution at a minimum flow rate (intensive stirring, or measurement in a flow through system). Because of the pH-dependence of the reaction – cf. eqn. (13) – the measurements are carried out in buffered solutions.

---

  * EC 4.1.1.–.
** EC 3.5.1.5.

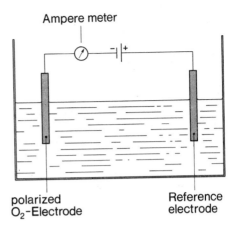

Fig. 4. Determination of oxygen at a polarized electrode.

polarized
O_2-Electrode

Reference
electrode

In 1956, *Clark* proposed an O_2-sensitive electrode in compact form[16,17] which offers protection against the deposition of solution constituents (e.g. proteins) on the polarized metal surface[1,18] (Fig. 5). Here, an oxygen-permeable membrane (Teflon®, polyethylene) separates the gold or platinum cathode and the silver anode from the material to be investigated. In the KCl electrolyte solution, the silver anode acts as an Ag/AgCl reference electrode. The membrane is 10 to 15 µm thick; it has nothing to do with the establishment of the potential.

This electrode has proved particularly valuable in the measurement of oxidase reactions:

(14) $$\text{glucose} + O_2 \xrightarrow{\text{GOD*}} \text{gluconic acid-}\delta\text{-lactone} + H_2O_2$$

(15) $$\text{uric acid} + O_2 + 2H_2O \xrightarrow{\text{urate oxidase**}} \text{allantoin} + H_2O_2$$

(16) $$\text{cholesterol} \xrightarrow[\text{oxidase***}]{\text{cholesterol}} \Delta^4\text{-cholestenone} + H_2O_2$$

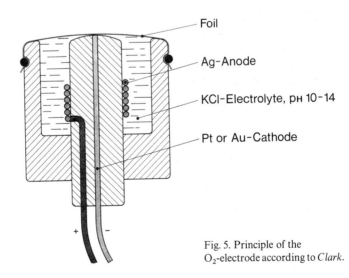

Foil

Ag-Anode

KCl-Electrolyte, pH 10–14

Pt or Au-Cathode

* EC 1.1.3.4.
** EC 1.7.3.3.
*** EC 1.1.3.6.

Fig. 5. Principle of the
O_2-electrode according to *Clark*.

Determination of glucose according to eqn. (14) is investigated most intensively. Earlier measurements determined proportional fractions of the total oxygen consumption in continuous glucose determinations[19]. Later, the kinetic procedure developed by Beckman (cf. p. 79 ff.) was offered in a semiautomatic instrument ("Beckman Glucose Analyzer")[20-22]; with this, uric acid[21,23] (15) and cholesterol[24,25] (16) can also be measured.

In all cases, a ready-made reaction mixture is saturated with atmospheric oxygen by vigorous shaking. After the addition of 10 µl of serum, the oxidation of the substrate begins. As in the BUN-Analyzer, the O_2-sensor reports the partial pressure of oxygen to the computer, which then determines the reaction rate and the initial concentration of the substrate.

The range of linearity extends up to 22 mmol/l (glucose), 1.25 mmol/l (uric acid), and 13 mmol/l (cholesterol)[25]. Sixty samples per hour can be measured.

The use of ion-selective electrodes is particularly interesting in combination with immobilized enzymes. Cf. p. 168 ff.

References

1 Ferris, C. D. (1974) *Introduction to Bioelectrodes*, Plenum Press, New York, London.
2 Ives, D. J. G. & Janz, G. J. (1961) *Reference Electrodes*, Academic Press, New York.
3 Bühler, H. (1975) *GIT-Fachz. Lab.* **19**, 653.
4 Johannesen, B. (1971) *Mitt. Dtsch. Pharmaz. Ges.* **41**, 3.
5 Rechnitz, G. A. (1967) *Chem. Eng. News* **45**, 146.
6 Buck, R. P. (1972) *Anal. Chem.* **44**, 270 R.
7 Buck, R. P. (1976) *Anal. Chem.* **48**, 23 R.
8 Moody, G. J. & Thomas, J. D. R. (1971) *Selective Ion Sensitive Electrodes*. Merrow Publishing Co. Ltd. Watford Herts England.
9 Bücher, Th., Hofner, H. & Rouayrenc, J.-F. (1974) in *Methods of Enzymatic Analysis* (Bergmeyer, H. U., ed.) 2nd edn., p. 254, Verlag Chemie, Weinheim & Academic Press, New York & London.
10 Näher, G. (1974) in *Methods of Enzymatic Analysis* (Bergmeyer, H. U., ed.) 2nd edn., p. 814, Verlag Chemie, Weinheim & Academic Press, New York & London.
11 Růžička, J. & Hansen, E. H. (1974) *Anal. Chim. Acta* **69**, 129.
12 Hansen, E. H. & Růžička, J. (1974) *Anal. Chim. Acta* **72**, 353.
13 Larsen, N. R., Hansen, E. H. & Guilbault, G. G. (1975) *Anal. Chim. Acta* **79**, 9.
14 Hansen, E. H., personal communication.
15 Tödt, F. (1958) *Elektrochemische Sauerstoffmessungen*, Walter de Gruyter, Berlin.
16 Clark, L. C., jr. (1956) *Trans. Am. Soc. Artificial Internal Organs*, **2**, 41.
17 Clark, L. C. jr. (1959) US Patent No. 2913386.
18 Mattson, J. S. & Smith, C. A. (1973) *Science* **181** (4104), 1055.
19 Kadish, A. H. & Hall, D. A. (1965) *Clin. Chem.* **11**, 869.
20 Kadish, A. H., Litle, R. L. & Sternberg, J. C. (1968) *Clin. Chem.* **14**, 116.
21 Alpert, N. L. (1973) *Lab. World* **24**, 40, Instrument Series Report No. 14.
22 Bünemann, C. & Kruse-Jarres, J. D., (1974) *Dt. Ges. f. klin. Chem. Mitteilungen* **2**, 56.
23 Meites, S., Thompson, C. & Roach, R. W. (1974) *Clin. Chem.* **20**, 790.
24 Noma, A. & Nakayama, K. (1976) *Clin. Chem.* **22**, 336.
25 Schuler, P., Hagen, A. & Bergmeyer, H. U., unpublished.

Microcalorimetry

Peter Schuler

Principles

Like most chemical reactions, enzymatic reactions take place at constant pressure. Consequently, the thermodynamics of isobaric changes of state applies to them and their energy conversion is described by the enthalpy of the reaction, ΔH. By this we mean the change in the internal energy ΔU less the work A performed by the system against the constant pressure p, as shown in eqn. (1). This causes an external change of temperature.

(1) $$\Delta H = \Delta U - A = \Delta U + p\Delta V \quad \text{J/mol}$$

By convention, ΔH carries a negative sign for exothermic reactions. Table 1 shows a comparison of reaction enthalpies of enzymatic reactions[1].

Table 1. Molar enthalpy of enzyme catalyzed reactions.

EC number	Trivial name	pH of the reaction	Substrates	$-\Delta$ (J/mol^{-1})	$-\Delta$ (cal/mol^{-1})
1.1.1.27	Lactate dehydrogenase	7.3	Na-pyruvate	$44\,380 \pm 1530$	$10\,600 \pm 365$
3.1.3.2.	Acid phosphatase	4.5	p-Nitrophenyl-phosphate	$26\,290 \pm 420$	$6\,280 \pm 100$
3.2.1.–	Glycoside hydrolases	4.5	Maltose Maltotriose Amylose	$4\,600$ $8\,830$ $4\,310 \pm 63$	$1\,100$ $2\,110$ $1\,030 \pm 15$
3.4.21.1	Chymotrypsin	6.6	Benzoyl-L-tyrosineamide	$24\,450 \pm 920$	$5\,840 \pm 220$
3.4.21.4	Trypsin	6.9	Benzoyl-L-arginineamide	$27\,840 \pm 840$	$6\,650 \pm 200$
3.5.1.1	Asparaginase	7.0	Asparagine	$23\,900 \pm 420$	$5\,710 \pm 100$
3.5.1.5	Urease	7.0	Urea	$6\,570$	$1\,570$

In any enzymatic reaction, therefore, a change in temperature – almost always a rise – is available as a measurable quantity. Consequently, a microcalorimetric detector could be used in all cases. Its combination with the selectivity of the enzyme would give an universal analytical concept.

The temperature changes in the case of enzymatic reactions on analytical scale are of the order of 10^{-2} K to 10^{-4} K. If, for example, the amount of glucose present in 10 µl of a solution with a concentration of 5.5 mmol/l (100 mg/100 ml) reacts with ATP and hexokinase, the enthalpy is about 3.5×10^{-3} J (0.82×10^{-3} cal). This can warm up 1 ml of water (or reaction solution) by about 0.8×10^{-3} °C. Measurement of these small temperature changes against random temperature fluctuations in the reaction solution is the true problem of microcalorimetry. It requires special thermostatting or thermal insulation to keep such fluctuations small in comparison to the measured quantity. This "signal-to-noise" ratio should be better than 100 : 1 for a reliable measurement. The temperature constancy of the solution in the present case would therefore have to be better than $\pm 0.5 \times 10^{-5}$ K. However, this also coincides with the resolution of the most sensitive temperature sensors (thermistors), so that fundamental theoretical limits are set to an improvement of the signal-to-noise ratio[2,3]. It is mainly these difficulties that have prevented routine application of microcalorimetry in enzymatic analysis.

Calorimeters

A distinction is made between adiabatic calorimeters and heat-flow calorimeters[4-8]. The ideal adiabatic calorimeter has perfect thermal insulation from its environment, so that there is no loss of heat. If an enzymatic reaction takes place in it, the reaction enthalpy serves entirely to heat the contents of the calorimeter. When the thermal capacity of these contents and the molar enthalpy of the reaction are known, the amount of substance reacted can be calculated from the rise in temperature.

In the heat-flow calorimeter, the reaction takes place in an ideally conducting chamber surrounded by a heat trap of constant temperature and infinite thermal capacity. The heat produced in the reaction chamber is therefore removed completely to the heat trap, the temperature of which does not change, until temperature equilibration is achieved (Fig. 1).

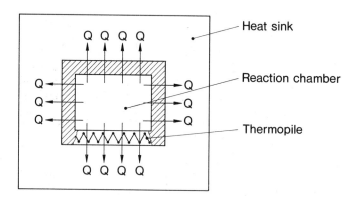

Fig. 1.
Heat-flow calorimeter.

The heat flux is proportional to the temperature difference ΔT.

$$(2) \qquad \frac{dQ}{dt} = k \times \Delta T$$

The apparatus constant k has the dimensions of power per temperature ($J \times s^{-1} \times K^{-1} = W \times K^{-1}$). The total amount of heat transferred until temperature equilibration is given by eqn. (3), in which ΔT has been replaced by the time-dependent function $f(t)$.

$$(3) \qquad Q = k \times \int_{t_1}^{t_2} f(t)\,dt \quad \text{with} \quad f(t) = \Delta T$$

The calorimeters used in practice are more or less close approximations to these two ideal types. The use of immobilized enzymes (cf. p. 168) concentrates the development of heat on a small area and thus results in a higher local temperature rise. This favours spot-like measuring temperature sensors (thermistors, *vide infra*). Moreover, the use of immobilized enzymes – e.g. in granular form in columns – opens up the possibility of measuring in flow-through systems. It is often difficult to classify such flow-through calorimeters as either heat-flow or adiabatic calorimeters. Generally, they come close to the adiabatic concept, because one attempts to utilize the liberated heat as completely as possible for warming a segment of the flowing fluid and to lead it to the temperature sensor (adiabatic column).

The selection of the suitable type of calorimeter has been discussed by *Schmidt* et al.[9] in connection with the determination of urea, lactate, and glucose. Due to their higher accuracy but longer measurement times heat-flow calorimeters are better suited to the exact determination of reaction enthalpies (cf. *Wadsö*[10] and literature cited there).

Temperature sensors

Thermistors and thermopiles are used for the temperature measurement[2,9]. Thermistors are temperature-sensitive resistors made from sintered ceramic semiconductors. They consist of a sintered mixture of metal oxides (Fe, Co, Ni) encapsulated in glass or plastic. Their temperature coefficient α is always negative and is of the order of 4% per K.

$$(4) \qquad \alpha = \frac{R_2 - R_1}{T_2 - T_1} \times \frac{1}{R_1} \quad K^{-1}$$

The parameter measured is therefore the voltage drop at the thermistor, which changes with the temperature. The Joule heat produced by the current must be smaller than the heat to be measured by the factor of the signal-to-noise ratio. Consequently, the thermistor is supplied with an appropriately low DC constant current, and the voltage drop is recorded via a DC amplifier. The Wheatstone bridge circuits used previously[2,9] do, indeed, allow a powerless measurement after the null adjustment, but up to that point they frequently cause unacceptable errors due to Joule heat.

Due to their sensitivity and high resolution (down to about 10^{-5} K), thermistors are most suitable for microcalorimetric measurements. They are often used in adiabatic calorimeters.

Thermopiles are thermocouples connected in series. They work on the basis of the *Seebeck-Peltier* effect, according to which a temperature-dependent contact potential arises at the surface of contact of two different metals. In far-reaching analogy to potentiometry (p. 155), this is a substance-specific EMF, the value of which again can be measured only in relation to a reference potential. For this purpose the potential of a junction of the same pair of metals brought to a

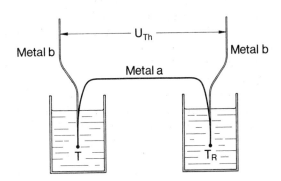

Fig. 2. Principle of the thermocouple.

reference temperature T_R (usually 273.15 K $\triangleq$ 0°C) is used (Fig. 2). By convention, lead is used as the reference metal to locate a metal in the "thermoelectric potential series". The temperature dependence of the thermoelectric EMF, U_{Th}, is linear over a wide range, the proportionality factor η according to eqn. (5) is called the thermoforce.

(5) $$U_{Th} = \eta \times (T - T_R) \quad V$$

Typical values of η are 3 μV/K (iron-lead) up to 120 μV/k (iron-constantan).

To construct thermopiles, short pieces of the two metals are soldered to one another in alternation. The soldered junctions must alternately be brought to the unknown and to the reference temperature. Consequently, the use of thermophiles is suitable in heat-flow calorimeters, since they can be incorporated in zigzag fashion in the heat-exchange layer (Fig. 1, p. 164). The temperature of the heat trap is then the reference temperature.

Applications

In contrast to conductometry (cf. p. 152), secondary reactions always cause an increase in signal yield in calorimetry. Often, the primary reaction produces protons which are then trapped by the buffer with evolution of heat. Tris buffer is used in such cases, because its heat of protonation is about 10 times as large ($\Delta H = -47.5$ kJ/mol) as that of phosphate buffer ($\Delta H = -4.74$ kJ mol)[12] for example. About two thirds of the total reaction enthalpy of the enzymatic phosphorylation of glucose by hexokinase* (HK) and ATP in tris-buffer is due to the protonation step (cf. eqns. (6) and (7)). Accordingly, the enthalpy of this reaction is strongly pH-dependent. *Goldberg* et al.[13-16] used a heat-flow calorimeter, and *McGlothlin* and *Jordan*[17] an adiabatic calorimeter to measure these enthalpies with dissolved HK. These authors found identical values after correction for different experimental conditions[14].

(6)   glucose + ATP $\xrightarrow{\text{HK}}$ glucose-6-phosphate + ADP + H$^+$

$$\Delta H = -27.6 \pm 4 \text{ kJ/mol}$$

(7)   Tris + H$^+$ $\longrightarrow$ Tris-H$^+$

$$\Delta H = -47.3 \text{ kJ/mol}$$

According to[17], in tris-buffer of 0.5 mol/l at pH 8.0 and 25°C:

$$\Sigma\Delta H = -74.9 \pm 1.5 \text{ kJ/mol}$$

The authors report satisfactory determination of glucose in serum with their particular apparatus. The sample volumes were 150 μl in[15] and 500 μl in[17,18], and a typical regression analysis[15] (reference: GOD-method, on AutoAnalyzer®) yielded the values of $a = -0.042$ mmol/l (-0.76 mg/ 100 ml) and $b = 1.06$ for the equation $y = a + bx$ (cf. p. 231). The linear range extended to about 22 mmol/l (400 mg/100 ml)[15] or 55 mmol/l (1000 mg/100 ml)[17], response time was 7 min[15] and 2 min[17,18] respectively.

Hexokinase is a nonspecific enzyme and acts on all hexoses. In another paper, *Goldberg* has described a correction technique for the determination of the true glucose content[19].

Subsequent reactions can also be induced artificially by enzyme coupling. For example, co-im-

---

* EC 2.7.1.1.

mobilization of catalase more than doubles the reaction enthalpy of the oxidation of glucose by glucose oxidase[9]:

(8)
$$\text{glucose} + O_2 \xrightarrow{\text{GOD*}} \text{gluconic acid-}\delta\text{-lacton} + H_2O_2$$
$$\Delta H = -83.7 \text{ kJ/mol}$$

(9)
$$H_2O_2 \xrightarrow{\text{catalase**}} H_2 + 1/2 O_2$$
$$\Delta H = -125 \text{ kJ/mol}$$
$$\Sigma \Delta H = -208.7 \text{ kJ/mol}$$

The catalase reaction also serves to re-supply oxygen for the primary reaction and thus prevents a soon loss of linearity due to lack of oxygen.

The technical specifications of an instrument employing an adiabatic column for the determination of urea have been described by *Canning* and *Carr*[20] (cf. also p. 172). Using a two-step thermostatting system, a temperature constancy of $\pm 3 \times 10^{-4}$ K was achieved. For 100-µl samples, the sensitivity of the system is ca. $3 \text{ K} \cdot \text{mol}^{-1} \cdot \text{l}$, so that a signal-to-noise ratio of $17:1$ to $83:1$ is obtained over the normal range from 1.7 mmol/l to 8.3 mmol/l (10 mg/100 ml to 50 mg/100 ml). Since only elevated urea values are of diagnostic significance, the required ratio of $100:1$ is very nearly reached in the critical concentration range in this case – though at a relatively high sample volume.

References

1 Brown, H.D. (1969) in *Biochemical Microcalorimetry* (Brown, H.D., ed.) p.149, Academic Press, New York, London
2 Praglin, J. (1969) in *Biochemical Microcalorimetry* (Brown, H.D., ed.) p.199, Academic Press, New York, London
3 Berger, R.L., Friauf, W.S. & Cascio, H.E. (1974) *Clin. Chem.* **20**, 1009.
4 Skinner, H.A. (1969) in *Biochemical Microcalorimetry* (Brown, H.D., ed.) p.1, Academic Press, New York, London.
5 Goldberg, R.N. & Armstrong, G.T. (1974) *Med. Instrum.* **8**, 30.
6 Prosen, E.J. & Goldberg, R.N. (1973) *NBS Report No. 73–180*, Washington, DC, National Bureau of Standards.
7 Ackermann, T. (1969) in *Biochemical Microcalorimetry* (Brown, H.D., ed.) p.235, Academic Press, New York, London.
8 Evans, W.J. (1969) in *Biochemical Microcalorimetry* (Brown, H.D., ed.) p.257, Academic Press, New York, London.
9 Schmidt, H.-L., Krisam, G. & Grenner, G. (1976) *Biochim. Biophys. Acta* **429**, 283.
10 Wadsö, I. (1976) *Biochem. Soc. Trans.* **4**, 561.
11 Pennington, S.N. & Brown, H.D. (1969) in *Biochemical Microcalorimetry* (Brown, H.D., ed.) p.207, Academic Press, New York, London.
12 Johansson, A., Lundberg, J., Mattiasson, B. & Mosbach, K. (1973) *Biochim. Biophys. Acta* **304**, 217.
13 Goldberg, R.N., Prosen, E.J., Staples, B.R., Boyd, R.N. & Armstrong, G.T. (1973) *NBS Report No. 73–178*, Washington, DC, National Bureau of Standards.
14 Goldberg, R.N. (1975) *Biophys. Chem.* **3**, 192.
15 Goldberg, R.N., Prosen, E.J., Staples, B.R., Boyd, R.N., Armstrong, G.T., Berger, R.L. & Young, D.S. (1975) *Anal. Biochem.* **64**, 68.
16 Prosen, E.J., Goldberg, R.N., Staples, B.R., Boyd, R.N. & Armstrong, G.T. (1975) in *Thermoanalytical Investigations by New Techniques* (Kambe, H. & Garn, P.D., eds.) J.Wiley & Sons, Inc., New York and Kodansha Scientific Ltd., Tokio.
17 McGlothlin, C.D., Jordan, J. (1975) *Anal. Chem.* **47**, 786.
18 McGlothlin, C.D., Jordan, J. (1975) *Clin. Chem.* **21**, 741.
19 Goldberg, R.N. (1976) *Clin. Chem.* **22**, 1685.
20 Canning, L.M. & Carr, P.W. (1975) *Anal. Letters* **8**, 359.

---

* EC 1.1.3.4.
** EC 1.11.1.6.

Measurement Techniques with Immobilized Enzymes

Peter Schuler and Hans Ulrich Bergmeyer

The applications of all the measurement techniques described so far, with their fundamentally different detectors, have been decisively affected by the advances in the development of immobilized enzymes. In enzymatic analysis, the enzyme is regarded as a reagent, and far too little attention is paid to its original significance as a catalyst.

Principles

A definite mass of enzyme with a definite catalytic activity can, according to the definition, catalyze an indefinitely large number of substrate reactions. However, the catalytic activity of *dissolved* enzymes is not completely utilized, since after the transformation of the substrate has taken place the enzyme is discarded. On the other hand, enzymes immobilized to insoluble supports continue to act catalytically until they are destroyed mechanically or chemically. Such immobilized enzymes are used for enzymatic steps of syntheses and in enzymatic analysis.

The immobilized enzyme

Enzymes immobilized to insoluble carriers should be compared with the insoluble structure-bound enzymes of the living cell (cytochrome oxidase, adenylate kinase, etc.). Such immobilized enzymes can be used in the same way as inorganic catalysts.

In principle, almost any enzyme can be bound to a carrier by covalent or heteropolar bonding or by adsorption, polymerized into plastics, cross-linked with low-molecular-weight bifunctional reagents, or incorporated into membranes (for reviews, see[1,2]). While for adsorptive and ionic bonds a wide variety of carrier materials are used, the following natural and synthetic polymers (which must be activated to bind the protein) have mainly come into use for covalent bonding: polysaccharides, polyacrylamide, nylon, and porous glass. The enzyme-loaded material is either converted to a granular form, or left in the form of rigid pieces, threads, or membranes.

Enzymes incorporated into gels, microcapsules, or threads have not yet gained acceptance, although they have high catalytic activity due to the presence of the unchanged enzyme protein. Enzymes locked into gel matrices or membranes can transform substrates of high molecular weight only to a limited extent because of diffusion problems. Enzymes bound in heteropolar fashion or by absorption are eluted from the matrix above certain ionic strengths and therefore can be used to only a limited extent. So far, enzymes immobilized to polyacrylamide, nylon, and glass have gained acceptance.

Use of immobilized enzymes

In enzymatic analysis, enzyme-loaded granules (as column fillers), nylon tubing with an enzymatically active inside wall[3,4] and gel membranes containing polymer-bound enzyme are used. As early as 1966, *Hicks* and *Updike*[5,6] used enzyme-loaded granules in columns, and in 1967 they used an oxygen-sensitive electrode whose surface was coated with a gel containing glucose oxidase.

The detectors are mainly those of potentiometry, polarography, and microcalorimetry (a review has been given by *Bowers* and *Carr*[7]). There is a very good reason for this. The choice of a detector depends on the reaction to be measured. For example, photocells will not be used if the primary reaction can be measured optically only via auxiliary and indicator reactions. Although in such cases the coenzymes can be regenerated with additional carrier-bound enzymes and substrates[8-10], photometry is generally avoided. Relatively expensive auxiliary and indicator enzymes as well as the systems for regenerating the coenzymes are thus spared. The remaining essential reactants are inexpensive, and it is quite permissible to discard them.

Applications

The combination of immobilized enzymes with detectors based on potentiometric, polarographic, and microcalorimetric principles of measurement may be of many types. Technical difficulties (gumming-up of the enzyme surface by sample constituents, long reaction times due to diffusion in the case of enzymatically active membranes, reduced catalytic activity due to bonding of the enzyme to the carrier, etc.) have so far been only partially overcome. Consequently, today, by no means all of the possibilities of using immobilized enzymes have been exhausted.

Immobilized enzymes as granular column fillers

Enzyme-loaded granules are most frequently used in the form of a reactor for flow-through measurements (Fig. 1). Closed and open systems are used.

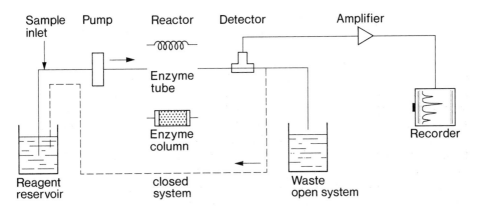

Fig. 1. Open and closed flow-through system.

Closed systems

In 1971, a principle of measurement was described[11-15] which contains a reactor (enzyme cartridge) in a closed recycling system with a measuring cell and a reservoir for the buffer solution. The sample (10 µl) is introduced as a plug of liquid by an automatically metering sample applicator and is measured at a detector (Fig. 2).

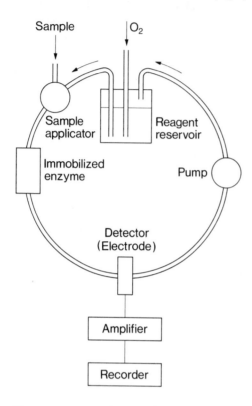

Fig. 2. Closed system for the determination of glucose with immobilized enzyme.

For oxygen-consuming reactions catalyzed by immobilized oxidases, an O_2-sensitive electrode is used as the detector.

The oxygen concentration of the buffer, when saturated with air, corresponds to a constant electrode potential (baseline). As the substrate is degraded in the column, consumption of oxygen leads to a break in the baseline so that a peak is recorded. The peak height is a measure of the substrate content of the sample.

The operating costs are extremely low. More than 10,000 determinations can be performed with 1 liter of buffer solution and one filling of the enzyme column.

Flow-through systems with sufficiently fast-responding electrodes and small tube diameters permit very short measurement times when dead volumes are avoided[16]. Figure 3 shows that the measured value (peak height) is available after about 20 s. The relaxation time of the system from the beginning of the potential jump to restoration of the O_2-saturation potential depends on the glucose concentration, but is less than 30 s in any case. Thus, a sample frequency up to 120/h can be achieved. Part of a series measurement with 60 samples/h is shown in Fig. 4, p. 171.

This procedure is limited in practice[17] mainly to methods using an O_2-sensitive electrode, i.e. to reactions that consume oxygen (e.g. determination of glucose with glucose oxidase, of cholesterol with cholesterol oxidase, or uric acid with urate oxidase, of amino acids with the ap-

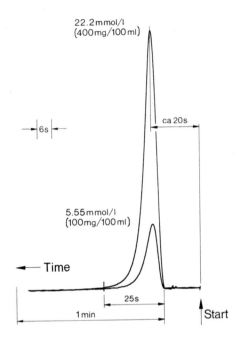

Fig. 3. Closed system. Relaxation time
at different glucose concentrations.

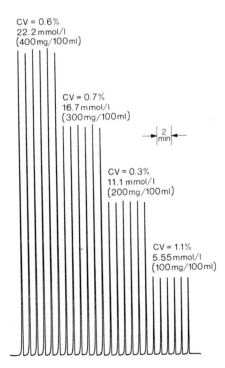

Fig. 4. Closed system. Measurement in series,
sample frequency of 60/h.

propriate oxidases, or of galactose with galactose oxidase, etc.). The linear range of measurement is sufficient for the determination of glucose, cholesterol, and uric acid in clinical chemistry[16]. The system has the advantage of high sample turnover and rapidity of individual determinations. It can be used day and night, and – due to the recycling process – consumes no reagents during operation pauses.

The life times of the buffer and the reactor are limited by the amounts of protein or particulate matter introduced with the samples. The enzyme-loaded granular filler finally becomes gummed up and the column becomes blocked. Enzymatically active tubes (see p. 173) instead of columns filled with enzyme-loaded granules may be advantageous.

In the case of photometric measurements in the closed system, accumulation of light-absorbing sample constituents leads to a continuously rising baseline of the recorded values. Consequently, photocells can be used as detectors only to a limited extent.

Open systems

In 1974, an open flow-through system with glucose oxidase fixed to glass and an O_2-sensitive electrode was described for the determination of glucose[18].

In 1975, *Carr* et al.[19] proposed an open microcalorimetric flow-through system for the determination of urea with immobilized urease. It corresponds essentially to Fig. 1. In a manner comparable with that of the closed system, the sample (120 µl) is passed through a column filled with immobilized enzyme which has a thermistor at each end. The thermistor at the inlet to the column provides the reference signal. When the heated solution passes the thermistor at the column outlet, the peak appears on the recording. Here again the peak height correlates with the urea concentration with sufficient accuracy.

The relaxation time of the system is 2 min and the maximum sample frequency is therefore 30/h. The flow rate is 1 ml/60 sec. The urea is degraded completely; phosphate buffer (0.5 mol/l, pH 7.4). The linear range of measurement ends at 25 mmol/l; with control serum, the coefficient of variation $CV = 0.5\%$. In comparison with the urease-indophenol method, values of $a = 0.994$ and $b = 0.06$ mmol/l have been obtained for the regression line $y = ax + b$, with a correlation coefficient $r = 0.990$. For explanations of the parameters of measurement and a discussion of the type of calorimeter, see p. 164.

In 1976, *Bowers* and *Carr*[20] reported a microcalorimetric determination of glucose in a flow-through system with immobilized hexokinase.

Using immobilized trypsin, *Mosbach* et al.[21,22] have succeeded in measuring the cleavage of benzoyl-L-arginine ethyl ester microcalorimetrically. Since hydrolyses of esters are practically free of enthalpy, the reaction was performed in tris-buffer, which traps the proton of the carboxylic acid formed with a pronounced evolution of heat (see p. 174).

Immobilized enzymes on rigid, shaped surfaces

In principle, there are no limits to the use of enzymes immobilized to solid surfaces. The advantage of this form of carrier-bound enzymes is that the diffusion difficulties that arise in the case of membranes disappear.

Thus, for the determination of urea in the air-gap electrode (see p. 159) *Guilbault* used urease gel fixed by nylon netting either to the bottom of the measuring chamber[23] or to the magnetic stirrer[24].

In the meantime, extensive use has been made of the possibility of fixing proteins – even enzymatically "inert" proteins – to the inside walls of plastic test tubes and centrifuge tubes (radioimmunoassay, p. 202, and ELISA-methods, p. 94, for the determination of insulin, insulin antibodies, digoxin, etc.). However, the fixing of enzymes to simple plastic apparatus such as test tubes, cuvettes, stirrers, mixing spatulas ("Plümper", see p. 124), as illustrated for the case of the "active" magnetic stirrer, has not so far been followed up further. Only enzyme-lined tubing has been the subject of further consideration.

"Enzyme" tubing with an enzymatically active internal surface can serve advantageously as a reaction pathway when the sample contains solid constituents, e.g. blood particles or a large amount of protein, which would block up or gum up enzyme-loaded granular column fillers. To determine glucose, uric acid, urea, and aspartic acid, tubing lined with the corresponding enzymes is connected directly to an AutoAnalyzer® system running according to the conventional flow-scheme[25].

Immobilized enzymes in membranes

The problem of using catalytically active membranes is the diffusion-dependent transport of substrate through the membrane to the sensor surface or, conversely, of reaction products through the membrane from the sensor surface (cf.[7, 26]). Apart from scientific investigations, immobilized enzymes in membranes are today used almost exclusively in the form of "enzyme electrodes".

Enzyme electrodes

These are ion-sensitive electrodes (cf. p. 158) whose surface has been coated with a thin layer of enzyme. Various proven techniques are available for their production (cf.[7, 27]). In the simplest case, the enzyme is made into a paste with a small amount of water and this is spread out on the electrode and covered with a piece of dialysis membrane. Nowadays use is made of enzymes polymerized into a matrix, generally polyacrylamide gel, with which the electrode surface is coated.

Enzyme electrodes are used for the determination of such substances as glucose, uric acid, urea, lactate, amino acids, and alcohol. Fig. 5 shows the systematic construction of the first GOD-electrode for the measurement of glucose concentrations.

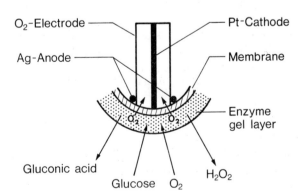

Fig. 5. Enzyme electrode for the determination of glucose according to *Updike* and *Hicks*.

An H_2O_2-sensitive electrode developed by *Clark*[28] has also come into use for the determination of glucose in a semiautomatic device (Yellow Springs Company)[29]. The electrode is coated with a membrane containing immobilized glucose oxidase. It has a useful life of about one week.

The urease electrode for the determination of urea is based largely on investigations by *Guilbault*[29]. The first trials[30.31] with an NH_4^+-sensitive glass electrode and a urease-polyacrylamide gel were unsatisfactory because of the cross-sensitivity of the electrode with respect to sodium and potassium. The principle was decisively improved by the use of the substantially more selective nonactin electrode[32, 33].

Enzyme thermistors

Thermistors coated with an enzyme gel can in principle also be used for the measurement of enzymatic reactions. A particularly simple arrangement[26] consists of two thermistors coated with an enzyme gel and immersed in a buffer solution at constant temperature. The gel layer of one electrode contains the active enzyme, and that of the other contains inactivated enzyme. The latter provides the reference signal. If the substrate of the immobilized enzyme is added to the solution, it is converted in the gel layer; the rise in temperature due to the enthalpy of the reaction (cf. p. 163) is the output signal.

Experiments have been carried out with immobilized glucose oxidase and hexokinase. They confirm a model calculation according to which the reaction enthalpy liberated in unit time depends linearly on the substrate (glucose) concentration.

References

1 Zaborsky, O. (1973) *Immobilized Enzymes*, CRC Press (a Division of the Chemical Rubber Co.), Ohio, Cleveland.
2 Nelböck, M. & Jaworek, D. (1975) *Chimia* **29**, 109.
3 Campbell, J., Hornby, W.E. & Morris, D.L. (1975) *Biochim. Biophys. Acta* **384**, 307.
4 Hornby, W.E. & Morris, D.L. (1975) in *Enzymology* (Weetall, H.H., ed.) Vol. 1, p.141, Marcel Dekker, New York.
5 Hicks, G.P. & Updike, S.J. (1966) *Analyt. Chem.* **38**, 726.
6 Updike, S.J. & Hicks, G.P. (1967) *Nature* **214**, 986.
7 Bowers, L.D. & Carr, P.W. (1976) *Anal. Chem.* **48**, 544 A.
8 Klose, S. & Hagen, A. (1975) DT-OS 2 526 558.
9 Fresenius, R.E., Woenne, K.-G. & Flemming, W. (1974) *Z. Anal. Chem.* **271**, 194.
10 Fresenius, R.E. & Woenne, K.-G. (1976) *Mitteilungen der GDCh Fachgruppe „Lebensmittelchemie"* **30**, 67.
11 Bergmeyer, H.U. (1971) *Atti del III Semposio Nazionali Sui Mettodi Enzimatici nella Diagnostica Clinica, Conegliano Veneto.* 26–28 Novembre 1971, Quod. Sclavo Diagn. **8**, 27.
12 Bergmeyer, H.U. & Hagen, A. (1972) *Z. Anal. Chem.* **261**, 333.
13 Hagen, A., Bergmeyer, H.U., Gruber, W. & Jaworek, D. (1975) DPB 2 130 340.
14 Hagen, A., Bergmeyer, H.U., Gruber, W., Beaucamp, K. & Jaworek, D. (1975) DPB 2 130 308.
15 Hagen, A., Gruber, W., Mewes, D. & Bergmeyer, H.U. (1975) DPB 2 130 287.
16 Schuler, P., Edelmann, H., Hagen, A. & Bergmeyer, H.U., unpublished.
17 Hoehne, W.E., Heitmann, P., Flemming, Ch. & Reichert, A. (1976) *Z. med. Labortechnik* **17**, 79.
18 Kunz, H.J. & Stastny, M. (1974) *Clin. Chem.* **20**, 1018.
19 Bowers, L.D., Canning, L.M., Sayers, C.N. & Carr, P.W. (1976) *Clin. Chem.* **22**, 1314.
20 Bowers, L.D. & Carr, P.W. (1976) *Clin. Chem.* **22**, 1427.
21 Johansson, A., Lundberg, J., Mattiasson, B. & Mosbach, K. (1973) *Biochim. Biophys. Acta* **304**, 217.
22 Mosbach, K. & Danielsson, B. (1974) *Biochim. Biophys. Acta* **364**, 140.
23 Guilbault, G.G. & Tarp, M. (1974) *Anal. Chim. Acta* **73**, 355.
24 Guilbault, G.G. & Stokbro, W. (1975) *Anal. Chim. Acta* **76**, 237.

25 Hornby, W. E. (1974) in *Insolubilized Enzymes* (Salmona, M., Saronio, C. & Garattini, S., eds.) Raven Press New York.
26 Weaver, J. C., Cooney, C. L., Fulton, S. P., Schuler, P. & Tannenbaum, S. R. (1976) *Biochim. Biophys. Acta*, **452**, 285.
27 Guilbault, G. G. (1975) in *Enzymology* (Wetall, H. H., ed.) Vol. 1, p. 293, Marcel Dekker, New York.
28 Clark, L. C. (1970) U. S. Patent 3 539 455.
29 Spencer, W. W., Sylvester, D. & Nelson, G. H. (1976) unpublished.
30 Guilbault, G. G. & Montalvo, J. G. (1969) *J. Am. Chem. Soc.* **91**, 2164.
31 Guilbault, G. G. & Montalvo, J. G. (1970) *J. Am. Chem. Soc.* **92**, 2533.
32 Guilbault, G. G. & Nagy, G. (1973) *Anal. Chim. Acta* **45**, 417.
33 Guilbault, G. G., Nagy, G. & Kuan, S. S. (1973) *Anal. Chim. Acta* **67**, 195.

The Automation of Analysis

Heinrich Netheler and Joachim Ziegenhorn

Automatic instruments are devices in which a given working process is carried out by self-acting control or in accordance with a program and therefore substantially independently of human intervention. Such devices can always be used economically when certain procedures have to be repeated frequently. In enzymatic analysis, they have thus far been used to the greatest extent in clinical chemistry laboratories, where large numbers of samples have to be analyzed in the same manner. This also applies to biochemical research procedures that require many identical working steps.

The first automatic device for the clinical chemistry laboratory was described in 1957 by *Skeggs*,[1] and was marketed by Technicon Instruments Corp. as the AutoAnalyzer®. This instrument was first used for the determination of substance concentrations with the aid of non-enzymatic methods of analysis. The technique of enzymatic analysis and its automation received its first impetus in the 1960's after the advantages of this process with regard to specificity and practicability had become recognized. At that time, in addition to the enzymatic determination of substance concentrations, the determination of activity concentrations of enzymes was becoming of increasing importance for diagnosis. This gave rise to the development of special systems for the measurement of the catalytic activity of enzymes (Eppendorf analyzers[2]). Today there is an increasing trend toward the design of automatic devices for enzymatic analysis that permit determination of both substance concentrations and activity concentrations of enzymes.

A new impulse towards the automation of enzymatic analyses came with the development of the GeMSAEC Fast Analyzer by *Anderson*[3] (see p. 193).

The development of automatic analyzers from analyzing machines to completely automatic devices is closely linked with the advances in the field of electronic control techniques and data processing. This development has been accelerated, above all, by miniaturization and the reduction in the cost of electronic components. Combinations of analyzers and computers were first used in the USA, and later also in Europe[4-9].Today the computer is an indispensable instrument for the automation of enzymatic analysis.

Automatic Devices for Enzymatic Analysis

The necessary means for the automation of enzymatic analysis can be subdivided into devices for:
- sample preparation and identification
- dispensing of samples and reagents, and mixing
- incubation and transport of reaction mixtures
- photometry
- process control and monitoring
- evaluation and documentation of the measured values.

Correct cooperation of all these devices is a basic problem in the design of automation. Various techniques have been developed for laboratory practice.

Partial mechanization as a transition from manual techniques to automatic devices

The mechanization of certain analytical steps is of practical importance as an intermediate stage in the transition from manual to automatic techniques. This relates to those analytical steps whose mechanization can be carried out with comparatively little effort and expense.

A characteristic feature for the partial mechanization of enzymatic analysis is the batchwise treatment of the samples to be measured. For this purpose the working area generally comprises

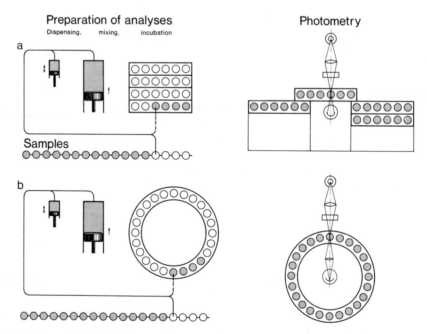

Fig. 1. Partially mechanized technique with groups of samples transferred manually from the preparation station to the measurement station. a) linear vessel transport, b) circular vessel transport.

a preparation station and a measurement station. Two or more racks, each of which takes one group of reaction mixtures are used. The cells in such a rack are filled with measured amounts of sample and reagent in the preparation station and are then transferred to the photometer for photometry. While one group of samples is being prepared for measurement at the preparation station, the second group is being measured (Fig. 1, p. 176). Sample/reagent dispensing and photometry are thus largely mechanized. Only the transfer of the reaction mixtures to be analyzed from the preparation station to the measuring station is done manually.

Given the multiplicity of enzymatic analyses, we always find different stages of mechanization side by side in a clinical chemistry laboratory. The economically acceptable degree of automation depends here on the number of analyses to be performed[10]. Rare operations are performed manually or are partially mechanized, while fully automatic devices are used for the analyses performed most frequently.

Automated Systems

In view of the multiplicity of the types of apparatus[11] on the market at present, only a few examples typical for the various techniques can be described below: the automatic analyzers of the Eppendorf, GeMSAEC, and ACA types, which use discrete vessels for each the reaction mixtures and the automatic instruments working on a continuous-flow basis, i.e. of the AutoAnalyzer® type.

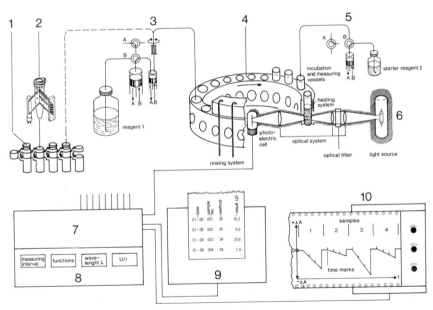

Fig. 2. Design of an automatic analyzer with discrete reaction vessels and dispensing of reagent from a liquid stock (Enzymautomat, Eppendorf Gerätebau). 1) Sample chain, 2) sample identification, 3) sample transfer and addition of reagents, 4) incubation and measuring turntable, 5) addition of starting reagent and mixing, 6) photometric measurement, 7) programmer, calculator, power supply, 8) control panel, 9) digital printer, 10) analog recorder.

Automatic analyzers of the Eppendorf type

At the suggestion of *Eggstein*, the technique shown in Fig. 2, p.177 for the determination of the catalytic activity of enzymes was developed by the firm of Eppendorf Gerätebau[2].

The samples to be measured are lined up in a chain. After recording by a reading device, the samples pass to the sampling position. Here, by means of a pump, a predetermined amount of the sample is removed quantitatively from the sample container and transferred together with the reagent to a reaction vessel on the incubation turntable. The incubation turntable is thermostatted with great precision, so that the sample in the reaction vessel assumes the working temperature. It is moved stepwise at a fixed cycle. The throughput of samples per hour is proportional to the working cycle. In order to make pre-incubation possible (temperature equilibration, expiration of interfering reactions), a starting reagent can be admixed to the sample. After photometrie measurement of the reaction mixtures the reaction vessels are washed or replaced.

The calculator determines the result of the measurement, referring either to a standard or to a molar absorption coefficient ("absolute measurement") (cf. p. 189). The orders necessary for the performance of a given method of analysis can be given via the calculator console. The results are documented by means of a printer. Connection to an electronic data-processing unit is possible. To check the results of the measurements, use is frequently made of a recorder that provides an analog display of the kinetics.

The above-described automation technique is used with more or less extensive modifications in many other automatic analyzers. These include the systems ABA-100® (Abbott Laboratories); AKES II (Vitatron Scientific); Autolab (Linson Instrument); C4, C4B, KA-150 (Perkin-Elmer); GSA II (Greiner Electronic); Hycel M® (Hycel); Kem-0-Lab®, Kem-0-Mat® (Coulter Scientific); Monomat®, SysteMatik (Braun Melsungen); TR (Beckman® Instruments); Ultrolab® (LKB); 3500 (Gilford® Instruments), and 5031, 5032 (Eppendorf Gerätebau).

Automatic analyzers of the GeMSAEC type

A survey of the operating technique of these automatic analyzers, which are on the market under the names of CentrifiChem® (Union Carbide), GEMSAEC Fast Analyzer, GEMENI® (Electro-Nucleonics), and Rotochem® II (American Instrument Company) is given on pp. 193–201.

Automatic analyzers of the ACA type

The automatic analyzers of the ACA type (Du Pont) are charaterized by the fact that they work with pre-measured quantities of reagents in plastic foil packs[12] (Fig. 3a). One pack is required for each analysis, and this serves both as an incubation chamber for the reaction mixture and as the photometric cell. The pack is designed with a high capacity for adaptation to the requirements

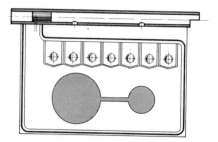

Fig. 3a. Test pack for the ACA analyzer (Du Pont).

of the various methods of analysis. It contains several compartments for the reagents. The pack header can, if required, include separating columns of various types, by means of which interfering substances can be eliminated prior to analysis. The individual packs bear a code that calls the required measurement program in the automatic analyzer.

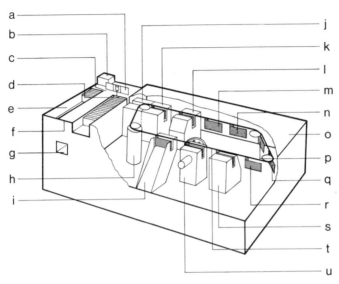

Fig. 3b. ACA analyzer (schematic). a) filling station, b) shuttle drive, c) patient's I.D. + printer, d) input tray for sample cups and analytical test packs, e) sample cups exit tray, f) printer, g) patient's report sheet exit tray, h) transport motor, i) expended pack remover, j) preheater 1, k) preheater 2, l) breaker-mixer 1, m) delay station 1, n) delay station 2, o) air heater with blower, p) delay station 3, q) delay station 4, r) delay station 5, s) breaker-mixer 2, t) transport chain, u) photometer.

The technique used in the ACA automatic devices is shown schematically in Fig. 3b. At the beginning of the analytical procedure, the machine injects an aliquot of the sample together with a predetermined amount of solvent into the pack. After warming up, the pack moves to an opening and mixing station where the compartments are opened by pressure and their contents thoroughly mixed with the solvent and the sample. Subsequently, the reaction mixture is allowed a certain period for temperature equilibration. If necessary, further reagents can be admixed to the reaction solution by opening the corresponding compartments. Finally, the automatic analyzer molds an optical cell from the transparent walls of the pack and measures the absorbance of the reaction mixture. The apparatus is calibrated by means of standard solutions or calibration sera. A computer evaluates the results of the measurements.

In addition to the ACA system, the semiautomatic CLINICARD Analyzer 368 (Instrumentation Laboratory), which works by a related technique, is used.

Automatic devices of the AutoAnalyzer® type

Automatic devices of the AutoAnalyzer® type (Technicon) work on the principle of *continuousflow* analysis[1,13]. An aliquot of the sample is fed into a continuously flowing stream of the reagent segmented by air bubbles (Fig. 4, p. 181). The reaction mixture is passed through mixing coils and the coils of a heating bath where the reaction takes place. A flow-through photometer then measures the change in absorbance. The measurement signals are evaluated by a calculator and displayed by a recorder. Any turbidity introduced by the sample can be eliminated by dialysis of the reaction mixture.

A characteristic feature of this system is that the measurement takes place in *steady state*[13]. Such a state exists when the concentration of the substance being measured in the flow-through cuvette of the photometer does not change with time. Under these conditions it is not necessary for the reaction to attain equilibrium.

It is a basic operating principle that *continuous-flow* systems must be calibrated with standard solutions or calibration sera; absolute measurements using a molar absorption coefficient cannot be performed with such apparatus. This is due, on the one hand, to the principle of *steady-state* measurement, and, on the other hand, to the sample/reagent-dispensing technique which, although it works reproducibly, does not yield defined volumes (cf. p. 185).

Automatic devices of the AutoAnalyzer® type are being used in several variations at present: AutoAnalyzer® I (single-channel apparatus), AutoAnalyzer® II (two-channel apparatus), and SMA® and SMAC® systems (multichannel apparatus).

Automatic analyzers for a spectrum of substances (multicomponent analysis)

Normally, several different activity or substance concentrations need to be determined in one sample. This problem offers a broad field of application for automated techniques.

Automatic analyzers of the ACA type (cf. p. 178) can in each case perform the desired analysis program serially on one sample. For this purpose, an analytical program is set up by assigning various reagent packs to the sample in accordance with the analytical problem. A characteristic feature is the high flexibility when the number of samples is not too large (e.g. night service, emergency service). At the present time, the costs of packaged reagents according to this technique are still higher than the costs for dispensing of reagents from larger liquid stocks.

If larger series of samples are to be analyzed, it is desirable to use automatic devices of the Eppendorf, GeMSAEC, or AutoAnalyzer® types (see above). With these instruments, a fairly large number of samples is first analyzed by one method, either serially or in parallel. The automatic analyzer is then set up for the next method, and the corresponding analyses are performed on those samples for which this is required. With some of these analytical systems it is possible to carry out a limited number of different analyses on one sample in succession before going on to the next sample.

With this operating techniques it is particularly important to ensure the correct assignment of the results to the individual samples after execution of the analytical program, since the automatic analyzer gives the results in chronological order according to the method of analysis. Electronic data processing can help to solve this problem.

In the case of very large numbers of samples, multiple analysis is used with analytical systems working in parallel, with each system taking aliquots of the sample from a sample container (SMA®, SMAC®, and GSA-II systems, see above). The assignment of the results to the measured samples in such automatic analyzers is simpler than in the case of several systems working independently of one another, since the samples need to be identified only once for the various methods.

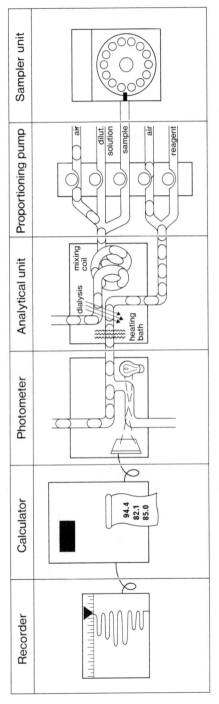

Fig. 4. Scheme of an automatic analyzer with the principle of continuous flow (AutoAnalyzer®, Technicon).

In principle, good efficiency with such multichannel analyzers working in parallel can only be achieved if all the methods possible are performed on all the samples supplied, or when at least a fairly uniform utilization of the various systems is ensured by an appropriate frequency distribution of the methods. For a large spectrum of analytical methods with a wide range of usage frequencies, the use of a number of different instruments is currently regarded as the most economical answer to the problem of multicomponent analysis.

Working Principles of Automatic Analyzers

Transport of samples

Samples for automatic analysis are generally prepared in plastic containers (cf. for example, Fig. 6b, p. 183). To guard against evaporation and contamination, the vessels are frequently closed by caps which are pierced for removal of sample aliquots. In most cases the vessels are discarded after being used once.

The most common systems of sample container movement are shown in Fig. 5. The turntable arrangement (Fig. 5a) was used particularly in the early stages of automation. With increasing numbers of samples, a changeover was made to linear arrangements of samples such as that shown in Fig. 5b or to arrangements in which the sample containers are made into the links of an endless chain (Fig. 5c). Both these configurations save space in comparison to the one shown in Fig. 5a.

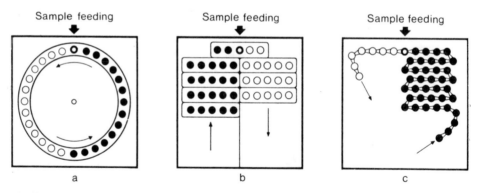

Fig. 5. Different sample transport techniques at the input of an automatic device. a) turntable carrier, sample holders along circumference, b) linear sample carrier for successive sample transport, c) chain with links serving as sample carriers.

Identification of samples

Usually, only a part of the specimen is available for enzymatic analysis. This applies particularly to the investigation of body fluids in the clinical chemistry laboratory. Here, in general, several analytical methods have to be used on a single specimen, and the specimens are therefore subdivided for the individual analytical procedures. When specimens are subdivided, the aliquots must be clearly labelled; the results must later be assigned accurately to the respective aliquots. Sample identification can today be done by machines, which reduces the margin of error in the assignment of analytical results to samples. Fig. 6 shows three different labelling techniques. The reading device of the automatic analyzer that records the sample label before aliquots are taken for analysis works optically in examples a and b (reflection scanning by means of light emitting diodes and phototransistors), and in case c by aperture scanning with piezoelectric elements. In systems b and c, the vessel is scanned while rotating around its axis. The information "read" by the reading device is fed into the computer of the automatic analyzer and allocated to the results after the analysis has been performed.

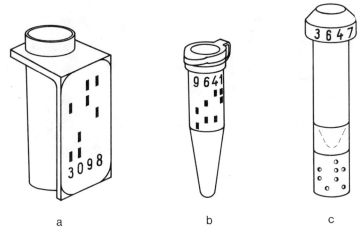

a   b   c

Fig. 6. Examples of machine-readable identification coding of sample containers. a) Technicon, b) Eppendorf, c) Siemens.

If the input of the automatic analyzer does not include a reading device, a bench list must be prepared. The samples must be lined up in the same order. The automatic analyzer gives the results of the measurements in the same sequence, and these are assigned to the respective samples according to the bench list.

Reaction vessels and transport technique

The incubation vessels for the reaction mixture and the transport technique selected fundamentally determine the external form of an automatic analyzer. The most common systems have already been shown in Figs. 2, 3 and 4, p. 177, 179, 181.

When discrete vessels are to be used, the question of whether photometry is to be carried out in the incubation system or the sample is to be transferred to a special cuvette for measurement must be decided prior to selecting a particular shape of container.

In the former case, all the incubation vessels also used for photometry must have an accurately defined (optical) path length. The material of which they are made must be transparent to the incident light. The vessel holder must be at the exact working temperature during the measurement, which requires good heat transfer from the holder to the vessel. Fig. 7 shows some common types of vessels for both incubation and photometry of reaction mixtures.

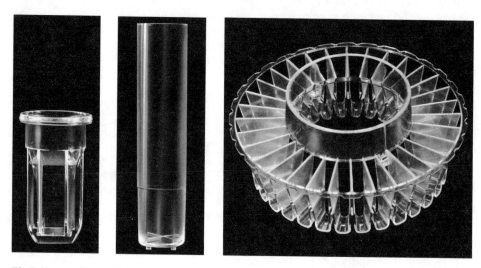

Fig. 7. Shapes of measuring vessels. a) cuvette Eppendorf, b) cuvette LKB 8600, c) multicuvette ABA-100.

If the reaction mixture is transferred to a measuring cuvette, the above requirements for transparency and defined path length apply only to the cuvette. On the other hand, a device for transferring the assay mixture is an additional expense. In practice, suction devices in combination with flow-through photometers are generally used for this purpose. If the incubation unit and the photometer are separated by a considerable distance, the connecting tubing must also be kept at the working temperature if kinetic measurements are to be performed with the automatic analyzer.

If the incubation vessels are to be used again by the automatic analyzer, thorough washing after use must be ensured. This also applies to the measuring cuvettes, which are often rinsed with part of the reaction mixture solution to be analyzed.

In continuous-flow systems, the reaction mixture is transported via a system of tubes. This must be adequately flushed between the individual reaction mixtures so that errors due to carryover are kept small. This is achieved by letting the sampler aspirate water between two successive dispensing steps. Furthermore, air bubbles are injected into the tubing at regular intervals, so that each reaction mixture introduced into the system is subdivided into several portions. Each liquid/air boundary surface passing through the tube corresponds to an emptying of the tube. The residual amount of one liquid segment remaining on the wall of the tube is partly taken up by the next liquid segment. Because of the frequent repetition of the flushing process, successive reaction mixtures are sufficiently free from cross-contamination[14]. The frequency of sample introduction is limited by the increase in carryover with higher flow rates.

Dispensing techniques

The most common mechanical dispensing devices for reagents are shown in Fig. 8.

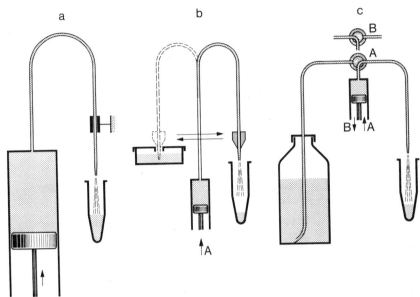

Fig. 8. Various reagent dispensing techniques. a) The reservoir is calibrated; the reagent is dispensed by a defined stroke of the piston. b) Change in volume by a change in the stroke of the piston. The volume of the tube is greater than the largest pump volume, so that the tube acts as a transfer vessel. The technique can be used only for small volumes. c) Reagent is dispensed from the storage bottle. The two-way valve is connected to the pump mechanism such that during the suction stroke (B) the line to the storage bottle is opened, and during the expulsion stroke (A), the outlet line is opened.

When the amount of reagent required is not too great, the stock solution can be placed in a calibrated cylinder (Fig. 8 a). If the piston movement is gouverned by a stepped motor, multiples of the volume corresponding to one step can be dispensed.

Another technical possibility is mechanization of the transfer process by means of a piston pump (Fig. 8 b). Air is present as the link in the tube connecting the piston pump and transfer cannula. When large amounts of reagent are required, it is preferable to dispense the solution from the storage bottle by means of a piston pump with a valve (Fig. 8 c).

Peristaltic pumps (cf. Fig. 4, p. 181) are used for continuous dispensing of the reagents in Auto-Analyzer® apparatus. This is substantially simpler, as regards the apparatus, than stepwise dispensing into separate vessels. On the other hand, the precision and accuracy of the measured volumes are lower with this method, since they depend on the elasticity of the tubing used in the pump.

One step in the operations that is particularly susceptible to error in the automatic performance of enzymatic analyses is the transfer of the usually very small amounts of sample from the sample container into the reaction system of the automatic analyzer. The percentage of sample in the final assay volume is about 1 % to 20 %, which corresponds in practice to a volume of 5 to 100 µl.

In dispensing such small volumes, it has proved useful to draw the samples from the sample container into a cannula at the end of a tube filled with water, physiological saline, or reagent, and then to rinse it quantitatively into the incubation vessel with the solution contained in the tube. Here use is made of a combination of two piston pumps, as has already been shown in Fig. 2. Fig. 9 shows the individual stages in this step of the analysis.

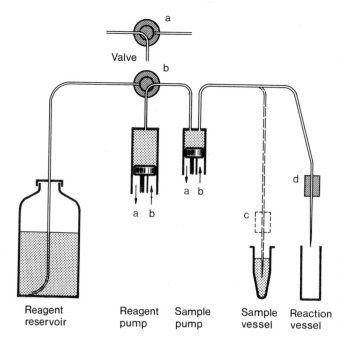

Fig. 9. The various steps in transferring the sample from the preparation table to the analytical cycle of the automatic analyzer. 1) Valve in position a), dispenser tip in sample vessel, 2) aspiration of sample (piston stroke of sample pump in direction a), 3) aspiration of reagent (piston stroke of reagent pump in direction a), 4) dispenser tip is shifted from position c to position d, 5) valve is set to position b, 6) expulsion of sample (piston stroke of sample pump in direction b), 7) expulsion of reagent (piston stroke of reagent pump in direction b), 8) valve is reset to position a.

In automatic devices of the AutoAnalyzer® type, the samples are dispensed by a peristaltic pump which feeds sample solution into the analytical system for a predetermined length of time (Fig. 4, p. 181).

Sample material adhering to the outside of the sampling tip is either wiped off when the tip pierces the plastic cap of the sample container, or is rinsed off with water before the tip is immersed in the next sample solution. Carryover between individual samples is thus avoided.

Mixing techniques

Correct and rapid mixing of sample and reagents is particularly important if the starter is added, since only a uniform distribution of the components can ensure satisfactory reaction kinetics. Some common mixing techniques are summarized in Fig.10, p.187. When using stationary stirrers (Fig.10b), care must be taken that the stirrer does not transfer any substance from one assay mixture to the next. In the AutoAnalyzer® system, the mixing of sample and reagent is effected by passage through a helical glas tube, which causes the liquid elements to rotate once in each turn of the helix (cf. Fig. 4, p. 181). Since the effect in one turn is small, a large number of turns must be connected in series.

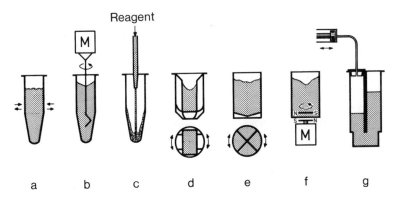

Fig. 10. The various mixing techniques. a) agitation perpendicular to the longitudinal axis of the vessel, b) motor-driven stirrer, c) injection of a second liquid, d) rotary acceleration of a vessel with rectangular cross-section, e) rotary acceleration of a cylindrical vessel with floor ribs, f) motor-driven magnetic stirrer, g) pneumatic mixing by alternate displacement and return of liquid.

Temperature control technique

The catalytic activity of an enzyme is strongly temperature-dependent (cf. p. 57). This leads to the requirement that the operating temperature be correctly adjusted to an accuracy of $\pm 0.05°C$ and kept constant during the measurement with a precision of $\pm 0.1°C$. Fulfillment of this requirement presupposes a suitable, efficient control technique as well as a good transfer of heat from the thermoregulatory medium through the walls of the reaction vessel to the substance undergoing the measurement. This is done most simply by means of a thermostatted water-bath or water-jacket. The inconvenience of dealing with systems containing water has led to the introduction of thermostatted metal blocks or graphite blocks with a Teflon coating, into which the reaction vessels are placed.

The thermal conductivities of various substances commonly employed in temperature control systems are as follows:

aluminium:	240	$(W/m \times K)$
quartz:	1.4	
OS glass:	1.0	
water:	0.6	
plexiglass:	0.2	
air:	0.03	

It is evident from the above that layers of air between the reaction vessel and holder offer high resistance to the transfer of heat. The thermal resistance of plastic vessel is also large. Even the aqueous solution in the cuvette may exhibit a temperature gradient because of its limited conductivity, if heat is lost on account of evaporation of water from the cuvette. The resulting temperature difference between the substance being measured and the temperature-controlled cuvette holder is the greater, the higher the heat-transfer resistance and the greater the difference between the working temperature and room temperature are.

At working temperatures of 25°C or 30°C, it is necessary in most cases to provide counter-cooling. If there is inadequate removal of heat, the apparatus may attain an overtemperature of 5°C to 10°C on account of the heat emitted by the electronic components, i.e. with a room temperature averaging 22°C, the working temperature would be exceeded.

The simplest source of coolant for counter-cooling is the water main. More expensive, but also more convenient, is closed water circulation with a built-in, electrically operated cooling unit. Since usually only a small cooling capacity is required, also *Peltier* elements can be used for cooling. These function by transferring heat unidirectionally along semi-conducting layers, so that a lowering of the temperature can be achieved. *Peltier* elements are small, noiseless, and require no maintenance.

Technique of photometry

In enzymatic analysis, the photometer generally has to perform the following three tasks: measurement of the absorbance change of the reaction mixture per unit time in the determination of the catalytic activity of enzymes, measurement of the difference between the absorbances of the assay mixture before and after the reaction in the determination of substance concentrations by the end-point method, and measurement of the absorbance change of the reaction mixture during a fixed-time interval in the determination of substance concentrations on a kinetic basis. For these purposes, essentially two techniques are employed in automatic analyzers:

1. The photometer measures the absorbance of the assay system continuously during a working cycle (Fig. 11 a). Since each sample passes through the photometer only once, the mechanical construction is simple.
2. The assay system passes through the photometer periodically over a relatively long space of time, so that several instantaneous values of the absorbance are determined (Fig. 11 b). This problem is solved technically with the aid of a turntable that holds the cuvettes (Eppendorf automatic analyzers[2]), a cuvette rotor (GeMSAEC automatic analyzers, cf. p. 194), or a series of cuvettes and incubation units alternating in succession (*continuous-flow* systems[15]).

In automatic analyzers having a fixed working cycle and limatated to one photometer, only the time of one working cycle is available for photometry. To achieve a high sample turnover, one will try to keep this cycle time as short as possible, although in the case of enzymatic reactions the changes in absorbance are then often very small. For example, in the case of the aminotransferases, 1 U/l corresponds to $\Delta A/\Delta t = 1 \times 10^{-3}$/min. This means, in particular, for automatic analyzers operating on the principle described under (1) above, that the photometer must reliably determine very small absorbance changes. Consequently, by means of various measures[16-19], the quality of the photometers used in modern automatic analyzers of that kind has already been increased to such an extent that absorbance changes of the order of $1 \times 10^{-4}/0.2$ min can be measured reproducibly. In practice, the precision of the measurement of very small absorbance changes is limited by the optical noise of the reaction mixture. Among others, this is due to impurities in the mixture which, above all come from turbidity in the sample.

Operational Control

The sequence of commands for the performance of the analysis by the automatic analyzer (process control) is laid down in a program. This information is stored mechanically, electronically,

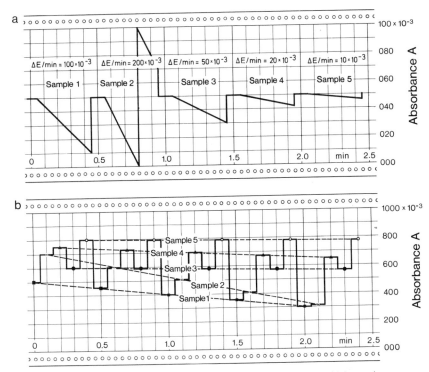

Fig.11. Analog recording of enzyme kinetics. a) continuous measurement, b) intermittent measurement (time-sharing).

or magnetically (e.g. banks of contact switches, drum controllers, flow diagrams, computer memory). The desired program is fed into the automatic analyzer according to the operating instructions before the start of the analysis via a keyboard, circuit plugs, code words, by setting up flow diagrams, etc. Alternatively, the entire operational sequence for one or more methods of analysis may also be programmed permanently into the automatic analyzer. This simplifies the operation of the instrument but reduces its flexibility.

The majority of automatic analyzers available at present make use of a combination of fixed and variable program elements. In general, the measurement is not affected by feedback from the controlling devices. Total automation, in which the analytical process is subject not only to simple, one-way control but also to monitoring and corrective measures (cybernetic control), so that reliable analytical results are always ensured, has not yet been realized. So far, selfcorrecting techniques in automatic analyzers have been used only for special applications (maintenance of constant temperature, voltage, speed of rotation, etc.).

Evaluation and documentation

Today, electronic calculators are widely used in automatic analyzers to evaluate the results of the measurements. In their simplest form, they can multiply, by a factor that is selectable or is permanently programmed, the absorbance differences measured by the photometer in unit time or in a predetermined time. The appropriate factor is obtained from the result of a standard run, or from the assay system and a molar absorption coefficient (cf. p.137ff.∴. The results are thus obtained in substance or activity concentration units.

Computers whit greater capacity can take over monitoring functions (testing the absorbance curve for linearity, marking of pathological values, testing of the initial absorbance of the reagent, etc.). In addition, more complicated computer operations, such as the storage and evaluation of curved calibration plots, can be performed.

The results determined by the computer are printed out digitally. In addition to the results, the identification code read in when the sample was introduced is given or printed out on a special sample-identification card which bears all the desired information concerning the sample and the party that ordered the analysis. Moreover, the results may be transferred directly for further use to a central electronic data processing unit (EDPU) or may be stored on a punched paper tape or other data carrier which is read into the EDPU at a desired time. Even if an EDPU is available, documentation of the measured values at the output of the automatic analyzer is required so that the laboratory can remain in operation and the required values will be available immediately even if the EDPU fails.

In addition to digital documentation, analog presentation of measured values is frequently used, it being customary to record the absorbance as a function of time. In this case the evaluation and documentation are performed manually, for example with the aid of an evaluating instrument with a calibrated scale.

Increasing the throughput of automatic analyzers

Reducing the assay volume

A general trend in the advance of automation is a reduction of the assay volume. This brings the following advantages:
– the use of methods with more expensive reagents
– reduction in the size of the apparatus and its space requirements
– an increased sample throughput because of the shorter time required per analytical step.
The third point is illustrated by Fig. 12.

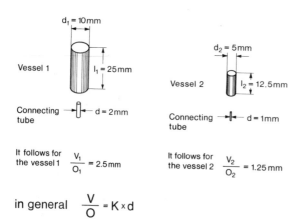

It follows for the vessel 1 $\dfrac{V_1}{O_1} = 2.5\,mm$

It follows for the vessel 2 $\dfrac{V_2}{O_2} = 1.25\,mm$

in general $\dfrac{V}{O} = K \times d$

Fig. 12. Cylindrical vessels: Vessel 2 has one half the volume/surface ratio of vessel 1, which has twice the diameter and length (d = diameter, l = length, V = volume, O = surface of the cylinder jacket, K = constant).

In cylindrical vessels with a definite ratio of length (l) to diameter (d), the volume increases as the third power and the surface as the second power of the vessel diameter. This brings decisive advantages for the important time-consuming steps of an analysis.

Temperature equilibration

If the liquid in the vessel is warmed above the surface, the volume (v) that can be heated above $1\,cm^2$ of the surface decreases linearly with the size of the vessel. When the diameter of the vessel is halved, the time required for temperature equilibration of the contents under otherwise identical conditions is also halved, to a first approximation.

Dispensing

A similar situation prevails in the dispensing of reagents. If a given rate of flow is assumed for the input conduit and the conduit cross-section is reduced commensurately with the cross-section of the vessel – in Fig. 12, the reduction in conduit diameter from 2 mm to 1 mm is indicated below the vessel – the filling time for vessel 2 falls to one-half of that for vessel 1, since the volume of vessel 1, with a conduit diameter of 2 mm, extends over twice the length compared with the volume of vessel 2 with a conduit diameter of 1 mm.

Mixing

The time required for the mixing of two substances is also smaller when the assay volume is reduced, because of the shorter distance to be covered by the individual particles.

Since the volume decreases as the third power when the diameter and the length of the vessel are reduced to one-half ($v_2/v_1 = \frac{1}{8}$), an approximate doubling of the sample throughput in unit time may be expected when the assay volume is reduced to $\frac{1}{8}$. There is a trend to reduce the assay volume from 5 ml–1 ml to 0.5 ml–0.1 ml. The reduction is at present limited by the difficulty of dispensing the corresponding small sample volumes with sufficient precision.

Increase in the precision of photometry

In addition to reducing the assay volume, an increase in the precision of photometric measurements of small absorbance changes is an important contribution to increasing the throughput of an automatic analyzer. For further details, see p. 188.

Introduction of analytical methods adapted for automatic analyzers

Apart from measures involving the apparatus, the throughput of automatic analyzers can be substantially increased by the use of methods suitable for automated analysis. These are methods which yield results in the shortest possible time, require only a few pipetting steps, and do not require a sample blank. Substance determinations on a kinetic basis (cf. p. 79) are examples of such methods.

References

1 Skeggs, L. T. (1957) *Amer. J. Clin. Path.* **28**, 311.
2 Bechtler, G. (1969) *Ärztl. Lab.* **15**, 86.
3 Anderson, N. G. (1969) *Anal. Biochem.* **32**, 59.

4 Hicks, G.P., Evenson, M.A., Gieschen, M.M. & Larson, F.C. (1969) in *Computers in Biochemical Research* (Stacy, R.W. & Waxman, B.D., eds.), Vol. III, p. 15–53, Academic Press, New York, London.

5 Eggstein, M., Kenzelmann, E., Knodel, W. & Allner, R. (1967) *Ärztl. Labor* **13,** 64.

6 Delbrück, A. (1968) *Krankenhausarzt* **41,** 265.

7 Gräser, W., Mieth, I., Porth, A., Knodel, W. & Eggstein, M. (1969) *GIT Labormedizin* **13,** 426.

8 Hjelm, M. (1969) *J. Clin. Chem. Clin. Biochem.* **7,** 96.

9 Keller, H. & Gessner, U. (1974) *Med. Progr. Technol.* **3,** 33.

10 Haeckel, R., Höpfel, P. & Höner, G. (1974) *J. Clin. Chem. Clin. Biochem.* **12,** 14

11 Keller, H. (1971) *Automaten im klinischen Labor*, Frank'sche Verlagshandlung, Stuttgart.

12 Nadeau, R.G. (1968) *Clin. Chem.* **14,** 778.

13 Smythe, W.J., Shamos, M.H., Morgenstern, S. & Skeggs, L.T. (1968) in *Automation in Analytical Chemistry*, Vol. I, p. 105-114, Mediad Inc., White Plains, N.Y. 10601.

14 Chaney, A.L. (1968) in *Automation in Analytical Chemistry*. Vol. I, p. 115–117, Mediad Inc., White Plains, N.Y. 10601.

15 Kessler, G., Morgenstern, S., Snyder, L.R. & Varady, R.H. (1975) *Clin. Chem.* **21,** 1005.

16 Cordos, E.M., Crouch, S.R. & Malmstadt, H.V. (1968) *Anal Chem.* **40,** 1812.

17 Atwood, J.G. & DiCesare, J.L. (1975) *Clin. Chem.* **21,** 1263.

18 DiCesare, J.L. (1975) *Clin. Chem.* **21,** 1448.

19 McQueen, M.J. & King, J. (1975) *Clin. Chim. Acta* **64,** 155.

Fast Analyzers

Norman G. Anderson*

Clinical chemistry has set itself high aims as a diagnostic aid. One of these aims is the provision of a complete miniature clinical laboratory for the bedside. Possible uses would be in night duty and emergency work, in paediatrics, in intensive care, and in the space laboratory (*Skylab*). The development of very small fast analyzers for clinical chemistry calls for the combination of technical advances in two directions, i.e. the miniaturization of photometers and computers and the use of entirely new principles for the handling of samples and reagents. These aims are now approaching reality.

In the following article, the basic principles of fast analyzers now coming into general use are described first[1-17]. Modifications and further developments[18-22] of this system are then discussed.

The fast analyzer was originally designed in 1968/1969[1-3]. It was assumed that small computers of suitable size would be available at low cost between 1975 and 1980. This forecast appears to have been realized already. Small, flexible *on-line* data collection systems are finding increasing use in clinical chemistry and in research laboratories.

Basic Principles

Definition of the problem

For the various activity and concentration determinations, it has been necessary until now to divide biological material from a patient into several portions. The test material from many patients leads to a large number of individual samples. This calls for a considerable amount of bookkeeping for sample identification, setting up of work lists, and recombination of the analytical data from various analytical systems or laboratories for the same patient. The system becomes even more complicated when several clinics are associated with one central laboratory.

This problem is overcome by the new system of analysis. A large number of different analyses are carried out in a very short time right next to the patient, without clerical work.

The rate of biochemical reactions is orders of magnitude slower than electronic data collection processes; the latter are limited only by the speed of light. To make use of fast data collection, the individual analyses must be performed more rapidly or else a large number of analyses must be carried out simultaneously. For the latter route, which is the more rational, all the reactions must be started at the same time, and measurements must be carried out in several equal time intervals (activity determinations) or, in the case of end-point methods, after a fixed interval. Analysis systems of this type for clinical chemistry and for research laboratories were described by us for the first time[8,13,14].

* Molecular Anatomy (MAN) Programme, Oak Ridge National Laboratory, operated for the U. S. Atomic Energy Commission by Union Carbide Corporation.

Solution of the Technical Problems

Reaction Initiation

To initiate the reaction, samples and reagents must be brought together in the cuvette. Centrifugal force is used for the simultaneous transport of these solutions. The samples and reagents are first automatically pipetted into a transfer disc (Fig. 1, upper diagram). The disc is then inserted in the cuvette rotor and accelerated. The solutions, which have remained separate until this time, flow radially into the corresponding cuvette, where all the reactions begin at the same time. Any air bubbles present are removed by the centrifugal force.

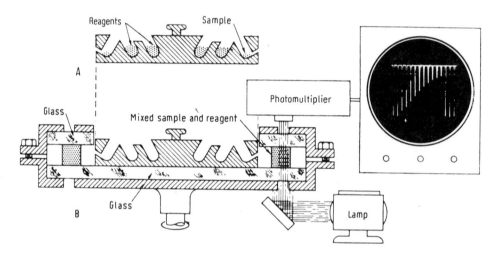

Fig. 1. Operating principle of the GeMSAEC* fast analyzer (acc. to[5]). Measured volumes of reagents and samples are placed in depressions in the fluorocarbon transfer disc (A). The depressions are so arranged that reagents and samples are unmixed while the disc is at rest, but can move radially without mixing with adjacent sets of reagents and samples. The transfer disc is placed in a cuvette rotor (B) and rotated. Centrifugal force moves all liquids outward into the rotor cuvettes, which proceed past a stationary light beam as shown in (B).

The signal received from the photomultiplier is continuously displayed on an oscilloscope. Fifteen separate reactions can be started simultaneously and followed continuously. Gross errors in pipetting or in the preparation of reagent or standard can be observed within a few seconds in the case of fast reactions.

Photometry

All cuvettes are scanned individually with a stationary light beam of a certain wavelength, and the absorbance is amplified by a photomultiplier and measured. During each revolution of the rotor, data are obtained for each cuvette, as well as a dark current reading (when the

---

* GeMSAEC=General Medical Sciences Atomic Energy Commission.

beam is interrupted by the solid part of the rotor). As can be seen from Figure 2, the combination of the dark current reading with the measured value is an extension of the double-beam principle of spectrophotometry.

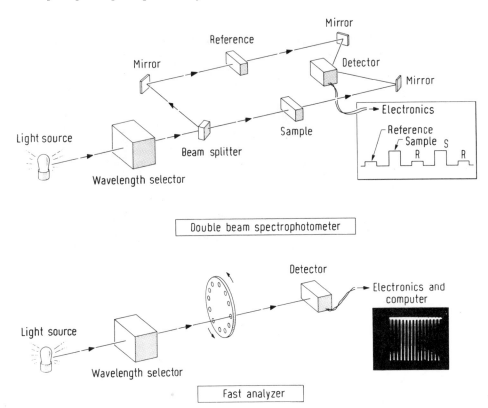

Fig. 2. Comparison of signal generation in a conventional double-beam spectrophotometer and in the multiple cuvette method in fast analyzers (acc. to[24]).

Emptying and Washing

Each cuvette in the cuvette rotor is provided with a siphon for emptying. By air pressure to the centre of the rotor or suction at the outer edge of the rotor, the cuvettes are emptied, washed, and air dried in 1–2 min during rotation[3]. For fast mixing of each analysis mixture at the beginning, the air is sucked back through the siphon.

Data Acquisition

A complete set of data (dark current, 100% transmittance, and all values for standards and samples) is obtained for each revolution. At 600 rpm, each revolution takes 100 m. For reactions that take longer, data are collected from several successive revolutions and averaged. In this way, electronic drift is eliminated and high precision is achieved. The photomultiplier is connected to an oscilloscope for immediate display of the reaction course in each cuvette (Fig. 3). Errors in dilution or reagent preparation and instrument defects can thus be observed

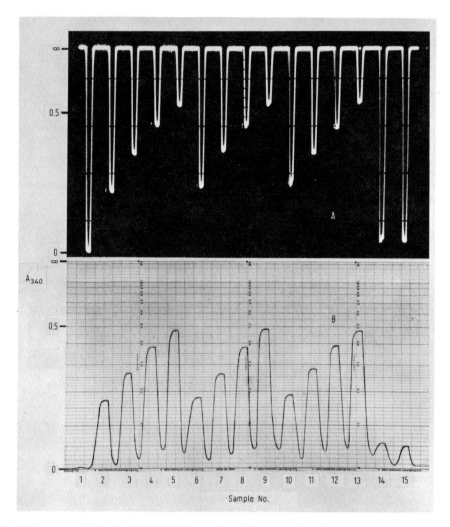

Fig. 3. Curves recorded by the GeMSAEC fast analyzer (A), comparison with curves of a *continuous-flow* analyser (B) (acc. to[5]). Lower curve: different baselines of different samples. Upper curve: total protein with Folin reagent.

Water blank (or sample) in cuvette 1. 50, 100, 150, and 200 µg of protein in a total volume of 500 µl in cuvettes 2–5. Repetition of this protein series in cuvettes 6–9 with addition of 1.08 mg of sucrose per cuvette, and in cuvettes 10–13 with addition of 2.48 mg of sucrose per cuvette. Cuvette 14 contains a reagent blank and cuvette 15 a reagent blank with 2.48 mg of sucrose.

Photograph taken 1 min after transfer of the liquid.

If a dye is destroyed (instead of being formed) in the analytical reaction in a continous-flow analyzer, the curve superficially resembles that obtained in the GeMSAEC system.

sooner. Figure 4 shows the data collected during each revolution. The *apparent* baseline is at the top. This line shows infinite absorption when the light beam is interrupted by the solid metal between two cuvettes.

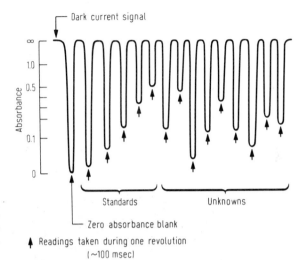

Fig. 4. Oscilloscope display and reading times during one revolution (acc. to[22]).
The dark current signal and the zero-absorbance blank are determined anew during each rotation, and all data collected during this rotation are referred to these two values. Since the entire process takes place in about 100 ms, the electronic drift is minimal.

The rotor informs the computer in three ways when a new rotation has started and when readings are to be taken from the tips of the peaks[10,12]:

1. The trigger signal is set at a point corresponding to 2/3 of the peak height; a reading.
2. The trigger signal is set immediately after the peak with the aid of a *sample-and-hold* circuit; reading of the maximum peak height.
3. Triggering of the first of several measurements at the start of the peak plateau; measurement of up to 16 values across the plateau; averaging.

When the last of these methods is used, 80 readings are recorded and averaged for each point during 5 successive rotations, i.e. with 20 measuring points for each of the 42 cuvettes in the large cuvette rotor, one obtains a total of 67,200 readings. The importance of *on-line* data collection is particularly obvious here.

Temperature

Different methods are used for temperature measurement and control in various fast analysis systems. All these methods give variations of only ± 0.1 to ± 0.3 °C in the range from 25 °C to 36 °C[11,14,19].

Addition of Reagents

In many analyses, one or more reagents must be added at intervals during the course of the reaction. By means of a special arrangement between the cuvettes, the reagent stream flowing into the spinning rotor is segmented and distributed between all the cuvettes[2,21]. Coriolis forces provide rapid mixing if the density differences between the individual liquids are not too large.

Programmes

A number of programmes exist for determinations of end points and catalytic activities (values in international units)[10, 12, 17]. These include *least-squares smoothing* to determine which portion of a curve is linear. The data are presented as plots of absorbance against time for all cuvettes (Fig. 5) or for each cuvette individually (Fig. 6). The intervals between the points and the number of points obtained (and hence the total reaction time) may be varied over a wide range.

For clinical chemistry, the programmes are stored on a disc and called for by a *Teletype* with the aid of a narrow paper tape. The tape carries the technician's name and the test to be carried out: the data and sample number are added from a keyboard.

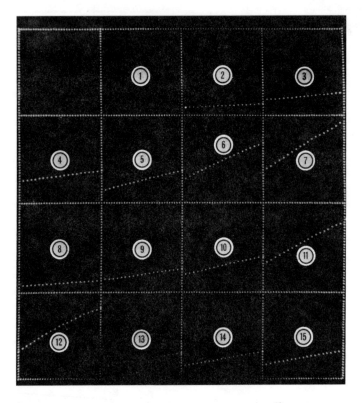

Fig. 5. Real-time display of the reaction rate in a 15-cuvette rotor (acc. to[22]).
Each square (except that in the upper left-hand corner) corresponds to one cuvette number. The ordinate of a given square corresponds to an absorbance range of from 0–2 on a linear scale, while the time is plotted on the abscissa. The first cuvette contains the water blank, and the curve therefore runs flat along the baseline. The other squares show the progress of the reaction.

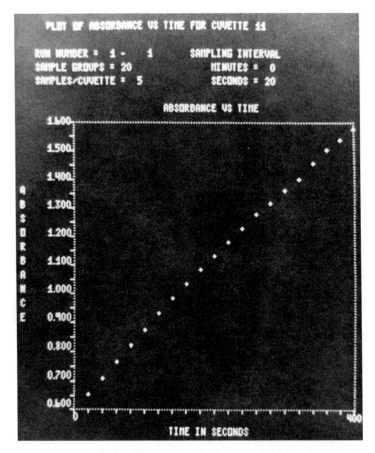

Fig. 6. Stored displays of results from cuvette 11 (acc. to[22]). The computer controls the abscissa display for agreement with the collected data. The absorbance range display can be controlled from the keyboard.

If readings are taken at very short intervals during the first part of the reaction, it is possible to extrapolate to time zero and to subtract the blank absorbance from the end-point absorbance. Using a PDP-8/I with an 8 K memory and a disc for programme and data storage, methods have been developed for the storage and processing of data from analytical runs. These allow the determination of V, K_m, and the pH optimum in very short time[23].

Miniature Systems for Individual Patient Analysis

The incentive for this work came from the needs of clinical chemistry for blood analysis in space on board the NASA Skylab[18-22]. Very small, disposable rotor discs that allow the addition of samples (including diluted whole blood) during rotation have been developed. The blood cells are centrifuged out during rotation. A measured quantity of diluted serum is transported into the cuvettes by suction or by air pressure[21]. A variety of reagents lyophilized in the cells and reconstituted before the addition of serum allow various assays to be carried out on one sample in a short time. Figure 7 shows a version of this system that is now under evaluation at the *Oak Ridge National Laboratory* and occupies only about 0.03 m³ of space. A mechanical data printer has been developed for this system[20], but within the next few years it will probably be replaced by a computer the size of the analyzer.

Fig. 7. G∅ (gravity zero) fast analyzer developed for use in space (acc. to[25]).
The plastic rotor disc contains 17 cuvettes. The photometric values of the analyzer are displayed on the oscilloscope on the left.

With suitably small computing systems and small replaceable read-only memories, the possibility exists not only for rapid data reduction but also of the conversion of data into the corresponding information, i.e. into suggested additional tests or possible diagnoses. Additional suggested tests may be incorporated into other rotor discs and carried out immediately.
A large part of medical costs is due to delay in laboratory analyses as a result of multiple patient/physician encounters and to costs associated with sample identification and data collection. Fast miniature analyzers capable of carrying out many different analyses rapidly on single samples may solve this problem.

Summary

Fast analysers allow the simultaneous solution of the following problems:

      – fast multiple sample analysis
      – high throughput

- precision absorbance measurement
- real-time reduction
- fast interaction with the operator
- decrease of sample and reagent volumes
- precision measurements on the basis of rate measurements or end-point determinations
- statistical analysis of the data collected
- storage and handling of data from consecutive runs.

The miniaturization of the entire system enables blood and urine analyses to be carried out during the diagnosis.

References

1 Anderson, N.G. (1968) *Anal. Biochem.* **23**, 207.
2 Anderson, N.G. (1969) *Anal. Biochem.* **28**, 545.
3 Anderson, N.G. (1969) *Anal. Biochem.* **32**, 59.
4 Anderson, N.G. (1969) *Anal. Biochem.* **31**, 272.
5 Anderson, N.G. (1969) *Science* **166**, 317.
6 Hatcher, D.W. & Anderson, N.G. (1969) *Am. J. Clin. Pathol.* **52**, 645.
7 Anderson, N.G. (1969) *Clin. Chem. Acta* **25**, 321.
8 Mashburn, D.N., Stevens, R.H., Willis, D.D., Elrod, L.H. & Anderson, N.G. (1970) *Anal. Biochem.* **35**, 98.
9 Anderson, N.G. (1970) *Am. J. Clin. Pathol.* **53**, 778.
10 Jansen, J.M., Jr. (1970) *Clin. Chem.* **16**, 515.
11 Burtis, C.A., Johnson, W.F., Attrill, J.E., Scott, C.D., Cho, N. & Anderson, N.G. (1971) *Clin. Chem.* **17**, 686.
12 Kelley, M.T. & Jansen, J.M. (1071) *Clin. Chem.* **17**, 701.
13 Fabiny, D.L. & Ertinghausen, G. (1971) *Clin. Chem.* **17**, 696.
14 Maclin, E. (1971) *Clin. Chem.* **17**, 707.
15 Tiffany, T.O., Johnson, G.F. & Chilcote, M.E. (1971) *Clin. Chem.* **17**, 715.
16 Burtis, C.A., Johnson, W.F., Mailen, J.C. & Attrill, J.E. (1972) *Clin. Chem.* **18**, 433.
17 Tiffany, T.O., Jansen, J.M., Burtis, C.A., Overton, J.B. & Scott C.D. (1972) *Clin. Chem.* **18**, 829.
18 Anderson, N.G., Burtis, C.A., Mailen, J.C., Scott, C.D. & Willis, D.D. (1972) *Anal. Letters* **5**, 153.
19 Burtis, C.A., Mailen, J.C., Johnson, W.F., Scott, C.D., Tiffany, T.O. & Anderson, N.G. (1972) *Clin. Chem.* **18**, 753.
20 Johnson, W.F., Mailen, J.C., Burtis, C.A., Tiffany, T.O. & Scott, C.D. (1972) *Clin. Chem.* **18**, 762.
21 Scott, C.D. & Mailen, J.C. (1972) *Clin. Chem.* **18**, 749.
22 Anderson, N.G. (1972) *Z. Anal. Chem.* **261**, 257.
23 Tiffany, T. O., Burtis, C. A. & Anderson, N. G. (1974) Fast analyzers for biochemical analysis, in *Methods in Enzymology* (Colowick, S. P. & Kaplan, N. O., eds.) Vol. 31, pp. 790–833, Academic Press, New York.
24 Anderson, N.G. & Burtis, C.A. (1974) GeMSAEC fast clinical analyzers, in *Clinical Biochemistry* (Curtius, H. Ch. & Rotte, M., eds.) pp. 521–543, Walter de Gruyter, Berlin, New York.
25 Burtis, C.A., Johnson, W.F., Mailen, J.C., Overton, J.B., Tiffany, T.O. & Watsky, M.B. (1973) *Clin. Chem.* **19**, 895.

Enzymatic Analysis with Radiobiochemicals

Alexander Hagen and Eric A. Newsholme*

Radioactively labelled substances can be used in enzymatic analysis for the determination of the concentration of substances and catalytic activity of enzymes. In both cases, the isotope technique can considerably increase the sensitivity in comparison with most conventional methods; it also allows determinations for which no other methods are available.

General

Handling of radioactive substances

The most important nuclides for enzymatic analysis are tritium [^{3}H], carbon-14 [^{14}C], phosphorus-32 [^{32}P], and sulfur-35 [^{35}S]. Activities below the level at which an official permit must be obtained will be sufficient in most cases, and the maximum will not exceed 10 times this limit; the danger of damage to health is therefore slight, and relatively modest safety precautions are adequate. The principal physical properties of the nuclides mentioned above, all of which are β-emitters, are listed in Table 1; the general physical laws connected with radioactive decay and radioactive radiation are described elsewhere[1].

Table 1. Physical properties of some nuclides.

Nuclide	Decay product	Half-life	Max. β-energy (MeV)	Max. range mg/cm^2** in Al
$^3_1$H	$^3_2$He	12.26 years	0.0186	<1
$^{14}_6$C	$^{14}_7$N	5760 years	0.158	36
$^{32}_{15}$P	$^{32}_{16}$S	14.3 days	1.71	800
$^{35}_{16}$S	$^{35}_{17}$Cl	87 days	0.167	38

The handlung of radioactive substances is controlled by law.
The maximum permissible concentrations of radioactive substances in effluent and exhaust gases also fixed by law (e.g. for the German Federal Republic, refer to Table 2).

Table 2. Maximum permissible values of radioactive substances in effluent and exhaust air for the German Federal Republic.

Nuclide	General legal limit		Max. concentration Effluent Exhaust air		Effluent Exhaust air	
	(μCi)	(s^{-1})	(μCi/ml)		(s^{-1} × ml^{-1})	
$^3_1$H	100	3.7×10^6	3×10^{-2}	2×10^{-6}	1.11×10^3	7.4×10^{-2}
$^{14}_6$C	100	3.7×10^6	8×10^{-3}	1×10^{-6}	2.96×10^2	3.7×10^{-2}
$^{32}_{15}$P	10	3.7×10^5	2×10^{-4}	2×10^{-8}	7.4	7.4×10^{-4}
$^{35}_{16}$S	10	3.7×10^5	6×10^{-4}	9×10^{-8}	22.2	3.3×10^{-3}

---

* Edited by Gerhard Michal, Klaus Stellner, and Werner Wolf.
** Normal manner of expressing the range of decay electrons as the maximum distance (cm) multiplied by the density (mg/cm^3) of the absorber.

For information about equipment and operation of an isotope laboratory, radiation-measuring equipment, reagents, purity criteria, and preparation of solutions and their stability, see[2].

Precision of Radioactivity Determinations

The accuracy of measurement in the radioactivity assay is affected mainly by two sources of error, viz., pipetting and the measurement of radioacitivity. The determination of the errors that arise in the measurement of radioactivity is briefly outlined below. For a more detailed description, refer to[3-5].

Standard deviation: The symbols used in the following discussion are

s	standard deviation	R_0	background counting rate
CV	coefficient of variation	R_p	counting rate for sample
N	number of counts measured	R_N	net counting rate
R	counting rate = counts per minute (cpm)	Re	purity number

Radioactive decay follows the laws of statistics. The decisive factor is the binominal distribution, which is represented approximately by the Poisson distribution in this case. Standard deviation and coefficient of variation are calculated according to eqn. (1):

$$\text{(1)} \qquad s = \sqrt{N} \qquad CV = \frac{\sqrt{N}}{N} \times 100\,[\%]$$

The standard deviation means that the actual count will lie within the limits given by

$$\text{(2)} \qquad N \pm \sqrt{N}$$

with a probability of approx. 0.68.
Also frequently used is the so-called 95/100 error with

$$\text{(3)} \qquad 2s = 2\sqrt{N}$$

The probability that the actual count will lie within the limits given by

$$\text{(4)} \qquad N \pm 2\sqrt{N}$$

is 0.95.
This must be taken into account for results that are of the same order of magnitude as the background. The total error is calculated from the root of the sum of the squares of the individual errors.

Example: Background 500 counts in 25 min. The background counting rate is

$$R_0 = \frac{500 \pm \sqrt{500}}{25} = 20 \pm 0.9\,(\text{cpm})$$

Sample count 1000 in 10 min. The counting rate for the sample is

$$R_p = \frac{1000 \pm \sqrt{1000}}{10} = 100 \pm 3.2\,(\text{cpm})$$

The net counting rate with the standard deviation is then

$$R_N = (100 - 20) \pm \sqrt{0.9^2 + 3.2^2} = 80 \pm 3.5\,(\text{cpm})$$

Checking the measuring system for statistical purity: This requires a large number of measurements on the same preparation. If the average of n individual measurements $N_1, N_2, ..., N_i$ is $\bar{N}$, the purity number is

(5)
$$Re = \frac{\left[\dfrac{(N_1 - \bar{N})^2 + (N_2 - \bar{N})^2 + \cdots (N_i - \bar{N})^2}{n - 1}\right]^{\frac{1}{2}}}{[\bar{N}]^{\frac{1}{2}}}$$

For a large number of events with statistical purity, the purity number Re approaches 1. In practice (about 20 to 30 measurements are necessary), Re values > 0.6 may be taken as indicating statistical purity. Re values < 0.5 point to a probable disturbance in the measuring arrangement. For measurements in a liquid scintillation spectrometer, the counting efficiency is determined by the "external standard" method or the "channel-ratio" method. For the magnitude of the error that arises here and its determination, refer to *E. Bush*[6]. A good survey of the general error calculation is provided by *Wittenberger*[7].

Determination of Substrates with Radiobiochemicals

For the determination of concentrations of substrates, three basic methods have gained acceptance: these are isotope dilution, specific enzymatic conversion, and enzymatic isotope dilution.

Isotope Dilution Principle

There are two variations of this method[8,9]. The principle is simple. A radioactive compound is mixed with the non-radioactive form of the same compound. The radioactivity per unit amount of this compound in the mixture (i.e. the specific radioactivity) is then smaller than that of the original radioactive compound. The decrease in the specific radioactivity depends on the non-radioactive compound, in accordance with the following equation:

(6)
$$X_S = X_0 \times \frac{M_0}{M_0 + M}$$

where

X_0 = specific radioactivity of the compound
X_S = specific radioactivity of the mixture of radioactive and non-radioactive compound
M_0 = amount of the radioactive compound
M = amount of the non-radioactive compound.

If the amount M_0 and the specific radioactivities X_0 and X_S are known, the amount M can be calculated. In practice, a sample of the mixture (radioactive and non-radioactive compound) is separated, and both the amount and the radioactivity of the compound in this sample are determined.

A disadvantage of this method is that in addition to the radioactivity of a compound, its amount must also be measured. If the latter is not possible, or is possible only with great difficulty, it is necessary to make use of another variation, the so-called "sub-stoichiometric isotope dilution principle"[10].

If the compound is removed in equal amounts from the solution prior to and after addition of the sample to determine the radioactivity, we have

(7) $$\frac{X_0}{X_S} = \frac{\text{counting rate for the pure radioactive compound}}{\text{counting rate for the mixture}} = 1 + \frac{M}{M_0}$$

The amount M can be calculated by comparing the radioactivity of the equal aliquots sampled with the amount M_0. Sampling is often carried out via reaction with an antibody or binding protein. For a general discussion, see[44].

If the volume of the radioactive solution is only negligibly altered by addition of the inactive sample to be determined, the amounts M_0 and M may be replaced by the corresponding concentrations $[S]_0$ and $[S]$, giving

(8) $$\frac{X_0}{X_S} = \frac{\text{counting rate for the pure radioactive compound}}{\text{counting rate for the mixture}} = 1 + \frac{[S]}{[S]_0}$$

The sub-stoichiometric principle has been used for the determination of proteohormones, e.g. insulin[11,12], growth hormone[13], glucagon[14], and thyroxine[15], but also for many other substances such as digitalis glycosides[16] and cyclic nucleotides[17].

Specific Enzymatic Reactions

Theoretically, any complete enzymatic reaction with two or more reactants can be used for the substance determination of substrates. The radiochemically labelled substrate is added in excess. The incorporation of the radioactivity into the product is proportional to the concentration of the other substrate. The practical application of this method necessitates complete separation of the radioactive substrate from the product, especially when the concentration of the radioactive substrate is high.

> *Example:* Determination of oxaloacetate[18,19].
> Citrate synthase catalyzes the conversion of oxaloacetate and $[^{14}C]$-acetyl-CoA into $[^{14}C]$-citrate. After incubation, the radioactive citrate is separated from the radioactive acetyl-CoA by cleavage of the acetyl-CoA to acetate and CoA at pH 12 and removal of the acetic acid by evaporation at 65°C. The radioactivity incorporated into the citrate is proportional to the concentration of oxaloacetate and can be calculated with the aid of a calibration curve.

Enzymatic Isotope Dilution Principle

A new principle, which combines an enzymatic reaction with the sub-stoichiometric isotope dilution principle, was developed in 1968[20].

A radioactively labelled substrate is specifically converted by an enzymatic reaction into a product that can be separated from the substrate and whose radioactivity can be determined. The enzyme reaction need only proceed far enough for the conversion of a small fraction (e.g. 20%) of the substrate into its product. This is achieved by stopping the enzymatic reaction after a fixed time. Determination of the substrate by the sub-stoichiometric principle of isotope dilution is therefore possible, since a correspondingly lower incorporation of radioactivity into the product is to be expected after the addition of the non-radioactive substrate.

If the substrate concentration is lower than that necessary for enzyme saturation, changes in the substrate concentration cause changes in the rate of product formation (because of the change in the catalytic activity of the enzyme); equimolar concentrations of the product then cannot be attained by the enzymatic reaction at various substrate concentrations.

The magnitude of the two effects, i.e. isotope dilution and the change in the catalytic activity of the enzyme, can be predicted quantitatively on the basis of the isotope dilution principle and the *Michaelis-Menten* equation.

According to *Michaelis-Menten* is valid:

(9)
$$v_i = \frac{V[S]_0}{K_m + [S]_0}; \qquad v_S = \frac{V([S]_0 + [S])}{K_m + ([S]_0 + [S])}$$

v_i and v_S denote the initial rates of the enzyme reaction at the substrate concentrations $[S]_0$ and $([S]_0 + [S])$, $[S]_0$ and $[S]$ denote the concentrations of the radioactive and of the non-radioactive substrate respectively, K_m is the Michaelis constant, and V the maximum rate.

Since

(10)
$$\frac{v_i}{v_S} = \frac{[P]_0}{[P]_S},$$

where $[P]_0$ and $[P]_S$ are the concentrations of the products formed in unit time when the concentrations of the substrates are $[S]_0$ and $([S]_0 + [S])$, it follows that

$$\frac{[P]_0}{[P]_S} = \frac{V \times [S]_0/(K_m + [S]_0)}{V([S]_0 + [S])/(K_m + [S]_0 + [S])}$$

(11)
$$\frac{[P]_0}{[P]_S} = \frac{[S]_0(K_m + [S]_0 + [S])}{(K_m + [S]_0)([S]_0 + [S])}$$

After isotope dilution, we have:

(12)
$$C_0 = [P]_0 \times X_0 \times V$$

(13)
$$C_S = [P]_S \times X_S \times V$$

where C_0 and C_S are the total radioactivities incorporated into the products P_0 and P_S and X_0 and X_S are the specific radioactivities of the radioactive substrate with the concentration $[S]_0$ and of the mixture of the radioactive and of the non-radioactive substrate with the concentration $([S]_0 + [S])$. V denotes the volume of the solution (the volume must be introduced because X_0 and X_S are defined as radioactivity per amount).

From equation (13) and equation (8), we obtain

(14)
$$C_S = [P]_S \times X_0 \times \frac{[S]_0}{[S]_0 + [S]} \times V$$

From equation (12) and equation (14):

(15)
$$\frac{C_0}{C_S} = \frac{[P]_0}{[P]_S} \times \frac{[S]_0 + [S]}{[S]_0}$$

If $[P]_0 = [P]_S$,

(16)
$$\frac{C_0}{C_S} = \frac{[S]_0 + [S]}{[S]_0}$$

The isotope dilution effect and the effect of the catalytic activity of the enzyme are combined by replacing $[P]_0/[P]_S$ in equation (15) by $[P]_0/[P]_S$ from equation (11)

$$\frac{C_0}{C_S} = \frac{[S]_0 + [S]}{[S]_0} \times \frac{[S]_0(K_m + [S]_0 + [S])}{(K_m + [S]_0)([S]_0 + [S])} ,$$

whence it follows that

(17)
$$\frac{C_0}{C_S} = 1 + \frac{[S]}{K_m + [S]_0}$$

Equation (17) is the mathematical formulation of the enzymatic isotope dilution principle. If the enzymatic isotope dilution principle is valid, a linear relation exists between C_0/C_S and $[S]$, the slope of the line being $1/(K_m + [S]_0)$; as $[S]$ approaches 0, C/C_S approaches 1. These predictions of the enzymatic isotope dilution principle have been checked experimentally, and good agreement was found between the theoretical predictions and the experimental observations[20].

So far, this principle has been used only for the determination of glycerol and glucose[20]. For details of the procedure for glycerol, see[21].

Determination of the Catalytic Activity of Enzymes with Radiobiochemicals

Radioactively labelled substances are used for the determination of catalytic activities of enzymes when the optical test fails. There are three general cases in which this happens:

a) The optical test is fundamentally impossible, since no link to a reaction in which light is absorbed or emitted can be stablished.
b) The optical test cannot be carried out in practice, owing to interference by side reactions.
c) The sensitivity of the optical test is too low.

Conventional Methods

Principle

The determination of the catalytic activity of an enzyme means the measurement of the enzyme-catalyzed transformation of substrate per unit time. If one of the substrates participating in the reaction is used in a radioactively labelled form, the reaction leads specifically to a radioactively labelled product. After a fixed time, the radioactive product must be separated from the radioactive substrate and the transferred or residual radioactivity measured. If the specific radioactivity is known, the quantity of substrate that has reacted can be deduced. The sensitivity of the determination can be varied by suitable choice of the reaction time, radioactivity, and specific radioactivity.

Separation Methods

The decisive question in the development of an isotope test is the ease of separation of the radio-active substrate from the product; a closely related problem is the choice of the method for determination of the radioactivity.

The separation method should generally be such that the radioactivity of the product can be determined directly, instead of being calculated from the residual radioactivity of the substrate. This is essential when the substrate can be further transformed by contaminating enzymes; the product must be separated from all the radioactive by-products formed

The following separation methods may be considered:

a) Evaporation of a volatile product (substrate), or of one that can be converted into a volatile form, from the non-volatile substrate (product).

   Examples: Liberated carbon dioxide [^{14}C] is absorbed in alkaline solution, in which the radioactivity is measured. Fixed carbon dioxide [^{14}C] can be determined after the unreacted bicarbonate [^{14}C] serving as the substrate is driven off with acid.

b) Solvent extraction of the product (substrate) from the aqueous phase. If the substrate and the product cannot be separated directly in this way, separation is often possible by formation, of a derivative.

   Example: Inorganic phosphate can be extracted as the molybdate complex from aqueous solution with isobutanol[22].

c) Precipitation of the product (substrate). The determinations of the activities of polysaccha-ride-, polypeptide-, and nucleic-acid-synthesizing enzymes are largely based on this princi-ple[23–25]. The enzymatically formed polymers are precipitated with organic solvents, the reac-tion being conveniently carried out on filter paper disks and stopped by immersion in organic solvents. The polymer is insoluble and remains on the support, while unreacted substrate is washed off. The radioactivity can be measured by placing the paper in a toluene scintillation solution in the liquid scintillation counter itself[26]. The counting efficiency for tritium can be considerably increased by the use of transparent supports made of glass fibre material[27]. Low-molecular-weight products can often be precipitated as sparingly soluble salts or deriv-atives[28].

d) Separation of product and substrate by ion exchange. This technique is used in many variations. In the simplest case, an ionic substrate is separated from a non-ionic product by passage through an ion-exchange column, and the radioactivity of the product in the eluate is measured.

e) Paper or thin-layer chromatographic separation of substrate or product. After the separation, the chromatogram may be evaluated with the aid of a scanner or by direct measurement of the activities of the cut-out paper strips in a liquid scintillation counter. The method is simplified by the use of solvent systems in which the product (substrate) remains at the starting position while the substrate (product) migrates with the solvent[29].

f) Other methods. Activated charcoal can be used for the adsorption of substrates containing purine and pyrimidine, for example. Thus, orthophosphate [^{32}P] can be rapidly separated in this way from nucleotides [^{32}P] and the activity of the unadsorbed substance, or that of the adsorbed substance after elution with ammoniacal ethanol, is then measured[30]. Polymeric components can be separated from low-molecular-weight components by gel filtration.

Optimum Conditions for Measurements

In contrast to the optical method, the course of the enzymatic reaction with time cannot be followed directly in the method based on the use of radioactive isotopes. The quantities of substrate that have reacted at various times must therefore be calculated from the radioactivity transferred. It is often sufficient in standardized routine tests to carry out a measurement after only one interval. The specific radioactivity should not be higher than is necessary for the radioactivity measurement. The handling of labelled substances with high activities can lead to considerable complications and give rise to errors (absorption due to radiolytic decomposition).

Calculation

The enzyme activity is calculated from equation (18)

$$(18) \quad \text{Enzyme activity (U)} = \frac{R_N}{2.22 \times 10^6 \times SA \times t \times E/100} = \frac{R_N}{2.22 \times 10^4 \times SA \times t \times E}$$

R_N Net counting rate (cpm) for the radioactive product
E Counting efficiency in percent
SA Specific radioactivity (microcurie/μmol $\hat{=}$ 3.7×10^4 s^{-1} μmol^{-1}) of the substrate
t reaction time (min)
2.22×10^6 factor for conversion from disintegrations per min.

Examples:

The following examples of the determination of catalytic activities of enzymes, which are taken from the principal classes, serve to illustrate the techniques.

Oxidoreductases: Enzymes from this group are generally determined by the optical method. However, if side reactions interfere, the following assay procedure can, for example, be used for 3-hydroxy-3-methylglutaryl-coenzyme A reductase[31].

$$\overset{*}{\text{HOOC}}-\text{CH}_2-\underset{\underset{\text{CH}_3}{|}}{\overset{\overset{\text{OH}}{|}}{\text{C}}}-\text{CH}_2-\text{COSCoA} + 2\,\text{NADPH} + 2\,\text{H}^+ \rightleftharpoons$$

$$\overset{*}{\text{HOOC}}-\text{CH}_2-\underset{\underset{\text{CH}_3}{|}}{\overset{\overset{\text{OH}}{|}}{\text{C}}}-\text{CH}_2\text{OH} + \text{CoASH} + 2\,\text{NADP}^+$$

5-[^{14}C]-HMG-CoA is converted into [^{14}C]-mevalonic acid in the presence of an NADPH-producing system with the aid of HMG-CoA reductase[†1], and the mevalonic acid is separated from unreacted HMG-CoA by ether extraction. After removal of the ether, the active mevalonic acid is quantitatively converted into 5-phosphomevalonic acid with ATP and mevalonate kinase[†2], in a second ether extraction, the 5-phosphomevalonic acid remains in the aqueous phase, where its radioactivity is measured. Other determinations from the oxidoreductase group are described in[32, 33].

[†1] Mevalonate: NADP oxidoreductase (CoA-acylating), EC 1.1.1.34.
[†2] ATP: mevalonate 5-phosphotransferase, EC 2.7.1.36.

Transferases: An example from this class is *Isselbacher's* method[34] for uridine diphosphategalactose pyrophosphorylase†[3].

$$UTP + \overset{*}{Gal}\text{-}1\text{-}P \rightleftharpoons UDP\text{-}\overset{*}{Gal} + PP_i$$

Uridine triphosphate is incubated with galactose-1-phosphate [^{14}C] and the enzyme. When the reaction is stopped, uridine diphosphate glucose is adsorbed on charcoal and eluted with an ammoniacal ethanol-water mixture, and the radioactivity of the eluate is determined.

For further examples from this class of enzymes, see [35, 36].

Hydrolases: This group includes the determination of phosphodiesterase†[4] in *E. coli*[37].

$$DNA^* \rightarrow 5'\text{-mononucleotide}^*$$

Deoxyribonucleic acid labelled with [^{32}P] is degraded to 5'-mononucleotides [^{32}P]. To separate the mononucleotides from unreacted DNA, the latter is precipitated with perchloric acid. The radio-activity can be measured directly in the supernatant fluid.

For further examples from this class of enzymes, see [38, 39].

Lyases and isomerases: Glutamic acid decarboxylase†[5] [40]. The micro method allows the determination of enzyme in freeze-dried tissue sections of only 3 to 15 µg.

$$HOOC-CH_2-CH_2-\underset{\underset{NH_2}{|}}{CH}-\overset{*}{C}OOH \rightarrow HOOC-CH_2-CH_2-CH_2-NH_2 + \overset{*}{C}O_2$$

The liberated carbon dioxide [^{14}C] is absorbed directly in the cuvette in Hyamine solution†[6], where it can be measured in a liquid scintillation counter after the addition of a scintillation liquid. For other methods see [41].

Ligases: This class of enzymes includes fatty acid synthetase†[7], the determination of which has been described by *F. Lynen*[42].

$$CH_3-CO-SCoA + n\,HOOC-\overset{*}{C}H_2-CO-SCoA + 2n\,NADPH + 2n\,H^+ \rightarrow$$
$$CH_3-(CH_2-\overset{*}{C}H_2)_n-CO-SCoA + n\,CoASH + n\,CO_2 + 2n\,NADP^+ + n\,H_2O$$

The enzyme that catalyzes the above reaction cannot be determined by the optical method in crude yeast extracts, since NADP is consumed too rapidly by side reactions. The incorporation of radio-active malonyl-coenzyme A into fatty acids is therefore measured, the fatty acids being separated from unreacted substrate by extraction with petroleum ether.

In vivo Methods

An interesting application of the isotope technique is the *in vivo* determination of catalytic activities of enzymes. According to *M. Wenzel* et al.[43], the activity of estradiol dehydrogenase can be determined in the human body.

$$\text{estradiol-17}\alpha\text{-}[^3H] + NAD(NADP) \rightarrow \text{estrone} + NAD[^3H](NADP[^3H])$$

$$NAD[^3H](NADP[^3H]) \xrightarrow[\text{chain}]{\text{respiratory}} H[^3H]O$$

---

†[3] UTP: α-D-galactose-1-phosphate uridylyltransferase, EC 2.7.7.10.
†[4] Oligonucleate 5'-nucleotidohydrolase, EC 3.1.4.1.
†[5] L-Glutamate 1-carboxy-lase, EC 4.1.1.15.
†[6] (Diisobutyl-cresoxyethyl)dimethylbenzylammonium hydroxide.
†[7] System number not yet assigned by the Enzyme Commission.

Estradiol-17α-[^{3}H] is administered and oxidized to the keto steroid by the 10-hydroxysteroid dehydrogenase present everywhere in the body.

The tritium added to the coenzymes NAD and NADP in the reaction is converted into tritiated water by the reactions of the respiratory chain. The tritiated water rapidly mixes with the body water (1–2 h). By determining the activity of an aliquot (blood, urine) that has first been distilled to separate other radioactive components, it is possible to deduce the total activity in the body water, and hence minimum activity of the dehydrogenase. Unlike all other metabolites, water may be assumed to be uniformly distributed in all parts of the body.

This principle may also be used for the *in vivo* determination of other dehydrogenases with suitably chosen tritiated substrates.

References

1 Schmeiser, K. (1963) *Radionuclide*, Springer Berlin–Göttingen–Heidelberg.
2 Hagen, A. & Newsholme, E.A. (1974) in *Methods of Enzymatic Analysis* (Bergmeyer, H.U., ed.) 2. edn., p.283, Verlag Chemie, Weinheim, and Academic Press, New York.
3 Fünfer, E. & Neunert, J. (1959) *Zählrohre und Scintillationszähler*, G.Braun, Karlsruhe.
4 Taylor, D. (1957) *The Measurement of Radioisotopes*, Menthuen & Co., London.
5 Overmann, R.T. & Clark, H.H. (1960) *Radioisotope Techniques*, McGraw-Hill Book Company, New York.
6 Bush, E.T. (1963) *Anal.Chem.* **35**, 1024.
7 Wittenberger, W. (1960) *Rechnen in der Chemie*, Springer Wien.
8 Broda, E. (1960) *Radioactive Isotopes in Biochemistry*, p.111, Elsevier, Amsterdam.
9 Gorsuch, T.T. (1968) *Radioactive Isotope Dilution Analysis*, Review 2, The Radiochemical Centre, Amersham, England.
10 Ruzicka, J. & Stary, J. (1964) *Atomic Energy Rev. Vienna* **2**, 3.
11 Yalow, R.A. & Berson, S.A. (1960) *J. Clin. Invest.* **39**, 1157.
12 Hales, C.N. & Randle, P.J. (1963) *Biochem. J.* **88**, 137.
13 Unger, R.H., Eisentraut, A.M., McCall, M.S. & Madison, L.L. (1961) *J. Clin. Invest.* **40**, 1250.
14 Hunter, W.M. & Greenwood, F.C. (1962) *Acta Endocrinol. Suppl.* **67**, 59.
15 Murphy, B.E.P. (1964) *Nature* **201**, 679.
16 Smith, T.W. & Haber, E. (1973) *Progress in Cardiology* **2**, 49–73.
17 Gilman, A.G. (1970) *Proc. Nat. Acad. Sci. U.S.A.* **67**, 408.
18 Löffler, G. & Wieland, O. (1963) *Biochem. Z.* **336**, 447.
19 Baird, G.D., Hibbitt, K.G., Hunter, G.D., Lund, P., Stubbs, M. & Krebs, H.A. (1968) *Biochem. J.* **107**, 683.
20 Newsholme, E.A. & Taylor, K. (1968) *Biochim. Biophys. Acta* **158**, 11.
21 Newsholme, E.A. (1974) in *Methods of Enzymatic Analysis* (Bergmeyer, H.U., ed.) 2. edn., p.1409, Verlag Chemie, Weinheim, and Academic Press, New York.
22 Harvey, R.A., Godefroy, T., Lucas-Lenard, J. & Grunberg-Manago, M. (1967) *Europ. J. Biochem.* **1**, 327.
23 de Wolf, H. & Hers, H.G. (1967) *Europ. J. Biochem.* **2**, 50.
24 Mans, R.J. & Novelli, G.D. (1961) *Arch. Biochem. Biophys.* **94**, 48.
25 Falaschi, A., Adler, J. & Khorana, G.G. (1963) *J. biol. Chem.* **238**, 3080.
26 Bollum, F.J. (1966) *Procedures in Nucleic Acid Research*, p.296, Harper & Row, New York.
27 Malt, R.A. & Miller, W.L. (1967) *Analyt. Biochem.* **18**, 388.
28 Oser, M.O. & Wood, N.P. (1964) *J. Bacteriol.* **87**, 104.
29 Ishimoto, N. & Strominger, J.L. (1966) in *Methods in Enzymology* (Colowick, S.P. & Kaplan, N.O., eds.) Vol. 8, p. 423, Academic Press, New York.
30 Ireland, D.M. & Mills, D.C.B. (1966) *Biochem. J.* **99**, 283.
31 Knappe, J., Ringelmann, E. & Lynen, F. (1959) *Biochem. Z.* **332**, 195.
32 Matsuhashi, S. & Strominger, J.L. (1966) in *Methods in Enzymology* (Colowick, S.P. & Kaplan, N.O., eds.) Vol. 8, p. 310, Academic Press, New York.
33 Anderson, R.L. (1967) *Biochim. Biophys. Acta* **144**, 18.
34 Isselbacher, K.J. (1958) *J. biol. Chem.* **232**, 429.
35 Brenner, J. & Norum, K.R. (1967) *J. biol. Chem.* **242**, 1744.

36 Slack, C.R. & Hatch, M.D. (1967) *Biochem. J.* **103,** 660.
37 Lehman, J.R. (1960) *J. biol. Chem.* **235,** 1479.
38 Winteringham, F.P.W. & Disney, R.W. (1962) *Nature* **195,** 1303.
39 Hers, H.G. (1964) *Advances in Metabolic Disorders*, Vol. I, 335, Academic Press, New York.
40 Roberts, E. & Simonson, D.G. (1963) *Biochem. Pharmacol.* **12,** 113.
41 Jourdian, G.W. & Roseman, S. (1962) *J. biol. Chem.* **237,** 2442.
42 Lynen, F., Hoppe-Kessel, J. & Eggerer, H. (1964) *Biochem. Z.* **340,** 95.
43 Wenzel, M. & Blum, K.U. (1967) *J. Clin. Chem. u. Clin. Biochem.,* **5.** 203.
44 Wunderwald, P., Jurz, G. & Michal, G. (1974) *Anal. Biochem.* **59,** 468–481.

Evaluation and Assessment of Experimental Results

The measuring techniques described in detail in the foregoing chapters yield experimental values that cannot be compared directly with one another and cannot serve by themselves as a basis for any conclusions. These values must first be used to determine the experimental results, which are then expressed as conventional, understandable quantities. The following sections were written with photometric measurements in mind, but their substance is also valid, in principle, for all other measuring techniques.

Experimental Data

Hans Ulrich Bergmeyer

The data provided by the measurements occasionally cannot be used directly, but they must often be corrected for one or more blank values. Frequently, they are meaningful only in combination with the results of other measurements (standard values, other reference magnitudes). Occasionally they are associated with large errors (for error theory, see p. 233). Gross errors are recognized by deviations from the expected course of the reaction. Two such phenomena are described below.

Non-constant end-point

In the determination of substance concentrations of substrates and coenzymes by the end-point method, the value of the physical parameter measured should not change after completion of the reaction. However, the absorbance occasionally changes slowly, i.e. it "creeps", for reasons that are not always apparent. Some of the causes are known. Thus the enzyme used may contain contaminating enzymes, which allow a slow reaction of other substances in the sample, or in NAD(P)H-dependent reactions the enzyme used may contain "NAD(P)H oxidase". An interfering reaction is therefore superimposed on the reaction to be measured. This may run in the same or in the opposite direction. Accordingly, instead of a constant end-point, there is an increase or decrease in the measured effect (Fig. 1, p. 214).

The additional absorbance, which normally shows a linear variation with time, can easily be eliminated by graphical extrapolation to t_0 (the time of the start of the reaction). If no recorder is used, absorbance readings are taken at regular intervals, e.g. one minute, the values are plotted against time, and the linear portion of the resulting curve is extended back to time t_0. The point of intersection with the ordinate axis at time t_0 gives the correct end-point and hence the true absorbance change ΔA.

Non-linear reaction curves

The form of the reaction curve is important in the determination of the catalytic activity of enzymes. By definition, the catalytic activity of an enzyme is given by the rate of the reaction that it catalyzes, and in particular by the initial rate v_i.

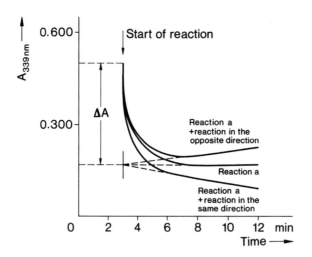

Fig. 1. End-point method for the determination of substance concentrations. Extrapolation when the end-point is not constant (schematic).

If the reaction curve is non-linear, however, the reaction rate $\pm \Delta c/\Delta t$ or $\pm \Delta A/\Delta t$ depends on the position of the measurement interval on the time scale[1]. Any curvature indicates that the rate changes during the reaction, the direction of the change usually being a decrease as the reaction progresses. The greater the curvature, the more difficult it is to determine the initial rate accurately. Approximate values, which are usually adequate for practical purposes, can be obtained from several experimental readings taken shortly after the start of the reaction. These values may be extrapolated graphically to $t = 0$ (Fig. 2b).

To obtain accurate values for the initial rate, a tangent is drawn to the curve at $t = 0$ (Fig. 2a), using a mirror ruler. This is a surface mirror perpendicular to the plane of the graph; it is placed

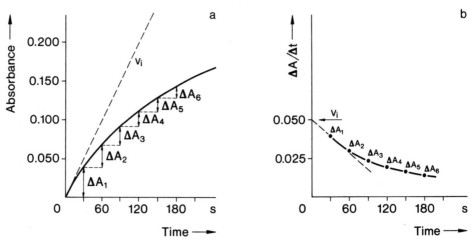

Fig. 2. Continuous measurement for the determination of catalytic activity of enzymes. Evaluation of the initial rate v_i when the reaction curve is non-linear. a) reaction curve with tangent at $t = 0$. b) Evaluation of v_i by extrapolation of the values for $\Delta A/\Delta t$ from the curve a versus $t = 0$. $t = 30\,s = $ constant.

across the reaction curve and pivoted until the mirror image forms an unbroken continuation of the curve. A line drawn along the edge of the mirror is perpendicular to the tangent. If measurements are not carried out at regular intervals (in the "two-point method"), the error increases with increasing curvature of the reaction curve (refer also to p. 77): In the case of a curve with a lag phase (cf. p. 16) – assuming there is no possibility of avoiding this type of curve – an approximate value for the "initial rate" is calculated from the slope of the tangent to the point of inflection (cf. p. 26).

Standard curves and standards

For a stoichiometric reaction, the experimental results can be calculated directly on the basis of the molar absorption coefficient, molar volume or other physical constants. If the reaction does not proceed to completion, standard curves must be constructed. It goes without saying that specified conditions of temperature, pH, and buffering must be maintained. Standard curves for determinations in biological material are best set up by adding the substance to be determined to the biological material, so that allowance may be made for any effects due to other compounds present in sample.

Standard curves should pass through the origin in a plot of the unit of measurement against concentration. If they intersect the ordinate (on which the unit of measurement is plotted), the system already contains traces of the substance to be determined (or of one of the intermediates in the case of coupled reactions), or else the reagent blank has been wrongly prepared and has given too low a value. Intersection of the calibration curve with the abscissa (on which the concentration or amount of the substance to be determined is plotted) is equivalent to intersection with the ordinate at negative values. This usually results from an excessively high reading for the reagent blank or from the presence of an impurity that reacts with the substance to be estimated so that the latter cannot be determined quantitatively.

Calibration points should lie on a straight line. When the curve is non-linear, the initial portion is often approximately linear; only this portion should be used. With non-linear calibration curves, there is no linear relationship between the values measured and the concentrations. One therefore tries to linearize curved calibration plots by using logarithmic, semilogarithmic, reciprocal, partreciprocal, or other graphical presentations.

Special care is necessary in the construction of standard curves for the determination of substrates by kinetics methods (refer to p. 79 ff.). Strict control of the conditions of measurement (particularly temperature, pH, and quantity of enzyme added) is very important. A single calibration point ("standard value") is sufficient if the "fixed-time" method can be used. The experimental data are referred to the standard (eqn. (4), p. 237).

Standard substances

The use of extremely pure standard substances is a prerequisite for the construction of a calibration curve. Because of the uncertainty associated with purity, the *International Union of Pure and Applied Chemistry* (IUPAC) has laid down the following classification of extremely pure substances[2]:

Grade A: Atomic-weight standard.

Grade B: Ultimate standard. A substance which can be purified to virtually atomic-weight standard.

Grade C: Primary standard. A commercially available substance of purity $100 \pm 0.02\%$.
Grade D: Working standard. A commercially available substance of purity $100 \pm 0.05\%$.
Grade E: Secondary standard. A substance of lower purity which can be standardized against primary (Grade C) material.

According to *Radin*'s recommendations[3], "primary standards" for clinical chemistry should be prepared from a product with $100 \pm 0.02\%$ purity. However, no primary standards are available for many biologically relevant compounds. In such cases, therefore, it is not possible to standardize a secondary standard against a primary standard. These standards should be termed "clinical standards"[3].

The *National Bureau of Standards* (NBS) offers a series of primary standard substances (Standard Reference Material, SRM).

References

1 Bergmeyer, H. U. (1952) *Biochem. Z.* **323**, 163.
2 Büttner, J., Borth, R., Boutwell, J. H. & Broughton, P. M. G. (1975) *Clin. Chim. Acta* **63**, F 25.
3 Radin, N. (1967) *Clin. Chem.* **13**, 55.

Experimental Results and Units of Reference

Hans Ulrich Bergmeyer, Erich Bernt, Marianne Grassl, and Gerhard Michal

The result of a measurement should provide specific information on the sample under investigation. For this reason, the processed data should be referred to the measured parameters of the sample (e.g. volume or mass).

Definitions

For metabolites, the result is usually expressed as a "concentration" (mol or g per unit volume of the sample), or else, with the unit weight of the sample as the reference quantity, as the "content" (mol or g per unit weight); in the case of purified substances, the result is given as the "purity" (in percent) based on the weight of substance used. *Bücher* et al.[1] give the following definitions for biological material (tissue): "The term 'metabolite content' of a tissue should be used when the analytical value is referred to the fresh weight of the tissue in question. No account is taken of the distribution of the metabolite within the tissue among the various types of cells and their intracellular compartments, the blood vessels, and the interstitial space. 'Metabolite concentration' is used when the reference quantity is the volume of a given tissue compartment in which it is distributed".

The result of the determination of the catalytic activity of an enzyme is expressed by the activity unit referred to the weight or the volume.

One unit (U) is the enzyme activity that transforms 1 µmol of substrate in 1 min under optimal conditions. This international unit will in future be replaced by the term katal (kat) as defined according to the SI-system (1 mol/s). Cf. pp. 9 ff. and 56. Description of the catalytic activity of an enzyme in terms of the rate of the catalyzed reaction is always possible, but difficulties occasionally arise with the term "mol of substrate converted" e.g. for some hydrolases that convert macromolecular substrates and for protein kinases where the molecular weight of the phosphorylated protein has not been established with sufficient accuracy. If an enzyme cannot be saturated with substrate (e.g. catalase), the concentration of the substrate should be given. For enzymes that catalyze definite equilibrium reactions, the substrate used for the measurement should be named. The terms "forward" and "reverse" reaction are not free from ambiguity. The activity of hydrolases, for example, is unambiguously defined only if one specifies which synthetic substrate (and there are many possibilities in some cases) was used (cf. p. 60). The temperature at which the measurements were carried out should also be mentioned, unless it is fixed by international agreement.

The activities of enzyme preparations are referred to the mass of enzyme protein (exceptions: when, as in the case of β-fructosidase, the enzyme is only about 25% protein, the remainder being polysaccharide, the activity is referred to the quantity of substance). The "specific catalytic activity" (U/g, kat/g, μkat/g) is thus obtained.

The quantity for the catalytic activity of an enzyme per unit volume, corresponding to the substance concentration of metabolites, is the "catalytic activity concentration" (U/l, kat/l, μkat/l). The following units are equivalent:

Metabolites			Enzymes		
Substance concentration		mol/l	Catalytic activity concentration		U/l; kat/l
		mmol/l			mkat/l
	or	g/l			μkat/l
		mg/l			n kat/l
Substance content		mol/g	Specific catalytic activity		U/g; kat/g
		mmol/g			
	or	g/g			mkat/g
		mg/g			μkat/g

In general, therefore, the experimental data should be converted to concentrations or concentration changes per unit time and referred to specified reference quantities. Only then can one speak of a "result".

Referring the experimental results to biological material

In the analysis of organ extracts, blood, serum, etc., the dilution resulting from deproteinization of samples must also be taken into account along with the fluid content of the sample. The following values give reasonable accuracy: blood 80% (w/w), tissue (liver, kidney, muscle, heart) 75% (w/w). Tissue samples are weighed out; a density of 1.06 is used for the conversion blood volumes into mass.

Apart from the volume (in the case of serum, plasma, blood, urine, etc.), other reference quantities that may be used for biological material are the fresh weight, dry weight, total nitrogen, protein content, protein nitrogen; cell count, e.g. erythrocyte count; hemoglobin content, cytochrome-c content, and dry weight of the cell-free sample solution.

Examples:

Determination of the dilution factor for blood.

The specific gravity of blood is taken as 1.06, and its water content is taken as 80% (w/w). 2 ml of blood are deproteinized with 3 ml of perchloric acid and centrifuged, and 2.5 ml of the supernatant are neutralized with 1 ml K_2CO_3 solution. The blood is therefore diluted by the following factor:

$$F = \frac{2 \times 1.06 \times 0.8 + 3}{2} \times \frac{2.5 + 1}{2.5} = \frac{1.696 + 3}{2} \times \frac{3.5}{2.5} = 3.29$$

The experimental result obtained with the neutralized blood extract must be multiplied by this factor to obtain the content of the metabolite in the blood.

Calculation of the dilution factor for multi-stage assay mixtures.
In the determination of maltose in biological fluids, the various reaction steps have different pH-optima. The assay begins with an incubation: 0.5 ml sample with 0.5 ml acetate buffer and 0.02 ml α-glucosidase. After inactivation of the enzyme, the second step is the determination of the glucose in 0.2 ml of the incubation solution ($V = 3.42$ ml). The dilution factor is thus:

$$F = \frac{0.5 + 0.5 + 0.02}{0.5} \times \frac{3.42}{0.2} = 2.04 \times 17.1 = 34.88 .$$

The experimental result, after division by 2 (1 maltose $\hat{=}$ 2 glucose), must be multiplied by this factor to obtain the maltose content in 1 ml of sample.

To calculate the metabolite content of the cells of a tissue, the metabolite content of the blood in this tissue must be taken into account.

The fraction by weight of blood in the tissue is determined according to *Bücher* et al.[1] from absorbance measurements at 578, 560, and 540 nm. Assuming that the proportion of oxyhemoglobin (HbO_2) in the circulating blood and the tissue is approximately the same, it follows that the fraction of blood x in the tissue is

$$x = \frac{\Delta A_{HbO_2} \times \text{dilution} \times d_1}{\Delta A'_{HbO_2} \times \text{dilution} \times d_2} \times 100\% \ (w/w)$$

where
ΔA_{HbO_2} = absorbance difference for tissue extract
$\Delta A'_{HbO_2}$ = absorbance difference for blood dilution
d_1 and d_2 = light paths of the cuvettes
ΔA_{HbO_2} and $\Delta A'_{HbO_2}$ are calculated[1] without the use of graphical methods from the absorbance measurements at 578, 560, and 540 nm, according to the formula:

$$\Delta A_{HbO_2} \text{ or } \Delta A'_{HbO_2} = (A_{578} - A_{560}) + [(A_{540} - A_{578}) \times 0.47]$$

If the metabolite concentration in the tissue sample is to be referred to the true volume of cellular fluid in order to give the physiological concentration[2], the result (in mmol/l of tissue extract) is multiplied by the following factor:

$$F = \frac{V_{\text{after neutralization}}}{V_{\text{before neutralization}}} \times \frac{\dfrac{\text{tissue weight}}{D} \times \dfrac{P}{100} + V_E}{\dfrac{\text{tissue weight}}{D} \times \dfrac{P}{100}}$$

P = vol.-percent (v/v) of liquid in the tissue, D = specific gravity of the sample. The latter quantity may be taken as unity in most cases. V_E = volume of reagent solution (e.g. $HClO_4$) used for deproteinization.

A similar calculation for erythrocytes has been published by *Bürgi*[3].

References

1 Hohorst, H.J., Kreutz, F.H. & Bücher, Th. (1959) *Biochem. Z.* **332**, 18.
2 Michal, G., unpublished.
3 Buergi, W. (1969) *J. Clin. Chem. u. Clin. Biochem.* **7**, 458.

Evaluation and Control of the Quality of Experimental Results

Fritz Stähler

Enzymatic analyses are performed with the aim of determining changes in biological systems. Interpretation of the experimental results is made more difficult by the fact that both biological and methodological variables can mask the true situation. Biological variability comprises the variation of biological parameters from individual to individual, while methodological variability results from variations in the analytical system, from isolation of the material for investigation through storage and preparation to the analysis proper.

The methods of mathematical statistics enable the demonstration of laws which are not directly apparent from the measurements. Statistics is basically a refinement of common sense, and allows an objective treatment of phenomena subject to fluctuation. Large amounts of data can be combined and characterized briefly and precisely with the aid of statistical concepts. Objective evaluation of the results of a small number of experiments can be performed only by statistical methods. These processes are particularly valuable in answering the question of whether any relationship exists between two variables.

The laws of mathematical statistics are derived from models of probability theory. As a rule, the measurements are compared with theoretical models. A meaningful comparison results when the model and the experiment satisfy the same assumptions.

A prerequisite for the study of biological variability and its susceptibility to experimental effects is the use of analytical techniques whose methodical variance is known and under control. In this article therefore, basic statistical concepts and methods will be discussed, followed by a description of the statistical quality control of analytical measurement techniques. References to the original literature have been largely avoided. A list of references treating the subject in greater detail[1-11] is appended.

Statistical Terms and Methods

Planning of experiments

Biochemical experiments are evaluated quantitatively by statistical methods, and it is thus possible to arrive at meaningful statements and rational decisions. When the conditions for certain calculating procedures are lacking, erroneous evaluations are obtained. The laws of statistics must be taken into account in all phases of the experimental work: in *formulation* of the problem (how accurate should the result be?), in the *planning* of the experiments (how many measurements are necessary?), in their *performance* (what methods and apparatus will be required?), and in the *evaluation* of the results (reading or recording processes, evaluation graphically or by calculation?).

To allow a definite statement to be made, a minimum number of experiments (samples) must be performed. The sample size depends on the preciseness of the desired experimental result and on the range of biological variation in the material under investigation. The sample size must be particularly large when it is desired to determine small differences significantly. Doubling of the exactness requires a fourfold increase of the sample size.

As a rule, a limited number of experiments *(samples)* will lead to the deduction of a law that is valid even when the experiment is repeated an unlimited number of times on the same *basic population*. Conclusions concerning the population that are derived from a sample are permissible only when there is a random selection. Each individual of the population must basically have the same, or at least an accurately predictable, chance of being sampled in the random experiment, and this is often difficult to achieve.

Evaluation of the experimental results

In descriptive statistics, experimental results are treated in three successive steps.

1. Tabulation of the results of observation, formation of classes, and determination of frequencies.
2. Graphical presentation: histogram, frequency curve.
3. Mathematical treatment: mean value, variance, distribution.

Tabulation of the observed results

All original data are organized synoptically in tabular form. This list is called the master list. It must contain complete and accurate information on all details of the experiment (worker, date, experimental arrangement, sequence of measurements, changes in the arrangement and/or performance of the experiments).

Class formation

In the case of comprehensive random samples with more than 30 values (n > 30), tabular representation is cumbersome. The range between the smallest and the largest values is divided into classes (grouping).

Frequency

The *absolute class frequency* gives the number of values in the interval (class) concerned. The *relative class frequency* is obtained by division by the size of the sample. This frequency as a function of the class means is called the *frequency function* of the random samples subdivided into classes.

Example:

Table 2 is obtained by grouping from a master list of 100 blood sugar values (Table 1).

Table 1. Analytical variability of the determination of glucose in serum (precision of the hexokinase/G6P-DH method, N = 100 single determinations on 100 days). Values in mmol/l.

4.37	4.13	4.46	4.45	4.73	4.20	3.64	4.15	3.96	3.61
3.71	4.05	3.70	4.21	4.35	3.89	3.67	4.50	4.16	4.07
4.31	4.08	3.65	4.23	4.00	4.58	4.30	4.42	3.90	4.36
3.93	4.14	3.76	3.82	4.16	4.17	4.30	4.18	4.56	3.93
4.60	3.94	4.32	4.55	4.40	4.55	4.82	4.56	4.19	4.52
4.38	4.36	3.69	4.04	4.40	3.98	4.38	4.00	4.08	4.16
4.10	3.84	4.03	4.58	4.20	4.37	4.58	4.14	4.88	4.21
4.11	4.31	4.27	4.31	4.62	3.80	4.08	4.05	3.85	4.21
3.87	4.05	3.94	4.23	3.95	4.32	4.03	3.91	4.18	4.23
3.84	4.03	3.56	3.81	3.93	4.28	4.03	3.74	4.27	4.72

Table 2. Class formation from the master list (Tab. 1).

Classes	Class means	Frequency absolute		relative	Additive frequency (relative)
3.50–3.67	3.59	‖‖	4	0.04	0.04
3.67–3.84	3.76	ЖТ ‖‖	9	0.09	0.13
3.84–4.01	3.93	ЖТ ЖТ ЖТ ‖	16	0.16	0.29
4.01–4.18	4.10	ЖТ ЖТ ЖТ ЖТ ‖	22	0.22	0.51
4.18–4.35	4.27	ЖТ ЖТ ЖТ ЖТ ‖‖	24	0.24	0.75
4.35–4.52	4.44	ЖТ ЖТ ‖	11	0.11	0.86
4.52–4.69	4.61	ЖТ ЖТ	10	0.10	0.96
4.69–4.86	4.78	‖‖	3	0.03	0.99
4.86–5.03	4.95	‖	1	0.01	1.00

If in an experiment two or more parameters (random samples) are investigated, all measured values are treated analogously.

Graphical presentation

The simplest form of graphical presentation is a histogram (Fig. 1, p. 222). This usually has the typical shape of a bell, which may be more or less biased toward the left of the right. Much rarer are distributions with two or more peaks. The width of the bell is a measure of the *variance* (see p. 222) of the measured values. The peak indicates the position of the frequency maximum of the random samples.

Frequency curve

With a sufficiently large number of random samples and a corresponding increase in the number of frequency classes, the shape of the histogram is smoothed out and a frequency curve is obtained (Fig. 2, p. 222).
The numerical value of the "average" that is used in the case of skew distributions is the *median* (the central value when the measured values are arranged in order of size). The median or central value has the probability p = 0.5. In symmetrical distributions, the median value coincides with the mean.

Normal distribution

Among the symmetrical frequency distributions, the normal distribution (*Gaussian* or probability curve) is characteristic for values scattered randomly around a defined mean value (Fig. 3, p. 223). The distribution of the individual figures must therefore be ascribed to chance and does not depend on systematic factors. Typical examples are methodical and technical errors (Fig. 2). The value of the abscissa corresponding to the peak of the curve gives the arithmetic mean $\bar{x}$. The perpendicular to the abscissa from either of the points of inflection of the two arms is the standard deviation (s).
The normal distribution is characterized by the fact that a definite percentage of values always lies within various multiples of σ (see Fig. 3 and Tab. 3, p. 223 for explanation of symbols):

$\qquad$ 68.3% of all values lie within $\mu \pm 1\sigma$
$\qquad$ 95.4% of all values lie within $\mu \pm 2\sigma$
$\qquad$ 99.7% of all values lie within $\mu \pm 3\sigma$

The normal distribution and its modifications are of great importance in biology (e.g. in comparative statistics and in the determination of reference values). In addition, "nonparametric" test processes are being used to an increasing extent. These have the advantage that the random samples need not exhibit any definite of distribution. The disadvantage is the lower resolution of

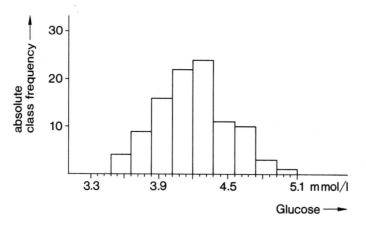

Fig. 1. Histogram of the random sample presented in Tab. 1.

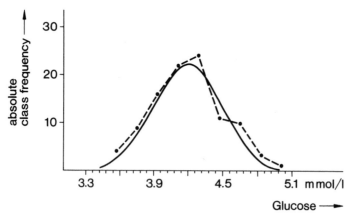

Fig. 2. Frequency curve of the histogram in Fig. 1 with the corresponding normal distribution (--- class means).

the corresponding tests with small sample sizes (n < 20). A condition for the validity of the "t" test that is often used in comparing mean values is, for example, that the sample consist of "normally distributed" values. If this condition is not fulfilled, which is often the case, the use of the t-test may lead to false interpretations.

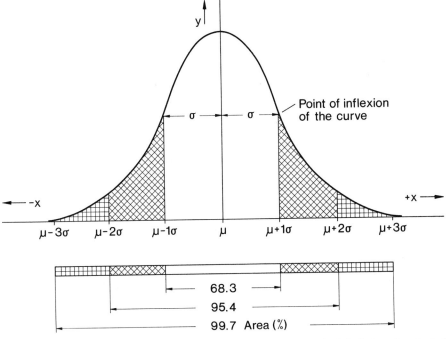

Fig. 3. Normal distribution of a basic population (mean value and standard deviation σ) and relative areas of μ ± 1σ, 2σ, 3σ (in a random sample x̄ = μ, s = σ).

Mathematical Evaluation of Experiments

Terms and symbols

Population and sample are characterized by *parameters* and *statistics*. Parameters belong to the population, statistics to the sample. The symbols differ accordingly.

Table 3. Parameters and statistics.

Term	Population Parameter	Sample Statistic
Sample size	N	n
Mean	μ	x̄
Variance	σ^2	s^2
Standard deviation	σ	s
Probability	P	–
Relative frequency	–	p
Correlation coefficient*	ϱ	r (ϱ̂)

* If there is no specific symbol for the sample statistic, the symbol is simply provided with the sign ˆ. Symbols with ˆ are therefore sample statistics.

Sample statistics

The *mean value* $\bar{x}$ of a random sample $x_1 \ldots x_n$ is defined as the arithmetic mean of values of the random sample:

$$(1) \qquad \bar{x} = \frac{x_1 + x_2 \cdots + x_n}{n} = \frac{1}{n} \times \sum_{j=1}^{n} x_j,$$

and is an estimate of the *true mean* (μ) of the population to which the random sample belongs. It approaches this value more and more closely, the greater the number of observations is. For $n \to \infty$, $\bar{x} \to \mu$.

The *variance* shows how widely the sample values are scattered around the mean value. It is denoted by s^2:

$$(2) \qquad s^2 = \frac{1}{n-1} \sum_{j=1}^{n} (x_j - \bar{x})^2$$

To calculate the variance, the following relation derived from eqn. (2) is used:

$$(3) \qquad s^2 = \frac{1}{n-1} \left[\sum_{j=1}^{n} x_j^2 - \frac{1}{n} \left(\sum_{j=1}^{n} x_j \right)^2 \right]$$

It gives an estimated value for the variance of the population:

$$(4) \qquad \sigma^2 = \frac{1}{n} \sum_{j} (x_j - \mu)^2$$

However, this can rarely be calculated exactly, since μ is practically always unknown.

In contrast to the variance of the population, the *sample* variance is referred to only $(n-1)$ observations. However, it can be shown that for $n \to \infty$, the value of s^2 tends to σ^2. The expression $(n-1)$ is also termed the number of *degrees of freedom*.

The *standard deviation* or mean error is the name given to the square root of the variance:

$$(5) \qquad s = \sqrt{\frac{\sum_{j} (x_j - \bar{x})^2}{n-1}}$$

It has the same dimensions as the measurements and should be regarded as the most probable error.

In practice, the quality of the analytical methods is characterized by the percentage error or *coefficient of variation* (CV), this being a specific measure of the imprecision of the measurement (cf. p. 234). It is the relative error:

$$(6) \qquad CV = \pm \frac{s_{\bar{x}} \times 100}{\bar{x}},$$

and is expressed as a percentage.

The arithmetic mean $\bar{x}$ is the best estimated value for the mean of the population, but in common with the individual observations, it is itself affected by an error. The average error of the mean is:

$$(7) \qquad s_{\bar{x}} = \frac{s}{\sqrt{n}}$$

The accuracy of the mean increases in proportion to $1/\sqrt{n}$. If it were desired to reduce $s_{\bar{x}}$ by a power of 10, the number of measurements to be performed would have to be increased hundredfold.

Confidence interval

The term confidence interval was defined in order to estimate the deviation of an approximate value (e.g. $\bar{x}$) from the true value (e.g. μ). The mean value $\bar{x}$ and the variance s^2 of a random sample are estimated values of the corresponding parameters of the basic population. The question is, how good are these approximate values inview of the errors attached to the experimental results? Since the sample statistics themselves belong to definite distribution functions, the followings can be postulated.

Let the mean value $\bar{x}$ and the standard deviation s of an approximately normally-distributed random sample be given. When the samples values are shown as a frequency distribution (see p. 223), it is apparent that, for example, 95.4% of the values occur in the interval $\bar{x} + 2$ s. Conversely, even on unlimited repetition of the experiment, one can expect to find, or "be confident" of finding, the mean value $\bar{x}$ in the interval $\bar{x} \pm 2$ s in about 95% of cases. Consequently, this interval is called the 95% confidence interval for the mean value $\bar{x}$. The limiting values are called *confidence limits*. The corresponding *confidence number* is denoted by γ. In biology, it is usually chosen as 95% or 99%.

If in a statistical investigation a parameter is to be estimated, the corresponding confidence limits should always be determined as well. Without confidence limits the credibility of an estimated result is zero.

The problem of outliers

Extremely high or low values within a series of measurements can probably be neglected under certain conditions. Errors of measurement, evaluation, and calculation, or a pathological case in the material of healthy subjects investigated can lead to extreme values which must be deleted, since they arise from populations different from that of the random sample.

A general rule[12] states that, given at least 10 individual values, a value can be rejected as an outlier if it lies outside the range $\bar{x} \pm 4$ s, when the mean value and standard deviation have been calculated without the outlier. The "4-sigma range" ($\mu \pm 4\sigma$) includes 99.99% of the values in the case of a normal distribution, in the case of other symmetrical single-peak distributions 97%, and in any other distribution 94% of the values.

Statistical Evaluation of Results

The testing of hypotheses

In evaluative statistics, a hypothesis is first set up as to how the random variable in question is distributed. For example: Let the null hypothesis (H_0) be that two characteristic magnitudes (e.g. mean values) do not differ significantly. Let an alternative hypothesis (H_1) state that there is a significant difference between the two characteristic magnitudes. If H_0 is accepted, H_1 must automatically be rejected.

If the hypothesis that the mean values μ_1 and μ_0 of two distributions do not differ is valid, then $\mu_1 = \mu_0$. Possible alternatives are

$$\mu_1 > \mu_0$$
$$\mu_1 < \mu_0$$
$$\mu_1 \neq \mu_0$$

In the case of the hypotheses $\mu_1 > \mu_0$ and $\mu_1 < \mu_0$, one-sided differences are investigated (e.g. whether the mean value of one random sample is larger than of the other). The hypothesis $\mu_1 \neq \mu_0$ tests for deviations in both directions; the question is two-sided. The question of a one-sided or two-sided deviation is of considerable importance in testing for significance.

The decision concerning the acceptance or rejection of hypotheses is made by comparing the experimentally determined characteristic magnitudes with "test distributions". A test magnitude is calculated from the experimental results; this must not be above or below a limiting value laid down by the investigator.

If in a series of investigations the differences between populations are to be elucidated and the appropriate tests reveal no significant difference, the statement is made that "On the basis of the random sample used, no (statistical) difference can be ascertained (for the assumed probability of error)".

Significance

Empirically, agreement has been reached on three levels of significance with the following probabilities of error (α).

1. $\alpha = 0.05$

   The null hypothesis (H_0) is erroneously rejected once in 20 measurements.

2. $\alpha = 0.01$

   The null hypothesis (H_0) is erroneously rejected once in 100 measurements.

3. $\alpha = 0.001$

   The null hypothesis (H_0) is erroneously rejected once in 1000 measurements.

The following rules apply to the selection of a significance level:

– If differences are to be discovered, a large probability of error is chosen, usually $\alpha = 0.05$.
– If a theory is to be drawn up which sets a specific scientific trend, a small probability of error is chosen, usually $\alpha = 0.001$.

Comparison of mean values

In testing whether the mean values of experimental groups differ substantially (significantly, with a previously specified probability of error), the choice of test procedure must be governed by the nature of the random samples. The conditions for the applicability of the appropriate test must be satisfied absolutely, since otherwise conclusions can be drawn which are seriously in error.

Comparison of the mean values of unequal random samples

Two normally distributed mutually independent random samples with random variances $(s_1)^2$ and $(s_2)^2$ and sample sizes n_1 and n_2 are to be compared with one another. Let the null hypothesis (H_0) be that their mean values $\bar{x}_1$ and $\bar{x}_2$ differ only by chance with the probability of error $\alpha (H_0 : \bar{x} - \bar{x}_2 = 0)$. The null hypothesis ($H_0$) is to be confirmed if, for α and the number of degrees of freedom $f = n_1 + n_2 - 2$, the calculated value t_0 for the test magnitude (t) is smaller than the tabulated value t_T (Table 4).

Table 4. Tabulated values of the t-distribution.

Degree of freedom f	Probability of errors $\alpha = 5\%$	$\alpha = 1\%$	Degree of freedom f	Probability of errors $\alpha = 5\%$	$\alpha = 1\%$
1	12.71	63.66	26	2.06	2.78
2	4.30	9.92	27	2.05	2.77
3	3.18	5.84	28	2.05	2.76
4	2.78	4.60	29	2.05	2.76
5	2.57	4.03	30	2.04	2.75
6	2.45	3.71	35	2.03	2.72
7	2.36	3.50	40	2.02	2.70
8	2.31	3.36	45	2.01	2.69
9	2.26	3.25	50	2.01	2.68
10	2.23	3.17	60	2.00	2.66
11	2.20	3.11	70	1.99	2.65
12	2.18	3.05	80	1.99	2.64
13	2.16	3.01	90	1.99	2.63
14	2.14	2.98	100	1.98	2.63
15	2.13	2.95	120	1.98	2.62
16	2.12	2.92	140	1.98	2.61
17	2.11	2.90	160	1.97	2.61
18	2.10	2.88	180	1.97	2.60
19	2.09	2.86	200	1.97	2.60
20	2.09	2.85	300	1.97	2.59
21	2.08	2.83	400	1.97	2.59
22	2.07	2.82	500	1.97	2.59
23	2.07	2.81	1000	1.96	2.58
24	2.06	2.80	∞	1.96	2.58
25	2.06	2.79			

The calculation is performed from the following equations:

$$(8) \qquad t = \frac{|\bar{x}_1 - \bar{x}_2|}{s_d} \times \sqrt{\frac{n_1 \times n_2}{n_1 + n_2}}$$

$$(9) \qquad s_d = \sqrt{\frac{s_1^2 \times (n_1 - 1) + s_2^2 \times (n_2 - 1)}{n_1 + n_2 - 2}}$$

Example:

In two groups of rats, average increases in weight per week of $\bar{x}_1 = 18$ and $\bar{x}_2 = 24$ g, were found in $n_1 = 20$ and $n_2 = 32$ experiments, respectively. The variances were $s_1^2 = 4$ and $s_2^2 = 6$. Do the two experimental groups differ if a probability of error $\alpha = 5\%$ is assumed ($H_0 : \bar{x}_1 - \bar{x}_2 = 0$; $\alpha = 0.05$).

For the test magnitude we calculate

$$t_0 = \frac{|18 - 24|}{\sqrt{5.24}} \times \sqrt{\frac{20 \times 32}{20 + 32}} = 9.20$$

The tabulated value of the t-distribution for a probability of error $\alpha = 5\%$ and $f = n_1 + n_2 - 2 = 50$ degrees of freedom is $t_T = 2.01$. Since $t_0 > t_T$, the null hypothesis (H_0) must be rejected, i.e. significant differences exist between the two mean values assuming a probability of error of 5%.

Comparison of the mean values of two random samples of normally distributed populations with the same known variance

The null hypothesis to be tested is that the random samples were taken from normally distributed populations with the same mean value ($H_0 : u_1 - \mu_2 = 0$ as compared with the alternative H_1: $\mu_1 \neq \mu_2$). Since the variance of the population is known, eqns. (8) and (9) given above for the test magnitude t reduce to

(10)
$$t = \frac{\bar{x}_1 - \bar{x}_2}{\sigma} \times \sqrt{\frac{n_1 \times n_2}{n_1 + n_2}}$$

As in the example relating to eqns. (8) and (9), it should be ascertained whether t_0 lies between the limits of the standard normal distribution given by the significance number α (see t-Table).

Testing whether the mean value belongs to a normally distributed population with a known variance

The mean value $\bar{x}$ of a normally distributed random sample of size n and variance s^2 is to be compared with the mean value μ of a normally distributed population of the same variance ($s^2 = \sigma^2$). The null hypothesis ($H_0 : \bar{x} - \mu_0 = 0$) that the two differ only by chance is to be accepted with a probability of error α (e.g. 5%) when the value t_0 calculated according to the test magnitude

$$t = \frac{|\bar{x} - \mu|}{s} \times \sqrt{n}$$

is smaller than the tabulated value t_T of the t distribution for α and the number of degrees of freedom $f = n - 1$.

Example:

In n = 30 blood samples the protein content was found to be $\bar{x} = 55$ g/l; variance $s^2 = 7$ g/l. The normal value is $\mu = 65$ g/l; $\sigma^2 = 7$. With a probability of error $\alpha = 0.05$, are the observed deviations fortuitous? The value of the test magnitude is

$$t_0 = \frac{|55 - 65|}{7} \times \sqrt{30} = 7.82$$

The tabulated value of the t-distribution for $\alpha = 0.05$ (5%) and $f = n - 1 = 29$ degrees of freedom is $t_T = 2.05$. Since $t_0 > t_T$, the null hypothesis (H_0) must be rejected. Significant differences exist between the mean value and the normal value.

t-Test for paired measurements

Paired measurements from the same experiment are to be compared. The principle of this test is that the control and test groups in the experiment differ only with respect to the parameter of interest. If no significant difference exists between the values of the control and test groups, positive and negative differences must cancel out.

It is known that most intermediate products in one individual are subject to smaller fluctuations than those observed between different individuals. Pair analysis reduces the error of these individual differences and the evaluation is thus made more effective and more meaningful from the biological point of view.

If with the given pairs of values $x_1, y_1; x_2, y_2; \ldots x_n, y_n$ the null hypothesis H_0 with $x_j - y_j = 0$ is to be tested against the alternative $x_j - y_j \neq 0$ ($\alpha = 0.05$), the mean difference d is

(11) $$\bar{d} = \frac{\Sigma d}{n}$$

The standard deviation s_d is calculated from the expression

(12) $$s_d = \pm \sqrt{\frac{\Sigma d^2}{n-1} - \frac{(\Sigma d)^2}{n \times (n-1)}}$$

The variance of the mean value of the differences is

(13) $$s_{\bar{d}} = \frac{s_d}{\sqrt{n}}$$

The test magnitude t is calculated from the equation

(14) $$t_0 = \bar{d}/s_{\bar{d}}$$

If the test magnitude t_0 is smaller than the tabulated value t_T (Table 4), the null hypothesis (H_0) is accepted, i.e. with a probability of error of 5%, no significant difference exists between the x_j and y_j values.

Example:

A new enzymatic procedure for the determination of uric acid is compared with the uricase method (reference method) on samples of human serum with different uric acid contents (Table 5).

Table 5. t-Test for paired data.

No.	x_j	y_j	$d = x_j - y_i$	d^2
1	2.9	2.8	−0.1	0.01
2	5.7	6.0	+0.3	0.09
3	3.3	3.7	+0.4	0.16
4	5.8	6.0	+0.2	0.04
5	4.4	4.3	−0.1	0.01
6	9.5	9.1	−0.4	0.16
⋮	⋮	⋮	⋮	⋮
20	11.3	11.0	−0.3	0.09
Σ	143.8	144.4	−0.1	1.21

The test magnitude t_0 of the values in Table 5 is calculated from eqns. (11)–(14) as $t_0 = 0.0912$. Since for 19 degrees of freedom and $\alpha = 0.05$ (5%), t_0 is smaller than the tabulated value $t_T = 2.09$, the null hypothesis is adopted on the basis of a probability of error of 5%. No difference exists between the analytical procedures.

Curve-fitting and the method of least squares

The relationship between two variables is to be represented, for example the dependence of the absorbance of a coloured solution on the concentration.

One begins with the collection of corresponding values. For the above example, the values of the concentration are denoted by $x_1, x_2, ..., x_n$ and the corresponding absorbances by $y_1, y_2, ..., y_n$, and the pairs of values $(x_1, y_1), (x_2, y_2), ..., (x_n, y_n)$ are plotted in a system of coordinates. A curve can be fitted through the results so plotted. This is a straight line if there is a linear relationship between the variables (see also Fig. 4).

Example:

The relationship between concentration and absorbance in an enzymatic determination of cholesterol is to be tested on the basis of measured values (Table 6) and their graphical representation (Fig. 4). Manual curve-fitting shows that a linear relationship exists between the two variables.

Table 6. Relationship between
concentration and absorbance

i	measurements x_i [mmol/l]	y_i (E_{546})
1	2.5	0.160
2	5.0	0.290
3	7.5	0.375
4	10.0	0.510
5	12.5	0.615

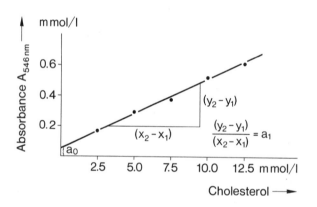

Fig. 4. Regression analysis of the relationship between concentration and absorbance in the enzymatic determination of cholesterol (data in Tab. 6).

Nonlinear relationships can frequently be linearized by plotting the results on a semilogarithmic or logarithmic scale.

Linear regression

Regression means movement backward, namely to the origin. If in an analytical process, for example a photometric procedure, the concentrations of the samples (random magnitudes x) are associated with absorbances (random magnitudes y), it is necessary to determine whether a

higher concentration is or is not associated, on average, with a greater absorbance, whether this relationship is linear (regresses), and what average concentration corresponds to a given absorbance *(regrettere)*. The calculation of regression is used to answer the second question.
The simplest linear fitting of a curve is a straight line with the equation:

(15) $$y = a_0 + a_1 x .$$

The additive term a_0 defines the point of intersection of the straight line with the y-axis (the *intercept*).

The constant a_1 defines the *slope* of the regression line, which is characterized by $\dfrac{y_2 - y_1}{x_2 - x_1}$ (Fig.4).

The method of least squares

In order to avoid individual evaluations in the fitting of straight lines or curves to the measured values, it is necessary to find an agreement on what is understood by the *best fitting*.
A measure of the quality of the fitting of the curve c to the given data is the sum of the squares of the deviations $(d_1^2 + d_2^2 + \cdots + d_n^2)$. The best-fitted curve is that for which the sum of the squares of the deviations is a minimum *(best fitting curve, least-square fit)*.

The least-square regression (least-square line)

The regression of the least-squares of the deviations for the points $(x_1, y_1, x_2, y_2, ..., x_n, y_n)$ has the equation

(16) $$y = a_0 + a_1 x .$$

The constants a_0 and a_1 are calculated from

(17) $$a_0 = \frac{\Sigma y - a_1 \Sigma x}{n}$$

(18) $$a_1 = \frac{n\Sigma xy - \Sigma x \Sigma y}{n\Sigma x^2 - (\Sigma x)^2} .$$

(In these equations, x, xy stand for x_j in the limits $j = 1 - n$; y, $x_j y_j$ in the limits $j = 1 - n$, etc.).

By calculation according to eqns. (17) and (18), the data in Table 6 yield the equation $y = 0.051 + 0.045x$. The correlation coefficient is calculated from eqns. (19)–(21); it is $r = 0.998$.

Correlation analysis

Correlation analysis investigates the degree of dependence between two or more random variables (experimental parameters). The most important measure of dependence is the correlation coefficient ϱ. An estimate of ϱ on the basis of a random sample is the correlation coefficient r; it can assume values between $+1$ and -1. If $r = 1$ or $r = -1$, a functional relationship exists between x and y. If $r = 0$, no relationship exists between x and y; the figures are uncorrelated. For non-normally distributed random variables with approximately linear regression, r is a measure of the degree of dependence between x and y.

Types of regressions are shown in Fig. 5.

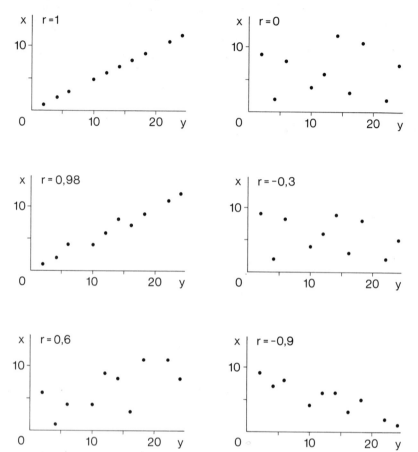

Fig. 5. Graphical representation of random samples with different values of the correlation coefficient r.

Calculation

Let a random sample of a two-dimensional xy-population be given. The random sample consists of n pairs of values $(x_1 y_1, x_2 y_2, \ldots, x_n y_n)$. Then $\bar{x} = (x_1 + x_2 + \ldots + x_n)/n$ is the mean of the x values in the random sample. The variance of these figures is

$$（19）\qquad s_x^2 = \frac{1}{n-1} \sum_{j=1}^{n} (x_j - \bar{x})^2 \, .$$

Correspondingly, $\bar{y} = (y_1 + y_2 + \ldots + y_n)/n$ is the mean of the values of y. The variance of the values of y is

$$s_y^2 = \frac{1}{n-1} \sum_{j=1}^{n} (y_j - \bar{y})^2 \, .$$

The product of the two deviations of the observed values (x, y) from the corresponding mean ($\bar{x}$, $\bar{y}$) is taken as a measure of the covariance (s_{xy}) of the random sample. This is calculated from

$$s_{xy} = \frac{1}{n-1} \sum_{j=1}^{n} (x_j - \bar{x}) \times (y_j - \bar{y})$$

The quotient

(20)
$$r = \frac{s_{xy}}{s_x \times s_y}$$

is called the correlation coefficient of the random sample. More suitable for calculation is the following formula:

(21)
$$r = \frac{\sum x_j \times y_j - \frac{1}{n} \sum x_j \sum y_j}{\sqrt{\left[\sum x_j^2 - \frac{1}{n}(\sum x_j)^2\right]\left[\sum x_j^2 - \frac{1}{n}(\sum y_j)^2\right]}}$$

(N.B.: r is not a measure of the dependence of y on x as such, but only for a linear dependence).

Quality Control

The aim of the analyst is to obtain correct results. However, no measurement is free from errors. Consequently, it is necessary to monitor and control all measurement procedures. The extent of errors in complicated analytical procedures and in the analysis of biological material in particularly large. Tissue constituents are usually present only in very low concentrations. In addition, substances in biological material to be analyzed are often unstable.

Because of the great importance of clinical chemical analyses for medical diagnosis, procedures for systematic quality control have been developed for this field[1,9].

The actual extent of the analytical errors can be seen if control samples of unknown concentrations are introduced into the daily routine over a long period. From a comparison of the results of various laboratories analyzing one and the same material, objective data are obtained on the actual analytical variability of types of analyses.

For better mutual understanding, international societies (e.g. the *International Federation of Clinical Chemistry*, IFCC) are attempting to unify the current technical expressions.

Types of error

According to *C. F. Gauss*, avoidable, gross, and systematic errors must be distinguished from basically unavoidable random errors. These types of errors can be clearly illustrated by the example of shooting at targets (see Fig. 6).

Gross errors are, for example, wrong technique, mix-ups of samples or reagents, and errors of calculation.

Systematic errors mean that all the results differ in one direction (positive or negative) from the target value.

Causes and examples

- wrong measurement temperature (especially in the determination of the catalytic activities of enzymes)
- contaminated, spoilt, or wrong standards
- incorrect dispensing (pipettes)

error types		random error	systematic error	gross error
	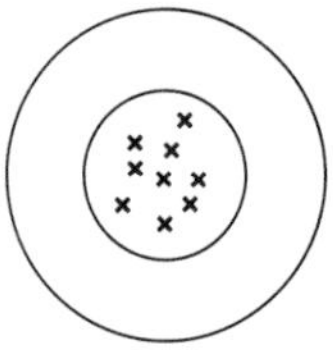	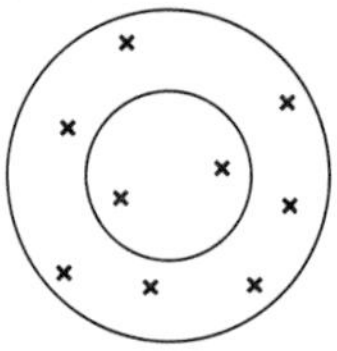	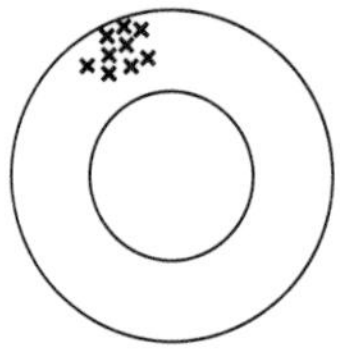	missed the target
precision	optimal	bad	good	–
accuracy	optimal	good	bad	–

Fig. 6. Random, systematic, and gross errors illustrated by the example of shooting at a target. Random errors lead to an uncertainty, systematic errors to inaccuracy (Büttner, Hansert, Stamm, 1974)[1].

Random errors arise from the unavoidable inaccuracy and variability of the analytical process. Only rarely are absolutely identical values obtained on repeated measurements.

Causes and examples

– errors of distribution (e.g. inhomogeneity of the sample)
– errors of volume (e.g. inaccuracy of dispensing devices within the tolerances)
– photometer errors (e.g. instability of the display, poor calibration of the wavelengths, slit width too large

Precision and accuracy

The quality of analytical procedures is characterized by their precision and accuracy. Both are determined from repeated measurements of samples of the same material for investigation, which must be stable and identical with respect to the parameters being investigated.

Precision

The term *precision* has qualitative significance and is dimensionless. Its conventional measure, the standard deviation or the coefficient of variation, corresponds to the conventional expressions variance and analytical variability; it is denoted by the word *imprecision*.

Imprecision is determined by repeated analyses of identical samples. The numerical value must always be characterized by specifying the type of experimental procedure (e.g. measured in series, from day to day, in different laboratories, etc.). See formulas on p. 224.

The standard deviation thus obtained mainly characterizes the random errors. As long as a given threshold value of the imprecision is not exceeded, *the precision is regarded as "under control"*. The determination of the permissible limits is guided by the state of the technique or pragmatically by the requirements of medical diagnosis. It is also advisable to take the biological variability into account.

Accuracy

By this is meant the agreement between the best-possible statement of the amount present (in the special case of enzymes, the catalytic activity) and the true concentration of the sample. Accuracy has no numerical value. The systematic deviation between the mean value of repeated measurements and the target value is known as the *inaccuracy*. The characterization of accuracy present difficulties.

Various methods have been proposed: the use of control sera, repeated measurements (on pure solutions or after addition of the substance to be determined), comparative investigations with known "correct" (reference) methods, and so on (e.g. reference to daily mean values of all investigated samples or comparison with reference values). Control sera and calibration standards can be used only if the true content of the sample is known (e.g. by weighing in pure substances). The inaccuracy should be zero within the random error of observation.

References

1 Büttner, H., Hansert, E. & Stamm, D. (1974) in *Methods of Enzymatic Analysis* (Bergmeyer, H. U., ed.) 2nd. edn., p. 318, Verlag Chemie, Weinheim & Academic Press, New York.
2 Campbell, R.C. (1971) *Statistische Methoden für Biologie und Medizin*, Georg Thieme Verlag, Stuttgart.
3 Documenta Geigy: *Wissenschaftliche Tabellen* (1975) 7th edn., Georg Thieme Verlag, Stuttgart.
4 Kreyszig, E. (1975) *Statistische Methoden und ihre Anwendungen*, 5th edn., Verlag Vandenhoeck Ruprecht, Göttingen.
5 Sachs, L. (1972) *Statistische Methoden / ein Soforthelfer*, 2nd edn., Springer Verlag, Berlin.
6 Spiegel, M.R. & Boxer, R.W. (1972) *Schaum's Outline of Theory and Problems of Statistics in the Units*, McGraw Hill, New York.
7 Walter, E. (1975) *Biomathematik für Mediziner*, Verlag Teubner, Stuttgart.
8 Weber, E. (1972) *Grundriß der biologischen Statistik*, 7th edn., Verlag Fischer, Stuttgart.
9 Haeckel, R. (1972) *Qualitätssicherung im medizinischen Labor*, Deutscher Ärzte-Verlag GmbH, Köln-Lövenich.
10 *Biomathematik für Mediziner* (1976), edited by: Kollegium Biomathematik NW, Springer Verlag, Berlin, Heidelberg, New York.
11 Sachs, L. (1974) *Angewandte Statistik*, 4th edn., Springer Verlag, Berlin, Heidelberg, New York.

Formulas

Hans Ulrich Bergmeyer

The use of the basic kind of quantities of the SI system (see p. 9) involves some changes in symbols, quantities and units, used formerly. For example, the base unit of length is the meter (m) and thousands or thousandths of it. The path length of a photometer cuvette is in general 10 mm (not 1 cm). Accordingly, the unit of the absorption coefficient also changes ($1 \times \mathrm{mol}^{-1} \times \mathrm{mm}^{-1}$, instead of $1 \times \mathrm{mol}^{-1} \times \mathrm{cm}^{-1}$).

For example, for NADH at 339 nm $\varepsilon = 6.3 \times 10^2 \, 1 \times \mathrm{mol}^{-1} \times \mathrm{mm}^{-1}$ instead of $6.3 \times 10^3 \, 1 \times \mathrm{mol}^{-1} \times \mathrm{cm}^{-1}$. For practical purposes it is proposed to use the path length $d = 10$ mm and the concentration c in mmol/l (μmol/ml). Then for NADH at 339 nm applies $\varepsilon \times d = 6.3 \, 1 \times \mathrm{mmol}^{-1}$.

The following symbols, kind of quantities and units are customary:*

ε	absorption coefficient, $1 \times \mathrm{mmol}^{-1} \times \mathrm{mm}^{-1}$	d	light path, mm
A	absorbance, 1	c	substance concentration, mol/l, g/l
ΔA	absorbance change, 1	b	catalytic activity concentration,
V	assay volume, l		U/l, kat/l
v	volume of sample used in assay, l	z	catalytic activity, U, kat
t	time, s	MW	weight of one millimole, mg/mmol
Δt	interval between measurements, s		

For experimental data obtained by fluorometric methods, F and ΔF are used instead of A and ΔA.

Metabolites

From Lambert-Beer law (p. 137) follows

(1) $$c = \frac{\log I_0/I}{\varepsilon \times d} = \frac{A}{\varepsilon \times d} \quad \mathrm{mmol/l}$$

Für chemical reactions this gives:

$$c_1 - c_2 = \frac{A_1 - A_2}{\varepsilon \times d}; \qquad \Delta c = \frac{\Delta A}{\varepsilon \times d} \quad \mathrm{mmol/l}$$

With complete conversion ($c_2 = 0$) it is

(1 a) $$c = \frac{\Delta A}{\varepsilon \times d} \quad \mathrm{mmol/l} \qquad\qquad \text{(in the cuvette)}$$

For the determination of the concentration of the sample the ratio of assay volume : sample volume (V : v) is to be considered:

---

* There are no generally recognized symbols for "content in the sample", "purity", or "specific catalytic activity".

(2) $$c = \frac{\Delta A \times V}{\varepsilon \times d \times v} \quad \text{mmol/l} \qquad\qquad \text{(in the sample)}$$

(3) $$c = \frac{\Delta A \times V \times MW}{\varepsilon \times d \times v} \quad [\text{mg/l}] \qquad\qquad \text{(in the sample)}$$

The result in relation to a standard is for the sample

(4) $$c = \frac{c_{\text{sample (measured)}}}{c_{\text{standard (measured)}}} \times c_{\text{standard (weighed out)}} \quad \text{mmol/l; mg/l}$$

or

(4a) $$c = \frac{A_{\text{sample (measured)}}}{A_{\text{standard (measured)}}} \times c_{\text{standard (weighed out)}} \quad \text{mmol/l; mg/l}$$

From the concentration of the substance in the sample solution (e.g. tissue extract) the content of the substance of the material under investigation is calculated by relating to its concentration in the standard solution:

(5) $$\text{Content} = \frac{c_{\text{sample (measured)}}}{c_{\text{standard (weighed out)}}} \quad \frac{\text{mmol/l}}{\text{mg/l}} = \text{mmol/mg}$$

(6) $$\text{Content} = \frac{c_{\text{sample (measured)}}}{c_{\text{standard (weighed out)}}} \quad \frac{\text{mg/l}}{\text{mg/l}} = \text{mg/mg}$$

If two or more moles of light-absorbing reaction product (e.g. NADH) are formed or consumed per mole substrate that reacts, the corresponding factor also appears in the denominator of the fraction in equations (2), (3), and in the following (7)–(9). If several moles of the substrate or reaction product go to form the unit of substance on which the measurement is based, the corresponding factor appears in the numerator (example: in the determination of peroxidase activity with guaiacol, the measurement is based on the product of dehydrogenation of guaiacol; the factor is 4).

Example:

Determination of fructose-1,6-diphosphate (F-1,6-P$_2$) (molecular weight: 340) in rat liver. Enzymatic analysis with aldolase/triosephosphate isomerase/glycerophosphate dehydrogenase. Two mole of NADH are transformed per mole of F-1,6-P$_2$. To prepare an "extract", 1 g of fresh liver was homogenized in 7.25 ml of HClO$_4$. With a value of 75% (w/w) for the fluid content of the liver, the volume of the extract is $7.25 + 0.75 = 8.00$ ml. To neutralize and remove perchlorate, 0.2 ml K$_2$CO$_3$ solution was added to 6 ml of the extract. The volume of the perchlorate-free extract is thus 6.2 ml. The dilution factor for the extract is $6.2/6.0 = 1.033$, and that for the tissue is $8 \times 6.2/6.0 = 8.267$. The experimental data must be multiplied by these values to express the results per 1 ml of acid extract or per 1 g of tissue.

The measured change in absorbance at 339 nm ($\varepsilon = 0.631 \times \text{mmol}^{-1} \times \text{mm}^{-1}$) was $\Delta A = 0.120$; the volume of the assay solution was 3×10^{-3} l, the volume of sample was 1.5×10^{-3} l, and the light path was 10 mm. The concentration in the perchlorate-free sample used for the assay was:

according to eqn. (2)

$$c = \frac{0.120 \times 3 \times 10^{-3}}{0.63 \times 10 \times 1.5 \times 10^{-3} \times 2} = 0.0190 \quad \text{mmol/l}$$

or according to eqn. (3)

$$c = \frac{0.120 \times 3 \times 10^{-3} \times 340}{0.63 \times 10 \times 1.5 \times 10^{-3} \times 2} = 6.48 \quad \text{mg/l}$$

Multiplication by the dilution factor gives the concentration in the acid extract:

$$c = 0.0190 \times 1.033 = 0.0196 \quad \text{mmol/l}$$

$$c = 6.48 \times 1.033 = 6.69 \quad \text{mg/l}$$

The content of F-1,6-P_2 in the tissue is

$$0.0190 \times 8.267 = 0.157 \quad \text{mmol/kg; } \mu\text{mol/g}$$

or

$$6.48 \times 8.267 = 53.57 \quad \text{mg/kg; } \mu\text{g/g}$$

Enzymes

For measurement of the catalytic activity z of enzymes the rate of the catalyzed reaction is used, the substrate conversion per time unit, μmol/min or mol/s. According to eqn. (1) it applies (conversion in mol* per time unit)

(7)   Catalytic activity

$$z = \frac{c \times V}{\Delta t} = \frac{\Delta A \times V}{1000 \times \varepsilon \times d \times \Delta t} \quad \text{mol/s (kat)}$$

(units: ε in $1 \times \text{mmol}^{-1} \times \text{mm}^{-1}$; V of the assay volume in l; d in mm; t in s)

(7a)

$$z = \frac{\Delta c \times V}{\Delta t} = \frac{\Delta A \times V \times 1000}{\varepsilon \times d \times \Delta t} \quad \mu\text{mol/min (U)}$$

(units: ε in $1 \times \text{mmol}^{-1} \times \text{mm}^{-1}$; V of the assay volume in l; d in mm; t in min)

The catalytic activity in a distinct volume is

(8)   Catalytic activity concentration $b = \dfrac{\Delta A \times V}{1000 \times \varepsilon \times d \times \Delta t \times v} \quad \text{mol/s} \times l \text{ (kat/l)}$

(units analog for eqn. (7), v in l)

(8a)

$$b = \frac{\Delta A \times V \times 1000}{\varepsilon \times d \times \Delta t \times v} \quad \mu\text{mol/min} \times l \text{ (U/l)}$$

(units analog for eqn. (7a), v in l)

The catalytic activity related to the mass of protein is

(9)   Specific catalytic activity $= \dfrac{\Delta A \times V}{1000 \times \varepsilon \times d \times \Delta t \times v \times c_{\text{protein}}} \quad \text{kat/g}$

(units analog for eqn. (7), c_{protein} in g/l)

---

* $c \times V$ (mol/l) $\times l =$ mol.

(9 a)   Specific catalytic activity $= \dfrac{\Delta A \times V \times 1000}{\varepsilon \times d \times \Delta t \times v \times c_{protein}}$ U/g

(units analog for eqn. (9), t in min)

Example:

Determination of the (specific) catalytic activity of an enzyme. The measurements were made at 339 nm; $\Delta A/\Delta t = 0.063/60$ s in a 3 ml assay mixture ($V = 3 \times 10^{-3}$ l). The volume of the sample was 2×10^{-4} l. The sample diluted thousandfold for measurement contained 10 g of enzyme protein per liter.

In the assay mixture the catalytic activity is according to eqn. (7) or (7 a), respectively

$$z = \frac{0.063 \times 3 \times 10^{-3}}{10^3 \times 0.63 \times 10 \times 60} = 5 \times 10^{-10} \text{ kat} = 0.5 \text{ nkat}$$

or

$$z = \frac{0.063 \times 3 \times 10^{-3} \times 10^3}{0.63 \times 10 \times 1} = 0.03 \text{ U}$$

In the solution of the assay mixture the catalytic activity concentration is according to eqn. (8) or (8 a), respectively

$$b = \frac{0.063 \times 3 \times 10^{-3}}{10^3 \times 0.63 \times 10 \times 60 \times 3 \times 10^{-3}} = 167 \text{ nkat/l}$$

or

$$b = \frac{0.063 \times 3 \times 10^{-3} \times 10^3}{0.63 \times 10 \times 1 \times 3 \times 10^{-3}} = 10 \text{ U/l}$$

In the sample solution the catalytic activity concentration is according to eqn. (8) or (8 a), respectively

$$b = \frac{0.063 \times 3 \times 10^{-3}}{10^3 \times 0.63 \times 10 \times 60 \times 2 \times 10^{-4}} = 2500 \text{ nkat/l}$$

or

$$b = \frac{0.063 \times 3 \times 10^{-3} \times 10^3}{0.63 \times 10 \times 1 \times 2 \times 10^{-4}} = 150 \text{ U/l}$$

Related to the mass of protein (dilution factor 1000):

$$\text{specific catalytic activity} = \frac{2500 \times 1000}{10} \frac{\text{nkat/l}}{\text{g/l}} = 250 \,\mu\text{kat/g}$$

or

$$\text{specific catalytic activity} = \frac{150 \times 1000}{10} \frac{\text{U/l}}{\text{g/l}} = 15 \text{ U/mg}$$

Statistics

For parameters and sample statistics see p. 233.
For mathematical evaluation of experiments (mean value, standard deviation, imprecision, inaccuracy) see p. 224.
For statistical evaluation of results, especially for regression analysis, see p. 225 f.

Appendix

Numbering and Classification of Enzymes

Extract* of the official Recommendations (1972) of the Commission on Biochemical Nomenclature on the Nomenclature and Classification of Enzymes, together with their Units and the Symbols of Enzyme Kinetics.

1. Oxidoreductases

1.1 Acting on the CH-OH group of donors

1.1.1	With NAD$^+$ or NADP$^+$ as acceptor
1.1.2	With a cytochrome as acceptor
1.1.3	With oxygen as acceptor
1.1.99	With other acceptors

1.2 Acting on the aldehyde or keto group of donors

1.2.1	With NAD$^+$ or NADP$^+$ as acceptor
1.2.2	With a cytochrome as acceptor
1.2.3	With oxygen as acceptor
1.2.4	With a disulphide compound as acceptor
1.2.7	With an iron-sulphur protein as acceptor
1.2.99	With other acceptors

1.3 Acting on the CH-CH group of donors

1.3.1	With NAD$^+$ or NADP$^+$ as acceptor
1.3.2	With a cytochrome as acceptor
1.3.3	With oxygen as acceptor
1.3.7	With an iron-sulphur protein as acceptor
1.3.99	With other acceptors

1.4 Acting on the CH-NH$_2$ group of donors

1.4.1	With NAD$^+$ or NADP$^+$ as acceptor
1.4.3	With oxygen as acceptor
1.4.4	With a disulphide compound as acceptor
1.4.99	With other acceptors

1.5 Acting on the CH-NH group of donors

1.5.1	With NAD$^+$ or NADP$^+$ as acceptor
1.5.3	With oxygen as acceptor
1.5.99	With other acceptors

1.6 Acting on NADH or NADPH

1.6.1	With NAD$^+$ or NADP$^+$ as acceptor
1.6.2	With a cytochrome as acceptor
1.6.4	With a disulphide compound as acceptor
1.6.5	With a quinone or related compound as acceptor
1.6.6	With a nitrogenous group as acceptor
1.6.7	With an iron-sulphur protein as acceptor
1.6.99	With other acceptors

1.7 Acting on other nitrogenous compounds as donors

1.7.2	With a cytochrome as acceptor
1.7.3	With oxygen as acceptor
1.7.7	With an iron-sulphur protein as acceptor
1.7.99	With other acceptors

1.8 Acting on a sulphur group of donors

1.8.1	With NAD$^+$ or NADP$^+$ as acceptor
1.8.2	With a cytochrome as acceptor
1.8.3	With oxygen as acceptor
1.8.4	With a disulphide compound as acceptor
1.8.5	With a quinone or related compound as acceptor
1.8.6	With a nitrogenous group as acceptor
1.8.7	With an iron-sulphur protein as acceptor
1.8.99	With other acceptors

1.9 Acting on a haem group of donors

1.9.3	With oxygen as acceptor
1.9.6	With a nitrogenous group as acceptor
1.9.99	With other acceptors

1.10 *Acting on diphenols and related substances as donors*
1.10.2   With a cytochrome as acceptor
1.10.3   With oxygen as acceptor

1.11 *Acting on hydrogen peroxide as acceptor*

1.12 *Acting on hydrogen as donor*
1.12.1   With NAD$^+$ or NADP$^+$ as acceptor
1.12.2   With a cytochrome as acceptor
1.12.7   With an iron-sulphur protein as acceptor

1.13 *Acting on single donors with incorporation of molecular oxygen (oxygenases)*
1.13.11   With incorporation of two atoms of oxygen
1.13.12   With incorporation of one atom of oxygen (internal monooxygenases or internal mixed function oxidases)
1.13.99   Miscellaneous (requires further characterization)

1.14 *Acting on paired donors with incorporation of molecular oxygen*
1.14.11   With 2-oxoglutarate as one donor, and incorporation of one atom each of oxygen into both donors
1.14.12   With NADH or NADPH as one donor, and incorporation of two atoms of oxygen into one donor
1.14.13   With NADH or NADPH as one donor, and incorporation of one atom of oxygen
1.14.14   With reduced flavin or flavoprotein as one donor, and incorporation of one atom of oxygen
1.14.15   With a reduced iron-sulphur protein as one donor, and incorporation of one atom of oxygen
1.14.16   With reduced pteridine as one donor, and incorporation of one atom of oxygen
1.14.17   With ascorbate as one donor, and incorporation of one atom of oxygen

1.14.18   With another compound as one donor, and incorporation of one atom of oxygen
1.14.99   Miscellaneous (requires further characterization)

1.15 *Acting on superoxide radicals as acceptor*

1.16 *Oxidizing metal ions*
1.16.3   With oxygen as acceptor

1.17 *Acting on -CH_2-groups*
1.17.1   With NAD$^+$ or NADP$^+$ as acceptor
1.17.4   With a disulphide compound as acceptor

2. Transferases

2.1 *Transferring one-carbon groups*
2.1.1   Methyltransferases
2.1.2   Hydroxymethyl-, formyl- and related transferases
2.1.3   Carboxyl- and carbamoyltransferases
2.1.4   Amidinotransferases

2.2 *Transferring aldehyde or ketonic residues*

2.3 *Acyltransferases*
2.3.1   Acyltransferases
2.3.2   Aminoacyltransferases

2.4 *Glycosyltransferases*
2.4.1   Hexosyltransferases
2.4.2   Pentosyltransferases
2.4.99   Transferring other glycosyl groups

2.5 *Transferring alkyl or aryl groups, other than methyl groups*

* Enzyme Nomenclature, Recommendations (1972) of the International Union of Pure and Applied Chemistry and the International Union of Biochemistry, Elsevier Scientific Publishing Company, Amsterdam 1973, p. 17–22.

Numbering and Classification of Enzymes (Continuation)

Atomic Weights*

International atomic weights based** on the value 12 for the relative atomic mass of the carbon isotope ^{12}C (according to***).

Element	Symbol	Atomic number	Atomic weight	Element	Symbol	Atomic number	Atomic weight
Aluminium	Al	13	26.9815	Molybdenum	Mo	42	95.94
Antimony	Sb	51	121.75	Neodymium	Nd	60	144.24
Argon	Ar	18	39.948	Neon	Ne	10	20.183
Arsenic	As	33	74.9216	Nickel	Ni	28	58.71
Barium	Ba	56	137.34	Niobium	Nb	41	92.906
Beryllium	Be	4	9.0122	Nitrogen	N	7	14.0067
Bismuth	Bi	83	208.980	Osmium	Os	76	190.2
Boron	B	5	10.811	Oxygen	O	8	15.9994
Bromine	Br	35	79.909	Palladium	Pd	46	106.4
Cadmium	Cd	48	112.40	Phosphorus	P	15	30.9738
Caesium	Cs	55	132.905	Platinum	Pt	78	195.09
Calcium	Ca	20	40.08	Potassium	K	19	39.102
Carbon	C	6	12.01115	Praseodymium	Pr	59	140.907
Cerium	Ce	58	140.12	Rhenium	Re	75	186.2
Chlorine	Cl	17	35.453	Rhodium	Rh	45	102.905
Chromium	Cr	24	51.996	Rubidium	Rb	37	85.47
Cobalt	Co	27	58.9332	Ruthenium	Ru	44	101.07
Copper	Cu	29	63.54	Samarium	Sm	62	150.35
Dysprosium	Dy	66	162.50	Scandium	Sc	21	44.956
Erbium	Er	68	167.26	Selenium	Se	34	78.96
Europium	Eu	63	151.96	Silicon	Si	14	28.086
Fluorine	F	9	18.9984	Silver	Ag	47	107.870
Gadolinium	Gd	64	157.25	Sodium	Na	11	22.9898
Gallium	Ga	31	69.72	Strontium	Sr	38	87.62
Germanium	Ge	32	72.59	Sulphur	S	16	32.06
Gold	Au	79	196.967	Tantalum	Ta	73	180.948
Hafnium	Hf	72	178.49	Tellurium	Te	52	127.60
Helium	He	2	4.0026	Terbium	Tb	65	158.924
Holmium	Ho	67	164.930	Thallium	Tl	81	204.37
Hydrogen	H	1	1.00797	Thorium	Th	90	232.038
Indium	In	49	114.82	Thulium	Tm	69	168.934
Iodine	I	53	126.9044	Tin	Sn	50	118.69
Iridium	Ir	77	192.2	Titanium	Ti	22	47.90
Iron	Fe	26	55.847	Tungsten	W	74	183.85
Krypton	Kr	36	83.80	Uranium	U	92	238.03
Lanthanum	La	57	138.91	Vanadium	V	23	50.942
Lead	Pb	82	207.19	Xenon	Xe	54	131.30
Lithium	Li	3	6.939	Ytterbium	Yb	70	173.04
Lutetium	Lu	73	174.97	Yttrium	Y	39	88.905
Magnesium	Mg	12	24.312	Zinc	Zn	30	65.37
Manganese	Mn	25	54.9381	Zirconium	Zr	40	91.22
Mercury	Hg	80	200.59				

* Lanthanides and actinides are incomplete.

** International Union of Pure and Applied Chemistry, Report of the 10th General Assembly, Ottawa 1960, p. 24.

*** International Union of Pure and Applied Chemistry, Compt. rend. de la 24e Conférence 1967, Butterworth, London 1967, p. 130.

The International System of Units (SI)

The General Conference of Weights and Measures (Conférence Générale des Poids et Mésures, CGPM) adopted as base units for a "practical system of units of measurement", the units of the following seven quantities: length, mass, time, electric current, thermodynamic temperature, luminous intensity, (10th CGPM 1954) and amount of substance (14th CGPM 1971), (table 1).

The 11th CGPM (1960) adopted for this practical system of units of measurement the name *International System of Units (Système International d'Unités)* with the international abbreviation SI and laid down rules for the prefixes (table 3), and the derived units (table 2) and other matters, thus establishing a comprehensive specification for units of measurement.

Table 1. Basic kind of quantities and base units.

Basic kind of quantities			Base units	
Name	Symbol	Dimension	Name	Symbol[b]
Length	l	L	meter	m
Mass	m	M	kilogram	kg
Time	t	T	second	s
Electric current	I	I	ampere	A
Thermodynamic temperature	T	Θ	kelvin	K
Luminous intensity	I	J	candela[a]	cd
Amount of substance	n	N	mole	mol

[a] stress on the "e"   [b] unit symbols do not change in the plural

The following terms are defined:

Quantity: A physically or chemically measurable property of a defined system.

Unit: A quantity of a defined size used as reference for other quantities of the same dimension.

Dimension: A product indicating the physical nature of a given quantity by showing its dependence on the dimensions of the seven basic kinds of quantities.

Base Unit: For each basic kind of quantity, one base unit is defined.

Derived Kind of Quantity: Given a certain set of basic kinds of quantities, other quantities are derived by algebraic equations (utilizing multiplication and division) between the basic kinds of quantities.

Coherent Derived Unit: When the product of base units constituting the derived unit contains no factors different from one, the unit is said to be coherent (e.g. mole per cubic meter; kilogram per cubic meter is coherent, in spite of the factor kilo $= 10^3$, because kilogram is a base unit).

Non-coherent derived Unit: As coherent derived units (and base units) do not always have a convenient size, subunits are constructed by using factors (e.g. milligram per cubic metre; mole per liter is SI non-coherent even if the name contains no factor because the liter is a non-SI unit (liter $= 10^{-3}$ m^3).

Table 2. Examples of derived SI units with special names.

Quantity			SI unit		Expression in terms of SI base units	Expression in terms of other units
Name	Symbol	Dimension	Name	Symbol		
Frequency	v	T^{-1}	hertz	Hz	s^{-1}	
Force	F	LMT^{-2}	newton	N	$m \cdot kg \cdot s^{-2}$	
Pressure	p	$L^{-1}MT^{-2}$	pascal	Pa	$m^{-1} \cdot kg \cdot s^{-2}$	N/m^2
Energy, work, quantity of heat	W, Q	L^2MT^{-2}	joule	J	$m^2 \cdot kg \cdot s^{-2}$	N $\cdot$ m
Power, radiant flux	P	L^2MT^{-3}	watt	W	$m^2 \cdot kg \cdot s^{-3}$	J/s

Table 3. Prefixes for unit symbols.

Factor	Prefix	Symbol	
10^{12}	tera	T	
10^9	giga	G	
10^6	mega	M	recommended
10^3	kilo	k	
10^2	hecto	h	
10^1	deka[c]	da	
10^{-1}	deci	d	not recommended
10^{-2}	centi	c	
10^{-3}	milli	m	
10^{-6}	micro	μ	
10^{-9}	nano	n	recommended
10^{-12}	pico	p	
10^{-15}	femto	f	
10^{-18}	atto	a	

[c] in the UK translation "deca"

Table 4. Kind of quantities and units.

Kind of quanity			Unit		Symbols of units and sub-units	
Name	Symbol	Dimension	Name	Class.	recommended	not recommended
Length	l	L	meter	basic	m mm µm nm	dm, cm µ, u mµ, mu, Å
Area	A	L^2	square meter	coherent	m^2 mm^2 $µm^2$	cm^2 $µ^2$
Volume	V	L^3	cubic meter	coherent	m^3	
			liter	non-coherent	l dm^3 ml cm^3 µl mm^3 nl pl fl $µm^3$	L cc, ccm λ, ul µµl, uul $µ^3$, u^3
Mass	m	M	kilogram	basic	kg g mg µg ng pg	Kg gr γ, ug mµg, mug γγ, µµg, uug
Amount of substance	n	N	mole	basic	mol mmol µmol nmol	M, eq, val, g-mol mM, meq, mval µM, µeq, µval nM, neq, nval
Mass concentration (of a com- ponent B)	ϱ_B	L^{-3}	kilogram per cubic meter	coherent	kg/m^3	
			kilogram per liter	non-coherent	kg/l g/l mg/l µg/l ng/l	g/ml %, g%, %(w/v), g/100 ml, g/dl %oo, g%oo, %oo (w/v) mg%, mg%(w/v), mg/100 ml, mg/dl ppm, ppm(w/v) µg%, µg%(w/v), µg/100 ml, µg/dl, γ% ppb, ppb(w/v) µµg/ml, uug/ml

Kind of quantity			Unit		Symbols of units and sub-units	
Name	Symbol	Dimension	Name	Class.	recommended	not recommended
Mass ratio (of a component B)	w_B	1	one	coherent	$\times 1$ $\times 10^{-3}$ $\times 10^{-6}$ $\times 10^{-9}$ $\times 10^{-12}$	kg/kg, g/g %, %(w/w) g/kg, ‰, ‰(w/w) mg/kg, ppm, ppm(w/w) μg/kg, ppb, ppb(w/w) ng/kg
Volume ratio (of a component B)	φ_B	1	one	coherent	$\times 1$ $\times 10^{-3}$ $\times 10^{-6}$	l/l, ml/ml %, %(v/v), % by vol ml/l, ‰, ‰(v/v), ‰ by vol μl/l, ppm, ppm(v/v)
Amount-of-substance concentration, molarity (of a component B)	c_B; [B]	$L^{-3}N$	mole per cubic meter mole per liter	coherent non-coherent	mol/m^3 mol/l mmol/l μmol/l nmol/l	 M, m, eq/l, val/l, N, n mM, meq/l, mval/l μM, uM, μeq/l nM, neq/l
Molality (of a component B)	m_B	$M^{-1}N$	mole per kilogram	coherent	mol/kg mmol/kg μmol/kg	m, mmol/g, μmol/mg mm μm, um
Amount-of-substance ratio, mole fraction (of a component B)	x_B	1	one	coherent	$\times 1$ $\times 10^{-3}$ $\times 10^{-6}$	mol/mol %, mol% mmol/mol, ‰, mol‰ μmol/mol
Thermodynamic temperature	T	Θ	kelvin	basic	K mK	°K, k°, grd
Celsius temperature	t, ϑ	Θ	degree Celsius	special derived coherent	°C, K m°C, mK	C, °, C°
Pressure	p	$L^{-1}MT^{-2}$	pascal (newton per square meter)	coherent	MPa (MN/m²) kPa (kN/m²) Pa (N/m²)	atm (1 physical atm = 101.3 kPa) bar, b (1 bar = 100.0 kPa) at (1 techn. at = 98.1 kPa) mmHg, Torr (1 Torr = 133.3 Pa) mbar, mb (1 mbar = 100 Pa) mmH₂O (1 mm H₂O = 9.81 Pa) μbar, μb (1 μbar = 0.1 Pa)

Kind of quantity			Unit		Symbols of units and sub-units	
Name	Symbol	Dimension	Name	Class.	recommended	not recommended
Energy, work, quantity of heat	W, Q	$L^2 M T^{-2}$	joule [dschul] newton × meter	coherent	kJ (kN · m) J (N · m)	kcal, Cal cal (1 cal = 4.1868 J) erg (1 erg = 10^{-7} J)
Time	t	T	second	basic	a Ms d h ks min s ms μs	Std., St. min., Min., m sec., s. us
Density	ϱ	$L^{-3} M$	kilogram per cubic meter kilogram per liter	coherent non-coherent	kg/m³ kg/l g/l mg/l	 g/ml mg/ml μg/ml
Relative density	d	1	one	coherent	× 1 × 10^{-3}	
Radio-activity	A	T^{-1}	reciprocal second	coherent	s^{-1}	Ci (1 Ci = 3.7×10^{10} s^{-1})
Specific radioactivity		$T^{-1} N^{-1}$	reciprocal second per mole	coherent	$s^{-1} \cdot mol^{-1}$	Ci/mol
Rate of a chemical reaction	v	NT^{-1}	mole per second	coherent	$mol \cdot s^{-1}$	

For kind of quantity and unit of a catalyst (enzyme) cf. p. 6–12.

References

The International System of Units (SI). NBS Special Publication 330 (1974 Edition) (Page, C.H. & Vigoreux, P., eds.) [(1974) National Bureau of Standards, U.S. Government Printing Office, Washington, D.C. 20402].

J. Clin. Chem. Clin. Biochem. (1974) **12**, 180–192.

Dybkaer, R. (1977) Enzyme **22**, 91–123.

Documenta Geigy (1975) Wissenschaftliche Tabellen 7. edn. p. 200 f., Georg Thieme Verlag Stuttgart.

Index